COMMITTED WORSHIP

A Sacramental Theology for Converting Christians

Volume II:
The Sacraments of
Ongoing Conversion

Donald L. Gelpi, S.J.

A Michael Glazier Book

✠ THE LITURGICAL PRESS
Collegeville, Minnesota

A Michael Glazier Book published by The Liturgical Press

Cover design by David Manahan, O.S.B.
Cover: Chrismon, SS. Gervase and Protase, Civaux, France

1   2   3   4   5   6   7   8   9

Library of Congress Cataloging-in-Publication Data

Gelpi, Donald L., 1934–
    Committed worship : a sacramental theology for converting Christians / Donald L. Gelpi.
        p.   cm.
    "A Michael Glazier book."
    Includes bibliographical references.
    Contents: v. 1. Adult conversion and initiation — v. 2. The sacraments of ongoing conversion.
    ISBN 0-8146-5825-3 (v. 1). — ISBN 0-8146-5826-1 (v. 2)
    1. Sacraments—Catholic Church.   2. Conversion.   3. Catholic Church.   Ordo initiationis Christianae adultorum.   4. Initiation rites—Religious aspects—Catholic Church.   5. Catechumens. 6. Catholic Church—Membership.   I. Title.
BX2203.G45   1993
264'.0208—dc20   92-40430
                                                                            CIP

Contents

Preface

Committed Worship sets into dialogue two exciting developments in the contemporary Church: the restored catechumenate, or RCIA (Rite for the Christian Initiation of Adults), and recent breakthroughs in the theology of conversion. In the process it lays systematic theological foundations not only for adapting the RCIA pastorally to the needs of the Church in the United States but also for effecting a much more broadly based parish and Church renewal that the restoration of the catechumenate presupposes as the condition for its ultimate success.

The first volume of this study focused on the experience of initial adult conversion, the RCIA, and adult initiation into the Church. The present volume examines the other sacraments in the light of the experience of ongoing Christian conversion. Since catechumens need systematic instruction not only in the demands of initial conversion but also in living authentic Christian lives, the issues treated in this volume have an important place in the work of the catechumenate itself. Since, however, we have reason to suspect that a significant number of baptized Christians have yet to transcend the limits of conventional religion and in the process to experience an initial adult conversion, the argument of both volumes has relevance as well for more general parish and Church renewal.

This second volume builds on the insights developed in the first. In other words, the argument presupposes the understanding both of conversion and of Christian initiation which the first volume proposed. The argument presupposes an understanding of the forms and dynamics of conversion, since the experience of ongoing conversion that the sacraments foster engages both. The argument presupposes a sound insight into the meaning of Christian initiation both because the other sacraments all renew the Christian covenant of initiation and because a sound theological insight into them develops and deepens many of the concepts that functioned in explaining Christian initiation.

As volume one explained, a traditional theology of conversion portrayed it as a religious event with moral and social consequences. In such an approach, conversion consists essentially in turning from unbelief to faith in God and from sin to obedience to the divine will. That essentially religious transformation has moral consequences because it commits one to living in ways that please God. It has social consequences because it culminates in entry into the Church. A traditional theology of conversion, therefore, linked the experience of conversion to only two sacraments: baptism, which admits one into the Church for the first time, or reconciliation, which readmits one into the Church after serious sin.

The new theology of conversion developed in these pages, by contrast, recognizes that conversion can occur not only in religious but in secular contexts. This new theology recognizes five forms of conversion in all: religious conversion, affective conversion, intellectual conversion, and two forms of moral conversion: personal and sociopolitical.

In addition, the new theology of conversion identifies and describes seven dynamics within the total process of Christian conversion. Affective conversion animates the other forms of conversion. Intellectual conversion orders the other conversions. Personal moral conversion helps orient the other conversions to realities and values that make morally ultimate and absolute claims. Christian conversion contributes two dynamics to the conversion process. It mediates between affective and moral conversion, and it transvalues the other conversions when they occur only naturally. Sociopolitical conversion deprivatizes the other forms of conversion, while they help supply norms and insights that authenticate sociopolitical conversion.

Instead of restricting the term "conversion" to the initial experience of religious encounter or to repentance from serious backsliding, in the manner of traditional theological reflection on the subject, the new theology portrays all five forms of conversion as a lifelong process that includes both initial and ongoing conversion.

The identification of five different kinds of conversion—one religious, the others secular—leads of necessity to an account of the analogy of conversion. The analogy of conversion shows how the different forms of conversion resemble one another and how they differ. In the first volume I suggested that all conversions involve turning from irresponsible to responsible behavior in some realm of human experience. Conversions differ in the realities to which they commit one and in the norms that each invokes for distinguishing between responsible and irresponsible behavior. Affective conversion commits one to cultivate emotional health and sensitivity to beauty. Intellectual conversion commits one to the search for sound logical and methodological principles for reaching the truth. Personal moral conversion commits one to living by the golden rule. Sociopolitical conversion commits one to seeking the common good. Religious conversion commits one to relate to a self-revealing God on the terms demanded by that revelation. Christian conversion exemplifies one form of religious conversion and commits one to responding to the God historically revealed in Jesus and in his Holy Breath.

Because each form of conversion transforms a different realm of experience, the theology of conversion also presupposes a specific understanding of experience as a process made up of three describable variables: 1) values, which develop in a continuum of feeling that stretches from sensation, to emotion, to imagination, and to hypothetical, deductive, and inductive inference; 2) actions, that express some evaluative response and that take the form of interaction, collaboration, or coercion; and 3) general tendencies, which result from actions. Autonomously functioning tendencies qualify as selves; selves capable of conversion qualify as human persons. The history of each spatio-temporal self defines what it is.

The reader will find all these points explained in considerable detail in the first volume as well as the definition of the key terms used in both volumes of this study in a glossary at the end of volume two.

In discussing each sacrament, the second volume, like the first, presents its biblical foundations, its historical development, the principal controversies that have marked that development, and the kind of religious commitment that each sacrament celebrates. Moreover, by its insistence on the necessity for political conversion in every act of sacramental worship, the second volume, like the first deprivatizes sacramental piety by insisting that, as in the case of the rites of initiation, sacramental worship commits one to living the social gospel in all of its radical demands.

Finally, the first volume presented in a schematic way the ecclesiology of Vatican II. The second volume uses the rest of the sacraments as a context for fleshing out the details of that sketch.

The argument of volume two begins with an examination of the two vocational sacraments: marriage and orders. Volume one explained confirmation as committing one to lifelong openness to the charismatic inspiration of God's Holy Breath. In marriage and ordained ministry we encounter charisms that need sacramental sanction before one can exercise them fully. The first part of this volume, therefore, shows how both sacraments deepen the initial conversion commitment that the rites of adult initiation originally sealed. A discussion of the converted responsibilities of Christian spouses to one another and to their children provides the appropriate context for examining the pros and cons of infant baptism. The foundational theology of the sacrament of orders developed in this section throws theological light on the origins and abuses of clericalism. Moreover, by interpreting both ordained ministry and the marriage covenant in the light of an integral, fivefold conversion, part one of this volume casts new light on such debated questions as divorce and remarriage, the ordination of married persons, and the ordination of women.

The final section of *Committed Worship* examines reconciliation, anointing, and the Eucharist as sacraments of ongoing Christian conversion. The discussion of the sacrament of reconciliation develops further the political interpretation of concupiscence presented in volume one of this study. That interpretation deprivatizes personal sin by showing that concupiscence American style all too effectively institutionalizes and systematically inculcates all seven of the capital sins. The discussion of anointing uses an insight into the relationship between illness and conversion to establish the sacramentality of this official Church ritual. That discussion also situates sacramental anointing within the Church's total ministry of charismatic faith healing. Finally, the discussion of the Eucharist shows how a sound understanding of the temporal structure of Eucharistic anamnesis throws important light on the intimate relationship between the real presence of Christ in the Eucharist, on the one hand, and the sacrificial and eschatological dimensions of Eucharistic on the other.

PART I

The Vocational Sacraments

CHAPTER I

The Evolution of Christian Nuptials

We are examining the ways in which an integral, fivefold conversion authenticates and transforms Christian sacramental worship. We have reflected on the rites of Christian initiation that seal an initial conversion to Christ. Initiation confers certain ecclesial rights and responsibilities on neophytes. Baptism endows them with a morally conditioned right to participate in the official public worship of the Church and to the means of sanctification. Confirmation confers the morally conditioned right to use the charismatic graces that the divine Mother confers for the good of the Church and of humanity.

Moreover, in sealing an experience of initial conversion, the sacrament of Christian initiation launches neophytes on the lifelong enterprise of ongoing conversion. Baptism commits them to prayerful sensitivity to the divine Mother's sanctifying inspirations that deepen hope, faith, love, and practical longing for justice. The rite of confirmation commits neophytes to lifelong responsiveness to whatever charisms of service she may bestow.

The Vocational Sacraments and Charismatic Ministry

Two forms of Christian charismatic ministry require official, public confirmation prior to their exercise: marriage and ordained ministry. The authentic exercise of any charismatic ministry, including that of the married and ordained, presupposes, of course, an initial conversion to Christ. As we shall see, both ordained ministry and the ministry of married Christians seek in addition to deepen conversion in the ministers and to foster it in others.

In the present chapter and in the chapter that follows, we will consider the ministry of married Christians and the rites that sanction it. This chapter deals with the Christianization of marriage and with some of the controversies that Christian marriage has occasioned. In the next chapter we shall reflect on the marriage covenant itself, on the commitment it embodies and on its consequences.

This chapter divides into three sections. The first section attempts to retrieve the biblical foundations of a theology of Christian marriage. The second traces the gradual Christianization of the ritual of matrimony. The third section examines some of the controversial issues that have arisen in the development of Christian marriage practices.

1. Biblical Foundations for a Theology of Christian Marriage. Jesus of Nazareth did not begin the institution of marriage. On the contrary, he seems to have insisted that the God who created human sexuality had (Mark 10:2-9; Matt 19:4-6). Jesus did, however, change the institution of marriage as he found it in three significant ways. First, he repudiated Mosaic divorce practices. Second, he demanded of his followers a certain quality of love that transformed the relationship of spouses to one another within marriage. Third, in sending the gift-giving Breath on Pentecost, he transformed Christian marriage into a form of charismatic ministry within the Church. Let us reflect on each of these innovations in turn.

a. Jesus Rejected Mosaic Divorce Practices. In the generation before Jesus' ministry, rabbinic opinion divided in its interpretation of the divorce law enunciated in Deuteronomy 24:1-4. The law allowed a husband to dismiss his wife from his house by writing and handing her a bill of divorce on the condition that he had found "something indecent" in her.

Rabbinic Debates about Divorce

Leading rabbis disagreed about the meaning of the crucial phrase "something indecent." Rabbi Hillel used his famous liberality in interpreting the law in order to render the phrase to the legal advantage of Jewish husbands and to the disadvantage of Jewish wives. He allowed that husbands could dismiss their wives for almost anything about her that displeased them. Rabbi Shammai, on the other hand, noted for his severe, conservative reading of the law, insisted that "something shameful" meant seriously immoral sexual conduct. His rigorous reading of the law gave Jewish wives more legal protection from the arbitrary whims of their husbands.

These rabbis' disciples prolonged the debate their teachers had begun in the generation before Jesus' birth. The famous Rabbi Akiba, a follower of Hillel, held that even something as trivial as a poorly prepared meal could justify dismissing one's wife; and other Hillelites expanded the list of justifying causes.

Jesus and Divorce in Mark

The Gospels of Mark and Matthew tell us that in the course of Jesus' ministry some Pharisees challenged him to take a stand on this debated question (Mark 10:1-12; Matt 19:3-12). Mark situates Jesus' judgment on Jewish divorce practices in an eschatological context. It occurs in "The Way" section of Mark's Gospel, in which Jesus predicts his own death three times and instructs his disciples in the meaning of discipleship. Moreover, Mark situates Jesus' teaching concerning marriage in Judea, as Jesus draws near to Jerusalem and to death and resurrection (Mark 10:1). For Mark, then, Christian discipleship interpreted in the light of the paschal mystery provides the proper theological context for understanding Jesus' teaching about marriage.

Mark describes how some Pharisees ask Jesus whether a Jewish husband is "permitted" to dismiss his wife (Mark 10:2). Jesus responds to their query with a question of His own. He asks them: "What did Moses command you?" (Mark 10:3) The Pharisees are looking upon the divorce legislation in Deuteronomy as permitting divorce; Mark's Jesus by contrast regards it as a command. Moreover, as the dialogue proceeds Jesus will make it clear that in his judgment the Mosaic command contradicts the will of God.

In Mark's account of the incident the Pharisees miss Jesus' distinction between "permission" and "command." They reply: "Moses permitted a man to write a writ of dismissal and send her away" (Mark 10:4). Jesus, however, immediately insists on the distinction he has made. He not only interprets the Deuteronomic legislation as a Mosaic command but as one improperly motivated by Jewish husbands' "hardness of heart" (Mark 10:5). Having done so, Jesus then attempts to shift the very terms of the discussion away from a choice between conflicting rabbinic interpretations of a badly motivated piece of legislation to a consideration of God's own will in the matter. He cites the account of the creation of humankind in Genesis and finds there a revelation of the divine intent concerning marriage. Jesus replies:

> Because of your hardness of heart he wrote that command for you. But from the beginning of creation "Male and female he made them." "For this reason a man shall leave his father and

mother and shall cleave to his wife, and the two shall become one body." So that they are no longer two, but one body. Therefore, what God has joined man must not separate (Mark 10:5-9).

Jesus is holding up to his interlocutors a lofty ideal of human marriage: one of enduring fidelity and loyalty. Through marriage husband and wife become "one body," that is, one person, before the Law and human society. That divine act of uniting takes precedence over any human legislation or legislative practice. Jesus therefore pronounces apodictically: let no man attempt to sunder what God has united.

Mark appends to this pronouncement a private conversation between Jesus and his disciples in which he clarifies for them its consequences. Jesus explains to the disciples: "Whoever dismisses his wife and marries another commits adultery against her. And if she dismisses her husband and marries another, she commits adultery" (Mark 10:11-12).

Jewish law did not allow wives to dismiss their husbands at the time Jesus lived and taught, but Roman law did. The exchange between Jesus and his disciples almost certainly expresses, therefore, Mark's own attempt to apply Jesus' teaching concerning Jewish divorce practices to the situation of the Gentile Christians for whom he wrote. Mark, in explaining to his Gentile audience how he thought Jesus would have reacted to Roman divorce law, portrays Jesus as forbidding both husbands and wives the right to divorce their spouses unilaterally. Mark's Jesus, however, remains silent on another point of Roman law, which allowed not only the unilateral dismissal of one spouse by another but also dissolved a marriage through the mutual consent of both spouses.

Jesus and Divorce in Matthew

Matthew's Gospel refers twice to Jesus' rejection of mosaic divorce practices. In the Sermon on the Mount Jesus teaches:

> It was also said, "Whoever dismisses his wife must give her a writ of dismissal." But I say to you, whoever dismisses his wife, except in the case of her uncleanness [*porneia*], makes her to commit adultery; and whoever marries a woman who has been dismissed, he commits adultery (Matt 5:31-32).

Matthew, however, inserts this saying into a series of similar teachings in which Jesus fulfills the law by demanding more, not less, of his disciples than the law did. Matthew, however, changes Jesus' prohibition by inserting the exceptive clause: "except for *porneia* (uncleanness)."

This exceptive clause has exercised Scripture scholars, who generally regard it as an interpolation by Matthew that seeks to clarify Jesus' original teaching. Unfortunately, however, exegetes have to date failed to agree on what the clarification means.[1] The phrase apparently attenuates in some way Jesus' original teaching. The terms of Matthew's qualification remain, however, obscure.

Matthew also records (in a slightly different version from Mark's) the story of Jesus' discussion of the Deuteronomic divorce law with a group of inquiring Pharisees. Matthew rephrases the question that the Pharisees put to Jesus. They ask: "Is a man permitted to dismiss his wife for just any reason?" (Matt 19:3).

Matthew notes the malice behind the query. The questioners tacitly acknowledge Jesus' liberal approach to the law on some issues and hope now to turn that same liberality to his discredit. The question as Matthew phrases it has more historical plausibility than Mark's version, since any Jewish male would have known that Mosaic law permitted husbands to divorce their wives. In Matthew's Gospel, however, Jesus' adversaries challenge him to take a stand with the disciples of Hillel.

Matthew's Jesus evades their trap, but he fails to insist on the need to interpret the Deuteronomic divorce law as a command in the way that Mark's Jesus does. Instead, the evangelist attributes this interpretation to Jesus' adversaries, an interpretation that Matthew's Jesus in contrast to Mark's will contest (Matt 19:7). In reply to his adversaries' original question, however, Matthew's Jesus plunges immediately to the heart of the matter:

> He said in reply: "Don't you know that he who created them in the beginning 'made them male and female'?" And he said, " 'For this reason a man will leave his father and his mother and will cling to his wife, and the two shall become one body.' So they are no longer two but one body. Therefore what God has joined man must not separate" (Matt 19:4-6).

Jesus shifts the terms of the debate from a choice between contradictory rabbinic interpretations of the Deuteronomic code to obedience

---

1. For a comprehensive survey of different scholarly renderings of the exceptive clause in Matthew, see Theodore Mackin, S. J., *Divorce and Remarriage: Marriage in the Catholic Church* (New York: Paulist, 1984), 60–66.

to the will of God revealed in his creation of human sexuality. Matthew's Jesus, like Mark's, asserts that the commitment of marriage transforms the spouses into a single moral person before the Law and before the rest of the community. He denies to Jewish husbands the right to sunder a union effected by God. Once again, however, Matthew's Jesus takes a less apodictic stand than Mark's. In replying to an objection from the Pharisees, who ask, "Why then did Moses command 'to give a writ of dismissal and so dismiss her'?" Matthew's Jesus responds:

> Because of your hardness of heart Moses permitted you to dismiss your wives. But in the beginning it was not so. I say to you that whoever dismisses his wife, except for her uncleanness [*porneia*], and marries another commits adultery (Matt 19:8-9).

Matthew once again inserts the exceptive clause into Jesus' interpretation of Jewish divorce practices. In the process he attenuates somewhat the absoluteness of Jesus' earlier pronouncement: "What God has joined man must not separate." Here too the exceptive clause derives most probably from the evangelist rather than from Jesus himself. Nevertheless, its citation for a second time does nothing to clarify its meaning.

Even thus qualified, however, Jesus' repudiation of Mosaic divorce practices strikes dismay into the hearts of his disciples, who object: "If this is the way it is with a man and his wife, it is better not to marry" (Matt 19:10). It fits the literary pattern of Matthew's Gospel for the disciples to misunderstand important sayings of Jesus and thus force him to clarify them. They do so in this case as well; Jesus replies to their objection:

> Not everyone can accept this teaching, but only those to whom it is given. Some there are who are eunuchs from their mother's womb; some have been made so by men; and some have made themselves so for the kingdom of God. Let him accept this teaching who can (Matt 19:11-12).

Does the metaphor "becoming a eunuch for the kingdom of God" allude cryptically to Jesus' own celibacy? Possibly. The phrase, however, certainly refers the disciples' willingness to renounce divorce. The metaphor is bracketed by two references to "this teaching": namely, the teaching he has just enunciated in his exchange with the Pharisees. Membership in the kingdom will, Jesus warns, demand sexual sacrifices. It will put a crimp in the Jewish male's freedom to replace one wife with another. Nevertheless, those "to whom it is given" will hear Jesus' words and respond.

While Mark situates Jesus' teaching about divorce in an eschatological context, Matthew links it to the kingdom. Membership in the kingdom, Matthew's Jesus warns, demands a revision of traditional Jewish perceptions of marriage and divorce. In the process it also forces a reevaluation of the relationship of husband and wife within marriage.

Jesus and Divorce in Luke

Luke deals with Jesus' teaching on divorce more cryptically than either Mark or Matthew. He omits any reference to the exchange between Jesus and the Pharisees. Instead Luke has Jesus state baldly: "Everyone who dismisses his own wife and marries another commits adultery; and anyone who marries a woman who has been dismissed by her husband commits adultery" (Luke 16:18). Luke's Jesus, then, contents himself with commenting on two possible forms of conduct available to the Jewish husbands of his day. Any husband who divorces his wife and remarries commits adultery; anyone who marries a divorced woman commits adultery.

Luke's Jesus fails to comment in any way on divorce initiated by a married woman. He says nothing about the marital status of adulterous men. He makes no statement at all concerning the indissolubility of marriage.

The Synoptic Gospels give us, then, no detailed insight into Jesus' thoughts on the significance of marriage. They leave us to judge for ourselves whether Jesus regarded the divorce law in Deuteronomy as a command or a permission. They do, however, assert clearly that Jesus, when confronted with the debate between the disciples of Shammai and Hillel, tried to shift the grounds of the argument from a choice between two rabbinic schools of thought to a consideration of the divine will revealed in the creation of marriage and sexuality. He denied to his male followers the freedom to dismiss their wives that the Hillelites sanctioned but did so on different terms from Rabbi Shammai. Jesus regarded such a dismissal, not as an illegitimate interpretation of the Deuteronomic code, but as a violation of the divine creative will itself. He seems also to have taught that the mutual marital consent of spouses transforms them into a single moral person.

b. Jesus Demanded a Special Quality of Love from His Disciples. In addition to repudiating the Mosaic divorce code, Jesus changed his disciples' perception of marriage by the quality of love he demanded of them. All three Synoptic Gospels record Jesus' endorsement of the great commandment. Mark gives the most extended account. A scribe asks Jesus which commandment of the Law qualifies as the greatest. Jesus replies:

> This is the first: Listen, Israel, the Lord our God is the one Lord, and you must love the Lord your God with all your heart, with all your soul, with all your mind, and with all your strength. The second is this: You must love your neighbor as yourself. There is no commandment greater than these.

When the scribe endorses Jesus' reply enthusiastically, Jesus assures him that he "is not far from the kingdom of God" (Mark 10:28-34).

New questers for the historical Jesus note that concern to identify the greatest commandment of the Law characterized more the piety of Diaspora Jews than that of Palestinian Judaism. On that basis some question whether Jesus ever took a position on the subject, even though they concede that his teaching on the two greatest commandments completely agrees with the rest of his doctrine. Since, however, Diaspora Jews came in large numbers annually to Jerusalem, we cannot rule out apodictically the possibility that one of them might have taken the opportunity to sound out one of the leading Palestinian rabbis on the subject. In other words, the incident narrated in the Gospels may well root itself in history. Moreover, both Mark and Matthew situate the incident in Jesus' final Jerusalem ministry, while Luke relocates it in Jesus' journey discourse.

The three Synoptic accounts, however, vary in dramatic details. Matthew and Luke offer abbreviated versions of the incident. Matthew's Jesus in citing Deut 6:5 and Lev 19:18 omits the phrase "with all your strength" from the first text. Moreover, he assures the scribe that "on these two commandments hang the whole Law, and the Prophets also" (Matt 22:34-40). Luke describes Jesus' questioner as a lawyer who asks him what one must do to obtain eternal life. Jesus challenges the lawyer to answer his own question; and when the latter cites Deut 6:5 and Lev 19:18, Jesus approves his response with the words: "You have answered right. Do this and you shall live" (Luke 10:25-28).

In Mark's account Jesus cites Deut 6:5 as the most fundamental commandment in the Hebrew Scriptures and links it to the love of neighbor commended in Lev 19:18. The pious Jew of Jesus' time would have interpreted the meaning of these two commandments in the light of the Torah. When, however, Mark's Jesus assures the scribe that in endorsing these two commands as the greatest he "is not far from the kingdom of God," Jesus is in fact suggesting an alternative way of understanding their meaning. Jesus is telling his questioner that one must interpret both commandments in the light of his own vision of the kingdom (Mark 12:28-34).

Jesus and the Great Commandment in Matthew

Matthew makes a similar theological move. His Gospel portrays Jesus as the divine lawgiver whose teachings give moral content to the new covenant. Moreover, in having Jesus remind the scribe that from these two commandments the whole Law and the Prophets all hang, Matthew tacitly reminds the reader as well that Jesus has come to fulfill both (cf. Matt 5:17). Jesus' vision of the kingdom, therefore, replaces the Torah as the context for interpreting the meaning of the two great commandments.

Jesus and the Great Commandment in Luke

Luke makes Jesus' endorsement of the great commandment a preface to the parable of the good Samaritan. The lawyer who had questioned Jesus, apparently embarrassed at having tacitly admitted to asking him a question whose answer he already knew, asks a second time in self-justification: "And who is my neighbor?" Jesus replies with the story of the good Samaritan.

The parable also makes it clear in its own way that the two great commandments must be understood in the light of Jesus vision of the kingdom. The love that he demands of his disciples must imitate the Father's own gratuitous love. It must like the Samaritan reach across social barriers. It must embrace anyone in need. It must effect both healing and social liberation (Luke 10:30-37).

Each of the Synoptic evangelists, therefore, uses different theological strategies in order to make it clear that the two great commandments of the old Law must be interpreted in the light of the new. For the converted Christian, then, love of God and of one's neighbor as oneself translates practically into the willingness to submit to the ethics of discipleship that Jesus proclaimed.

We obey the great commandments when we allow trust in the Father's providential care to free us from attachment to our worldly possessions in order that we might share them with the needy, the alienated, and the dispossessed. We live the two great commandments by imitating Jesus' own table fellowship with sinners, by reaching out to the marginal and oppressed, by seeking to obliterate the social barriers that divide people from one another. Love of God and of neighbor demands too the willingness to forgive one another with the same gratuitous, atoning love as God has revealed to us in a crucified and risen savior.

By deriving the moral content of the two great commandments from the other teachings of Jesus, the Synoptic evangelists make it theologically irrelevant whether or not the historical Jesus ever cited Deuteronomy and Leviticus.

As we have seen, the Fourth Gospel does not reproduce Jesus' moral teaching with the same detail as the Synoptics. John the evangelist, however, clearly looks upon Jesus Himself as the ultimate revelation of the meaning of both divine and human love. John's Jesus gives his disciples a "new commandment": "Love one another just as I have loved you" (John 13:33).

Christian Marital Love

The first Christians recognized that loving one another in the name and image of Jesus transformed every human relationship including familial ones. We find that recognition reflected in Christian modifications of the household codes commonly employed in the first century to describe domestic relationships. For example, the household code in the Letter to the Colossians reminds the reader six times in the course of nine verses that in Christian families people ought to relate to one another "in the Lord" (Col 3:18–4:1). In other words, Jesus' vision and example must transform from within the way the members of Christian households deal with one another on a day-to-day basis. That insistence mutes somewhat but not entirely the traditionally patriarchal tone of such codes.

The household code in Colossians, for example, includes the following exhortations:

> Wives be subject to your husbands, as is fitting in the Lord. Husbands, love your wives, and do not be harsh to them. Children obey your parents in everything, for this pleases the Lord. Fathers do not provoke your children, lest they become discouraged (Col 3:18-21).

The passage subjects wives to husbands and children to parents in the manner of the traditional household codes, but it qualifies that subjection in both cases. Wives should be subject only "as is fitting

in the Lord." The phrase suggests that Christian wives should interpret their subjection to their husbands in the light of gospel values.
Moreover, in urging husbands to love their wives, the author of the
letter uses the characteristically Christian verb agapan, which designates gospel-inspired love. In other words, husbands should love their
wives in the ways that Christian love demands. Moreover, both in
the relationship between spouses and in that between parents and
children a reciprocity of love and responsibility obtains.

The Letter to the Ephesians makes a similar point. It compares
the love of two spouses to the love relationship between Christ and
his Church.

> Be subject to one another out of reverence to Christ. Wives, be
> to your husbands, as to the Lord. For the husband is the head
> of the wife as Christ is the head of the Church, his body, and is
> himself its Savior. As the Church is subject to Christ, so let wives
> be in everything to their husbands. Husbands, love your wives,
> as Christ loved the Church and gave himself up for her, that he
> might sanctify her, having cleansed her by the washing of water
> with the word, that he might present the Church to himself in
> splendor, without spot or wrinkle or any such thing, that she
> might be holy and without blemish. Even so husbands should
> love their wives as their own bodies. He who loves his wife loves
> himself. For no man ever hates his own flesh, but nourishes and
> cherishes it, as Christ does the Church, because we are members
> of his body. "For this reason a man shall leave his father and
> mother and be joined to his wife, and the two shall become one
> flesh." This mystery is a profound one; I speak with regard to
> Christ and the Church. Nevertheless, let each of you love his wife
> as himself, and let the wife see that she respects the husband (Eph
> 5:21-33).

The passage begins by insisting on the mutual subjection of Christian spouses to one another within marriage. It then invokes the relationship of Christ to the Church to clarify the terms of that subjection.
Wives should "be toward" their husbands as the Church relates in
subjection to Christ. Husbands should relate to their wives as the servant Messiah related to his Church: He suffered and died in order
to purify and beautify it. Moreover, Christ's love for the Church transforms it into his body. Christ and his body constitute a single moral
person in a manner analogous to the way marriage transforms husband and wife into a single moral person.

Clearly, the mutual subjection of spouses for which the letter
calls excludes any hint of power or domination in their relationship.

Rather, it binds husband and wife together in a reciprocity of love that seeks to imitate the redeeming, forgiving love of Christ. They cooperate within marriage freely and willingly. The husband does not exercise "headship" over the wife in the manner of other husbands. As subjected to their wives in mutual service husbands can exercise headship only with the self-sacrificing love of the servant Christ. Wives for their part should seek to love and serve their husbands with the same love that draws the Church to Christ.

Here, moreover, we should note that in this exhortatory passage the Letter to the Ephesians makes no statement whatsoever about the metaphysical indestructability of sacramental marriage, as a later medieval theology would claim. Instead, the author of the letter simply holds up Christlike love as a moral ideal for Christian spouses. In so doing the passage gives eloquent testimony to the realization that the quality of love that Christian discipleship demands redeems and transforms the relationship between husband and wife.

c. By Sending the Gift-giving Pentecostal Breath, the Risen Christ Transformed Christian Marriage into an Ecclesial Ministry. The Apostle Paul realized that the charismatic character of Christian marriage also distinguishes it from other marital unions. He made the point in his First Letter to the Church at Corinth.

The Corinthian community had sent him by letter several questions that they wished him to clarify. Among other things they asked him about the advisability of practicing sexual abstinence within marriage as a way of fostering prayer. Paul conceded the legitimacy in principle of a couple deciding by mutual consent to abstain from sex, but conscious of the multiple temptations to promiscuity that the city of Corinth afforded, he cautioned Christian spouses against starving one another sexually, especially for prolonged periods of time. Instead, both husband and wife should show concern to satisfy one another's sexual needs (1 Cor 7:1-6).

Paul concluded these reflections with the remark: "I wish that all people were as I; but each has his own gift [*charisma*] from God, one this, another that" (1 Cor 7:7). By way of clarification, he would explain later in the same letter that he found apostolic advantages in the celibate life he himself lived: it freed him for the work of the kingdom (1 Cor 7:25ff.). Nevertheless, in describing Christian marriage as a charism Paul insisted on its graced character. The Holy Breath anoints Christian spouses to live together as husband and wife. Their graced union in Christ gives concrete expression to the saving gift bestowed on us in Jesus' death, resurrection, and mission of the Holy Breath.

We have reflected on the biblical foundations for a theology of Christian marriage. Let us, then, examine the way Christian marriage practices evolved.

2. The Christianization of the Rites of Marriage. We have no detailed knowledge of the marriage customs of the first Christians. Moreover, during the first three centuries we find only sporadic references to marriage in the writings of the fathers. In A.D. 110 Ignatius of Antioch counseled believers not to get married without first obtaining episcopal approval, but we have no way of knowing the extent to which people actually adhered to such a practice at the time that he wrote (*To Polycarp,* 5). In the second century, Athenagoras of Athens alluded to the existence of Christian marriage procedures (*Legatio,* 33); and in the third, Clement of Alexandria spoke of a blessing used in Christian marriages. Tertullian described marriages that "the Church arranges, the Sacrifice strengthens, upon which the blessing sets a seal, at which angels are present as witnesses, and to which the Father gives his consent" (*Ad Uxorem,* 2.8.6-9).

Tertullian's description provides some evidence that by the third century Christians had significantly transformed pagan marriage customs. Instead of a relative or close friend arranging the marriage, as pagans did, the Church now made the arrangements. The Christian Eucharist replaced a pagan sacrifice as the marriage rite's confirming ritual. The couple received a Christian, not a pagan, blessing. Angels replaced the household gods as witnesses to the event. God the Father sealed the union. Tertullian also argued for the appropriateness of celebrating Christian weddings in church.

Despite the thinness of the evidence, we may, then, infer with some confidence that during the first three centuries Christians gradually transformed the domestic marriage ritual of the pagans into a church service presided over by either a presbyter or a bishop. Moreover, while Christian marriages seem to have derived their structure from pagan ritual, the Church Christianized the rite by systematically replacing pagan with Christian symbols.

Fourth Century Developments

In the fourth century, Christian marriages, like the other rites of the Church, underwent symbolic embellishment. We find some evidence of a period of betrothal, sometimes ritualized by the gift of a ring. Ordinarily a presbyter or bishop presided at the marriage and blessed it. In addition, however, we find the use of psalmody and of the epithalamion, a marriage prayer in hymnic form. During the marriage ceremony near relatives held crowns over the couple's head (or sometimes over the bride's head only). In Syria the ceremony included an imposition of hands (Basil of Caesarea, *Hexameron,* 7.5; Gregory of Nazianzus, *Oratio 4, On Holy Baptism,* 18; John Chrysostom, *Homily on 1 Tim 9, In Gen. Hom.,* 48.6; Ephraem the Syrian, *Commentary on the Gospel,* 2.26). In both Syria and Palestine Christians seem to have adopted the Jewish custom of seven days of feasting during nuptial celebrations (John Chrysostom, *Bapt. Inst.,* 6.24, *De res. dom.,* 50).

By the fourth century, the Latin Church had also adopted the marriage blessing but tended to restrict its use to first marriages (Ambrosiaster, *Liber quaestionum,* 50.400, *In Ep. I ad Cor.,* 7.40, *In Ep. I ad Tim.,* 3.12; Ambrose of Milan, *Exp. in Lucam* 6.1386.9; Paulinus of Nola, *Carmen* 25). Ambrose of Milan spoke of a period of betrothal sealed by a kiss (*Exp. in Lucam,* 7.231, *De poenitentia,* 2.3.18, *De Isaak et anima,* 1.8). Instead of crowns the western Church ordinarily preferred the symbolic use of a veil during the wedding ceremony. Sometimes the celebrant veiled the bride during the nuptial blessing (Pope Siricius I, *Ep. I. 4, ad Himerium*); sometimes the veil was draped over the shoulders of both the bride and groom (Paulinus of Nola, *Carmen* 25; Augustine, *De peccato originali,* 36.41). In the Latin Church we also find evidence of signed legal documents attesting to the wedding contract (Sidonius Apollinaris, *Ep. 7,* 2.7; Augustine, *Ennaratio in Ps.* 80, 21). As the liturgical year took shape, the western Church discouraged marriage during Advent and Lent.

Medieval Marriage Rituals

Roman sacramentaries laid the foundations for medieval marriage rituals. They situated the wedding in a Eucharistic context and in addition to nuptial blessings provided special collects,[2] secrets,[3] and other prayers. The sacramentaries give evidence of the use of extemporaneous prayers on traditional religious themes: creation, especially, the creation of the sexes; God's blessing of Adam and Eve; prayers for a successful marriage and for the virtues it requires; prayers for fecundity; prayers urging the imitation of Old Testament couples.

---

2. The collect, a prayer pronounced by the celebrant, terminated the introductory rites of Eucharistic worship.

3. Because the Eucharistic celebrant ended the preparation of gifts with a silent prayer, it took the name "secret."

As Roman ritual evolved, it diverged from other Christian liturgical traditions by restricting the nuptial blessing to the bride.

The early Middle Ages brought a rich flowering of marriage rituals with the emergence of Anglo-Norman, Mozarabic, and Roman Rites. Despite considerable variations from one region of Europe to another, certain ritual patterns emerge. (1) The posting of banns, a triple public announcement of the wedding, ordinarily preceded the ceremony itself. (2) We find the first reference to the use of marriage rings in Spanish Mozarabic ritual. As the custom of blessing and exchanging rings spread, it first followed the nuptial Eucharist as an optional ritual then preceded the Eucharist as a prescribed rite. A formula for the exchange of rings first appeared in England, but it quickly spread to the rest of Europe. We can trace the use of two rings in the ceremony no earlier than the eleventh century. (3) The formal ritual exchange of consent acquired enhanced importance and eventually replaced the reading of the dowery [*dos*], which in the earliest medieval rituals symbolized the tacit consent of the couple. The exchange of vows tended to follow a basic Roman formula. As the formal exchange of marital consent acquired enhanced liturgical importance, the rite of betrothal tended to fall into obsolescence. (4) In contrast to the eastern Church, western marriages emphasized the differentiation of sex roles and contained special prayers for the bride. (5) In French and German ritual, the priest played a somewhat more active role; often he handed the bride over to the groom before the couple pronounced its consent to the marriage. (6) British marriages abounded in marriage blessings. (7) The German church usually celebrated marriages outside the Eucharist.

During the early Middle Ages in the East, the Byzantine, Armenian, Coptic, Ethiopic, and old Syriac rites developed distinctive marriage rituals. Here again, however, certain liturgical patterns emerge: (1) The crowning ceremony in marriage gained universal acceptance and acquired rich and diversified liturgical symbolism. It became the focus of many prayers and hymns. We find little tendency to adopt the western practice of veiling. (2) The rites of marriage include both betrothal and marriage in fairly close succession. (3) The eastern Church always celebrated marriage publicly and embellished the ceremony with priestly blessings and prayers that addressed the needs and aspirations of the couple. (4) The absence of an eastern equivalent of the Latin "low Mass," tended to dissociate the celebration of marriage from a Eucharistic context. (5) Oriental rituals show a willingness to incorporate folkloric elements into Christian ritual, like the Ethiopic custom of hair cutting or the Chaldean use of penitential ashes. (6) One finds the occasional survival of domestic rituals, the liturgical residue of practices that preceded weddings in churches. (7) Oriental ritual tends to emphasize the spiritual significance of marriage, often with references to Eph 5 or to John 2. (8) In contrast to the western Church which tended to acquiesce in gloomy Augustinian assessments of human sexuality, the oriental Church preserved a positive biblical attitude toward both marriage and sex.

Marriage in Protestant and Anglican Ritual

Pastoral concern during the Middle Ages had motivated the increased use of vernacular prayers during the wedding ceremony. In the sixteenth century, the Protestant reformers translated the entire ritual into the vernacular. Luther shortened the ceremony but preserved more of the medieval ritual than Calvin. Lutheran weddings used different parts of the church, retained the ring ceremony and the ritual joining of hands at the exchange of vows. Lutheran marriage ritual invited local embellishment but tended toward the austere. Calvin eliminated the ring ceremony and the joining of hands, expanded the marriage promises, and stressed liturgically the couple's need for divine grace.

In England Cranmer devised a two-part ceremony. The first part began with a long exhortation. The celebrant then gave public opportunity for the lodging of a marriage impediment. The couple exchanged vows and (unblessed) rings. They then joined hands as the priest blessed their union. The second part of the ceremony began with a *Kyrie* followed by the Our Father. It ended with four prayers: a blessing filled with Old Testament allusions, a optional prayer for offspring, a prayer that reinforced the woman's changed social status, and a prayer with allusions to Adam and Eve. Methodist ritual adopted Cranmer's ceremony with minor modifications. John Knox, however, copied the austere Geneva rite, but in time the Presbyterian Church expanded it somewhat.

Marriage in the Catholic Church

The Council of Trent did little to revise the Christian rite of marriage. It asserted the Church's right to regulate marriage discipline and abolished clandestine marriages (DS 1797–1816).

In the twentieth century, Vatican II sanctioned the vernacular celebration of marriage, mandated the revision of the marriage rite along with the other sacraments, and encouraged the celebration of marriage within a Eucharistic context (*Sacrosanctum Concilium,* 62–63, 77–78). The revised rite of marriage amplified the liturgical readings and number of vow formulas and gave enhanced importance to the celebrant's homily during the wedding ceremony.

We have considered some of the important stages in the evolution of Christian marriage ritual. That evolution helps contextualize some of the controversies that have surrounded Christian marriage. In the section that follows we shall examine some of the issues that those controversies raised.

3. Issues in the Development of Christian Marriage. We can identify three principal areas of controversy in the development of Christian marriage practices. First, while some theologians and Churches defend the sacramentality of the marriage ritual, others deny it. Second, while canonical legislation in the Roman Catholic Church regards a ratified, consummated marriage as indissoluble, other Christian traditions have taken a less rigorous stand on this issue. Third, theologians diverge in their interpretation of the values that Christian marriage seeks to embody. Let us reflect on each of these controversies in turn. As we shall see, they tend to overlap.

a. Is Marriage a Sacrament? It took theologians twelve centuries to include marriage in the canon of the sacraments. Why the delay? It resulted from a convergence of cultural forces.

Augustine on the "Goods" of Marriage

Although Augustine of Hippo included sacramentality among the "goods" of marriage, nevertheless, as we have already seen, he espoused a dim view of human nature in general and of human sexuality in particular. He portrayed marriage as providing an outlet for concupiscent sexual desires. He held, however, that spouses who indulge in sex for lustful motives rather than for the procreation of children commit sin. He therefore deemed it likely that the use of sex even within marriage would provide husband and wife with an occasion for committing venial sin (Augustine, *On Marriage and Concupiscence, On the Good of Marriage,* I, xvii–xviv).

Augustine's gloomy assessment of human sexuality enjoyed wide acceptance during the Middle Ages. As a consequence, theologians found themselves loathe to include in the canon of the sacraments a contract whose fulfillment placed men and women in a proximate occasion of sin.

The Canonical Definition of Marriage

In the twelfth century the decision of medieval canonists to define Christian marriage as indissoluble certainly encouraged the inclusion of marriage in the canon of the sacraments. We shall examine below the theological motives that led canonists to take such a stand. Once, however, medieval theologians had convinced themselves that a ratified, consummated Christian marriage gives symbolic expression to the indestructible love of Christ for his Church, they found themselves better disposed to regard the rite of marriage as a sacrament of the Church.

In the twelfth century Peter Lombard included marriage in his list of Christian sacraments (Peter Lombard, *The Book of Sentences,* IV, d.31, a.1). So too did Hugh of St. Victor (Hugh of St. Victor, *On the Sacraments,* II, xi, 1-7); and the great scholastic theologians followed suit (Bonaventure, *Commentary on the Book of Sentences,* IV, d.31, a.1, qq.1-2; Thomas Aquinas, *Commentary on the Book of Sentences,* IV, d. xxvi, q.2, aa.1-3; John Duns Scotus, *Oxford Commentary on the Book of Sentences,* IV, d.31, a.1, qu.un.).

The fifteenth century saw marriage officially canonized as a sacrament of the Church in the decrees of the Council of Florence (DS 1327).

The Protestant Denial

The following century, however, Zwingli, Luther, and Calvin all denied the sacramentality of marriage (Ulrich Zwingli, *Commentary on True and False Religion,* 15; Martin Luther, *Works,* 36:92-94; John Calvin, *Institutes of the Christian Religion,* IV, 19, 34) Predictably, the Council of Trent, which defended late medieval sacramental piety at the same time that it tried to reform it, responded by vindicating the sacramentality of Christian marriage (DS 1797–1812). Protestants and Catholics have remained divided on this issue ever since.

b. The Indissolubility of Christian Marriage. The Gospels remind Christians of every generation that Jesus had in his day repudiated Mosaic divorce practices, but every generation of Christians has had to apply Jesus' teaching to pastoral situations more complex than the one he addressed. As one might expect, over the centuries theologians and pastoral leaders have not always agreed on the best way to interpret Jesus' injunction against divorce.

New Testament Exceptions

Even during the apostolic age Church leaders had wrestled with the pastoral application of Jesus' teaching in situations very different from first-century, Palestinian Judaism. Whatever the intent of Matthew's exceptive clause, it sought to clarify the apparent rigor of Jesus' teaching. Paul the Apostle had allowed Christians to separate from pagan spouses who refused to live with them in marital peace. In effect he counselled that Christians not obstruct civil divorce proceedings initiated by the troublesome non-Christian spouse (1 Cor 7:12-16). Moreover, he did so with full awareness of Jesus' repudiation of Deuteronomic divorce laws (1 Cor 7:10-11).

Divorce and Remarriage in the Eastern Church

The Fathers of the Church in their day puzzled over the meaning of Matthew's exceptive clause. They, however, erroneously attributed the clause's authorship to Jesus himself, as would medieval theologians after them. Moreover they interpreted the exceptive clause as sanctioning the divorce of an adulterous spouse.

Accordingly, during the first four centuries, theologians generally allowed Christian husbands the right to dismiss their wives when the latter committed adultery. Most conceded the same right to the wife of an adulterous husband. Most of the Fathers censured severely a man who divorced his wife for her adultery and then remarried, but some Church authorities seem to have tolerated the practice as the lesser of two evils. Moreover, a few of the Fathers conceded cautiously that the dismissing spouse could remarry provided that adultery had in fact justified the dismissal. The guilty party, however, would sin if he or she attempted marriage after dismissal. Moreover, even though in the eastern Church those who ignored Church discipline by obtaining a civil divorce and then remarrying were treated as adulterers and required to do penance; nevertheless, the patristic Church regarded the second marriage as legal and binding.[4]

It should, then, come as no surprise that oriental Christianity came to adopt a more tolerant discipline in dealing with divorce and remarriage than would the Latin Church. The oriental Church itself grants no divorces, but it does allow Christians who obtain civil

---

4. For a careful, scholarly treatment of the development of Church legislation concerning divorce, see Theodore Mackin, S. J., *Marriage in the Catholic Church: Divorce and Remarriage* (New York: Paulist, 1984).

divorces to remarry in the Church. This second marriage is looked upon as real but not as sacramental.

Divorce and Remarriage in the Latin Church

In the West, however, Jerome and especially Augustine laid the theological foundations for a more rigorous interpretation of the indissolubility of Christian marriage. They regarded dismissal for adultery not as a true dissolution of marriage but only as a separation of the spouses that leaves the marriage bond intact. Augustine recognized, of course, that not all married couples have children and that spouses do in fact separate. He taught, however, that when other goods of marriage fail "something matrimonial" (*quiddam matrimoniale*) nevertheless survives. He failed, however, to explain the nature of this matrimonial something, a lapse for which medieval theology would attempt to supply (Augustine, *On the Good of Marriage*, I, xvii–xxiv).

In the chaos that ensued upon the collapse of the Roman Empire, the legal regulation of marriage fell more and more to local episcopal courts; and in the early Middle Ages we find a growing body of ecclesiastical legislation that sought to bring both sexual mores and local marriage customs into closer alignment with Christian ideals.

The penitential manuals of the period give some insight into the kinds of pastoral problems that confronted Church leaders and missionaries. The manuals were compiled unofficially to aid confessors in assigning penances when administering the sacrament of reconciliation. Different manuals handle the question of divorce and remarriage with differing degrees of severity, but they generally allowed husbands to dismiss unfaithful wives and to remarry. Some manuals allowed remarriage in the case of one spouse abandoned by another who had chosen to pronounce the vows of religion. A freed slave whose spouse remained in bondage could also contract marriage with a second free partner. Couples separated when one was carried off in war could remarry.

Alarmed by the laxity with which the manuals handled the question of divorce and remarriage, popes made repeated attempts to impose a Roman contractual interpretation of marriage north of the Alps and to restrict the right to divorce; but until the twelfth century they lacked the effective authority to compel assent to their position.

Moreover, during the twelfth century theologians and canonists in the Latin tradition began moving toward a theological and legal definition of marriage. Roman theology, taking its inspiration from one strain in Roman law, held that the marriage contract creates the marriage.[5] The Germanic tribes in the north held that sexual intercourse did. In 1140 the canonist Francis Gratian combined the two traditions by teaching that sexual intercourse consummates the marriage contract, which in and of itself creates only an inchoate marriage; for prior to intercourse, the marriage contract, which confers upon spouses rights over one another's bodies, goes as yet fulfilled. He also held that the Church could dissolve inchoate marriages. Subsequent popes would claim that right.

Sacramental Indissolubility

The twelfth century brought another important transformation of a Latin understanding of Christian marriage. Augustine, as we have seen, had described Christian marriage as a *sacramentum.* By that he had meant that before God Christian spouses bind themselves with an unbreakable pledge to share their lives with one another. He had also spoken of a mysterious "matrimonial something" that survives even after spouses separate. In the twelfth century, canonists identified these two realities. They held that the sacrament of marriage survives the separation of the spouses because, once it is consummated, it images forth the unbreakable union of Christ and his Church. In other words, the unbreakable union of Christ and his Church makes marriage both a sacrament and indissoluble. The papacy of Alexander III transformed this interpretation of Christian marriage into Church law. Henceforth, western canonists would regard a consummated Christian marriage as intrinsically and extrinsically indestructible.

Eventually these medieval distinctions found codification in the 1917 Code of Canon Law. It defined a sacramental marriage as essentially one and indissoluble (*Codex Juris Canonici,* 1013). In other words, by legal fiat it built indissolubility into the very essence of a ratified, consummated marriage (*Codex Juris Canonici,* 1015); but it also reserved to the papacy in virtue of the "power of the keys" competence to dissolve certain kinds of marriages: nonconsummated sacramental ones and under certain conditions consummated, nonsacramental marriages.

5. Another strain in Roman law defined marriage as the blending of two lives (*consortium vitae*), but it would take the Church several centuries to adopt the latter approach to the institution of marriage.

More specifically, the papacy claims the right to dissolve non-sacramental marriages in the following two cases: (1) when two non-Christians contract marriage and when one of them subsequently seeks baptism and then desires freedom from the first marriage in order to marry sacramentally (the Pauline privilege, *Codex Juris Canonici,* 1120); (2) when an unbaptized person contracts marriage with a non-Catholic Christian and then desires the dissolution of the first marriage in order to seek baptism and marry sacramentally (the Petrine privilege, or privilege of faith, *Codex Juris Canonici,* 1127).

A strict canonical understanding of marriage finds no connection whatever between the legal creation of a marriage and the mutual love of the contracting spouses. A marriage exists objectively and indissolubly whenever ratified and consummated by two persons with the baptismal character on their souls. From a canonical standpoint, the marriage contract's essential indissolubility causes its sacramentality because it reproduces symbolically the absolute indissolubility of the bond uniting Christ and his Church. Such a marriage cannot therefore be dissolved by any power except the death of one of the partners.

Contemporary Debate over Indissolubility

Subsequent to the promulgation of the 1917 Code of Canon Law, Catholic theologians began to question the theological presuppositions that underlie this canonical interpretation of the indissolubility of Christian marriage. Critics complained that a purely canonical view of marriage reduces it to an impersonal, objective, metaphysical entity divorced from the human relationships that actually constitute a marriage's living reality. The critics argued that consent creates a marriage and that, while Christians *ought never* to withdraw such consent, in their limitation and sinfulness, nevertheless, they can and sometimes do—and in ways that destroy marriages permanently. When that occurs, the claim that an indestructible bond continues to unite two separated and mutually alienated spouses certainly, under present ecclesiastical discipline, prevents them from ever remarrying publicly in the Church; but, the critics argued, it does not in fact preserve the original marital bond in any meaningful sense of that term.

Critics of a purely juridical notion of marital indissolubility also claim (correctly) that when the Letter to the Ephesians compares Christian marriage to the relationship between Christ and the Church, it holds up to Christian spouses a moral ideal; but the letter does not in any way assert the absolute indestructibility of a ratified, consummated marriage. The critics therefore contend that the canonical legislation on divorce invokes dubious biblical and theological justification.

Before we can begin to understand the implications of this debate, however, we need to consider theological discussion of the "goods" of marriage.

c. The Goods of Marriage. Augustine of Hippo shaped decisively the ways in which theologians in the Latin tradition came to interpret the "goods" of marriage. By the goods of marriage they meant the values it ought to embody. Augustine discovered four goods in marriage: offspring, the mutual support of the spouses, the alleviation of concupiscence, and the *sacramentum* (sacrament). By the sacrament of marriage Augustine meant, as we have seen, the solemn and irrevocable pledge that spouses make before God to share their lives together till death parts them (Augustine, *On the Good of Marriage*, I, xvii–xxiv).

Medieval theologians commented variously on Augustine's theory of the goods of marriage; and eventually in the fifteenth century the Council of Florence assigned to sacramental marriage three goods: the conception and education of children, the mutual fidelity of the spouses, and indissolubility (DS 1327). By the fifteenth century for reasons discussed in the preceding section theologians had subsumed the sacramentality of marriage under the idea of its indissolubility. Accordingly, the council collapsed sacramentality and indissolubility into a single good.

The Personalist Interpretation of Marriage

Not until the twentieth century do we discover a significant attempt to rethink the values that Christian marriage seeks to incarnate. As we have seen, medieval theology looked upon marriage as a contract in which two parties bind themselves to perform a mutual service: namely, they consent freely to have sexual relations with one another. The act that creates the contract, the mutual consent of the spouses, ratifies the marriage; but only when the spouses deliver what they have contracted by having intercourse for the first time, do they consummate the marriage. At that point the marriage becomes intrinsically and extrinsically indestructible because it reproduces symbolically the indissoluble union of Christ and his Church. So taught medieval canonists.

Personalist theologians like Dietrich von Hildebrand and Herbert Doms argued that a medieval contractual theory of marriage failed to do justice to the interpersonal character of marital relationships. Personalist theology questioned the medieval assumption that procreation provides marriage with its primary end. They found such a description of marriage too impersonal and instrumental. Moreover, they insisted that marriage involves much more than making babies. They interpreted marriage as the interpersonal blending of two lives. They regarded the interpersonal union of husband and wife within marriage as a good in itself and not simply as a means of ensuring the survival of the human race.

In a personalist understanding of marriage sexual intercourse seeks in the first instance to effect and complete the union of two spouses. Every sexual act achieves this primary purpose of marriage whether or not it results in the conception of a child. In personalist theory, however, the union of husband and wife within marriage looks to two further ends: their growth and fulfillment as persons and the conception of the offspring that symbolize and express their union.[6]

Vatican II on the Goods of Marriage

Although at first the Vatican reacted negatively to a personalist reformulation of the purpose of marriage, that same formulation received a more favorable reception in the decrees of Vatican II. *Gaudium et spes* referred to marriage as "a community of love," as an "intimate partnership," as an institution created by the "marital covenant" (*Gaudium et spes*, 47–49). In other words, in describing the consent that creates a marriage Vatican II invoked the richly interpersonal, biblical notion of a "covenant" instead of the traditional, functional, legal notion of a "contract." The council also described the marital covenant as an act of interpersonal consent that binds a man and a woman to one another irrevocably. Once they consent to the marriage covenant, neither party can take that consent back nor can they give it back. Within the marriage covenant the two spouses give themselves to one another as persons. Moreover, the mutual self-gift that the marriage covenant embodies ought to pervade every aspect of Christian married life (*Gaudium et spes*, 48–49).

6. Dietrich von Hildebrand, *Marriage* (New York: Longmans Green, 1942); Herbert Doms, *The Meaning of Marriage,* translated by George Sayer (London: Sheed and Ward, 1939).

Clearly, the human capacity to enter into a marriage covenant of the kind that Vatican II described demands much more than the bare legal competence to make a contract about having sexual intercourse.

Humanae Vitae on the Values of Marriage

In his encyclical letter *Humanae vitae* Pope Paul VI endorsed a personalist approach to marriage. He wrote:

> By means of the reciprocal personal gift of self proper and exclusive to them, husband and wife tend towards the communion of their beings in view of mutual personal perfection, to collaborate with God in the generation and education of new lives (*Humanae vitae*, 8).

The Pope described conjugal love as human, total, faithful, exclusive, and fecund (*Humanae vitae*, 9). Augustine had spoken of four goods of marriage; the 1917 Code of Canon Law, echoing and embellishing his thought, had described marriage's primary end as the procreation of children and its secondary ends as the mutual support of the spouses and the remedying of concupiscence (*Codex Juris Canonici*, 1013). Pope Paul VI, in a dramatic shift away from a strictly teleological understanding of the purpose of marriage, spoke instead of the meanings, or intentionalities, present in marriage (*Humanae vitae*, 12).

Clearly, Vatican II began an important shift in the way Catholics think about marriage. More recent canonical legislation on marriage suggests, however, that the theology of marriage has a long way to go before it completes that shift. In speaking of Christian marriage the language of the revised Code of Canon Law sometimes reflects the influence of Vatican II by calling marriage a covenant, but sometimes the new code also reverts to the more traditional term "contract" (*Code of Canon Law, 1983*, 1055, 1058). When read in the light of Vatican II, the term "covenant" has biblical and personalist connotations. It suggests that the reality of marriage includes much more than a contract to have sex. The term "covenant" also blurs the clear distinction made in the 1917 code between the primary and secondary ends of marriage. Nevertheless, the revised code still invokes the medieval criterion of a "ratified and consummated" marriage in order to establish its validity (*Code of Canon Law, 1983*, 1061). In other words, the latest canonical legislation on marriage mingles traditional canonical categories with biblical and personalist categories.

After the publication of the new code, these ambiguities found an echo in the decisions handed down by the Roman marriage tribunals. More recent decisions, however, suggest a growing willingness on the part of canonical judges to mitigate the rigor of earlier court decisions, particularly in granting marriage annulments.

We have examined the relationship between three important theological debates about Christian marriage. As we have seen, the way one evaluates the sacramentality of marriage depends in part on the way one understands both its indissolubility and the values it seeks to embody. In the chapter that follows we shall attempt to respond to all three of these debates. First, however, we need to examine more closely the kind of faith commitment that Christian marriage seeks to embody.

CHAPTER II

The Marriage Covenant

In the preceding chapter we considered the way in which Christian nuptials evolved historically. In the present chapter we will be searching for a strictly normative insight into Christian marriage. A strictly normative approach to marriage needs to take into account the ritual's historical evolution, but such an approach does not finally ask how Christian marriage has evolved or has been interpreted over the years. Instead, strictly normative theological thinking asks, how ought one to understand the reality of Christian marriage? To reach a strictly normative insight into any Christian ritual, one must grasp its relationship to initial and ongoing conversion; for the dynamics of conversion supply the norms that measure the strictly normative behavior of Christians.

Our reflections in the present chapter divide into five sections. The first suggests ways in which sin and concupiscence have distorted the institution of marriage. Those distortions pose a serious challenge to Christian spouses, who must with the divine Mother's guidance overcome them if they are to discover in marital union a humanizing realm of grace. The second section examines how Christian conversion ought to prepare couples to approach marriage responsibly in faith. The third focuses on the significance of the revised rite of Christian marriage. Reflection on the marriage ritual itself will provide an occasion to respond to some of the controversies that surround Christian marriage. The fourth section examines the Christian family as a dynamic realm of grace that seeks to nurture spouses to mature holiness and their offspring to initial conversion. The discussion of Christian nurture also reflects on the significance of infant baptism and on the responsibilities it imposes on Christian parents who practice it. The fifth and final section of this chapter attempts to speak to those controversies surrounding the rite of Christian marriage that we failed to address in part three.

1. Marriage, Concupiscence, and Sin. Any institution as ancient as marriage has been shaped by a variety of historical forces, among them concupiscence and sin.

As we saw in chapter six, the term "concupiscence" designates those forces in the situation of the baptized that come from sin and lead to sin. The forces of concupiscence include ideologies, which rationalize situations of oppression as preordained and unavoidable. Three ideologies have left a significant mark on the institution of marriage: sexism, patriarchalism, and Victorian morality.

Sexism in Marriage

Male sexism surely ranks among the most ancient ideologies. Male sexism arranges the institution of marriage to the advantage of husbands and to the disadvantage of wives. It subjects women to their husband's authority in infantilizing ways. In extreme cases sexism degrades women to chattel and endows husbands with the power of life and death over them. In mitigated forms of sexism wives exist in order to satisfy the personal and sexual needs of their husbands.

Sexist marriages allow men rights that they deny to women. Inheritance passes automatically to the male heir; only in his absence can wives and daughters inherit. In sexist unions not only does childbearing rank among a wife's primary duty, but wives are also expected to produce the male heirs who will perpetuate their father's name. In sexist unions only husbands have the right to own property; even wages earned by the wife belong legally to her spouse. Sexism allows only husbands the right to initiate divorce proceedings. It winks at their sexual escapades outside the marriage bed, at the same time that it strictly forbids the same license to women.

Patriarchal and Victorian Marriage

Forces other than sexism have shaped the institution of marriage. In the eighteenth century, marriages in this country followed a patriarchal pattern, in which the family functioned as an economically cooperative unit. Husband, wife, and children worked side by side in order to ensure the economic success of the family farm or shop. The father regulated peace and order in the family, decided his children's occupations and marriage choices, and controlled his wife's property and wages.

In the nineteenth century the industrial revolution with its attendant ideologies redefined sexual roles within the family. The Victorian family curtailed the father's authority over his children, who now ordinarily chose their own spouses and careers. Victorian mores assigned home and hearth to the wife as her proper sphere. Victorians sentimentalized women's role within the family, portraying wives as "the angel in the house," as paragons of virtue entrusted the task of preserving moral values but strictly within the home. By privatizing morality and confining it to the hearth, a liberal Victorian ethos simultaneously sanctioned the right of men to deal ruthlessly with one another in politics and in the marketplace. In other words, while patriarchalism gave husbands license to exploit their wives, Victorian mores also gave them license to exploit and traduce one another.

As Christian couples approach marriage, therefore, they need to face frankly the fact that, as traditionally institutionalized, marriage demands more of women than of men. Worse still, concupiscent ideologies like sexism, patriarchalism, and *laissez faire* liberalism can transform marital relationships themselves into a serious occasion of sin and injustice.

Marriage and Sin

Moreover, besides the forces of concupiscence, sin itself distorts the institution of marriage. Criminal actions of one spouse against another occur in fifty percent of the marriages in the United States. Wife beating, marital rape, child abuse, abortion, incest, and infidelity can transform family life into a living hell. Some marriages breed pathology: anxiety, depression, insomnia, obsession, alcoholism, drug abuse. Divorce and the wage gap between men and women advance the feminization of American poverty, while slick pornographic magazines sing the praises of open marriages. The 1980 census showed that on the average American marriages last no more than seven years.

These bleak facts pose a serious challenge to Christian spouses. With the divine Mother's guidance they must undertake the responsibility of redeeming marriage and the family from the dehumanizing, oppressive forces of sin and concupiscence. They will succeed in that enterprise only to the extent that they themselves have experienced integral conversion before God.

2. Conversion and Human Sexuality. With biological inevitability, boys and girls mature physically into sexually mature men and women; but only the fully converted mature in sexually responsible ways.

Human Adolescent Development

The growing spurt that marks the beginning of sexual maturation inaugurates the adolescent crisis of identity, but the emotional
ambivalence that adolescents normally experience results from more
than physical causes. Teenagers manifest a capacity for rational
thought impossible for small children, and that capacity opens to
them the complex world of adult thinking whose skills they need to
master.

Teenagers also display a new capacity for social relationships.
The process of socialization has already taught them as small children to transcend their spontaneous egocentrism and to see the world
from another's perspective. A friend of mine, for example, once told
me that his universe changed radically the day he discovered the milk-
man had a family; prior to that he had assumed that the man existed
solely to satisfy his own need for food. In adolescence, however, that
capacity to see the world from another's standpoint takes on a self-
conscious character. Teenagers understand in a way that younger
children do not how other people view the adolescent's own relationship to them. In other words, instead of just being able to say:
"I see the way you see things," adolescents can now say: "I see you
seeing me seeing you."

During adolescence young people also begin to move out of
the close circle of the family into the more threatening, competitive
milieu of adult life. They need to make important vocational options
and to acquire the skills proper to their adult calling.

Romantic Love

Finally, as if all of these major life transitions did not pose
enough of a problem, maturing young adults also need to integrate
into an increasingly complex pattern of life their own newly acquired
capacity to engage in the genital expression of love. No wonder adolescents experience a crisis of identity!

Initial conversion marks the point of transition from the relatively carefree life of childhood to responsible adult living. It also
grounds responsible sexual conduct. As a way of illustrating the relationship between conversion and human sexuality I shall in the
paragraphs that follow attempt to explore the implications of the
following two propositions: (1) The natural forms of conversion—
affective, intellectual, moral, and sociopolitical—humanize sexuality. (2) Christian conversion suffuses human sexuality with sacramental significance.

a. Affective Conversion Humanizes Sexuality by Healing It. Every human activity, including genital acts, expresses human evaluative processes. As a consequence, sexual acts can embody every variety of human emotion: love, craving, prurience, rage, hatred, contempt, terror, guilt. Moreover, genital activity also engages and expresses the unconscious mind; and it can do so in either healthy or unhealthy ways.

Personality Dysfunction

As we have seen, the repression of the negative emotions breeds personality dysfunction. "Nervousness" gives way to more costly impairments of smooth adaptive response to environmental stimuli. As the psyche deteriorates further, it explodes in destructive, antisocial behavior. Hospitalization and suicidal tendencies complete the painful spiral into ultimate psychic fragmentation.

Psychic dysfunction can express itself in genital activity as well. Unconscious emotional conflicts can motivate sexual impotence. Repressed rage and resentment can erupt in rape and in other sadistic acts of sexual violence. Guilt and self-loathing can help motivate a life of sexual promiscuity. Affective conversion humanizes sexuality by bringing to conscious healing the repressed rage, fear, and guilt that distort and degrade human sexual activity with rapine, lust, and promiscuity.

Emotionally integrated children are spared the pain of dealing with serious sexual disorders, but even they need during adolescence to learn how to integrate overtly sexual feelings into their relationships with other persons. Moreover, during the emotional turmoil that sexual maturation triggers, erotic emotions repressed during childhood frequently surface and require conscious integration into the emerging adult personality. Taboos and inhibitions unconsciously absorbed from adults need to be faced and brought into emotional perspective.

The Development of Human Love

By healing emotional dysfunction and freeing young people to express the sympathetic emotions, affective conversion enables human love to mature into marital love. Children begin to learn to love by sharing in the intimate affection that binds families together. The process of socialization teaches them the meaning of friendship. Adolescence brings with it the capacity for romantic involvement. Romantic love finds mature expression in marital commitment.

Affection, friendship, and romance all blend together in mature marital love. Recent studies indicate that among the things that endow marriages with permanence, a deep, developing friendship between the spouses ranks very high. In stable marriages, spouses like one another as people. They want the relationship to succeed. They laugh together often and know how to express love and affection. They agree on mutually satisfying ways to express their love for one another sexually, but their mutual love and commitment transcends sexuality. In stable marriages spouses confide in one another and take genuine pride in one another's achievements. They recognize one another's faults but take even greater satisfaction in their partner's virtues. They respond sensitively to one another's needs. They know how to forgive.

Affective conversion brings to human sexual relationships the kind of emotional self-understanding and honesty that makes such marital love possible. It suffuses marital relationships with zest and imagination. In the process, affective conversion both heals and humanizes sexuality.

b. Intellectual Conversion Humanizes Sexuality by Suffusing It with Intelligence. A thoroughly humanized use of sexuality engages every facet of the human personality including human intelligence. Humane sexual activity springs from an understanding of human sexuality, its purposes, and its place within the total human enterprise. Not everyone, of course, need understand sex with the technical thoroughness of a genetic engineer. All children do, however, need basic sex education and protection from destructive misinformation concerning human sexuality. Similarly, responsible parenthood requires family planning and the means to go about such planning intelligently. Responsible scientific investigation into human sexuality can contribute significantly to the healing of sexual disorders and to the clarification of misunderstandings about sex.

More than anything, however, an intelligent approach to human sexuality demands the ability to put it into perspective, to integrate it into a balanced philosophy of life. That ability expresses wisdom rather than book learning. It springs from a reverent appreciation for human life in all of its complexity and for the place of sexuality within the human enterprise. In successful marriages spouses share such a philosophy of life and have agreed on the place that sex occupies within it.

Clearly, then, when the kind of flexible intelligence that intellectual conversion nurtures informs sexual activity, it humanizes it.

c. Moral Conversion Humanizes Sexuality by Teaching It the Ways of Responsible Love. Moral conversion relativizes human sexuality by subordinating it to realities and ideals that lure the conscience even as they stand in judgment upon its decisions. Ethical realities and values make, as we have seen, absolute and ultimate claims. The morally converted individual knows that human sexual activity too must submit to similar moral constraints.

Moral conversion teaches us to treat other persons as persons. Humans achieve full personhood through conversion, through the decision to take adult responsibility for their own lives and for the consequences of their own decisions. An ethical use of sexuality ought, then, to flow from an integral, fivefold conversion and to encourage it in others. It must, therefore, transcend mere egocentric self-gratification. It must express and encourage in others a thoroughly responsible attitude toward sexual activity.

The morally converted stand accountable to other persons and to society at large for their sexual conduct. They avoid romantic entanglements that will produce either destructive consequences for other persons or the irresponsible creation of human life. They value the family as the most fundamental unit of human society and avoid any form of sexual conduct that would undermine or destroy family relationships. They eschew sexual conduct that springs from emotional disorders and oppose every form of personal sexual exploitation.

Studies of successful marriages show that they require a certain quality of moral commitment. In a successful marriage spouses dedicate themselves to the enterprise of marriage on a long-term basis and with the determination to make it work. The divorce rate in this nation since 1970 suggests that a growing number of young Americans for a variety of reasons lack the ability to sustain such a commitment, although more recent studies of marriages suggest that more young Americans have the will to work at making their marriages succeed. Nevertheless, the recent erosion of family life in this country suggests that we are passing through an ethical crisis that threatens not only the American family but the very moral fabric of American life.

Clearly, then, by teaching humans to restrict sexual activity to actions that express commitment to other persons as persons and by creating the capacity for a stable marital relationship, moral conversion contributes significantly to the humanization of sexuality. Within marriage it teaches spouses fidelity as well as mutual personal sensitivity and respect.

d. Sociopolitical Conversion Humanizes Sexuality by Freeing its Use from Institutional Exploitation and Degradation. Human institutions give public sanction to habitual patterns of behavior. Sexual behavior too undergoes habitual routinization and institutionalization. Not every form of institutionalized sexual conduct expresses, however, an integral fivefold conversion. We also institutionalize sexual perversion, destructive sexual taboos, and different forms of sexual neurosis and exploitation. In addition, we create other institutions that threaten to undermine healthy institutionalizations of human sexuality. In contemporary society sexism in all of its various institutional forms oppresses and dehumanizes both women and men. Poverty and hunger also undermine and destroy the family. The sociopolitical convert encourages institutional policies that foster responsible sexuality and stands in opposition to every form of institutionalized sexual oppression.

Sexual Archetypes and Sexual Stereotypes

Sexism gives evidence of extending deep roots into the human unconscious. Among the archetypal images that shape human sexual conduct in unconscious ways, images of masculinity and femininity play, predictably enough, an important role. Moreover, conscious and unconscious sexual images both motivate the institutionalization of sexual conduct and are themselves conditioned by existing institutional structures.

Sexist imagery transforms the archetypes of masculinity and of femininity into rigid social stereotypes. In typical tales of heroic derring-do, the archetypal male hero is called from obscurity to undertake a dangerous quest. In the course of his adventures often he must slay a dragon or destroy some other figure that symbolizes inhibiting parental relationships.[1] He must secure the object of his quest and rescue a maiden in distress. He then returns home with both, where he marries the maiden, enjoys the fruit of his adventures, and lives happily ever after.

The archetype of the hero interprets through narrative the experience of masculine coming of age. The maturing young male emerges from the anonymity of childhood to begin the enterprise

---

1. In archetypal theory dragons and serpents are associated with the figure of the mother. They lay eggs and crawl upon Mother Earth. When they devour their prey, they become distended like a pregnant woman; as a consequence they symbolize the Terrible Mother who destroys her own children.

of adult living. In order to establish an adult male identity he must separate himself from parental control, especially from maternal ties. His slaying the dragon symbolizes that separation. The young male must also prove before the world his ability to function as a grown-up (succeed in his quest) and develop the capacity to relate tenderly to a sexually mature woman (rescue and marry a maiden).

In hero myths, however, only men play the part of the protagonist. Women play only passive roles. They require rescuing and marrying. Once married they serve no other dramatic function than to admire the exploits and prowess of the successful hero.

Sexist societies transform such nursery tales into oppressive stereotypes. Such societies exclude women systematically from competition with men. Sexist discrimination in education ensures that women will lack the skills that would enable them to compete. Sexist mores bar women from politics, from the marketplace, from positions of power and influence. Worse still, sexism through advertising, pornography, and prostitution encourages the exploitation of women as sex objects by tacitly and sometimes actively accepting and encouraging women's degradation and physical abuse (including rape). More primitive sexist cultures not only ostracize women but treat them as chattel. Among the poor, sexism only exacerbates the misery born of destitution.

Sociopolitical converts recognize male sexism as an unjust institutional perversion of human sexuality and as an intolerable form of social oppression. In the struggle against this particular form of injustice, they also show concern, however, not to fall into a reverse sexism that rigidly and automatically stereotypes all men as male chauvinist pigs.

The Erosion of American Family Life

In addition to opposing sexual oppression and exploitation of every kind, sociopolitical converts also need to defend the family against those forces in contemporary society that threaten to destroy it. Too often and tragically, poverty and racism have disrupted the shared lives of American black families. The individualism and narcissism that infects our consumerist culture supplants moral altruism and saps human willingness to sustain a lifelong marital commitment. Abortion on demand perpetuates the massive slaughter of innocent children and deprives marriage of its fruit. The nuclear family puts unrealistic stress on intrafamilial relationships. The migration of refugees fleeing war, violence, and hunger also destroys family life.

Studies of successful marriages indicate that in lasting marital unions instead of exploiting one another both spouses value one another as persons and encourage one another's achievements. In stable marriages both spouses also value the family itself as a source of stability within human society and are willing to make the sacrifices necessary to see to it that their own family survives. Sociopolitical conversion extends a similar concern to other families as well. Indeed, as we shall soon see, the defense of family life constitutes one of the major apostolates of Christian families.

e. Christian Conversion Endows A Humanized Sexuality with Sacramental Significance. We have been reflecting on the ways in which the four natural forms of conversion—affective, intellectual, moral, and sociopolitical—humanize sexuality. As we have also seen, these same forms of conversion instill the kinds of attitudes and commitments that produce stable, successful marriages. Studies of lasting marriages indicate, however, that in addition to embodying a humane and balanced approach to human sexuality, lasting marriages must also rest on a religious foundation. In successful marriages, both spouses tend to look upon their marriage vows as a sacred commitment made before God.

Christian conversion provides marriage with a religious context. As we have seen, Christian conversion contributes two important dynamics to the total experience of conversion. By mediating between affective and moral conversion it opens the convert to the triune God in an attitude of global, justifying faith that engages every aspect of the convert's life: heart, mind, conscience, social and institutional relationships. As a consequence, Christian conversion also effects the transvaluation in faith of the other four forms of conversion. Christian conversion transforms affective conversion into the theological virtue of hope, both affective and intellectual conversion into the theological virtue of faith, moral conversion into the theological virtue of love, and sociopolitical conversion into the Christian search for justice.

Marital Love

Christian conversion also transvalues sexual coming of age. As we have seen, affective conversion heals the repressed rage, fear, and guilt that deform and degrade human sexual activity. At the same time, it releases the capacity for affection, friendship, and romantic love that blend together in order to form the rich texture of mature marital love.

Christian conversion transvalues marital love by demanding that in addition to affection, friendship, and romance it also express the love of charity. As we have seen, both the vision of the kingdom and the example of Jesus' own love for us provide Christian love with its moral content. We shall examine presently the ways in which a Christian ethics of discipleship transforms the Christian family into a saving realm of grace. Here, however, we concern ourselves only with reflecting on the ways in which charity differs from and transvalues natural marital love.

Marital love blends three forms of love: affection, friendship, and romance. Charity blends three other forms of love: atoning love, contemplative love, and the love born of need.

To some degree the three forms of love that blend into charity function within natural marital love. Marital friendship combines an atoning, self-giving love with a contemplative love by teaching friends mutual support and forgiveness as well as shared enthusiasm. Marital romance unites needy love with contemplative love: erotic lovers need one another profoundly and rejoice in one another's beauty. Marital affection expresses mutual need and mutual self-giving. In other words, marital love includes elements of atoning love, of contemplative love, and of needy love because these three forms of love function within the friendship, romantic involvement, and affection that comprise natural marital love.

The Love of Charity

The love of charity, however, blends atoning love, contemplative love, and the love born of need as its primary and constitutive components. Moreover, it does so in an attitude of religious self-transcendence. The love of charity springs from faith. It discovers the full meaning of atoning love in the divine love embodied in Jesus: in his incarnation, death, glorification, and mission of the divine Mother into a sinful Church. Atoning love suffers the consequences of sin without sinning. Like the love of God revealed to us in Christ, atoning love stands ready to excuse, to hope, to trust, and to endure whatever comes. It abides all rejection with forgiveness: before the offense is committed, while it is being performed, before any sign of repentance.

Mystics exemplify most perfectly the contemplative dimension of Christian charity. Charity flows from a heart enthralled with the beauty of God revealed to us in Jesus and in people who resemble him. It yearns for union with the divine and seeks that union by prayer and by performing the deeds of love. Authentic charity recognizes that it flows from God as a free gift. Christians therefore look to God to effect within them the love that unites them to the divine family. Mystics have advanced in the love of charity so far that it constitutes the most fundamental way in which they know God. In the grace of infused contemplation love replaces image and concept as the primary way of knowing God.

Because Christian charity transvalues natural human love, however, it never transcends human need. Instead, the love of Christ draws us into a community of faith sharing that acknowledges the neediness of all of its members with compassion. Indeed, Christian love demands that we acknowledge our need for one another not only in order to live a humane life but also in order to attain its ultimate purpose: union with the triune God in love. Hence, in addition to atoning and contemplative love Christian charity includes the love that springs from human neediness. Christians do not exchange love in community out of a position of impregnable strength. Rather in moments of strength one reaches out in compassion to those needier than oneself. In moments of need one accepts with grateful love the ministry of others.

The Gracing of Marital Love

As Christian charity transvalues marital love it suffuses it with the atoning love of Christ. Readiness for Christian marriage requires therefore the capacity in both partners to forgive with Christlike compassion the remnants of sin in one's own heart and in one's spouse. Mature marital love requires, of course, that spouses forgive one another. Charity, however, requires of them that they do so with the same quality of forgiveness as God has revealed to us in Jesus.

Christian charity also teaches romantic lovers to approach marriage contemplatively. Not only must Christian couples look upon the marriage covenant itself as a religious vow made before God, but they must also pray their way into marriage. They need to find in their own prayer a divine call to blend their lives in Christ, and they need to find that charism confirmed by other members of the Christian community. Marital love draws them into shared living informed by faith and prayer.

Finally, because Christian charity blends atoning and contemplative love with the love that need inspires, it also teaches romantic lovers to approach marriage as a form of mutual Christian ministry. All marital love includes love born of need. If husbands and wives did not need one another they would never consent to blend their lives. Christian marriage requires in addition that spouses minister to one another's needs with the tenderness and compassion of Christ.

Moreover, because Jesus' vision of the kingdom helps provide Christian charity with its moral content, the graced transvaluation of romantic love requires that it submit to the moral demands of life in the kingdom. Christian romantic lovers need to relate to one another not just as mutually attractive men and women but also and specifically as Christians. Their mutual commitment to one another must, therefore, express the desire to share together their possessions and persons freely and gratuitously. That sharing should express their trust in the providential care of the God who calls them to marital union. As a Christian couple they stand committed to reach out to those in greatest need and to labor in order to break down the sinful social barriers that separate people from one another. As a Christian couple they commit themselves to one another in a marriage that advances the kingdom. They commit themselves to a life together nurtured by both private and shared prayer, and they recognize that only the love of atonement authenticates Christian prayer.

Finally, because they regard marriage as a form of charismatic ministry within the Church, Christian couples recognize that they cannot undertake the responsibilities of marriage as Christians unless the divine Mother calls them to do so. Charismatic graces, as we have seen, differ from the graces common to all Christians by their particularity. The charism of marriage provides no exception to this rule. It binds together two unique individuals in a lifetime of shared ministry to one another, to their children, to the Church, and to humanity. That call like every other form of charismatic ministry needs to submit to the discerning judgment of the Christian community.

As we have seen, events take on a sacramental character when they acquire saving significance. Both the graced transvaluation of romantic and marital love in Christlike charity and the charismatic transformation of marriage into a form of Christian ministry suffuses human sexual relationships with ultimate religious significance. In the process a sexuality humanized by the four forms of natural conversion undergoes a sacramentalization that the rite of marriage itself celebrates.

The sacramentalization of marriage involves, moreover, more than the graced transformation of the love between a man and a woman. It requires as well the social redemption of marriage and the family. A Christian marriage covenant demands, therefore, the repudiation of sexism, reverse sexism, or any other oppressive institutional distortion of human sexual relationships not only as morally evil but as the embodiment of Antichrist. It also commits Christian spouses to defend their own marriage and the institution of marriage itself against any sinful forces in society that would seek to undermine and destroy it.

3. The Marriage Ritual. We are attempting to understand the ways in which an integral, fivefold conversion transforms both human sexual relationships and the institution of marriage itself. In this section we shall first reflect on the preparations that should precede the ritual celebration of Christian nuptials. Then we shall reflect on the rite of marriage itself.

a. Marriage Preparations. Some people may approach adult initiation with that degree of converted maturity and commitment that Christian marriage requires. One must, however, judge marriage preparedness case by case; for ordinarily Christian marriage requires a much deeper level of conversion than does the rite of adult initiation. Ritual initiation seals and celebrates an initial conversion to Christ. It commits one to lifelong growth in holiness and to lifelong responsiveness to the divine Mother's charismatic call. Readiness for Christian marriage, however, presupposes that those who approach it have matured sufficiently in holiness that they can also undertake responsibly the founding of a Christian family. It also presupposes that the Christian couple has in fact discerned their charismatic call to the ministry of marriage.

The excitement of falling in love can prevent lovers from appreciating the fact that a responsible approach to marriage marks a major transition in an individual's life. Such periods of passage ordinarily advance in three stages: a time of separation, a time of marginality, and a time of reintegration. During the period of separation, one abandons one way of living and begins to adopt another. As the transition to a new way of life advances, one enters a period of marginality in which one makes multiple personal readjustments. The time of marginality ends, of course, with marriage, which begins the period of reintegration.

Human Readiness for Marriage

The marital passage begins when two people fall in love. As the divorce rate in this country tragically proves, however, not every man and woman who experience mutual sexual attraction have the capacity to create a stable marriage. A sound insight into the dynamics of conversion offers, moreover, a practical set of pastoral norms for judging a couple's readiness to undertake a Christian marriage. Ordinarily, such testing should transpire during the period of betrothal. Inevitably, betrothal introduces them to a time of marginality, which the rite of marriage itself terminates. Moreover, as a couple moves toward marriage, they gradually learn how to abandon independent living for a life of mutual commitment in every area of their lives.

A Christian couple needs first of all to show signs of human readiness for marriage. They should display a healthy degree of the emotional integration that ongoing affective conversion produces. They should have faced and dealt with any serious emotional disorders that might undermine the marriage. They need to exhibit the capacity for deep friendship and for the easy exchange of affection.

In addition, betrothal introduces a couple into a time of mutual emotional adjustment. Moreover, in their relationship with one another Christian couples should experience more than sexual attraction. They must show the concrete capacity to blend their lives in a deep and long-lasting friendship. They also need to have reached a common, realistic understanding about the place that the genital expression of love will have in their lives. In order to do that effectively, Christian couples should share a common appreciation for the significance of human sexuality. The experience of learning how to respond in responsible ways to the emotional needs of another sexually mature adult ordinarily challenges one to new emotional honesty with oneself. In the process one learns new kinds of responsible affective behavior that ordinarily deepen affective conversion.

In order for two lovers to move responsibly to marital union, they also need to exhibit the capacity for the kind of moral commitment that Christian marriage requires. They must have decided unconditionally to make their relationship work and must accept in advance the sacrifice that that may entail. They must value one another as persons and genuinely desire to foster conversion in themselves and in one another. They need to find joy in one another's accomplishments and in simply being together. They should have renounced any desire to dominate one another. They should value the family as a fundamental human institution and stand committed to defend it against the forces that threaten it. Clearly, one cannot assume the responsibilities involved in lifelong commitment to a concrete person and to founding a family without in some way deepening in moral conversion.

Moreover, the more ideals and values a couple shares in common, the easier they will find it to make their marriage work. Since, however, no two individuals share the same history, very likely as two people explore the common ground they share for building a permanent personal relationship, they will find that they challenge one another to grow not only affectively but intellectually, morally, and even politically as well. As a consequence, the period of marginality called betrothal, when used responsibly, promises to deepen initial conversion at every natural level.

Readiness in Faith for Marriage

Moreover, besides human readiness for marriage, Christian couples also need readiness in faith. They need to stand committed to one another with the atoning love of Christ, to love one another with a commitment of forgiveness that is simply there, ready for claiming at any time. Both personal and shared prayer should inform their relationship; and the hope, faith, love, and longing for justice common to all Christians must inform their lives together. They need to show a capacity to respond to one another's needs with Christlike compassion.

They also need to recognize marriage as a form of charismatic, Christian ministry. They need to have discerned together the divine Mother's particular call to them to undertake such a ministry and to have found that call confirmed by the Christian community and its pastoral leaders. As they learn how to nurture faith in one another and how to assume new ministerial responsibilities, Christian couples inevitably deepen their initial commitment to Christ and to the Christian community.

Discerning Readiness for Marriage

Clearly the adequate discernment of a call to Christian marriage takes much more time and care than our culture ordinarily allows or encourages. It requires of Christian couples the willingness not only to explore every dimension of their relationship to one another before marrying but also to have reached agreement as far as possible about every detail of their lives together.

Successfully married spouses have the best qualifications for assisting young couples in discerning their call to the ministry of marriage, but the ordained leaders of the Church cannot for their part responsibly witness a Christian marriage without having first thoroughly discerned the couple's readiness to make such a commitment.

The ritual of marriage terminates the marginal period of betrothal and begins a reintegration of life for the newlyweds. In the section that follows, we shall reflect on the rite of marriage and on the kind of commitment it embodies.

b. The Rite of Matrimony. We have reflected on the ways in which Christian conversion authenticates preparation for marriage. In the present section we will reflect on the ways in which it transforms the marriage commitment itself.

Preliminary Rituals

When a couple celebrates the rite of matrimony during a nuptial Eucharist, the celebrant greets the bridal couple at the entrance to the church, congratulates them, and expresses to them the joy that the Christian community feels in their union (Roman Catholic Rite of Marriage, 19; hereafter abbreviated as RCRM).

After the procession into the church, the Liturgy of the Word is celebrated in the ordinary manner but may contain three readings selected from the lectionary by the bridal couple. During the homily the celebrant reflects on the significance of Christian marriage: on its mystery and dignity, on its graces and responsibilities. He should also relate his reflections to the particular circumstances of the couple whose marriage he is witnessing (RCRM, 21–22).

The rite of marriage itself advances in four stages. First, the Eucharistic celebrant reminds both the bridal couple and the assembled community of the meaning of the marriage ritual. Second, the bride and groom publicly declare their intention to live up to the responsibilities of Christian marriage. Third, the bride and groom exchange their marriage vows. Fourth, their union is sealed symbolically by blessing and exchanging the wedding rings. Let us reflect briefly on the significance of each of these ritual actions.

The Homily

The new rite of marriage gives enhanced importance to the role of the homily. It suggests that in explaining to the bridal couple and to the assembled community the meaning of the marriage ritual, the Eucharistic celebrant should insist on its public ecclesial character. As in the case of the rites of initiation, Christian marriage gives public, ecclesial sanction to a maturing faith commitment: the decision of two baptized Christians to commit themselves both to one another and to the charismatic ministry of marriage in the name and image of Jesus.

The Eucharistic celebrant should also insist on the specifically Christian character of the act that the bridal couple is about to perform. They commit themselves to one another not merely as man and woman but also and specifically as a Christian man and woman. The celebrant should therefore also remind the couple that the Christian character of their mutual commitment to one another flows directly from their prior initiation into the Church. An insight into the dynamics of Christian conversion explains the link between marriage and initiation. A Christian couple's commitment to love one another as God has loved them in Christ flows directly from the baptismal moment in the rite of initiation, which, as we have seen, consecrates Christians to lives of ongoing sanctification in Jesus' image. That the bride and groom exchange marriage vows in response to the divine Mother's charismatic call flows directly from the second moment in the rite of initiation, which commits Christians to live in lifelong openness to whatever charism of service the third person of the Trinity chooses to bestow upon them.

Finally, the Eucharistic celebrant should remind the bride and groom that because they commit themselves to one another in the name and image of Jesus, their love for one another must exhibit the same unconditioned character as his commitment to us. It therefore binds them in mutual and lifelong fidelity (RCRM, 23).

The Exchange of Vows

The Eucharistic celebrant then invites the bride and groom to declare publicly to the assembled Christian community their willingness to accept the responsibilities of Christian matrimony. More specifically, they must attest that they are entering into marriage freely and without constraint, that they will give themselves to one another without reservation, that they will honor one another as husband and wife for the rest of their lives, and that they will rear their children in accordance with the law of Christ and of his Church (RCRM, 24).

The bride and groom then pronounce the vows of matrimony according to one of the formulas that the new ritual provides. After they have done so, the priest as the official representative of the Christian community receives their consent publicly and blesses it, reminding the spouses of Jesus' command that humans should not divide what God has joined (RCRM, 25–26).

The Exchange of Rings and the Nuptial Blessing

The Eucharistic celebrant then blesses the rings, consecrating them as a symbol of the spouses' mutual love and fidelity. They then place the rings on one another's fingers pledging lifelong love and faithfulness (RCRM, 27–28).

When marriage is celebrated during the Eucharist, after the Our Father the Eucharistic celebrant pronounces the nuptial blessing over the two spouses; and at the end of the Eucharist, before blessing the people, the priest gives the couple a special blessing of their own (RCRM, 32–37). The blessings emphasize the equality and mutual commitment of the two spouses and implore God to grace their union and make it fruitful.

c. The Marriage Covenant. An analysis of the ways in which Christian conversion transforms and transvalues the human institution of marriage sanctions calling the Christian exchange of marriage vows a covenant. Let us reflect briefly on some of the reasons why.

The Christian Covenant

In Christian initiation converts seal a covenant of faith with God. Jesus' preaching and ministry help supply the new covenant with its moral content, but the new covenant also draws Jesus' followers into the paschal mystery. At the Last Supper Jesus referred to his immanent death as a covenant sacrifice (Mark 14:24; Matt 26:28; Luke 22:20; 1 Cor 11:25). Moreover, his resurrection, his historical manifestation as Lord, and his mission of the divine Mother manifested the new covenant's full scope; for these events seal the new covenant decisively and reveal its ultimate purpose: graced transformation in the image of the risen Christ. The covenant sealed in Jesus' blood reveals, then, the absolute and unconditioned character of God's commitment to us sinners in love (Rom 8:31-39). Through conversion and sacramental initiation Christians respond to that divine commitment with a faith that seals the new covenant in their hearts.

When Christians exchange the vows of marriage as Christians they enter by that act into a sacred covenant with one another because they cannot pronounce the vows of marriage as Christians without simultaneously reaffirming the religious commitment they made in their covenant of initiation. In committing themselves to love one another in Jesus' name and image they renew the commitment they made in baptism to live in obedient imitation of God's obedient Son by taking on the responsibility of nurturing holiness in one another. In consenting to the charism of marriage they reaffirm the commitment they made in confirmation to respond in faith to whatever charism the divine Mother would choose to give them.

Marriage as Christian Covenant and Sacrament

The marriage covenant, however, commits Christian spouses to responsibilities that go beyond the covenant of initiation. It commits them to a lifelong marital union and to founding a Christian family. The marriage covenant goes beyond the covenant of initiation by rendering it more specific. It focuses the love of charity to which all baptized Christians stand committed upon the person of one's spouse and on the children that will flow from marital union, and it specifies the open-ended commitment to charismatic ministry made in confirmation by consecrating two spouses to the particular ministry of marriage. Not that marriage exhausts the charisms bestowed on Christian spouses, but it does help contextualize the other personal gifts that they exercise in ministering to others.

Moreover, the fact that one cannot enter into Christian marriage without simultaneously reaffirming one's baptismal covenant transforms Christian marriage into a sacrament. In the preceding section I suggested a strategy for trying to resolve the dispute between Protestants and Catholics concerning the number of the sacraments. I suggested that we derive from those rituals that all the Churches recognize as sacramental a descriptive definition of the term "sacrament." We found that if one accepts adult baptism and the Eucharist as sacramental actions then one can legitimately describe a sacrament as a symbolic, ritual act of new covenant worship (1) that expresses the shared faith of the Church universal, (2) that is celebrated in God's name by a person authorized to do so by the Christian community, (3) that derives in some way from the ministry of Jesus, (4) that gives access in faith to the paschal mystery because it challenges one prophetically to faith in Jesus' Lordship, in the Father he proclaimed, and in the Holy Breath he sends, and (5) that effects the grace it signifies to the extent that it expresses faith and deepens faith.

When a man and woman commit themselves to one another in the Christian marriage covenant, they perform an act that possesses all of the above traits. Their act qualifies as a symbolic, ritual act of new covenant worship because it reaffirms their baptismal covenant while simultaneously conferring upon them the rights and responsibilities of Christian spouses. The Christian community has discerned and sanctioned a particular couple's calling to the charismatic ministry of marriage; the bride and groom therefore administer the ritual to one another with official, ecclesial authorization to do so in the name of the triune God. They commit themselves irrevocably to one another with the intention of submitting in obedience to Jesus' command that humans should not sunder two persons united by God. Christian spouses also commit themselves to love one another with the atoning love of Christ and in response to the divine Mother's charismatic anointing. The marital vows that they exchange have therefore been radically redeemed and transformed by Jesus' ministry, and in sealing the marriage covenant Christian spouses enter more deeply into the paschal mystery by the selflessness with which they give themselves to one another. In exchanging vows before the Church, they also challenge one another publicly to fidelity (because they act with the Church's official sanction) and prophetically (because they also act in the name of the triune God). Finally, the exchange of marriage promises effects the grace it signifies because it both expresses and deepens the couple's faith.

Finally, we note that taken together, both the sacramental character of Christian marriage and the fact that in exchanging marriage vows Christian spouses reaffirm their covenant of initiation make the celebration of Christian nuptials during the Eucharist extremely appropriate; for, as we have seen and as we shall see in greater detail in the final chapter, in every Eucharist Christians reaffirm personally and collectively their covenant of initiation.

4. The Christian Family. Ever since the days of Augustine of Hippo, Catholic theology in the West has discovered four values in Christian marriage: offspring, the mutual support and sanctification of Christian spouses, the alleviation of concupiscence, and sacramentality. We have no reason to regard this list as exhaustive. In fact the Second Vatican Council pointed to another value that Christian marriage embodies: its ministerial outreach. In the documents of Vatican II marriage and the family rank as an important expression of the lay apostolate. Moreover, anyone who studies the history of Christian marriage must concede that our theological understanding of the values it incarnates evolves constantly.

In the present section of this chapter we shall examine four values that Christian marriage attempts to embody: the mutual support of Christian spouses, the transformation of marriage into ministry, the alleviation of concupiscence, and the procreation and nurture of offspring.

a. The Mutual Support and Sanctification of Spouses. If we view marriage as a natural, human institution, the mutual support of spouses qualifies as its most basic benefit. Biological causes may prevent spouses from bearing children, but they can always blend their lives in mutual love, affection, and caring. Moreover, the mutual love and commitment of spouses helps create the only healthy social matrix for the responsible rearing of children. In this sense too it ranks as more fundamental.

Similarly, if we view marriage as a Christian institution, the mutual sanctification of the spouses provides it with its most fundamental benefit; for their advancement in holiness creates the realm of grace that nurtures holiness in their children and staves off the evil influences of concupiscence.

Converted Mutual Support

A theology of conversion gives practical meaning to the support that spouses give to one another within marriage. It also gives practical meaning to their ongoing sanctification. Let us try to understand how.

Spouses support one another to the extent that they encourage one another to advance in the natural forms of conversion. The responsible exchange of marriage vows presupposes, as we have seen, considerable emotional maturity. Nevertheless, even ego-integrated persons harbor unconscious neurotic tendencies. Moreover, every marriage passes through predictable periods of transition that bring their own kinds of emotional pressure. After the glow of the honeymoon fades, for example, couples must face with new realism the day-to-day challenge of making their marriage work.

Affective Support

The arrival of children can bring great joy to parents, but it also creates its own kinds of emotional stress, as does their departure from the family to begin their own adult lives. In this context I think of a young professor of American literature, wakened at two in the morning for the sixtieth night running by the hungry crying of his first child. He and his wife took turns feeding the infant. That night, as he lay in bed listening to his wife take her turn, he suddenly came to the blinding insight that his son was Moby Dick: an irrational, amoral presence that had suddenly erupted into their lives. A man with an ironic sense of humor, the next day he bought the boy a grinning, stuffed white whale, which the infant used to flail about with as though wielding a club. Or I think of a couple, who used to look forward to rediscovered freedom once their children left home for college, only to find themselves supporting one another through a time of wistful sadness when the event actually occurred.

Other forces may put spouses under emotional pressure: one's career, economic distress, the ordinary challenges of emotional maturation, and marital infidelity, should it occur. Here I think of a marriage in which both husband and wife worked in professional jobs on opposite coasts of the United States. Their marriage succeeded but not without considerable effort and sacrifice on the part of both of them.

Moreover, no child of Adam and Eve escapes some form of the mid-life transition with its attendant crisis of generativity and shifting sexual needs. No one escapes the emotional challenge of aging and dying. Sickness and unforseen tragedies bring other kinds of emotional distress. Take, for example, a young couple whose first son died at the age of four of a genetically inherited bone disease. Together they fought the child's death with every resource they had. When they neared the limits of their own, they made a public appeal for help from others and received it, but to no avail. The child died in their arms. They emerged from this tragic loss more deeply bonded than ever by the love and mutual support they had shared in facing it.

Spouses support one another emotionally when they encourage one another in the enterprise of ongoing affective conversion. That kind of encouragement presupposes a depth of mutual trust that frees husbands and wives to share with one another their moments of emotional vulnerability: the fears, the frustrations, the hurts that burden them and make life difficult. Indeed, deep affective bonding between spouses results from the willingness to stand by one another in times of emotional crisis and trauma. Drug abuse has, for example, wrecked more than one family in this country. Those who have supported addicted spouses through rehabilitation have learned through experience that it takes tough love to give effective support and avoid sentimental cooption into codependency.

Intellectual Support

The friendship that unites husband and wife ought ideally to lead them to develop common intellectual interests as well. Shared cultural concerns provide couples with a lifetime of enjoyable conversation topics. Moreover, their ability to investigate together matters of common interest and concern and to do so from a variety of perspectives adds intellectual depth and zest to their relationship. At the very least couples need to encourage one another to develop intellectually and to take genuine pride in one another's speculative achievements. In this context, I think of a couple I know whose passion for literature and art not only generated delightful conversations around the dinner table but bore fruit in shared scholarly work as well.

Moral Support

Spouses also need to give one another moral support. They should help one another face and resolve not only personal moral dilemmas but also the moral crises that confront them as a family. The willingness to encourage one another to moral courage and to the responsible exercise of freedom will demand the willingness to talk through all of life's major decisions. The moral crises that families face can have sociopolitical causes. Hence, spouses must also help one another advance in sociopolitical conversion and support one another in the search for social justice. Here I think of a husband whose wife experienced sexist discrimination in hiring. The incident radicalized both of them, and they fought together for years against the discriminating institution, with some success.

Christian conversion sanctifies marital union when it informs and transvalues the progress that spouses make in the other four forms of conversion. Christian conversion transforms the family into a community of hope in which the free sharing of the physical supports of life expresses radical trust in God's providential care. That same trust frees Christian families to reach out in compassion to others and to welcome in Christian hospitality persons in need. Think of those families who have adopted orphans and welcomed refugees in Jesus' name. Here I think of an incredible couple in California who decided that they did parenting best and enjoyed doing it most. In addition to their own children they adopted a whole brood of physically handicapped children who brought incredible joy to their home.

The Charismatic Family

As we have seen, the shared faith consciousness of the Church universal results from sharing the divine Mother's charismatic inspirations in community. Similarly, the shared faith consciousness of the Christian family results from sharing the gifts within the home. Shared prayer and shared healing in faith create within the home a sense of the divine presence. Parents may lack the gift of prophecy personally, but they can attend to prophetic voices within the Church and echo them within the family. In teaching their children the Christian story and basic Christian doctrine, they endow their family with a sense of its concrete religious identity. Acts of ministry undertaken by individual family members or by the family as a whole make its shared faith a conscious, lived reality. Here I think spontaneously of a family of Catholic anarchists I knew who ran a Catholic Worker soup kitchen and of a politically active suburban couple whose son tested out the second most politically radical student in his entire high school.

The gift of discernment teaches Christian families to form their consciences in faith. At the same time, Christian conversion ensures that the love that bonds the members of a family include more than natural love. Christian families are called to incarnate the atoning love of Christ. The vision of the kingdom must inform everything the family and its members do. Mutual sensitivity to human needs within the family and outside of it should inspire personal and shared deeds of charity. I think in this context of a couple who spent hours talking through every major decision while trying to understand in detail how the different options they faced would change the lives of each member of the family.

The Family Commitment to Justice

Finally, Christian conversion ought to inspire the family's passionate concern for the establishment of God's just reign in human social institutions. Parents should model Christian social and political activism for their children. I think in this context of a San Francisco family who during dinner regularly debated the moral pros and cons of every major political issue. Most of the children wound up in some kind of public advocacy work or as professors of moral theology.

Clearly, when spouses support one another in the process of ongoing conversion, they transform their lives together into Christian ministry. To this topic we turn in the section that follows.

b. Marriage as Ministry. The Second Vatican Council, as we have seen, has augmented the traditional list of the values that Christian marriage incarnates by portraying married life as a form of Christian ministry and as an important expression of the lay apostolate. In discussing marriage as ministry, one needs, however, to distinguish between ministry within the Christian family and ministry outside its confines. One must also distinguish between the ministry of individual family members and the ministry of the family as such.

Individual Ministry in the Family

The mutual support of spouses and the Christian nurture of their offspring constitute the most fundamental forms of ministry within the family. The charism of marriage, however, does not exhaust the personal charismatic endowments of Christian spouses. The use of those charisms extends the apostolate of Christian spouses outside the sphere of the family itself. After marriage, however, Christians need to coordinate the other forms of ministry in which they engage with the responsibilities that flow from their marriage covenant.

The Family as a Ministerial Team

Moreover, in addition to the ministry that individual members of Christian families perform, sometimes the family itself can function as an apostolic team in ministering to others. That occurs, for example, in the exercise of ordinary Christian hospitality, in the adoption and care of orphans, in extraordinary hospitality to strangers, refugees, and aliens, in the care of the aged and of troubled or needy adolescents. Moreover, married life can itself prepare one to engage in other forms of apostolic work like assisting young couples in their marriage preparation and supporting other families in times of crisis (*Apostolicam actuositatem,* 11). Here I think of hundreds of Christian families who provided homes for Vietnamese and Cambodian refugees, of couples who had devoted weekends to organizing Marriage Encounters, of Christian men and women I have known who have done outstanding work as teachers and Newman chaplains. One could multiply the list almost indefinitely.

c. The Alleviation of Concupiscence. The light that a theology of conversion throws on the first two sets of values that Christian marriage seeks to incarnate also illumines what it means to say that Christian marriage alleviates concupiscence. By the alleviation of concupiscence, however, I mean something very different from what that phrase has traditionally connoted. In saying that Christian marriage seeks to alleviate concupiscence, I do not mean that it gives Christian spouses a legitimate outlet for their lust. Instead, I mean that the Christian marriage covenant commits spouses to transforming marriage and the family into a realm of grace unmarred by the effects of human sinfulness.

Through mutual Christlike love Christian spouses must find the means to purge their life together of oppressive patriarchal and sexist distortions. In sharing their lives and possessions they must purify the family of economic inequity. Their love must banish violence and exploitation from home and hearth. In their ministerial concern for others married Christians must labor to defend both marriage and the family from the sinful forces that erode and corrupt it. Through passionate concern for Christian social justice, parents by word and example teach their children to identify the forces of sin and to arm themselves against their onslaught.

In other words, the effective mutual support of Christian spouses, their loving transformation of the family into a realm of saving grace, and their active ministerial concern as married people for the needs of others and for a just social order all combine to undo the oppressive distortions with which sin and concupiscence infect marital and familial relationships. This graced redemption of marriage and the family also creates the kind of environment needed to nurture children to full Christian maturity.

d. Christian Nurture. The generation and nurture of offspring provides Christian marriage with its fourth fundamental value. As we have seen, Vatican II, in an attempt to undo the misunderstandings that resulted from past theological and canonical attempts to portray the generation of offspring as the primary end of marriage, ranked procreation and nurture on a par with the mutual support of Christian spouses. As the preceding analysis makes clear, however, the ministerial involvement of Christian spouses and their active concern to counteract the influence of concupiscence on their family's shared life combines with their mutual love and support to create the kind of environment that grounds the possibility of successful Christian nurture.

The Aims of Christian Nurture

The dynamics of conversion supply Christian nurture with its fundamental aims and goals. Christian parents seek to educate their offspring to take adult responsibility for their lives. Since conversion marks the passage to adult responsibility in every area of human experience, Christian education seeks to lead young people to an integral, fivefold conversion.

By modeling such a conversion for their children Christian parents transform the home into a safe realm of grace in which children can advance by stages toward adult maturity. Since, however, parents require assistance in the enterprise of educating their offspring, the Christian community to which the family belongs must also bear part of the burden of providing young Christians with a nurturing matrix of faith in which to grow and develop.

As Christian children mature emotionally, they need to grow in the supernatural virtue of hope. As they mature appreciatively and intellectually, they need to grow in the supernatural virtue of faith. As they mature morally, they need to grow in Christian love. As they mature socially, they need to commit themselves to the Christian search for social justice. Let us reflect in more detail on how this occurs.

Children need to establish very early a bond of trust with their parents. As they develop the capacity to relate to God, they need to transfer to the divine persons an analogous trust. Here the work of James Fowler illumines in theologically significant ways the religious development of young children. His researches suggest that children develop a capacity to relate to God very early and that their own religious attitudes are shaped profoundly by the adults who people their world. As young children begin to struggle with feelings of guilt, shame, and inferiority, parental love, acceptance, and forgiveness can communicate effectively the reality of a divine love that seeks to nurture the young to full maturity in Christ. Similarly, with the onset of the adolescent crisis of identity, young Christians need with the support of both their parents and the Church to discern the ways in which God is calling them to serve others in Jesus' name.

As Christian children mature intellectually, they need to deepen in their understanding of their relationship to God. At first the Christian story and ritual will provide them with their most fundamental religious categories. As they develop the capacity for rational thought, however, they will need to learn how to think theologically. They should understand something of the richness of the Christian tradition and begin to deal with the tensions within it. As they advance toward adulthood, they need a sound insight into the dynamics of conversion and into the practical demands that responsible Christian living makes upon them.

As Christian children mature morally, they need to grow in the love of Christ. With parental love and encouragement young children need to learn how to transcend the innocent egocentrism of childhood and respond to the needs of others. As children develop an initial capacity for moral commitment, they need deepened perceptions of the covenant of love that God has made with us in Christ and of the moral demands of life in the kingdom. The preadolescent and adolescent child need to develop a personal friendship with Jesus and to ponder the ways in which the great saints have lived out that friendship. Jesus' vision of the kingdom calls the young adult's conscience beyond the constraints of law and order to concern with God's own justice.

As Christian children mature socially, they need to commit themselves more and more actively to the Christian search for social justice. Here too parental attitudes have the capacity to shape a child's social prejudices profoundly; but beyond developing sound social instincts, children need insofar as they can to confront important issues of faith and justice that trouble contemporary society. As adolescence approaches, developing young adults need to judge the adult world they are about to enter with the mind and heart of Jesus. They need to take responsibility for confronting that world prophetically in the name of God and of Christ.

Christian maturation should, then, transform every facet of a young child's life. Initially the Christian family provides the immediate realm of grace in which children can begin to grow to Christian maturity. The larger Christian community augments that realm and supports maturing children in their transition from the security of the family to the world of converted, responsible, adult living.

The Question of Infant Baptism

The preceding reflections throw theological light on the vexed question of infant baptism. In reflecting on Christian initiation, I promised that we would deal with this issue in discussing the responsibilities of Christian parents. The time has come to do so.

Infant baptism ensures that a newborn child will mature as a member of the life-giving realm of grace created by the shared faith of the Christian community, by parental faith, and by the graced environment of the family.

As we have seen, not all the Christian Churches practice infant baptism. Those that do not baptize infants equivalently require children to undergo an extended catechumenate that culminates eventually in adult baptism. The Catholic Church has taken a minor step toward permitting such a discipline by including in the revised rites of Christian initiation ceremonies for advancing children not baptized as infants through all stages of initiation: catechumenate, initiation, and mystagogy (RCIA, 252–330).

The relatively high incidence of infant mortality in the ancient world certainly encouraged the practice of baptizing infants. Moreover, in parts of the world in which infant mortality remains high,[2] the baptism of infants still makes sense. The restoration of the catechumenate and the official establishment of a catechumenate for unbaptized children raises the question, however, about the pastoral advisability of postponing the baptism of children whom death does not threaten so that they might, after proper catechetical instruction, enter the Church as committed adults.

While I would favor controlled pastoral experimentation in this direction, I myself see no decisive advantage to either form of Church discipline. Children baptized as infants have the advantage of growing up with a clearly defined religious identity, since they have already been accepted in a preliminary fashion into the Church. Moreover, they have the opportunity of consciously ratifying their own baptism when they begin to communicate in the Eucharist and especially (as we shall see) when they are confirmed. When Church discipline allows the postponement of baptism, children nurtured in such a tradition have the advantage of consciously choosing to join the Church with a measure of adult maturity and in a way that preserves the integrity of the rite of initiation.

In my opinion the quality of the child's religious education counts far more than the timing of baptism. In the absence of quality religious education, neither discipline works.

Churches that practice infant baptism elect to initiate the offspring of Christian parents into the Christian community in stages; for, as we have seen, one ought to regard baptism, confirmation, and first Holy Communion as three stages in a single rite of initiation rather than as three distinct sacraments. Infant baptism only begins the ritual process of initiation. When children reach sufficient maturity they receive first Holy Communion. The rite of confirmation, in my opinion, ought then to conclude the initiation process when

2. We need to include the United States in the list of nations with high infant mortality. By some estimates we rank fifteenth in the world in infant deaths, many of which result from lack of proper nutrition. A child born in Hong Kong has a better chance of surviving than one born in the United States.

the child has reached sufficient maturity in faith. Clearly, the practice of infant baptism would in that case reorder the second and third stages of initiation. One can, however, argue that the revised order corresponds pastorally to the growth needs of baptized children. Let us reflect briefly on the reasons why.

Infant Baptism and Original Sin

The Churches that practice infant baptism justify it on the basis of the fact that the ritual takes away original sin. In adults baptism removes both personal and original sin. In the case of infants it removes original sin alone. Infants have committed no personal sins, but they are born into a sinful world. As we have seen, we need to understand both original sin and concupiscence situationally and perspectivally. We need to understand them perspectivally because my personal sins contribute to the experience that other people have of original sin and concupiscence; their sins contribute to my experience of original sin and concupiscence. No one, therefore, experiences sin and concupiscence in exactly the same way or from the same angle of vision. We need to understand original sin and concupiscence situationally because they create the sinful environment in which we live. That environment includes institutional sin.

Baptism, as we have seen, takes away original sin by changing one's environment. It does so by introducing one into the Church, into the realm of divine grace that sensitizes one to the existence of situational sin and supplies one with the means to resist it. In the process, as we have also seen, baptism changes original sin into concupiscence, into those forces in the situation of the baptized recognized as coming from sin and as leading to sin.

As an act performed by Christian adults, infant baptism brings with it the responsibility of providing the matrix of grace that the baptized child needs in order to grow to Christian maturity. Both the child's parents and the baptizing Church commit themselves by that act to nurturing the infant to an integral, fivefold conversion.

As we have already seen and shall see in greater detail in the last chapter, through shared Eucharistic worship Christians reaffirm on a regular basis their original covenant of initiation. This sacrament more than any other seeks to nurture in Christians ongoing conversion to God. It makes sense, therefore, that baptized children should begin to take advantage of this sacramental help to advance to full adult conversion as soon as they can understand its significance and participate in Eucharistic worship with genuine commitment, probably around the age of eight or nine but sooner if they should manifest the capacity for intelligent participation in faith.

Confirming the Infant Baptized

Confirmation would then complete the ritual introduction of baptized infants into the Christian community. That fact would also determine the ritual's pastoral timing. Full sacramental incorporation into the Christian community presupposes an integral, fivefold conversion. Christians baptized as infants should not, then, receive confirmation until they have achieved the same degree of converted commitment that the restored catechumenate demands of adult converts. Since, moreover, confirmation commits one to lifelong openness to the divine Mother's charismatic inspirations and since a Christian vocation needs charismatic inspiration, ideally confirmation ought to occur before young Christians baptized as infants have made a major vocational option, normally toward the end of high school or in the first two years of college. That a baptized child would have the capacity to experience an integral, fivefold conversion prior to that age seems to me highly unlikely, since the child would lack the personal wherewithal to take adult responsiblity for itself, for its world, and for its responses to God.

Theological confusion concerning the purpose of confirmation has certainly contributed significantly to the premature administration of this ritual. As we have already seen, in the contemporary debate over confirmation we find a variety of theological approaches to the ritual and to date little or no consensus. We have discovered two principal areas of disagreement: theologians dispute both the significance of the ritual and its timing in the case of those baptized as infants. Confronted with this theological disarray, current Church discipline allows the confirmation of those baptized as infants once they reach the age of reason, although the precise age at which confirmation occurs varies considerably from diocese to diocese.

We have already suggested a way of resolving the dispute over the significance of confirmation. The time has come to reflect on the role and timing of this ritual in the religious maturation of those baptized as infants.

Some theologians, as we have seen, push for the restoration of the "liturgical integrity" of the rite of initiation even in the case of those baptized as infants. By that they mean either the administration of both confirmation and Communion at the time the infant receives baptism or the confirmation of the baptized child before the administration of first Communion. In the latter case confirmation would ordinarily occur at about the age of eight or nine.

In my own opinion, those who push for the restoration of the "liturgical integrity" of the rite of initiation in the case of those baptized as infants often fall into the triple fallacy of historicism, formalism, and abstractionism. They seem to assume the normativity of fourth-century sacramental worship for twentieth-century Christians. They seem to ignore the functional character of ritual by valuing aesthetic symmetry and rubrical uniformity more than the religious needs of living people. Finally, they tend to try to understand sacramental worship in abstraction from a strictly normative insight into the demands of Christian conversion. Unfortunately, however, when liturgical theology advances in abstraction from foundational thinking it tends to produce aesthetes and rubricists rather than theologians and pastors.

A restoration of the "liturgical integrity" of adult initiation by a return to fourth-century sacramental practice would make sound pastoral sense, in my opinion, only if the Churches that currently practice infant baptism decided to abolish the practice and baptize only adults. In the case of those baptized as infants, however, it does make sound pastoral sense to allow them to receive Holy Communion as soon as they would benefit from active participation in Eucharistic worship and to complete the rite of initiation with confirmation.

Even, however, if the Churches would decide to make adult baptism the norm and infant baptism the exception, it seems unlikely that one could eliminate infant baptism altogether. The Church ought to baptize infants on the brink of dying. Infant mortality, moreover, stalks the First as well as the Third World. The United States to its shame ranks fifteenth in the world in infant deaths. In the case of baptized infants who recover health, the present discipline of the Church would probably suit their religious needs better than the reception of the full rite of initiation administered to a child who lives in total oblivion of its significance for them and for their lives.

The Timing of Confirmation for the Infant Baptized

When, however, Churches that baptize infants terminate the process of initiation prematurely they act with pastoral irresponsibility. The termination of initiation including those baptized as infants ought to seal an adult conversion to Christ and orient young Christians to active charismatic service in the Church and in the world. We have solid reason to doubt that children at the age of eight or nine have the capacity to make such a commitment, although they can and should begin by that age to participate actively in the Eucharist. The premature confirmation of those baptized as infants (and by that I mean their confirmation prior to having experienced an integral, fivefold conversion) makes it seem as though the Church does not really require of them either integral conversion to Christ or an adult readiness to serve charismatically in his image as the condition for full Church membership. If, then, the bishops at Vatican II acted correctly in restoring the catechumenate, they should take responsibility for the consequences of that decision and not allow the completion of the rite of Christian initiation until those baptized as infants have reached the level of conversion that one would require of baptized adults. In most cases, therefore, baptized Christians would probably need to wait until the end of high school or the early years of college before receiving confirmation.

Liturgical purists will no doubt object that in that case confirmation would seal the rite of initiation rather than the Eucharist, as it did in the fourth century and as it now does in the RCIA. To that I would reply that in the case of those confirmed after first Holy Communion the Eucharist would in fact seal the rite of confirmation as long as pastors take care to see to it that confirmation ordinarily occurs at a Eucharist. True enough, in that case one's confirmation would not find its liturgical seal in the confirmed Christian's first Holy Communion, but in a subsequent Holy Communion. That, however, seems to me a trivial rubrical price to pay for a celebration of initiation that actually meets the religious needs of those baptized as infants.

In other words, confronted with a choice between those liturgical historicists, formalists, and abstractionists who insist on restoring the "integrity" of the rite of initiation, on the one hand, and those who urge a more pastoral approach to this question, on the other, I side with the latter. Moreover, I would argue that the foundational theology of Christian initiation presented in this study provides theological justification for adapting sacramental rites pastorally to the needs of people rather than people to the abstract exigencies of academic liturgists.

5. Facing the Issues. In the course of reflecting on the history of Christian nuptials, we discovered three issues about which theologians and Churches disagree. They dispute about the sacramental character of Christian marriage, about the values it embodies, and about its indissolubility. In reflecting on the commitment embodied in the marriage rite, we began to address the question of sacramentality; and we have reflected in some detail on the values that Christian marriage incarnates. Does the attempt to understand Christian marriage in the light of the dynamics of conversion further illumine these disputed questions?

a. The Sacramentality of Christian Marriage. In the course of reflecting on the rite of matrimony, I argued that the commitment it embodies renews the Christian covenant of initiation and reproduces all the defining characteristics of a sacrament. Such an argument builds on ecumenical consensus. It first takes the two Christian rituals whose sacramentality no one disputes and analyzes their fundamental traits. It then identifies as sacramental any other Christian ritual that reproduces the same characteristics.

One may, however, approach the sacramentality of Christian marriage from another theological perspective. Sacramental rituals celebrate sacramental events of grace that both reveal and conceal the saving presence of the triune God. Christian marriage qualifies as such an event because, when properly celebrated, it seals publicly the graced commitment of a man and a woman whose mutual love has been transformed and transvalued in the saving love of Christ and whose desire for matrimony flows from the divine Mother's charismatic anointing.

Marriage as a Sacramental Event

As we have seen, no one should pronounce nuptial vows in the Church who lacks both human readiness and readiness in faith to assume the responsibilities of married life. Human readiness for marriage demands the affective, intellectual, and moral maturity to build a healthy relationship between the spouses and to found a family. It demands as well a sound understanding of the importance of family life and a determination to defend it against those institutional forces that seek to undermine it. Human readiness for matrimony flows, then, from the four forms of natural conversion. It ordinarily presupposes not only initial conversion but a measure of ongoing conversion as well; for Christian spouses take on serious social responsibilities in addition to those they assumed on entering the Church. Finally, human readiness for marriage also demands that romantic involvement has matured into marital love.

Readiness in faith to pronounce the vows of matrimony demands, then, much more than legal competence to make a contract about enjoying genital sex with another person. It demands not only an initial conversion to Christ but also signs of growth in Christian holiness. The love of charity, which blends the atoning love of Christ, the visionary love of the mystic, and the needy love of a child, must have already transvalued to a significant degree the shared marital love of a Christian man and woman before they pronounce the vows of matrimony. Moreover, their mutual love in Christ must give promise of binding them to one another for life. In addition, readiness in faith to pronounce marriage vows also presupposes that a Christian couple has not only discerned that God has called them to the vocation of marriage in general but also that the divine Mother has called them specifically and concretely to marital union with one another.

In other words, unless two baptized Christians commit themselves to one another with a marital love informed by the love of Christ and unless their mutual love and commitment flows from the divine Mother's charismatic anointing, their marriage vows lack a sacramental character because they fail to seal a sacramental event of grace.

In addition, the full sacramentality of Christian marriage encompasses all the graced human values that the Christian family embodies; for, when two spouses love one another with a Christlike love that frees both of them to advance in an integral, fivefold conversion, the divine Mother acts in them to create a sacramental realm of grace that not only sanctifies their union but also nurtures their children to a similar conversion before God. In addition, the sharing of the divine Mother's charisms within the family transforms it sacramentally into a ministerial instrument for the spread of the kingdom. Finally, the gracing of family life also mitigates the impact of situational sin upon the lives of its members and arms them to resist both sin and concupiscence. All of these graced consequences of Christian marriage suffuse Christian family life with saving, sacramental significance. The sacramentalization of marriage poses then a practical moral challenge that precludes understanding its sacramentality as a metaphysical given.

The Family as Icon

Moreover, the sacramentalization of married life points to an even deeper mystery. As we have seen, Christians may legitimately imagine the reality of the triune God as a divine family. Christians imagine the first person of the Trinity as the divine Father and the second person as the divine Son. Both Scripture and tradition sanction imagining the third person of the Trinity as the divine Mother.

When Christian families love one another with Christlike charity, their mutual loving gift of themselves to one another in faith imitates the eternal self-gift of the divine persons to one another, a self-gift that unites them in an identity of divine life. In other words, the love that unites Christian families transforms them into a sacramental revelation, a created icon, of the divine family.

The preceding reflections also throw light on the institution of the sacrament of matrimony. The sacramentality of marriage flows from its Christianization. Jesus Christ may then be said to have instituted marriage as a sacrament when he rejected divorce as sinful, when he demanded of his disciples a quality of atoning love that transforms human marital relationships, and when he sent the divine Mother to transform marriage charismatically into a form of Christian ministry; for these saving events of grace endow Christian marriage with saving and therefore with sacramental significance.

b. The Indissolubility of Christian Marriage. If the sacramentality of Christian marriage flows from the transformation of marital love that Christian conversion effects, then the absence of conversion may desacramentalize married life as well. When spouses refuse to forgive one another with the love of atonement, when they relate to one another out of sinful self-reliance rather than from faith, when they selfishly withhold from one another parts of themselves or their personal possessions, when their lives together embody secular, class values rather than the vision of the kingdom, then their relationship to one another ceases to image forth the life of God.

The Erosion of Marital Commitment

Moreover, the absence of affective, intellectual, moral, and sociopolitical conversion may also suffuse a Christian marital commitment with a destructive inauthenticity that can gradually erode and destroy it. The refusal to deal with repressed aggression, fear, and guilt can lead spouses to acts of mutual spite or freeze them in mutual enmity. A fundamentalistic rigidity of mind can put serious strains on a marriage relationship. Moral irresponsibility can betray spouses into using or abandoning one another. The absence of affective and moral conversion can also motivate sinful marital infidelity. Materialism, sexism, individualism, and all the other rationalized forms of institutional sin can infect a marriage and gradually deprive it of graced, sacramental significance.

Not only can the absence of conversion erode the sacramentality of a Christian marriage, but experience also teaches that it can tragically destroy the marriage itself. The sinful destruction of a marriage would, however, seem to contradict Jesus' prohibition of divorce. How, then, should one interpret that prohibition?

Moral and Metaphysical Indestructibility

If we examine the history of Christian marriage, we find that the first Christians, those historically closest to Jesus, seem to have regarded marriage as morally but not as metaphysically indestructible. By the moral indestructibility of Christian marriage, I mean that two spouses cannot destroy a Christian marriage without sinfully and grievously violating solemn vows pronounced before God. By the metaphysical indestructibility of marriage, I mean its inability to be destroyed by anything other than by the death of one of the spouses.

The first Christians treated those who divorced and remarried as adulterers, but they do not seem to have denied that the divorce had destroyed the first marriage or that the second marriage qualified as a real marriage.

The moral indestructibility of a sacramental marriage has sound theological justification. It flows inevitably from the quality of love that Christian conversion demands. Spouses who love one another in the name and image of Jesus commit themselves to one another unconditionally before God.

The Fallacies of Metaphysically Indestructibility

The attempt to prove the metaphysical indestructibility of a ratified, consummated marriage rests, by contrast, on arguments that do not conclude. Nor does their repetition in official, though fallible, Church documents render them any more conclusive. The traditional proof of the metaphysical indestructibility of sacramental marriage invokes an inadequate understanding of Christian marriage, an inadequate grasp of its sacramentality, an inaccurate interpretation of Scripture, and two logical fallacies.

The canonical interpretation of Christian marriage formulated in the twelfth century derives from pagan rather than from Christian sources: Roman civil law and from Germanic tribal customs. Roman law taught the medieval canonical mind to define marriage as a contract (not as a covenant). Germanic tribal customs taught canonists to define marriage as a contract to have sexual intercourse. In redefining Christian marriage as an interpersonal, covenant commitment rather than as a contract, Vatican II has, I believe, officially set aside a medieval, canonical definition of marriage as theologically inadequate.

The traditional defense of marriage's metaphysical indestructibility also rests on an inadequate interpretation of the sacramentality of Christian marriage. In a medieval, canonical interpretation of marriage, its sacramentality flows automatically from the sexual union of two married Christians who have a baptismal character on their souls. The baptismal character alone cannot, however, guarantee the sacramentality of Christian marriage; for it confers, as we have seen, only a morally conditioned right to engage in acts of Christian worship. The full and actual sacramentality of those ritual actions results from the fulfillment of those moral conditions. In the case of Christian marriage, its sacramentality flows from the fact that its vows express the mutual, Christlike love of the spouses and their charismatic call to blend their lives in the name of the triune God. Any theory of the sacramentality of marriage that grounds it in a single act of intercourse labors, then, under serious theological inadequacies.

A medieval canonical defense of the metaphysical indestructibility of Christian marriage also rests on an inadequate biblical foundation. It contends that the indestructible union of Christ and his Church described in Ephesians 5:21-33 causes the metaphysical indestructibility of the ratified, consummated marriage of two baptized Christians because the consummated union of two spouses symbolizes the union of Christ and his Church. As we have seen, however, Ephesians 5:21-33 does not assert the metaphysical indestructibility of Christian marriage. Rather, it holds up the love uniting Christ and his Church as a moral ideal for Christian spouses to imitate.

Finally, a medieval, canonical defense of the metaphysical indestructibility of Christian marriage rests on two logical fallacies. It argues *a priori,* and it confuses a factual statement with a statement of obligation.

In what sense does the traditional defense of the metaphysical indestructibility of marriage argue *a priori*? Medieval canonists defined marriage in such a way that indestructibility belongs to its very essence. In other words, they made it indestructible by legal fiat. Like all *a priori* definitions, however, this one, to the extent that it makes an assertion about human social relationships, qualifies only as a fallible hypothesis, not as the validated conclusion it claims to be. It finds validation or invalidation in the concrete behavior of Christians. That behavior suggests that humans have the moral capacity to destroy marriages.

Moreover, in appealing to Ephesians 5:21-33, medieval canonists attempted to derive a factual conclusion from an ethical premise. From an ethical premise, however, only ethical conclusions follow. If Christians ought to love one another with the same kind of love that unites Christ and his Church, then it follows logically that, if they fail to do so, they sin; but one cannot derive from such a premise any conclusion whatever about the metaphysical permanence of the marriage covenant.

In addition, one may question whether the union between Christ and his Church should be described as metaphysically indestructible since it roots itself in a free and mutual moral commitment. God's commitment to us in Christ always abides, because God keeps his promises; but individual Christians can and sometimes do withdraw their commitment to Christ in faith. Even, however, when Christians keep that commitment, their union with Christ remains morally free rather than metaphysically necessary.

The Indissolubility of Marriage in Canon Law

These reflections point to the need for the further revision of Catholic legislation concerning sacramental marriages. As we have seen, even though the new Code of Canon Law at times defines Christian marriage as a covenant (*foedus*) rather than as a contract, in other respects it reaffirms the traditional canonical legislation. Another revision of the code will not happen tomorrow; until it happens, Catholics need to find ways to deal with canonical realities. In the meantime they can also try to imagine an alternative to present Church discipline.

The vows of matrimony bind two Christians to an unconditioned love that requires them to bend every effort to save their marriage; but when that effort fails, one can imagine two possible pastoral strategies for dealing with the situation. An investigation of a failed marriage might reveal that the original marriage commitment lacked sacramentality either (1) because the contracting parties did not possess the personal maturity in faith required to enter into a Christian marriage covenant or (2) because they had failed to discern adequately their charismatic call to marital union with one another. Nonsacramental marriages can be annulled.

In the case of two Christians who sinfully destroy a sacramental marriage, canon law might well decide one day to deal with this serious sin in the same way that it handles other serious sins: with the rite of reconciliation. Church leaders in the West may also one day agree with Orthodox Christians that lifelong prohibition from ever contracting another marriage punishes the divorced too severely just as permanent exclusion from Eucharistic Communion punishes the divorced and remarried too harshly for the sin they have committed.

6. Conclusion. In this chapter and in the one that preceded it we have considered the first of two vocational sacraments: Christian marriage. We have examined its historical development and some of the important controversies it has occasioned. We have also considered the ideals to which integral conversion challenges Christian spouses, and we have pondered the forces that can make married Christians fall short of those ideals. Most Christian marriages lie somewhere between the gospel ideal and sinful reality. Christian spouses will meet the challenge of Christian marriage, not by denying the ideal to which Christ summons them, but by allowing the divine Mother to teach them how to transform their lives together creatively and imaginatively until they approximate ever more fully the ideals of marital union to which Christians aspire.

In the two chapters that follow we shall attempt a similar analysis of the second vocational sacrament: ordination to public Church leadership.

CHAPTER III

The Development of Ordained Ministry

In the course of the preceding chapter we reflected on the charismatic ministry of married Christians. We examined the ways in which the ministry of Christian spouses flows from Christian initiation. We saw how the graced sacramentalization of human sexual relations transforms the rite of marriage into a sacramental covenant. We also considered the values Christian marriage embodies in the light of the dynamics of conversion and discovered in the Christian family a realm of grace that sanctifies spouses, nurtures children to integral conversion, and advances the work of the kingdom.

Like the ministry of the married, the ministry of official, pastoral leadership in the Church also requires ritual confirmation. As we shall see, like the call to Christian marriage the call to ordained leadership deepens the commitment to Christ embodied in the rites of initiation. It presupposes and extends the conversion of the ordained ministers themselves and empowers them to encourage others in the enterprise of initial and ongoing conversion. Christian ordination also brings with it new pastoral responsibilities that go beyond those effected by the rites of initiation.

Our reflections on the development of the rite of ordination divide into three sections, with corresponding subsections. The first section reviews briefly the biblical foundations for a theology of Christian priesthood. As we shall see, those foundations hold the key to resolving many of the controversies that surrounded ordained leadership. The second section examines the way in which the ritual of ordination has evolved over the centuries. The third section of this chapter attends to some of the theological disputes that accompanied that ritual development.

1. Biblical Foundations for a Theology of Christian Priesthood. A New Testament theology of priesthood derives its categories largely from the Hebrew Scriptures, even though the experience of Jesus and of the paschal mystery eventually forced a radical reinterpretation of those categories. We find priestly images scattered throughout the New Testament, but the Letter to the Hebrews develops them into an extensive meditation on the priesthood of Jesus and argues that it transcends and replaces the Levitical priesthood. In order to understand both that meditation and other New Testament allusions to Christian priesthood, one needs, then, to know something about the Levitical priesthood that Jesus' priesthood was destined to replace.

a. The Levitical Priesthood. We find the name of Levi listed among the twelve patriarchs and among the twelve tribes of Israel (Gen 29:31–30:24; 35:23-26; 49:3-27; Exod 1:1-5; Deut 27:12-13; 33:6-29; Ezek 48:31-34; 1 Chr 2:1-2). Scripture scholars debate, however, whether the sons of Levi always functioned as priests of Israel or whether the tribe of Levi began secular and only subsequently acquired a sacral, priestly status.

Psalm 99:6 calls Moses a priest, but nowhere in the whole of the Pentateuch do we find the designation repeated. Instead, Moses consecrates Aaron and his sons to priestly office (Exod 29:20-21; Lev 8:23-24). Moses, however, enjoyed a personal access to God denied to the other practitioners of Mosaic religion. The Levitical priesthood resulted from the need to make the God of Moses humanly accessible.

The Rise of the Levitical Priesthood

The title "priest" (*kohen*) and the Hebrew understanding of priestly responsibilities derive from the urbanized culture of the Canaanites, whose worship developed around religious cultic centers. After the conquest of Canaan the Hebrew priesthood also took shape around sanctuaries over which priestly families presided.

In the ancient Middle East kings patronized the priestly caste in expectation that the latter would lend religious sanction to the monarchy. Early in his reign King David transported the ark of the covenant to Jerusalem and appointed Abiathar and Zadok to preside over worship in his capital city (2 Sam 6:1-23; 8:17). He chose Abiathar as the sole surviving heir of one of the most influential priestly families in Israel (1 Kgs 1:5-8, 44; 2:26-27). An obscurer figure, Zadok may have functioned as the Jebusite priest of Jerusalem before David conquered the city.

The Priesthood under David

David's location of the ark of the covenant in Jerusalem and his desire to house it in a suitable Temple expressed more than personal piety. By transforming "the City of David" into the cultic center for all twelve tribes, the Davidic monarchy sought to consolidate popular assent to the belief that God sanctioned its hegemony over the whole of Israel (2 Sam 6:1–7:17). Solomon fulfilled his father's dream of Temple building (1 Kgs 6:1-14). When, after Solomon's death, the other tribes rebelled against the Davidic monarchy, Jeroboam, the rebel king, recognized the political implications of Temple worship in Jerusalem and transformed Bethel into the cultic center of the northern kingdom (1 Kgs 12:20-33). In other words, the establishment of Temple worship in the capital cities of Judah and of Israel began the politicization of priestly ministry.

The Josiahan Reform

In 621 B.C. the righteous king Josiah abolished all local shrines with their attendant priests and centralized cult in the Jerusalem Temple. The Temple priesthood evolved a complex, male, hierarchical structure over which the high priest, a descendent of Zadok, presided (2 Kgs 12:10; 22:4, 8; 23:4). A "second priest" administered the temple, while other priests, "keepers of the threshold," took charge of finances. The heads of the different priestly families comprised the "elders of priests." Finally, beneath the priests, singers and gatekeepers helped with the details of cult. In other words, the centralization of cult in Jerusalem not only tied the fate of the Levitical priesthood more tightly to that of the monarchy, but it also endowed the Levitical priesthood with a more clearly defined power structure.

The Levitical Priesthood after the Exile

In 587 B.C. the highest priestly classes were deported into exile in Babylon. The Babylonians razed the Temple and put a temporary end to its cult, but after the return from exile the Zadokite aristocracy reasserted its control of temple worship. The Zadokite priesthood required proven descent from Aaron as a precondition for exercising priestly office. It thus demoted other members of the priestly caste to the status of Levites (Num 18:6; 16:1-11).

In 172 B.C. the Hasmonean rulers of Israel ended Zadokite domination of Temple cult when they replaced Jason, the last Zadokite high priest, with appointees of their own. Religious purists like the Pharisees questioned the legitimacy of these priestly appointments, and not without reason. By the time of the Roman Empire the high priesthood had degenerated into a political nomination that made no pretense of enjoying genealogical legitimacy. Rome appointed the high priest of the Jews.

The Functions of the Levitical Priest

In the course of its development, the Levitical priesthood performed three religious functions: it presided over cult, delivered oracles from God, and interpreted the Law.

As a cult leader, Levitical priests offered sacrifices to God (Exod 29:38-42). Once a year on the Day of Atonement, the high priest offered a sacrifice for the sins of all Israel. On that occasion he functioned as the supreme mediator between God and the people (Lev 16:1-34; Sir 50:5-21). Priests also presided over rites of consecration, like the anointing of kings (1 Kgs 1:39; 2 Kgs 11:12), and rites of purification of mothers after delivery (Lev 12:1-8), of lepers after their cure (Lev 14:1-32), and of defiled places (Lev 14:33-57).

Up until the time of David, priests also delivered oracles through the use of the Urim and Thummim, two objects kept in the ephod, an apronlike vestment that priests wore. By drawing forth the Urim and Thummim, priests pronounced in God's name positive or negative answers to questions posed them (1 Sam 14:36-42; 30:7-8; Deut 33:8). After the reign of David we find no mention of this practice.

Finally, Levitical priests proclaimed and interpreted Torah. On feast days they read to the people the narratives that grounded Israel's faith (Exodus 1–15). At covenant renewals they proclaimed the Law (Exod 24:7; Deut 27:9; Neh 8:1-18). The priestly caste supervised the final redaction of the Pentateuch. After its public proclamation by Ezra in 445 B.C., it commanded the obedience as sacred Scripture and Law (Neh 8:1-18). The Levitical priest also functioned as an ordinary, authoritative interpreter of the Law (Deut 33:10; Jer 18:18; Ezra 44:23; Hag 2:10-14). By the time of Jesus, the rabbis who presided over synagogues had largely taken over this particular priestly function. As a consequence, the Levitical priesthood functioned almost exclusively in the realm of cult.

The Levitical priest, then, lived set apart from the rest of the people. He belonged to an elite professional caste within Israel. Membership in that religious elite depended on ancestry, not upon personal endowments. The Levitical priest presided over cult at some religious sanctuary, interpreted the Law, and, until the time of David, delivered oracles that informed Israel of God's intentions. The holiness and transcendence of God gave the priestly office its purpose. Priests helped worshippers commune with a distant deity and called down upon them the assurance of his blessing. They purified the legally defiled. The priesthood's association with the monarchy led to its politicization. The centralization of cult generated a hierarchical power structure within the Temple priesthood. During the intertestamental period, the high priesthood degenerated into a pure political appointment.

b. The Ministry and Priesthood of Jesus. Jesus did not belong to the tribe of Levi, nor did he in the course of his life function as a Levitical priest. His disciples called Him "Rabbi," teacher. Teach he did, but not as the other rabbis did. He spoke with a charismatic authority inspired by the Breath of God and by his own experience of God as *Abba.* Attuned to the apocalyptic aspirations of his people, he proclaimed the coming reign of God and validated his authority to speak in God's name by the miracles of healing and by the exorcisms he performed.

Contemporary Scripture scholars often prefer to describe the historical Jesus as the head of a movement rather than as the founder of a Church. Nevertheless, the historical Jesus did give rudimentary institutional shape to the new Israel he was in process of founding when he appointed the Twelve to function as its judges (Mark 3:13-19; 10:28-31; Matt 10:1-4; 19:27-29; Luke 6:12-16; 18:24-27).

While Jesus preferred parabolic language to the high poetry of the Hebrew writing prophets, his ministry of teaching also had prophetic overtones. He foretold the destruction of Jerusalem and the end of Temple cult (Luke 19:41-44; 21:5-6; John 2:19; Mark 13:1-4; 14-20; Matt 24:1-3) and performed prophetic gestures like cleansing the Temple (Mark 11:15-19; Matt 21:12-17; Luke 19:45-48; John 2:14-16). On the night he was betrayed he performed another such gesture. He communicated to his disciples the meaning of what he was about to suffer by giving them bread and wine to eat and drink as his Body and Blood. Moreover, the words he used on that occasion portrayed his death as a covenant sacrifice (Mark 14:22-25; Matt 26:26-29; Luke 22:15-20; 1 Cor 11:23-25).

Jesus' Death as Sacrificial

Throughout the New Testament we find Jesus' death interpreted in sacrificial imagery that echoes the words he himself used in instituting the Eucharist. Paul the Apostle describes Jesus' death as a passover sacrifice that effects a new liberation by purging believers of the old leaven of sin (1 Cor 5:7). The First Letter of Peter echoes the image when it portrays the baptized Christian as purified by the sprinkled blood of Christ, the passover lamb without blemish (1 Pet 1:18). The Letter to the Romans proclaims that Jesus offered his life in sacrifice in order to reconcile Jew and Gentile alike to God in faith (Rom 3:25). In a similar theological vein, the First Letter of John describes Jesus' death as a propitiation for sins, while the Letter to the Galatians portrays the effects of Jesus' sacrificial death as extending to the individual believer (Gal 2:20). The Letter to the Ephesians holds up the love embodied in Jesus' sacrificial death as an example for Christians to imitate (Eph 5:2).

Jesus the New High Priest

The Letter to the Hebrews, however, transforms these sacrificial images into a profound Christological meditation on the priesthood of God's incarnate Son. Through his incarnation, death, and glorification, the author of the letter insists, the Son of God was consecrated to function as the high priest of the new covenant. Moreover, he exercises a priesthood so different from and superior to that of the old Law that it terminates once and for all any need for the Levitical priesthood.

The meditation on Jesus' priesthood in Hebrews begins by contrasting Jesus' fidelity to God with that of Moses and by insisting that the superiority of Jesus' fidelity forces a choice between the "house" in which Moses served and the "house" of God, the Church, which Jesus brings into being by his faithful ministry (Heb 3:1-6). Both Moses and Jesus sought to lead people to share in God's rest. Moses sought to lead a rebellious and unbelieving people to rest in the Promised Land; Jesus seeks to lead an obedient people to share in the eternal rest of God in heaven (Heb 3:7–4:11).

The author of Hebrews contrasts the high priesthood of Jesus with the high priesthood exercised under the old covenant. Under the former dispensation, consecration to the office of high priest set a man apart from the rest of the people and dedicated him to perform sacred tasks that no one else could do. Jesus, however, became the high priest of the new covenant, not by joining a sacred power elite, but by identifying totally with humanity in its suffering and need. He differs from us only in his sinlessness; but even his sinlessness brings him all the closer to us, because sin divides humans from one another. In approaching the sinless Christ we know that absolutely nothing separates him from us, including the barrier of sin (Heb 4:12-15).

Under the old dispensation the high priest mediated between God and the people. As the high priest of the new law, Jesus mediates between God and humanity, not distantly, but in virtue of being God's incarnate Son. As high priest he needs to understand humanity in all of its frailty in order that he can represent effectively its needs before God. This understanding he acquired by assuming the human condition personally. At the same time, the high priest of the new covenant needs to be divinely appointed to speak to humankind in God's name and to mediate to us the blessing of salvation. In sending us his own Son to speak for him, God endowed him with the needed priestly authority.

The Superiority of Jesus' Priesthood

Moreover, Jesus' death and glorification reveal the full scope of that authority. In submitting to a humiliating death he experienced the human condition in all of its misery and weakness. That act of self-sacrifice expressed the perfection of his sinless obedience to God. In addition, however, even as he submitted obediently to death, he also prayed to the God who had power to deliver him. His glorification effects that deliverance and reveals the efficacy of his priestly prayer. If, then, his obedient submission to the cross discloses the perfection of his sinless obedience to God, his glorification discloses the perfection of his high priestly authority and intercession (Heb 5:1–6:20).

Appointed high priest of the order of Melchizedek, Jesus' priesthood abides forever. Like the mysterious Melchizedek, the king of righteousness and peace to whom Abraham offered tribute, the high priest of the new covenant has "no father, mother, or ancestry, and his life has no beginning or ending" (Heb 7:1-3). Arguing allegorically, the author of Hebrews sees in the tribute that Abraham paid to Melchizedek and in the blessing that Melchizedek gave to Abraham a revelation of the superiority of the priestly order of Melchizedek to the Levitical priesthood that Abraham was destined to father. The letter then argues from the superiority of Jesus' priesthood to its difference in kind from the priesthood of Levi and of his descendants (Heb 7:4-10).

The superior supplants the inferior. Since, moreover, the Levitical priesthood served the old covenant, Jesus' revelation as high priest in the order of Melchizedek signals the replacement of the old covenant by the new. The Law of Moses gives way to "the hope that brings us nearer to God" (Heb 7:11-19).

The eternity of Christ's priesthood guarantees his power to save with utter certainty, since he intercedes forever for all those who approach God through him. We know this because the sinless Son of God by a single self-sacrificial act atoned for sin once and for all and was therefore exalted to the heavenly throne of God, where no sin abides. Having no need to offer sacrifice for his own sins, as the high priests of the old Law did, he pleads instead for the sinners for whom he died (Heb 7:20-28).

Jesus therefore exercises a new kind of priesthood. Levitical priests offered ritual sacrifices again and again. He, however, sacrificed his very self and experienced as a consequence a personal transformation in God that placed him once and for all on the throne of grace and establishes him eternally as the high priest of the new covenant. The passion perfected his solidarity with humanity; his glorification perfects his solidarity with God. His unique priesthood results directly from his divine filiation, which his resurrection reveals historically.

Both the qualitative uniqueness of Jesus' priesthood and its superiority to the Levitical priesthood also stand revealed in this, that Jesus' priesthood begins the future. Jesus has entered into the sanctuary of heaven, which the sanctuary of the Jerusalem Temple only dimly foreshadowed. He bears into the presence of God, not the blood of animals, but his own blood. Having offered himself once and for all through the eternal Breath of God, he now begins the future by sending her to purify from all sin the hearts of those who believe in him. This efficacious purification seals the new covenant and begins the last age of salvation, which the second coming of Christ will terminate. Having dealt with sin during his first coming, the victorious Christ will come again to reward with salvation those who wait for him. In other words, by the strength of one single act of self-oblation, the high priest of the new covenant now effects through the Breath he sends a liberation from sin that puts an end to the need for any further sin offering. It therefore replaces the futilely repetitious and inefficacious sin offerings of the Levitical priesthood. Moreover, Jesus' own glorious entry into the heavenly sanctuary paves the way for those who will follow him (Heb 8:1–10:18).

c. The Priestly People of God. All of the Gospels portray the priestly caste in Jerusalem as the ones chiefly responsible for Jesus' murder. It should, then, come as no surprise, that the first leaders of the Christian community felt loathe to take them as role models. We find, as a consequence, no indication within the New Testament of a priestly caste within the apostolic Church similar to the Levitical priesthood.

If, however, the first Christians did not think of their leaders as Levitical priests, the First Letter of Peter gives evidence that they regarded themselves as the priestly people of God. The Book of Exodus promised the people of the covenant that they would exercise a priestly function (Exod 19:1-15). The First Letter of Peter finds that promise fulfilled in the Christian community, which offers "spiritual sacrifices" made acceptable to God through the death and glorification of Jesus. The action of God within the Church transforms it into a living Temple. Christians become this Temple by incorporation into the new Israel that reconciles Jew and Gentile in Christ. The nations, therefore, have come to share in a holy priesthood once reserved for Israel alone (1 Pet 2:4-10).

The First Letter of Peter does not assert that all Christians share equally in the priesthood. The author of the letter does recognize the existence of official Church leaders, or presbyters, but does not look upon their role in the community as priestly in any privileged sense of that term.

The Book of Revelation echoes in its own way some of these insights. It portrays Jesus as the victorious Lamb, slain for our sins, but the Lamb receives worship rather than offers it as a priest. The victorious Christ does, however, transform the Christian community into a royal priesthood purified from all sin whose prayers enter into the heavenly liturgy celebrated before the throne of God and of the Lamb (Rev 4:1–5:14; 14:1-5; 19:1-10).

d. The Ideal of Christian Leadership. As we have seen, the Synoptic Gospels portray Jesus repudiating secular messianism as a form of idolatry. He himself supplied his disciples with the example of leadership they were expected to imitate. Moreover, Jesus' conception of leadership in the new Israel he was founding set him at odds with the Twelve, who found the way of power politics more congenial. Jesus, however, insisted that leadership in the new Israel demands the willingness to serve as the least of all in imitation of a servant Messiah who lays down his life for his disciples. It demands renouncing the arrogance of pagan rulers and embracing the way of powerlessness (Mark 9:33-37; 10:35-45; Matt 20:27, 20:24-28; Luke 22:24-27; John 13:1-20). Leaders in the new Israel must therefore live ready to suffer the same kind of persecution that Jesus himself experienced at the hands of the rich and powerful of this world (Matt 10:17-20).

Nevertheless, within the new Israel, the Twelve exercise genuine authority to bind and loose, to welcome new members and to exclude backsliders. Moreover, Peter, in virtue of his confession of Jesus as Messiah, enjoyed a preeminence among the rest of the Twelve (Matt 16:18-19; 18:18). The Twelve also participated in Jesus' own charismatic authority to proclaim the kingdom with power by healing illnesses and casting out demons (Mark 6:7-13; 11:27-33; Matt 10:5, 8, 9-14; 21:23-27; Luke 9:1-6; 20:1-8).

The shift from the Old Testament to the New Testament marks a major transition in a biblical theology of priesthood. As we shall see, other analogous transitions would also occur within postbiblical theology as the Christian understanding of priesthood evolved. In order to understand postbiblical reflections on priestly ministry, however, we need to understand how the structures of ordained Christian leadership and the rite of ordination itself evolved; for that evolution helps us contextualize the theological shifts that they precipitated.

2. The Development of Ritual Ordination. By choosing the Twelve and by associating them closely with his own ministry, Jesus left the new Israel with rudimentary structures of leadership that would eventually evolve into ordained ministry as we know it. The risen Christ also sent the divine Mother to transform Christian leadership into a charismatic ministry within a charismatic Church. In this twofold sense, then, Jesus Christ may be said to have "instituted" orders within the Church.

Public Ministry in the Apostolic Church

In the apostolic Church public leadership took a variety of forms. The Twelve exercised the judicial role Jesus had assigned them in part by functioning in times of dispute as a last court of appeal (Acts 15:1-2). Missionary apostles like Paul testified to the resurrection of Jesus in the power of the Holy Breath. Their authority derived from their experience of the risen Lord, from their charismatic commissioning to bear witness to him, and from their having founded local Churches (Rom 1:1; 1 Cor 4:15; 9:1; 12:28; Gal 1:16; 2:1-10). Prophets and teachers also exercised an influential ministry within the community (1 Thess 5:19-22; 1 Cor 4:6-12; Eph 4:11). Prophets addressed the Church with words from God and in some Churches presided at the Eucharist (*Didache*, 10).

Some Scripture scholars think that the Apostle Paul may have reserved the pastoral governance of the Corinthian community to himself. If so, his letters to that chaotic church suggest that his experiment in ecclesial government failed. To maintain good order, missionary apostles found it necessary to establish on-the-spot, local leadership. In the New Testament these local leaders are called by a variety of names: leaders (Heb 13:7), elders (*presbyteroi*) (1 Pet 5:1; Jas 5:14; Acts 11:30), presidents (*proistamenoi*) (Rom 12:8; 1 Thess 5:12-13), overseers (*episkopoi*) (Acts 20:17, 28; Phlm 1:1; Titus 1:5-9), and assistants (*diakonoi*) (Phil 1:1; 1 Tim 3:1-2). Among Christians the New Testament reserved the title of hieratic, sacrificial priest (*hiereus*) to Jesus alone. In English, however, the term "priest" designates both the hieratic sacrificial priest and the office of oversight exercised by presbyters and bishops. Nevertheless, the two offices differed significantly in the apostolic Church, and their conflation would take several centuries.

The Emergence of Deacons

The appointment of the Seven as deacons of the Church in Jerusalem illustrates both the spontaneity and the care that went into creating Church leadership structures (Acts 6:1-7). One should not, however, confuse the Seven with the office of deacon that evolved elsewhere. The latter served under the local Church overseer or governing board of elders in ministering to the needs of the community. The Seven, by contrast, may have exercised a certain administrative authority over the Gentile Christians in the Jerusalem Church. They were chosen democratically on the basis of their good reputation, charismatic gifts of leadership, and wisdom. Similarly, in the Pauline Churches, overseers were also expected to give evidence of being charismatically called to serve the community (2 Tim 1:6).

In the Acts of the Apostles and in the pastoral epistles we find, moreover, a simple pattern in the transfer of authority from the apostles to the Church leaders who succeeded them. The apostles designated local leaders who were charged with preserving and handing on the apostolic tradition. Normally, a ritual imposition of hands conferred the responsibility of leading the Christian community in humble imitation of the servant Messiah. The rite also confirmed the tested charismatic competence of the new leader (2 Tim 1:6).

Early Church order derived in part from the synagogue, which was governed by a group of elders led by an administrative president.

The Christian presbyterate seems to have been organized originally along similar lines.

The Rise of the Monepiskopos

In the second century, however, we begin to observe the emergence of the *monepiskopos,* or single bishop presiding over a local Church, who replaced the elders as the governing authority in the local Church. In times of crisis communities governed by a board of presbyters looked increasingly to the president of the board to make executive decisions. The growth of episcopal authority corresponded, then, to genuine pastoral needs and tensions within the Church. Internal dissensions over doctrine and discipline demanded pastoral action, and individual bishops responded more effectively in times of crisis than did a committee of elders.

Rome preserved government by a board of elders longer than did most of the other Churches but eventually elected its own *monepiskopos.* The establishment of the patriarchal sees, which traced their foundation to one of the apostles, transformed the bishop of Rome into the Patriach of the West.

Moreover, the emergence of the monarchical episcopate changed temporarily the purpose of the diaconate. The first deacons had been considered servants of the community. Now they functioned as assistants to the overseers, or bishops. As the authority of the bishop and deacon waxed, the prestige of the presbyterate waned, at least temporarily.

Episcopal Ordination in the Second and Third Centuries

During the second century, however, the Church still expected the ordained to exhibit charismatic competence to lead the community before receiving authority to do so through the ritual imposition of hands. Episcopal leadership involved not only the pastoral supervision of a local community, much in the manner of today's parish pastors, but also concern for the unity of the Church universal and for the integrity of the faith it professed. Except in Alexandria, where presbyters ordained their bishop, ordinarily a bishop or group of bishops ordained another bishop with a double imposition of hands, first silently, then with a prayer of consecration. The kiss of peace and a Eucharistic celebration immediately followed (*Apostolic Tradition,* 2–4).

During the second century episcopal supervision of community worship expanded to include cultic leadership. Normally, at Eucharistic celebrations the bishop presided flanked by his priests. As a consequence, the community came to perceive the rite of ordination as conferring not only the responsibilities of Church leadership but also the right to preside at Christian worship, even though some communities at least refrained from interpreting this episcopal right in narrowly exclusive terms. As we have seen, in some sections of the early Church prophets presided at the Eucharist; and well into the second century in Africa, we find evidence of lay Eucharistic presiders in the absence of an ordained minister (Tertullian, *De Exhort. Cast.,* 7.3; *De Praescriptione,* 41.5-8).

The first Christians did not practice universal ordination in the manner of most contemporary Christian Churches. Instead, ordination consecrated one to serve a specific local community which had tested and confirmed the ordinand's pastoral competence prior to the imposition of hands. By the third century, bishops ordained both priests and deacons. At this point, presbyters, who copresided at the Eucharist with the bishop, still functioned as a board of elders governing a local Church in collegial solidarity with the bishop. Deacons still functioned as the bishop's personal administrative assistant.

In the third century the ordination of bishops expanded to include a rite of enthronement in addition to the traditional imposition of hands. By the end of the fourth century the rite required the imposition of the Book of Gospels on the nape of the ordinand's neck in the course of his consecration. More elaborate prayers of consecration also accompanied the rite of ordination.

Fourth Century Developments

During apostolic times women numbered among the leaders of the Christian community (1 Cor 16:19; Rom 16:1, 3, 7; Acts 9:36; 18:26; John 20:17), and into the fourth century women routinely served as deaconesses. The Council of Nicea, however, officially excluded women from the ranks of the clergy, and eventually the office of deaconess disappeared altogether.

The fourth century also saw the beginning of the transformation of the priestly board of elders into parish priests. The rapid numerical expansion of the Church that followed upon imperial patronage, partly motivated the shift. Bishops of large urban communities found it impossible to preside personally at every Eucharist. Deacons could not preside at the Eucharist, but priests already functioned as copresiders with the bishop during Eucharistic worship. They therefore began to serve as the principal celebrant of Eucharists and baptisms that the bishop could not attend. Presbyters also represented urban bishops in rural communities and presided at their Eucharists.

As the presbyterate acquired enhanced liturgical importance, the office of deacon gradually disappeared as a separate ministry. By the fifth century the diaconate had degenerated into a stepping stone to the priesthood; by the sixth century the permanent diaconate had virtually disappeared.

The Church's emergence from the catacombs during the fourth century inaugurated a period of elaborate liturgical development. Ordination proved no exception to this rule. In the Byzantine rite of episcopal ordination, for example, the candidate was presented to the ordaining bishop to whom he professed his desire for ordination. The bishop elect then made a long profession of faith, received the pastoral staff of office, and after the singing of the *trisagion* (thrice holy) entered the sanctuary. There he knelt with his head bowed to touch the altar. The coconsecrating bishops held the open Book of the Gospels on the nape of his neck while the presiding bishop recited the prayers of consecration. After the consecration the new bishop donned the garments of his office while the clergy and people acclaimed him worthy. The kiss of peace and the enthronement of the new bishop then followed. Priestly ordination followed a somewhat similar pattern, though the prayers and vestments of office differed and the ritual lacked, of course, the rite of enthronement.

Ordination in the Roman Rite

In Rome the rite of episcopal ordination proceeded with much more simplicity. During the Eucharist, after the *Kyrie,* which at this point followed the epistle as a formalized prayer of the people, the pope recited the prayers of consecration over the bishop-elect and after the consecration exchanged with him the kiss of peace. The newly ordained bishop then joined the other assembled bishops for the rest of the Eucharistic celebration.

In the Roman Rite priests and deacons were ordained after the gospel. The candidates were presented to the pope, then prostrated themselves as the congregation prayed the litany of the saints over them. The pope then imposed hands on each candidate and recited ordination prayers for the deacons. The ceremony closed with the kiss of peace.

During the Middle Ages, however, this spare Roman ritual of ordination underwent considerable elaboration north of the Alps. The resulting ritual fused many different liturgical traditions. The ordination of bishops, priests, and deacons each began with an allocution by the ordaining prelate. In the ordination of a bishop the allocution was followed by a prayer and by the ritual of consecration. The new bishop was then anointed, given a ring and staff as symbols of his office, and enthroned. The ceremony ended with a blessing.

The ordination of priests and deacons followed an analogous pattern: an allocution, a prayer following the laying on of hands, clothing in the liturgical vestments of office, the handing over of the liturgical instruments that the ordinand would handle during the Eucharist, an anointing of the priest's hands, and a final blessing. The vesting, handing over of the liturgical instruments, and anointing of the hands both reflected and nurtured medieval perceptions of the priest as the principal agent of the Christian sacrifice.

These new rituals developed in the Gallican Church, but in the tenth century Rome adopted the Gallican ritual with minor modifications. Official adoption in Rome fixed the structure of the rite.

Protestant Ordination

In the sixteenth century the Protestant reformers, who generally rejected the sacramentality of orders, showed little patience with elaborate ordination rituals. Lutheran ordinations, for example, began with a prayer for the candidate, an address by the presiding minister on the responsibilities of Church ministry, and an imposition of hands accompanied by the Lord's Prayer and a prayer of ordination. Calvin omitted the ritual imposition of hands and consecrated the ministerial candidate with a simple prayer.

Ordination in Vatican II

After the Reformation we find little change in the rites of ordination until the Second Vatican Council. Vatican II called for a revision and simplification of the Catholic ordination ritual as a part of its liturgical reforms. It also reestablished the permanent diaconate.

We shall examine the structure of the new rituals below, when we ponder their significance. Before doing so, however, we need to reflect on some of the major debates about the meaning of ordained ministry.

3. Issues in the Development of Ordained Leadership. The theological interpretation of the purpose and scope of ordained ministry within the Church has evolved over the centuries, and as one might expect controversy has punctuated that evolution. We shall reflect briefly on five debates: disagreement over reordination and its theological fallout, shifts in the understanding of Christian priesthood, Reformation arguments over the sacramentality of the rite of ordination, the debate over mandatory clerical celibacy, and the contemporary disagreement over women's ordination.

a. The Reordination Controversy. As we have already seen, the Donatist controversy which divided the African Church during the fourth and fifth centuries gave decisive shape to the theological understanding of Christian baptism. The Donatists required the rebaptism of backsliders; the orthodox did not. That debate motivated Augustine's distinction between the grace of the sacrament and the baptismal character.

Donatist Ordination

The Donatist controversy also shaped theological understanding of the rite of ordination. The Donatists appealed three times to the emperor for political support. Each time that support failed to materialize. Finally, the emperor compelled the Donatists' acquiescence in the orthodox position.

Reconciliation did not come easily. The controversy had dragged on for generations and had been marked by violence. The Circumcellians, the radical wing of the Donatist Church, periodically lynched orthodox Christians. Once the Donatists capitulated, not all of the orthodox welcomed the prospect of attending Eucharists celebrated by former Donatist priests, and the question inevitably arose concerning their worthiness to preside at the Eucharist without reordination.

The Character of Ordination

Desirous of peace, Augustine once again invoked the notion of a sacramental character in order to argue against the need for reordination. Like the baptized, the ordained, he argued, are also permanently marked by the ritual of ordination even though they fall from grace. As a consequence, in order to function again as sacramental ministers, they need only sacramental reconciliaton to the Church, not reordination (*Against Parmenian,* 2, 13; *On the Good of Marriage,* 24).

Augustine left the meaning of the character vague, but during the high Middle Ages scholastic theologians interpreted it in a variety of ways. Albert the Great believed that it designated one as a prelate of the Church (Albert the Great, *On the Sacraments,* Tr. VIII, q. 4, a. 3). Bonaventure described it as a sign of spiritual power (Bonaventure, *Commentary on the Book of Sentences,* IV, d. xiv, p. 2, a. 1, qq. 1-3). Aquinas held that the character of ordination conferred the power to administer the sacraments (Thomas Aquinas, *Summa Theologiae,* III, lxiii, 1–6).

During the sixteenth century, however, the Protestant reformers could make no sense of this mysterious spiritual mark on the soul of the ordained. Luther found it unintelligible (Luther, *Works,* 36:110-111, 160, 201). So did Zwingli (Zwingli, *Commentary on True and False Religion,* 20).

The Council of Trent for its part reacted to such scepticism by committing Catholic theology to a defense of the character imposed at ordination. It asserted that ordination confers a character but failed to explain in what it consists (DS, 1774).

Any contemporary theologian who holds for the reality of the character conferred by ordination must, then, offer a plausible account of its cause and nature.

b. Shifting Perceptions of Priesthood. As we have seen, in apostolic times official church leaders seem not to have conceived their office primarily in cultic terms. Nevertheless, over several generations bishops gradually evolved into cult leaders. Moreover, as we have also seen, the fourth century transformed presbyters into Eucharistic celebrants.

These ritual developments signaled a gradual sacralization of Church leadership. Sacralization brought with it elitist tendencies. By the third century we find increasing references to the ordained as clergy, i.e., as "specially chosen," "set apart." With increasing regularity we also find bishops and occasionally presbyters described as cultic priests. In the fourth century these impulses bore fruit in a theological movement called sacerdotalism.

The Emergence of Sacerdotalism

In the fourth century, the clergy joined the empire. In 313 Constantine recognized Christianity as an official state religion. He hoped to enlist the help of the Christian clergy in reforming a corrupt civil bureaucracy. Accordingly, after 318 ecclesiastical courts enjoyed imperial sanction. That sanction transformed bishops overnight into imperial bureaucrats.

Soon, however, those bishops began to suspect that in accepting imperial patronage they may have taken a tiger by the tail. In 325 the pagan emperor Constantine summoned the Council of Nicea to deal with the Arian heresy. The bishops complied with the emperor's summons; but the more thoughtful, like Basil of Caesarea, recognized the need to erect strong theological barriers against imperial meddling in the Church's internal affairs. In the process of constructing these defenses, Basil helped lay the foundations for a new understanding of episcopal leadership.

A trained rhetorician, Basil used his Athenian schooling to exhort the emperor not only to live according to Christian ideals but also to respect the bishops' right to govern the Church without imperial interference. Both the emperor and the bishops participated directly in divine authority, Basil argued. The emperor did so in secular matters, the Christian clergy did so in governing the Church. In telling the emperor that he derived his authority to govern from the triune God, Basil had spread his theological nets to catch a king. As the secular image of God, the emperor must never forget that he counted *only* as an image and should never accept idolatrous worship from his subjects, as some of his predecessors had. Moreover, since the emperor governs in the name of the Christian God, he must take care to live as a paragon of Christian virtue. Eventually this line of thinking would transform subsequent caesaro-papist emperors into the thirteenth apostle.

The same thinking transformed Christian bishops into the high priests of the new covenant. Ecclesiastical authority, Basil argued, differs in its origin and purpose from civil authority. Bishops participate directly and immediately in the priestly authority of Christ to which the Letter to the Hebrews eloquently testifies. Episcopal authority qualifies, therefore, as sacred rather than secular. It brings spiritual healing as well as direction and guidance to the Christian Church. Moreover, in the world of Christian Platonism, bishops participated immediately in the priesthood of Jesus in a way that set them apart from and over the rest of the Church.[1]

1. For a lucid exposition of Basil's thought on this point, see Gerard F. Reilly, C.SS.R., *Imperium and Sacerdotium According to Basil the Great* (Washington, D.C.: Catholic University Press, 1945).

The Ironies of Sacerdotalism

Fourth-century sacerdotalism exhibited some speculative ironies. While it appealed to the priesthood of Christ expounded in the Letter to the Hebrews, it drew from that exposition theological conclusions that contrast sharply with those drawn by Hebrews itself. As we have seen, the Letter to the Hebrews argued that the utterly unique and transcendent character of Christ's priesthood had put an end to the Levitical priesthood. Fourth century sacerdotalism by contrast argued that because bishops participate in the priesthood of Christ, they must be regarded as the quasi-Levitical priests of the new covenant. Hebrews portrayed Jesus' priesthood as a priesthood of identification with humanity, especially with the poor, the outcast, and the marginal. Sacerdotalism significantly advanced the sacralization of the clergy and their separation from the secular, more profane laity. Not only, then, did sacerdotalism mark a major departure from a New Testament theology of priesthood, but it also ran the risk of holding up as role models for the episcopacy the very priestly, power elite whom the New Testament principally blames for Jesus' death. Given the political character of the Levitical priesthood, it comes as no surprise that sacerdotalism not only paralleled but also in part rationalized the imperial politicization of the episcopacy.

Other elitist tendencies marked in fourth-century sacerdotalism. It exhorted the clergy, especially bishops, to look upon themselves not only as the high priests of the new covenant but quite explicitly as a moral and spiritual elite. These exhortations also sprang in no small measure from political concerns. As imperial judges, the bishops would encounter the same temptations to bribery that had corrupted the civil courts. As a consequence, sacerdotalist theology held up to bishops the highest standards of moral and religious conduct lest they yield to the blandishments of the world.

These exhortations, however, only enhanced the sacral aura beginning to surround Church leadership. So too did the imposition of episcopal celibacy. It comes, then, as no surprise that the first forms of clerical dress made their appearance in the fourth century.

The fourth century witnessed, therefore, a profound transformation of Christian perceptions of the meaning of priesthood. That transformation advanced the systematic clericalization of ordained leadership. Other forces in other times and places would, of course, contribute to the advancement of clerical privilege; but sacerdotalist thinking provided clericalism with its first systematic rationale. By the clericalization of ordained ministry I mean transformation from a service to a power elite.

The Emergence of Hierarchicalism

In the sixth century, an obscure Syrian theologian laid the speculative foundations for a second important shift in the theological understanding of ordained ministry. The theologian in question wrote under the pseudonym of Dionysius the Aeropagite, an Athenian whom Paul the Apostle had converted to Christianity (Acts 17:34). Scholars call him Pseudo-Dionysius.

Pseudo-Dionysius's vision of ordained leadership blended biblical angelology with Platonic metaphysics. He organized the different choirs of angels mentioned in the Bible into three hierarchies, each subdivided into three tiers. By a "hierarchy" Pseudo-Dionysius meant "a holy ordinance," an eternal, divinely established principle of order that gives unchanging, intelligible structure to the universe (Pseudo-Dionysius, *The Celestial Hierarchy*, III, 1). The first angelic hierarchy included the choirs of Seraphim, Cherubim, and Thrones; the second, Dominations, Powers, and Authorities; the third, Principalities, Archangels, and Angels. Following his fantasy, Pseudo-Dionysius imagined that the angelic capacity for grace and enlightenment diminished as one descended the hierarchical ladder. Seraphs enjoyed more capacity than cherubs, cherubs more than thrones, and so forth (*Ibid.*, V, 1-IX, 2). This may all sound far removed from a theology of ordained leadership. Nevertheless, Pseudo-Dionysius invoked the Platonic belief that changing, material things participate in eternal, spiritual realities in order to argue that the structures of Church governance must reproduce the eternal, unchanging structures of the angelic hierarchies (*Ibid.*, I, 3).

The Ecclesiastical Hierarchies

Pseudo-Dionysius divided the Church into two hierarchies: the clerical and the lay. The bishop stands on the supreme rung of the clerical hierarchy. As supreme hierarch, he confronts the Church as "a deified and divine person, instructed in all holy knowledge, in whom the entire hierarchy that depends on him finds the pure means of perfecting and expressing itself" (Pseudo-Dionysius, *The Ecclesiastical Hierarchy*, I, 3). Priests rank below the bishop, deacons rank below the priests. The lay hierarchy contains religious, laity, and catechumens.

As in the case of the angelic hierarchies all grace and enlightenment in the Church flows from the top of the hierarchical ladder to the bottom: grace and light descend from the bishop to priests, from priests to deacons, from the clerical hierarchy to the lay, from religious to ordinary laity, from the ordinary laity to catechumens (*Ibid.*, V). Since the catechumenate had by this time disappeared, for all practical purposes the laity stood on the bottom rung of the Church's two hierarchies.

Pseudo-Dionysius's hierarchical vision of the Church did more than assert subsidiarity within Church leadership structures. It also interpreted subsidiarity in such a way as to reduce the laity to a position of total passivity within the Church.

Medieval Hierarchicalism

As we shall see, in the twentieth century the Second Vatican Council would set aside the quaint hierarchical vision of Pseudo-Dionysius as theologically unacceptable, but the claim of this sixth-century Syrian to speak as one of the original converts of the great Apostle of the Gentiles endowed his writings with considerable authority during the Middle Ages. (Thomas Aquinas, for example, cited only one authority more frequently than Pseudo-Dionysius: the great Aristotle himself.) Because scholastic theologians mistook him for a disciple of Paul, they simply assumed that Pseudo-Dionysius described first-century Church order. They found his vision of the Church congenial for another reason: it described fairly accurately the way medieval Church order worked.

Medieval Debates over Episcopal Ordination

During the Middle Ages, a hierarchical, sacerdotalist understanding of ordained ministry also transformed theological perceptions of the character conferred by ordination. Late medieval Eucharistic piety perceived priests as the principal agents of the Christian Eucharistic sacrifice. Moreover, medieval debates over the real presence in the Eucharist had focused theological attention on the transformation of the bread and wine that Eucharistic consecration effects. As a consequence, scholastic theologians depicted ordination to the priesthood as the ritual empowerment to transform bread and wine into the Body and Blood of Christ. Priestly ordination also empowered priests to administer the sacraments of baptism and penance and to anoint the sick and the dying. Episcopal ordination conferred jurisdictional power to govern the Church and the sacramental power to ordain and to confirm. The sacramental character conferred by ordination came, then, to be conceived as a spiritual mark on the soul that conformed the ordained to Christ, the great high priest of the new covenant, empowered them to function as sacramental channels of grace to the laity, and advanced them up the hierarchical ladder (Albert the Great, *On the Sacraments,* Tr. VIII, q. iv, a. 3; Bonaventure, *Commentary on the Book of Sentences,* IV, d. xiv, p. 2, a. 1, qq. 1-3; Thomas Aquinas, *Summa Contra Gentiles,* IV, lxxiv–lxxvi, *Summa Theologiae,* III (Suppl.), xxxiv–xl).

During the fourth century bishops had functioned more like parish priests than medieval princes of the Church. By the high Middle Ages, however, they had for all practical purposes joined the aristocracy and relegated the major burden of pastoral and sacramental ministry to presbyters. As a consequence, the great scholastics looked upon ordination to presbyterial ministry as conferring priesthood. They interpreted the episcopacy, not as a sacrament, but as a rite conferring jurisdictional authority and extending sacramental authority. Because the Council of Trent in the sixteenth century left the issue of the sacramentality of episcopal ordination unresolved, the matter would not reach settlement until the twentieth century. Then the Second Vatican Council, hearkening back to fourth-century sacerdotalist theology would not only proclaim the sacramental character of episcopal ordination but would find in the episcopacy the fullness of ordained priesthood.

Reformation Debates over Priesthood

While hierarchicalism combined with sacerdotalism to shape medieval perceptions of ordained ministry in a variety of ways, the polemics of the Reformation were destined to transform once again the theology of ordained ministry.

In the sixteenth century, Luther laid the foundations for a Protestant understanding of ordained leadership. Luther argued, quite correctly, that he could find no hint in the New Testament of the presence within the apostolic Church of a quasi-Levitical priesthood. He placed the proclamation of the gospel rather than cultic leadership at the heart of official Church ministry (Luther, *Works,* 36. 113). Nevertheless, while the Lutheran interpretation of ordained ministry stressed the ministry of proclamation, it did assign cultic responsibilities to the ordained. The Augsburg Confession described the church as "the congregation of the saints in which the Gospel is rightly preached and the sacraments are rightly administered" (*Augsburg Confession,* 16).

Luther also rediscovered the New Testament doctrine of the priesthood of all believers. Moreover, he denied any qualitative difference between the priesthood of the ordained and that of the baptized. For Luther baptismal faith unites the soul to Christ; the two then become one. Since Christ reigns over the Church as king and priest, all believers share in his royal priesthood (Luther, *Works*, 36. 116).

Calvin also recognized that in addition to proclaiming the word, the ordained exercise a liturgical, sacramental function. He, however, refused both to regard the Eucharist as a sacrifice and to call ordained leaders priests. Moreover, he rightly discovered in the early Church a variety of ministries. He regarded the proclamation of the gospel as the chief responsibility of pastors. Elders and deacons administered the affairs of the Church (Calvin, *Institutes*, IV, xix, 22–33). Zwingli recognized no priesthood except Christ's (Zwingli, *Commentary on True and False Religion*, 21).

Priesthood in the Council of Trent

In responding to Protestant interpretations of ordained ministry, the Council of Trent opted to defend and reform the medieval synthesis. It insisted on the hierarchical structure of official Church leadership and on a qualitative difference between the priesthood of the ordained and that of the baptized. In contrast to the Protestants Trent emphasized the cultic responsibilities of the ordained over their responsibility to proclaim the Word. The council insisted that ordination confers power to consecrate and offer the Eucharist and to forgive sins and denied that ordination merely commissions one to preach the gospel. Finally, the council affirmed that ordination did indeed confer a character; but it failed to explain its nature (DS, 1767–1769, 1771, 1774).

With the Council of Trent, sacerdotalist thinking reached its historical high-water mark. Fourth-century sacerdotalism had portrayed bishops primarily as the quasi-Levitical high priests of the new covenant. Trent expanded sacerdotalist theology to include the presbyterate as well, even though by the late Middle Ages many theologians questioned the sacramental character of episcopal consecration because they had come to regard the episcopacy primarily as an administrative ecclesiastical office. Not until Vatican II, however, would the sacramental character of the episcopacy receive conciliar endorsement. Moreover, the embittered polemics of the Reformation and the hatred inspired by the Wars of Religion left Catholic and

Protestant theology entrenched in lopsided perceptions of ordained ministry until ecumenical dialogue led both to soften their positions. Protestants emphasized proclamation, Catholics emphasized cult.

Vatican II on Priesthood

Ecumenical dialogue influenced significantly the theology of priesthood promulgated at Vatican II. Although the Second Vatican Council defended the priesthood of the ordained, it took a more irenic tone in its assessment of Protestant perceptions of ordained ministry than had the Council of Trent. Instead of insisting defensively on the cultic responsibilities of the ordained, it situated sacramental ministry within the context of a ministry of proclamation. The council also recognized the priesthood of the faithful. It held that through baptism all the faithful both ordained and unordained participate in Jesus' threefold ministry of priest, prophet, and king, although with different pastoral responsibilities (*Lumen gentium,* 10).

Vatican II took exception, however, to two aspects of Luther's account of the priesthood of the faithful. The council insisted that the priesthood of the ordained differs qualitatively from that of the baptized. In contrast to Calvin, the council also taught that the ordained exercise a genuinely sacerdotal ministry.

Moreover, although Vatican II continued to use the term "hierarchical" to designate ordained leadership, it set aside the hierarchicalism of Pseudo-Dionysius as theologically inadequate. Instead of portraying the hierarchy as standing over the Church, Vatican II situated the ministry of the ordained within the Church. Instead of describing the ordained as the exclusive channel of divine grace between God and the laity, the council insisted on the lay apostolate's immediate charismatic inspiration. The divine Mother gives gifts to whomsoever she wills. The hierarchy have the responsibility of evoking and coordinating those gifts through sacramental ministry and the proclamation of the Word, but they have no right to suppress the Holy Breath's authentic inspirations (*Lumen gentium,* 10; *Apostolicam actuositatem,* 3, 30).

The Shifting Theology of Priesthood

We can, then, discover five major shifts in the theological understanding of priestly ministry. The first occurred within the Bible itself as a New Testament theology of priesthood supplanted the Levitical priesthood. The shift from the New Testament to fourth-century sacerdotalism marked a second major shift in the theological perception of priestly ministry. The third shift, which fused a sacerdotalist with a hierarchicalist understanding of priesthood, began in the sixth century and found general theological acceptance during the high Middle Ages, even though, as we have seen, by the late Middle Ages theologians often challenged the sacramental character of episcopal consecration. A fourth shift occurred as medieval consensus about the meaning of priesthood gave way to the entrenched polemics of the Reformation. A fifth and final shift occurred in Catholic theology when ecumenical dialogue forced Vatican II to revise both medieval and Tridentine perceptions of the priesthood.

During the Reformation, a Catholic and a Protestant theology of ordination divided over yet another important point: its sacramentality. To this argument we turn next.

c. The Sacramentality of Orders. From the fourth century on, the rite of ordination began to appear in the lists of the Church's sacraments, although some of the early scholastic theologians failed to name it as a sacrament. After the twelfth century, however, theologians agreed on the sacramentality of priestly ordination; and in the fifteenth century the Council of Florence officially canonized orders along with the other six rituals whose sacramentality had gained general theological acceptance (DS 1326).

Zwingli, Luther, and Calvin all denied the sacramentality of orders (Zwingli, *Commentary on True and False Religion,* 15; Luther, *Works,* 36.106-116; Calvin, *Institutes,* IV, xix, 28). The Council of Trent, however, reaffirmed the position taken at Florence and denied that ordination merely designated one to preach the gospel (DS 1173).

In the post-Tridentine Church, theologians continued to debate whether or not one should regard episcopal consecration as a sacrament. Vatican II decided the issue when it decreed that episcopal consecration confers the fullness of the sacrament of orders (*Christus Dominus,* 15). As we shall see, however, tensions between a biblical and sacerdotalist understanding of priesthood suggest revising the theological terms that the council invoked in affirming the sacramentality of episcopal consecration.

Moreover, since the Reformation, ecumenical dialogue has produced broad areas of consensus concerning the scope of ordained ministry. The Churches now agree on its charismatic foundation and that the rite of ordination confirms that gift. In addition, we find some consensus concerning the responsibilities of ordained leadership and the significance of ordination (*Baptism, Eucharist, and Ministry: Faith and Order Paper No. 111,* Geneva: World Council of Churches, 1982). We have yet, however, to reach full ecumenical agreement either about the purpose of ordination or about the sacramentality of the rite of ordination.

d. The Debate Over Clerical Celibacy. The first attempt to legislate celibacy for the Christian clergy occurred in A.D. 309 at the local Council of Elvira. A convocation of the clergy of Spain to deal with internal Church discipline, Elvira conducted its business in the manner of a Roman court of law. At Elvira the clergy arraigned, judged, and assigned appropriate penances to Christians found guilty of moral turpitude. The clerical judges reserved the severest penalties for other offending clerics.

Elvira dealt with sins of gambling, fornication, adultery, divorce, prostitution, homosexuality, idolatry, and disobedience to or betrayal of Church leaders. One half of the cases considered dealt with sexual immorality. The acts of Elvira testify to the pastoral concern of the Spanish clergy to oppose sexual promiscuity and perversion, to preserve marital fidelity, and to discourage marriages between Christians and pagans.

The Emergence of Clerical Celibacy

As a way of validating its own right to demand greater sexual restraint from lay Christians, the clergy of Spain adopted an elitist solution. They decided to impose even greater restrictions on their own sexual conduct than those they legislated for the laity. Elvira required all Spanish clerics to abstain in the future from having sexual relations with their wives. It banned unmarried clergy from contracting matrimony. It ordered defrocked any cleric convicted of fathering a child.[2]

Moreover, sacerdotalist elitism also encouraged clerical celibacy. If Levitical priests had had to refrain from sexual activity before leading Jewish worship, the high priests of a new and better covenant should, the elitists argued, renounce sexuality altogether. The fourth century saw the emergence of a celibate episcopate as well as the attempt to extend celibacy to the presbyterate as well.

Not all the clergy, however, looked with favor on the latter proposal. At the Council of Nicea the abbot Paphnucius, himself a celibate and awesome ascetic, successfully led the opposition to the

2. For a lucid study of the council of Elvira, see Samuel Laeuchli, *Power and Sexuality* (Philadelphia: Temple, 1972).

imposing celibacy on all the clergy; and to this day priests of the Oriental Church can marry. In the West the attempt to impose celibacy on priests did not succeed effectively until the twelfth century. In 1123 the First Lateran Council forbade marriage to the ordained and required married clerics to abandon cohabitation with their wives. Fifteen years later the Second Lateran Council declared clerical nuptials invalid (DS 711).

Nevertheless, economics more than spiritual elitism seems finally to have motivated the legal imposition of clerical celibacy in the West. The bishops took the action they did at Lateran I and II largely in order to ensure that the Church not lose priestly benefices through inheritance.[3]

The Protestant Rejection of Clerical Celibacy

In the sixteenth century the Protestant reformers rejected clerical celibacy; but the Roman Catholic tradition continued to require it of all its clergy until Vatican II, when it admitted married men to the newly restored, permanent diaconate. The council, however, still held priests and bishops to celibate lives.

We shall have occasion to reflect on some of the pros and cons of clerical celibacy below. Here it suffices to note the fact of the contemporary debate and to put it into an historical context. One final debate deserves our attention before we attempt to understand the significance of ordained ministry: the dispute over women's ordination.

e. The Debate Over Women's Ordination. The struggle for women's rights in this country emerged from the abolitionist movement. Nineteenth-century women who fought for the liberation of blacks realized that they were demanding rights for Southern slaves that they themselves did not enjoy. They began to agitate for women's rights. Eventually American women won for themselves the right to vote, but they remained the victims of other forms of sexist oppression.

The fight for women's rights in the Church has focused on the ordination of women as an issue that symbolizes the clerical exclusion of women from the centers of ecclesiastical power and influence. To date the Roman curia has responded to the demand for women's ordination with conflicting signals. The Papal Biblical Commission

---

3. Cf. Charles A. Frazee, "The Origins of Clerical Celibacy in the Western Church," *Church History* 41 (1972) 149–67.

published a study that concluded that nothing in the New Testament forbids the ordination of women. The Sacred Congregation for the Doctrine of the Faith has, however, issued a contradictory statement condemning the ordination of women; but the theological community as a whole has not received with favor its arguments from Scripture, tradition, and reason. John Paul II has made his opposition to women's ordination clear more than once. Nevertheless, official opposition to the ordination of women has not silenced its proponents. Clearly, any contemporary theology of ordained ministry must attempt to address this vexed issue. We shall therefore return to it in the next chapter.

We have reflected on biblical foundations for a theology of Christian priesthood. We have traced the development of ritual ordination and examined some of the principal theological controversies that have surrounded the evolution of ordained ministry. The time has come to seek a normative insight into the responsibilities of official Church leadership, an insight that will allow us to address and hopefully to resolve some of the debates that surround this sacrament. One reaches a normative insight into ordained ministry by interpreting it in the light of an adequate theology of conversion. To this complex problem we turn in the chapter that follows.

CHAPTER IV

Ordained to Serve

In the preceding chapter we reflected on the development of ordained ministry in the Church. We examined the way in which the rite of ordination evolved. We also took a look at some of the controversies that have surrounded this particular ritual.

In the present chapter we shall attempt to understand the kind of commitment that ordination embodies. We shall explore the responsibilities of ordained ministry, and we shall attempt to respond to the questions that its history raises.

Our reflections divide into five sections. The first examines the generic responsibilities common to all those who exercise ordained ministry in the Church. The second reflects on the ordination and specific responsibilities of deacons; the third, on the ordination and specific responsibilities of priests; and the fourth, on the ordination and specific responsibilities of bishops. The fifth and final section responds to unanswered questions that the history of ordained ministry poses.

1. The Responsibilities of Ordained Christian Leaders. All authority in the Church roots itself partly in a divinely sanctioned commission, partly in the divine Mother's charismatic enlightenment. Jesus' own authority derived from the mission he received from his Father and from the divine Mother's charismatic inspiration (Mark 1:9-11; Matt 3:13-17; Luke 3:21-22). She endowed his preaching with compelling authority and inspired his miracles, the works of power that confirmed the divine authority of his words (Mark 1:22; Matt 7:29; Luke 4:32; John 5:26).[1]

---

1. For a lucid explanation of the relationship between Jesus' authority and the action of the Holy Breath within him, see C. K. Barrett, *The Holy Spirit and the Gospel Tradition* (London: S.P.C.K., 1947). See also James Dunn, *Jesus and the Spirit* (Philadelphia: Westminster, 1975).

In a like manner, apostolic authority derived from a commission of the risen Christ to bear witness to the resurrection and from the divine Mother's charismatic guidance of Church leaders (Matt 28:16-20; Luke 24:46-49; John 20:20-23; Acts 1:7-8; 2:1-21). The apostles in their turn commissioned Church leaders to hand on the apostolic tradition intact (Acts 20:17-38; 1 Tim 6:3-16; 2 Tim 2:14–3:17), but the authority of the successors to the apostles derived also from their charismatic giftedness (2 Tim 1:6).

The Evolving Character of Ordained Leadership

History testifies that from the beginning leadership structures in the Church evolved in response to pastoral needs. Ultimately, however, those structures root themselves in Jesus' call of the Twelve. He associated them with him in his own ministry and designated them judges in the New Israel. As a consequence, authentic Church leadership like the ministry of the Church as a whole must always prolong Jesus' own ministry and extend historically his proclamation of the kingdom.

The fact that all authentic ordained ministry extends Jesus' own ministry in space and time provides an important norm for measuring the authenticity of the different leadership structures that have developed in the Church over the centuries; for unless those structures embody the mind of Jesus, unless they extend the reign of God he proclaimed, unless they incarnate the paschal mystery and draw others into that mystery, they spring from some other source than Jesus Christ and from the Holy Breath he sends.

Ordination and Conversion

As we have seen, Christian conversion contributes two dynamics to the conversion process as a whole: initial conversion mediates between affective and moral conversion, while ongoing conversion transvalues the other forms of conversion. Together these two dynamics mediate lifelong commitment to the ethics of discipleship that Jesus lived and proclaimed. As we have seen, fidelity to that moral commitment transforms natural into supernatural hope, intuitive and inferential perceptions of reality into faith, and sound judgments of conscience into personal charity and the Christian search for social justice.

That same moral commitment demands that Church leaders take Jesus and Jesus alone as the norm and model of the meaning of Christian leadership and of Christian priesthood. Hence, any interpretation of ordained leadership, any theology of priesthood that in its meaning or consequences compromises the moral commitment that authentic Christian leadership demands fails to pass theological muster and must be consigned to the dust heap of invalid theological hypotheses.

In this section of the present chapter, we are reflecting on the ways in which converted commitment to Christ imposes generic moral responsibilities on anyone ordained to Church leadership: whether deacons, priests, or bishops. In considering the processes of ongoing conversion, we saw that initial conversion to Christ ought to mature into some charismatically inspired ministry to others. Hence, after considering the generic moral demands that conversion to Christ makes of all of the ordained, we shall show how the specific charism that grounds each kind of ordained ministry imposes specific moral responsibilities on those who respond to it.

Generic Responsibilities of the Ordained

In examining the generic responsibilities of all the ordained, we shall reflect on the following propositions: (a) Ordained ministry requires ongoing conversion of all Church leaders. (b) Ordained Church leaders have the responsibility of extending in space and time Jesus' own ministry of proclamation. (c) The ordained leaders of the Church participate in some way in the authority to bind and loose that Jesus conferred on the Twelve. (d) Ordained Church leaders have the responsibility of serving the Christian community in collegial solidarity. (e) Ordained Church leaders have the obligation to conduct their ministry in responsiveness to the Divine Mother's charismatic inspirations operative not only in their own lives but also in the Church as a whole.

a. Ordained Ministry Requires Ongoing Conversion of All Church Leaders. The Twelve discovered the true scope of leadership in the new Israel by being drawn into the paschal mystery. As we have seen, the Gospels all testify to the fact that they clung tenaciously to the illusions of secular messianism and that their tenacity set them at odds with Jesus. He insisted that leadership in the new Israel demands that one become the least of all, the servant of all. In their ministry the Twelve must take Jesus himself, not the princes of this world, as their role model (Mark 10:35-45; Matt 20:20-28; Luke 22:24-27).

The Dark Night of the Apostolate

Jesus' passion and death revealed to the Twelve the full cost of discipleship. It also taught them the full meaning of leadership in the service of atonement. As leaders of the new Israel, they must be willing to risk all and, if necessary, to lay down their lives for God's little ones.

The transformation of the Twelve into apostles demanded of them a profound religious conversion. That conversion began when they first responded to Jesus' call to discipleship, but it culminated in a transforming encounter with the risen Christ and in their charismatic commissioning on Pentecost. The Apostle Paul underwent a similar conversion. His encounter with the risen Lord transformed him from a zealous persecutor of Christians into a committed believer and eventually into the Apostle of the Gentiles.

As we have seen, Christian conversion claims one totally. Jesus' vision of the kingdom must inform a convert's hopes, beliefs, conscience, and search for social justice. The ordained leaders of the Church cannot summon others responsibly to an integral, fivefold conversion without having experienced such a conversion themselves. Moreover, competence to lead the Christian community presupposes much more than the initial conversion that the rites of initiation seal. It demands as well significant advancement in the capacity to act responsibly and in holiness.

The Five-Fold Conversion of the Ordained

Affective conversion, as we have seen, heals the heart's violence and sensitizes it to beauty. It frees one to respond to others with affection, sympathy, friendship, compassion. It frees one from personal sexism, racism, anti-Semitism, and other forms of bigotry. It promotes emotional balance and integration. It enables the emotions to judge persons and situations accurately and thus instills the natural prudence that grace can transform into discernment. It suffuses human life with realistic vision and emotional zest. It teaches the heart and the imagination playfulness and humor. Anyone who aspires to Church leadership needs to have advanced far down the therapeutic path to which affective conversion leads.

Intellectual conversion frees the mind from the shackles of fundamentalism. It enables one to approach problems with a variety of methods and from a variety of perspectives. The Church leader who lacks intellectual conversion runs the risk of promoting the kind of religious fascism and fundamentalism that flourishes among some right-wing Catholics. The Church leader advanced in the skills that intellectual conversion fosters can deal flexibly and wisely with the different traditions and doctrinal viewpoints that enrich the life of the Christian community.

The Church legitimately requires high moral standards of its leaders. Moral conversion alone ensures only the minimal ethical integrity that responsible Church leadership demands; for gospel living, as we have seen, requires more than natural morality. Nevertheless, moral conversion schools the conscience in prudence, justice, courage, temperance, and all the other human virtues. It ensures that the ordained cultivate the kind of personal selflessness that responsible leadership requires.

Sociopolitical conversion consecrates one to the pursuit of social justice. Responsible Church leadership recognizes the ways in which institutionalized sin conditions human conduct, including that of the ordained. Church leaders need to be able to identify institutionalized neurosis, see through obfuscating political and economic ideologies, demand moral accountability of politicians, businesspeople, and other social leaders. In a word, they need to summon the principalities and powers of this world to repentant moral responsibility. They also need to redress and reform sinful and oppressive Church structures.

In addition, Church leaders need to show signs of a Christian conversion that transforms and transvalues the other four forms of conversion. The vision of the kingdom and the promise of salvation revealed in the paschal mystery must have taught the hearts of the ordained a passionate hope in God that they can share enthusiastically with others. A living and articulate faith must inform their proclamation of the gospel. Wholehearted submission to the moral constraints of discipleship must have taught their consciences the meaning of Christian love. They must have learned to judge personal and institutional sin with the mind of Christ and must measure institutional injustice by the divine justice that Jesus incarnated and proclaimed.

b. Ordained Church Leaders Have the Responsibility of Extending in Space and Time Jesus' Own Ministry of Proclamation. Jesus summoned his contemporaries to repentance and to obedient submission to the reign of God. He associated the Twelve with him in that ministry of proclamation. Moreover, the risen Christ sent the apostles forth to bear witness to his resurrection under the the divine Mother's empowering illumination. The ordained, therefore, prolong the ministry of Jesus and of the apostles by summoning others to repent, to submit to the moral demands of life in the kingdom, to believe in the risen Christ as savior and Lord, to accept baptism in water and the Holy Breath, and to live in lifelong openness to the Divine Mother's charismatic inspirations.

Inevitably, then, the rites of Christian initiation together with the fivefold conversion they seal help define the scope of ordained ministry in the Church. Church leaders have the responsibility to proclaim the gospel to all creatures by summoning all people to the kind of initial conversion that culminates in ritual incorporation into the Church. In addition, Church leaders have the responsibility of fostering the ongoing conversion of Christians by proclaiming the good news in season and out.

Like Jesus and the first apostles, those who aspire to ordination should, then, give evidence of an ability to proclaim the gospel in power. Minimally, their preaching should effect initial and ongoing conversion in their auditors; but ideally one would hope that ordained Church leaders would also enjoy a charismatic capacity to summon others to affective and physical healing in faith. Such signs of healing authenticate the word they proclaim.

c. The Ordained Leaders of the Church Participate in Some Way in the Authority to Bind and Loose That Jesus Conferred on the Twelve. Conversion effects personal liberation. Christian conversion introduces one into the liberating realm of grace we call the Church. Church leaders loose those caught in the bonds of sin and death by summoning them to an integral Christian conversion and by introducing them into the Christian community, where they can share in the liberty of God's children. Church leaders bind people when they exclude them from Eucharistic communion.

Binding and Loosing in the Church

In binding and loosing, Church leaders exercise sacramental authority. Deacons exercise that authority when they baptize. Priests and bishops do so when they baptize and when they readmit serious sinners to Eucharistic Communion. Moreover, canon law reserves the most serious sins of backsliding Christians to episcopal absolution.

Acts of binding and loosing seek the common good of the Christian community. Serious sinners by their bad example undermine the commitment of the rest of the community and need to be summoned to repentance and renewed gospel living. If they fail to respond to that summons, they must be excluded from Eucharistic Communion until they do.

The Ambiguities of Excommunication

Liberal Christians often find the notion of excommunication repugnant. Church leaders should certainly invoke it only as a last resort. Nevertheless, sometimes it offers the only means of preventing serious scandal. I think, for example, of the racists whom the archbishop of New Orleans excommunicated in the early fifties. Many of them received Communion daily while practicing the most overt acts of racial oppression and bigotry. They resisted every call from Church leaders to repent and mend their ways. Had the archbishop not excommunicated them, he would have equivalently told a local Church culturally conditioned to acquiesce in racism that one could in conscience participate in the Eucharist while ruthlessly oppressing black people.

One may legitimately question, however, whether all the institutions of the Church foster the kind of freedom in the Lord that Christian baptism promises. As we saw in the preceding chapter, one can argue plausibly that current marital legislation in the Church imposes too harsh a penalty on many who have already suffered the pain of a failed marriage. Even the revised code of canon law refuses to deal adequately with the personal and ecclesial rights of the baptized. One can question whether the Church's judicial procedures adequately ensure due process and protect Christians adequately from the threat of fundamentalism in high places.

Closing one's eyes to the presence of injustice in the Church does not make it go away. As a consequence, all of the ordained have the responsibility to see to it that Church institutions foster the responsible liberty they should. When human limitation and sinfulness spawn unjust Church laws or oppressive forms of Church discipline, all the ordained share the responsibility for abolishing these sinful structures. Ultimately, of course, bishops bear the principle responsibility for ongoing Church reform. When institutional inertia postpones necessary structural reforms within the Church, the ordained have a pastoral responsibility to minimize the destructive impact of unjust Church structures on the lives of the baptized.

At the same time, the gospel makes very specific moral demands; and the ordained can never lie about the demands of gospel living or about the difference between genuine sin and Christian virtue. Nor can they lie about the kind of moral commitment demanded by Eucharsitic worship. The Christian community must move decisively to correct abuses in Church discipline and purge it of needless harshness and injustice. Nevertheless, were the ordained to abrogate any right to bar serious sinners from the Eucharistic table, the Christian community would forfeit its right and responsibility to distinguish credibly between Christian and un-Christian conduct among the baptized. The Church, then, will always need processes of excommunication that respect due process as well as the ritual means to reconcile excluded but repentant sinners to Eucharistic Communion.

d. Ordained Church Leaders Have the Responsibility of Serving the Christian Community in Collegial Solidarity. Jesus called twelve men to judge the new Israel he was in process of founding. Among the Twelve, he gave Peter special responsibilities of leadership. Nevertheless, the Acts of the Apostles portray the Twelve as exercising their judicial function in mutual solidarity (Acts 11:1-18, 21b-23; 15:1-35). Paul the Apostle insisted that the Father and Jesus had commissioned him to proclaim the gospel; but he, too, showed concern to exercise that ministry in solidarity with the other apostles (Gal 1:1–2:2).

The Common Good of the Church

The bishops have succeeded functionally to the apostles as a college concerned for the common good of the Church. The common good of the Church includes its fidelity to the mission it has received from the risen Christ to proclaim his resurrection to every creature in the divine Mother's empowering enlightenment. In other words, the college of bishops secures the common good of the Church (1) when they defend the basic human rights of Christians, (2) when they see to it that every Christian can participate in the benefits of Church membership in a ready and adequate manner, and (3) when they advance the work of evangelization. Needless to say, the bishops alone cannot convert the world. Rather they need to facilitate the collaboration of all believers in ensuring the church's common good.

The benefits of Church membership include ready access to instruction and to shared sacramental worship. As a college, therefore, the bishops have a grave responsibility not only to exercise a personal ministry of teaching and sanctification but also to ensure that the Church always has access to an adequate number of sound teachers and of competent sacramental ministers.

The benefits of Church membership also include the right and responsibility to respond to any of the divine Mother's charismatic inspirations. The ordained, especially the bishops, have, therefore, the responsibility of seeing to it that Church discipline does not arbitrarily exlude from any form of Church ministry any individual whom the Breath of God might call to community service.

Finally, the common good of the Church demands the Christianization of human society. As a college, therefore, bishops need to foster constantly the apostolate of the laity and of the clergy who assist the laity in establishing God's just reign on earth as in heaven.

The common good of the Church requires bishops to undertake the task of Church leadership, not as isolated individuals, but as a college; for no single bishop acting as an individual enjoys the wherewithal to secure the Church's common good. The evangelization of all peoples, the instruction and sanctification of all Christians, and the Christianization of secular society pose challenges so massive that, unless bishops respond to them in collegial solidarity and with the active support of the rest of the Christian community, they will surely fail in their fundamental mission to the Church and to the world.

Priests and deacons also seek to foster the common good of the Church under the authority of the bishops and in collegial solidarity with them. Priests and deacons contribute their personal charisms to the corporate ministry of the ordained. They represent their bishop to the local communities they serve and those communities to the bishop; they mediate between the local Church and the needs and concerns of the Church universal.

e. Ordained Church Leaders Have the Obligation to Conduct Their Ministry in Responsiveness to the Divine Mother's Charismatic Inspirations Operative Not Only in Their Own Lives But Also in the Church as a Whole. Every authentic proclamation of the gospel seeks to open people to the divine Mother's gracious inspirations. As we have seen in reflecting on the rites of initiation, she sanctifies believers by teaching them to put on the mind of Christ in their interpersonal dealings and in their search for God's own justice in human society. She also inspires them by her gifts of mutual service.

Preaching the Word with Power

In other words, all authentic preaching, including that of the ordained, exhorts Christians to claim the graces that Christian initiation promises. By proclaiming the gospel, the ordained leaders of the Church seek, then, to evoke and coordinate the charisms. Success crowns their preaching when it motivates Christians to serve God's Word and the needs of other people and to advance the common good of the Church.

The authentic exercise of any charism requires that its owner respect the divine Mother's action in the lives of other members of the Christian community. The authentic exercise of the charism of Church leadership labors under the same constraint. On Pentecost the divine Mother came, not to isolated individuals but to the Christian community as a whole. Moreover, as we have seen, the shared faith of the Church results from the active sharing of all the charisms in community. The ordained need, therefore, to hear the prophetic voices raised in the Church and to rely on those with a tested charismatic ministry of teaching for a sound interpretation of the gospel. The ordained must seek the wisdom of individuals with approved gifts of discernment in reaching pastoral decisions. They must lean on those with gifts of healing in dealing with human woundedness. They must profit from the insights of those gifted with prayer.

The Need for Discernment

I am not suggesting that Church leaders rubber-stamp every impulse in the Church that claims charismatic inspiration. Quite the contrary, in addition to gifts of teaching Church leaders also need to exercise personal gifts of discernment in dealing pastorally with any human impulse that claims charismatic inspiration. They also need to show a personal capacity for making sound pastoral decisions.

A sound insight into the dynamics of conversion will, moreover, supply them with sound criteria for judging whether or not this or that impulse can legitimately claim divine inspiration. Such an insight will help them distinguish authentic Christian hope from neurosis and self-deception. It will give them norms for distinguishing authentic faith from the rationalization of unbelief. It will reveal to them the moral demands of Christian love. It will help them distinguish the authentic Christian search for a just social order from privatized piety. Nevertheless, I am suggesting that Church leaders, including the pope, have in the exercise of their office a serious pastoral responsibility not to rely exclusively on their own personal gifts but to profit instead from the tested charisms present in the communities they lead and in the Church as a whole.

Deacons, Priests, Bishops

We have considered the responsibilities common to the three principal forms of ordained ministry: the diaconate, the presbyterate, and the episcopacy. These responsibilities flow from commitment to living in the image of Jesus by putting on his mind. Other specific responsibilities accrue to ordained ministry in virtue of the specific charism that that ministry embodies. To these specific responsibilities we turn in the sections that follow. We will examine the ritual ordination and responsibilities proper to all three Church offices. We will consider first the ordination and responsibilities of deacons, then the ordination and responsibilities of priests, and finally the ordination and responsibilities of bishops.

As we have seen, ordinarily Christian conversion matures into a sense of charismatic call, into a vocation to minister to others in the name and image of Jesus. Of necessity, however, the Church's institutional structures will condition the responsibilities of the ordained, for their vocation inserts them into the official, public leadership of the Church.

As we have also seen, not only have the rites of ordination evolved; but the Church's understanding of the episcopacy, presbyterate, and diaconate has also developed over the centuries. In the sections that follow we will, then, ponder these Church ministries in their present state of evolution. As we shall see, the documents of the Second Vatican Council supply us with a normative insight into the specific responsibilities of contemporary ordained Church leaders.

2. The Ordination and Responsibilities of Deacons. Ordination to the diaconate should ordinarily occur on a Sunday or feast day when a large number of the faithful attend the Eucharist. The candidate processes into the church preceded by a deacon who carries the Book of the Gospels and followed by the ordaining bishop (Roman Catholic Ordination of a Deacon, 1–5; hereafter this ritual will be abbreviated as RCOD).

The Rite of Diaconal Ordination

The rite of ordination follows the gospel. The candidate is summoned by a deacon and presented to the ordaining bishop by a priest. After the bishop inquires publicly into the candidate's worthiness and chooses him for membership in the diaconate, the congregation signifies its consent by an appropriate gesture, ordinarily by applause (RCOD, 9–13).

The ordaining bishop then instructs the candidate and the congregation in the responsibilities of deacons. The revised ritual insists on the charismatic inspiration of diaconal service to the community and speaks of the threefold ministry of deacons: a ministry of the Word, a liturgical ministry, and a ministry of charity. As ministers of the Word deacons are ordained to proclaim the gospel to both believers and unbelievers. As liturgical ministers they preside over public prayer, baptize, witness marriages, administer Holy Communion, bring viaticum to the dying, and lead paraliturgical worship and the rites of burial. Deacons also assist bishops and priests in the celebration of the Eucharist. Finally, as ministers of charity deacons serve the needy in the community, especially the poor (RCOD, 14).

The bishop examines the candidate and elicits from him a public promise to discharge the office of deacon faithfully in obedience to the bishop or to his religious superiors (RCOD, 15–17).

The deacon then prostrates himself while the congregation prays the litany of the saints over him. The bishop closes the litany with a prayer for the candidate. He then imposes hands and prays the prayer of consecration.

The prayer recalls the consecration of the sons of Levi to the service of the tabernacle and the election of the Seven narrated in Acts to serve as deacons in the Jerusalem community. As we have already seen, we have reason to question whether the office of deacon derives from the ministry of the Seven; and, as we shall soon see, we have even more reason to question whether ordained ministry in the Christian Church should model itself on the Levitical priesthood. As a consequence, these allusions in the prayer of consecration need revision (RCOD, 18–21).

After the prayer of consecration, the deacon is invested with a stole and dalmatic as symbols of his office. The bishop then presents him with the Book of the Gospels with the charge: "Receive the gospel of Christ, whose herald you are. Believe what you read, teach what you believe, and practice what you teach." The rite of ordination ends with the kiss of peace (RCOD, 22–25). During the rest of the Eucharistic celebration, the deacon assists the bishop at the altar (RCOD, 27–28).

The Permanent Diaconate Restored

As we have seen, both the diaconate and presbyterate have evolved over the years. In restoring the permanent diaconate the bishops at Vatican II sought to alleviate the shortage of priests in segments of the Church. Moreover, while they continued to require celibacy of priests and bishops, in opening the diaconate to married males, they consciously mitigated the law of clerical celibacy imposed at the First and Second Lateran Councils (*Lumen gentium,* 29).

Permanent deacons can and do supplement the ministry of priests and serve in important ways not only where the supply of priests has dwindled but also where priestly vocations abound. Moreover, in mitigating clerical celibacy the bishops took an historic step. One may question, however, whether the establishment of the permanent, married diaconate fully solves the pastoral problems it addresses. Deacons can supplement the pastoral work of priests through preaching, through limited sacramental ministry, and through practical service to the community; but they cannot celebrate the Eucharist. Moreover, the legal imposition of clerical celibacy on the rest of the clergy continues to pose a serious obstacle to the recruitment of priests and to the union of the Christian Churches.

3. **The Ordination and Responsibilities of Priests.** The ordination of priests follows the same pattern as the ordination of deacons but with appropriate symbolic differences. The candidate processes into the church clothed in an alb and diaconal stole and followed by the ordaining bishop. As in ordination to the diaconate, after the gospel the candidate is summoned to ordination and presented to the bishop who chooses him for the office of priesthood. The faithful signify their approval by applause (Roman Catholic Ordination of a Priest, 1-13; hereafter this ritual will be abbreviated at RCOP).

The Rite of Priestly Ordination

The bishop instructs the candidate and the congregation in the responsibilities of priestly ministry (RCOP, 14). The candidate then professes publicly his determination to live up to the responsibilities of his office and promises obedience to the bishop or to his religious superiors. As in the ordination of deacons, the candidate prostrates himself while the congregation prays the litany of the saints over him. After imposing hands the bishop recites the prayer of consecration (RCOP, 15–22). The new priest is then clothed in stole and chasuble, the liturgical vestments of the priesthood. His hands are anointed. The gifts for the Eucharistic celebration—the paten, chalice, and Eucharistic bread and wine—are then presented to the bishop who entrusts them to the newly ordained priest. The rite of ordination closes with the kiss of peace (RCOP, 23–27). The new priest then concelebrates the rest of the Eucharist with the bishop (RCOP, 29).

The Pastoral Responsibilities of Priests

Vatican II in contrast to the Council of Trent ranks the proclamation of the gospel first among the responsibilities of priests (*Presbyterorum Ordinis,* 4). Priests have the responsibility of proclaiming the gospel to Christian and non-Christian alike. That proclamation should contextualize their liturgical ministry of baptism, reconciliation, healing, and the Eucharist. They should, indeed, regard the Eucharist as the source and apex of their ministry of proclamation (*Presbyterorum Ordinis,* 5).

Priests wield genuine authority in the Church, but in subordination to the bishop, with whom they collaborate in serving the community. Like the bishops, priests must foster Church unity (*Lumen gentium,* 28; *Presbyterorum Ordinis,* 2). Priests represent the bishop to the communities they serve (*Presbyterorum Ordinis,* 5). They minister to others in collegial solidarity with him. By participating in priests' senates they function as Church elders and advisers to the bishop (*Presbyterorum Ordinis,* 7).

Priests also minister in collegial solidarity with one another. They serve not as isolated individuals but as members of a corporate ministry in the Church to which they contribute their personal gifts. Older priests should help and encourage younger ones. They should welcome one another in hospitality and foster common life among themselves in the places where they serve (*Presbyterorum Ordinis,* 8, 10).

Finally, priests minister in solidarity with the laity whose apostolates they are called to foster (*Presbyterorum Ordinis,* 9). They should seek as well to promote ecumenical dialogue and the ultimate reconciliation of the Christian Churches (*Presbyterorum Ordinis,* 9).

Priests should seek to advance the central mission of the Church: the conversion of all people to Christ. Chosen from the people of God, they function in their midst as servants of the community. In order to minister to the human condition in Jesus' name and image, they need like him to know it personally. Priests should strive constantly to imitate the servant Christ in whose name they serve God's people, and they should have a profound love of the Church and a sense of the mystery of grace that it embodies. Their ministry requires of them goodness and sincerity of heart, strength and constancy of character, a passion for justice, civility and gentleness in dealing with others, and an openness to all good things (*Presbyterorum Ordinis*, 3; *Optatem Totius*, 8–9, 13–14).

The Charismatic Priesthood

Vatican II insists on the charismatic foundations of all priestly ministry: one must be gifted for it by the divine Mother. Moreover, in exercising their ministry priests must respect her action in the Christian community. They should assist lay Christians in discerning their own call to minister and take the formation of community as one of their principal duties (*Presbyterorum Ordinis*, 5–6).

Priestly ministry brings with it the responsibility to strive after holiness under the divine Mother's charismatic inspiration. It also demands empathy with every genuine human value (*Presbyterorum Ordinis*, 12, 17). It demands, in other words, an ongoing fivefold conversion, daily self-examination and prayer, the devout assimilation of sacred Scripture, and pastoral discernment in relating the gospel to problems in contemporary culture (*Presbyterorum Ordinis*, 18).

4. The Ordination and Responsibilities of Bishops. The revised rite of episcopal ordination requires that at least two other bishops assist the principal consecrating bishop. If the ordination takes place in the bishop-elect's own church, the principal consecrator may ask the newly ordained bishop to preside over the celebration of the Eucharistic liturgy (Roman Catholic Ordination of a Bishop, 2-10; hereafter this ritual will be abbreviated RCOB).

The Rite of Episcopal Ordination

As in the case of ordination to the diaconate and priesthood, the ordination of bishops should ordinarily occur on Sunday or on a feast day when large numbers of the faithful can attend. The consecrating bishops together with the bishop-elect process vested into the church at the beginning of the Eucharist. The ordination follows the gospel (RCOB, 1, 6, 10, 13).

At the presentation of the bishop-elect for consecration, the principal consecrating bishop asks publicly whether the Holy See has mandated the ordination. After the mandate is read, the people indicate their approval of the appointment by some appropriate gesture, normally by applause (RCOB, 16–17).

The principal consecrating bishop then instructs the congregation and the bishop-elect in the responsibilities of episcopal service. The revised ritual portrays the bishop as servant of the community, as its faithful overseer and guardian, as a shepherd called to imitate the Good Shepherd, as priest, and as father and brother to those he serves. He must show special concern for the poor, the alien, and the marginal in society. He must encourage and support the priests and deacons who collaborate with him in leading the Christian community. He must encourage the apostolate of lay Christians and seek their counsel in ministering to the Church. He must encourage the spread of the gospel. He must show pastoral concern for the universal Church and support other Churches in special need (RCOB, 18).

After the bishop-elect professes publicly his willingness to discharge faithfully the responsibilities of his office, he prostrates himself while the community prays the litany of the saints over him. The litany closes with a prayer for the bishop-elect. The consecrating bishops then impose hands, and the Book of the Gospels is held over the new bishop's head during the prayer of consecration (RCOB, 19–26).

The principal consecrator then anoints the bishop's head with oil and presents him with the Book of the Gospels that he is to proclaim with "unfailing patience and sound teaching" (RCOB, 27–30). The new bishop is invested with a ring that symbolizes fidelity to those he pastors and with the miter and pastoral staff of office. His enthronement follows. The ceremony closes with the kiss of peace (RCOB, 31–35). After communion the *Te Deum* is sung, and the Eucharist concludes with a solemn blessing of the community by the presiding bishop (RCOB, 38–39).

Episcopal Authority

The bishops govern the Church as a college in functional succession to the apostles. Episcopal consecration incorporates one into the college of bishops (*Christus Dominus,* 1–3). As a college bishops minister to the Church as a whole and seek to ensure its common good (*Christus Dominus,* 1, 5–6).

In addition, a bishop exercises pastoral jurisdiction over a diocese. He has the responsibility of proclaiming the gospel to those he serves and of administering Church properties faithfully. He should defend the freedom and bodily integrity of those to whom he ministers, promote the unity and stability of family life, support causes that benefit society as a whole, and foster inculturated evangelization (*Christus Dominus,* 11–14).

The documents of Vatican II describe bishops as possessing the fullness of the priesthood. As pastors, bishops serve patiently both the Church and the human community. They should show openness to every good work, welcome and support the priests and deacons with whom they collaborate, foster the lay apostolate, and work for the union of the Christian Churches. They must show special concern for the marginal, poor, and oppressed. While they administer the affairs of the Church independently of civil authority, they must show willingness to collaborate with civil officials in worthy projects (*Christus Dominus,* 15–20).

In serving his diocese a bishop must rely on the assistance of collaborators. He may require the assistance of one or more auxiliary bishops. Vicars supervise different diocesan works. The episcopal curia assists in the ongoing administration of diocesan affairs. A senate of priests advises the bishop on diocesan policy. Priests, especially pastors, collaborate in the practical task of ministering to the people of God. Religious orders and congregations also advance the life of the Church at a diocesan level, and lay apostles assist not only with Church ministries but also in the Christianization of secular society (*Christus Dominus,* 25–35). In other words, the pastorally effective bishop evokes and coordinates the charismatic ministry of the community he serves. Indeed, a wise bishop would do well to establish lay senates to advise him in managing the diocese and in conducting the affairs of the Church.

Bishops also need to collaborate as a college in governing the Church as a whole. Richer dioceses should come to the aid of poorer ones. Through the activities of episcopal conferences, local synods, and ecumenical councils bishops give collective pastoral guidance to the Church (*Christus Dominus,* 36–44).

As official Church teachers, bishops have the chief responsibility for achieving consensus in doctrine, morals, and discipline, and for promulgating that consensus. The episcopacy in the United States has in recent years given an admirable example of the way that bishops ought to go about evoking consensus from the community. Their pastoral letters on nuclear disarmament and on the United States' economy emerged from free and open debate of pressing moral issues. The bishops sought and received expert opinion from both clergy and laity, from theologians, from those schooled in the secular sciences, and from other experts. They published the drafts of the pastorals and invited critical comment on them. Through the very process of composing the documents they educated the consciences not only of the Church but of the nation as a whole concerning the principles of Christian moral conduct that must govern two important areas of national policy. In a word, the bishops used modern communications effectively in order to elicit a sense of the believing Church before pronouncing as a conference on important pastoral problems.

5. Facing the Issues. In the course of examining the development of orders in the Church, we noted several controversies that that development engendered. Do the preceding reflections on the commitment demanded of ordained Church leaders cast light on those traditional theological disputes? I believe that they do. Accordingly, in this fifth and final section of the present chapter I shall attempt to respond to each of the following questions: (a) Should orders be considered a sacrament? (b) Should the ordained be looked upon as priests? (c) Have sacred orders a hierarchical structure? (d) Do orders confer a character; and, if so, in what does it consist? (e) Should clerical celibacy be imposed by law? (f) Should the Church ordain women?

a. Should Orders Be Considered a Sacrament? As we have seen, not until the high Middle Ages did theologians reach a clear consensus concerning the sacramentality of orders, even though the rite begins to appear in lists of sacraments from the fourth century on. Zwingli, Luther, and Calvin, on the other hand, denied the sacramentality of the ritual and greatly simplified its celebration, even though Luther and Calvin both agreed that official Church leadership dedicated one to the ministry of the word and to cultic leadership.

In judging the sacramentality of the rite of orders I will use the same strategy that I employed in deciding the sacramental status of Christian marriage. I will first argue from ecumenical consensus by trying to show that one cannot consent officially and publicly to official Church leadership without implicitly renewing the sacramental commitment one made in becoming a Christian while simultaneously taking on new and more extensive public responsibilities in the Church. As a consequence, the religious commitment embodied in the rite of orders incarnates the same characteristics that define the two rituals that all the Churches accept as sacramental: adult baptism and the Eucharist. Second, I will try to show that because the rite of ordination confirms a charismatic call to exercise responsibilities that go beyond mere membership in the Church, it enjoys a special sacramentality of its own.

The Argument from Ecumenical Consensus

We saw in chapter four that, viewed as sacraments, adult baptism and the Eucharist incarnate the following traits: (1) They ritualize symbolically an act of new covenant worship. (2) They must, therefore, be celebrated by someone whom the Christian community has authorized. (3) They derive in some way from the ministry of Jesus. (4) They give access in faith to the paschal mystery of Jesus' death, glorification, and sending of the Holy Breath because they challenge one prophetically to faith in Jesus' Lordship, in the Father he proclaimed, and in the Holy Breath he sends. (5) They effect the grace they signify to the extent that they express faith and deepen faith.

The rites of ordination reproduce all of the above traits but in a different ritual context from the rites of initiation. The sacraments of initiation incorporate one into the Church; the rites of ordination incorporate one into the ranks of public Church leadership. Moreover, as we have just seen, the three ordination rituals differ in that each confirms a different charism while conferring different kinds of leadership responsibilities.

The rites of ordination qualify as acts of new covenant worship because in publicly consenting to lead the Church ordinands reaffirm the commitment they made when they first sealed the new covenant sacramentally. In joining the church they committed themselves to lifelong openness to the divine Mother in putting on the mind of Christ and in responding to whatever charisms of service she might choose to give them. In the rite of ordination the Christian community confirms the ordinands' charismatic calling to official Church ministry and consecrates them to leadership in the service of atonement. The rite of ordination requires, moreover, that the ordained lead the Church in the image of a servant Messiah who proclaimed the reign of God and who laid down his life for his disciples. One cannot make such a religious commitment without simultaneously renewing one's baptismal covenant with the triune God, but one does so in the context of assuming new ecclesial responsibilities.

Someone officially qualified must do the ordaining in the name of God and of the Christian community. Moreover, the celebration of the ritual has been appropriately reserved to bishops: appropriately because bishops succeed the apostles and bear chief responsibility for securing the common good of the Church.

The rite of ordination derives remotely from Jesus' designation of the Twelve as judges of the new Israel. It derives more proximately from the commission of the risen Christ to the apostles to proclaim his resurrection in the power of the Holy Breath and in this way to establish local Churches. The apostles in turn transferred their responsibility to lead the Church to bishops and presbyters probably through the ritual of laying on of hands.

The rite of ordination draws one into the paschal mystery. It commits one to lead the Christian community in the image of the crucified Christ. It dedicates one to a ministry of proclamation in which one embodies the Word one proclaims. Ordination therefore challenges the ordained prophetically to an ever deepening faith in the triune God. It also charges them to ensure the Church's fidelity to the apostolic witness through lives of hope, faith, love, and dedication to the pursuit of God's justice. The ordained must proclaim by word and example the Lordship of Jesus, the Fatherhood of God, and the divine Mother's saving presence. Finally, the rite of ordination effects the grace it signifies to the extent that it expresses and deepens faith in the fidelity of God who raises up in each generation official leaders of his people.

A ritual that reproduces all the defining traits of a sacrament deserves to be included in the canon of the sacraments. Ordination qualifies as such a ritual.

Nevertheless, the sacramentality of orders goes beyond that of the rites of initiation, even though the commitment it embodies flows directly from them. Ordination dedicates one to speaking and acting publicly in the name of the Christian community. That dedication endows the public ministry of the ordained with a special sacramental visibility. The official acts of the ordained express publicly the shared faith of the Church as they lead its sacramental worship and as they evoke and proclaim the faith of the Christian community. Bishops have an official, personal responsibility to teach pastorally; but they bear the chief responsibility for evoking, formulating, and promulgating statements of doctrinal consensus. The rest of the ordained, especially priests, have the responsibility of assisting the bishops in that ministry. Moreover, once promulgated, such creedal professions endow the shared faith of the Church with concrete sacramental visibility.

In this respect official Church teaching differs from the charismatic ministry of teaching exercised by individual Christians. All authentic Christian teaching should express the Church's shared faith, and anyone charismatically inspired speaks in some sense in God's name. Nevertheless, charismatic teachers do not have the responsibility of speaking publicly and officially for the Church in the way that the ordained do.

In addition, the ordained confront the Church in the name of the risen Christ. Anyone who ministers under the divine Mother's charismatic guidance confronts the Church in God's name and speaks with a divine authority. The ministry of the ordained, however, prolongs in space and time the judicial ministry of binding and loosing that Jesus conferred upon the Twelve and that the apostles exercised in the name of the risen Christ. The ordained exercise that ministry in a variety of ways: in sacramental acts of binding and loosing, through their ministry of proclamation that prolongs the divine judgment begun in Jesus' own ministry, and through pastoral decisions taken for the spread of the gospel and for the common good of the Church.

The Vocational Sacraments Compared

Finally, as in the case of Christian marriage, the rite of ordination seals publicly the graced, sacramental transformation of a human life. Marriage certifies that a couple has advanced sufficiently in holiness to respond responsibly to the divine Mother's call to the ministry of marriage. Ordination certifies that an individual has advanced sufficiently in holiness to respond responsibly to the divine Mother's call to lead the Christian community publicly and officially in the service of atonement. It also confirms one's charismatic call to such a ministry and one's tested possession of the gifts that that ministry requires.

Indeed, by comparing and contrasting the two vocational sacraments of marriage and orders, one can come to a sense of the analogy that obtains among the sacraments. Both marriage and orders transform preexisting institutional structures. Jesus found the institution of marriage already existing in the world as he knew it; but he sanctified it by repudiating Mosaic divorce practices, by requiring his disciples to love one another with an atoning love like his, and by sending the divine Mother to transform Christian marriage into a charismatic ministry. Jesus created the institution of the Twelve; but then he transformed it by rising from the dead, by commissioning the Twelve along with the other apostles to bear witness to his resurrection, and by sending the divine Mother to anoint Christians to the ministry of leading the Church in the service of atonement.

Both marriage and orders seal a process of communal discernment that certifies the competence of Christians to minister publicly in the Church. Both rites attest to the ongoing conversion and charismatic calling of those to whom they are administered.

Married Christians serve the Church by transforming the family into a realm of divine grace and practical ministry. The rite of ordination commits one to serve the Church universal in some local Church by summoning it to that responsiveness to the divine Mother's inspirations that transforms it into a converting and healing realm of grace.

Both rituals, moreover, seal a sacramental event of grace. As a sacramental event marriage encompasses the experience of ongoing conversion, the charismatic calling of two persons to the ministry of marriage, and the gracious transformation of two lives blended in Christlike love. Similarly, as a sacramental event ordained ministry embraces the ordinands' personal growth in holiness, their charismatic call to Church leadership, and the ministry that flows from that call. The rite of orders endows the life of the ordained with new sacramental visibility. The ordained speak not just as individuals but in the name of the Church. They also speak with the apostolic authority of Jesus Christ.

b. Should the Ordained Be Looked Upon as Priests? As we have seen, in the apostolic Church ordained leaders were looked upon as overseers and elders rather than as quasi-Levitical priests. As we have also seen, the Letter to the Hebrews grounds the priesthood of Jesus in the fact of the incarnation and proclaims his priesthood unique. Hebrews teaches that Jesus' priesthood transcends utterly the Levitical priesthood and insists that the priesthood of Christ has terminated once and for all the need for Levitical priests.

The State of the Question

We have also seen that during the patristic era, the transfer of cultic responsibilities into the hands of the ordained caused theologians to portray first bishops and sometimes elders as the priests of the new covenant. This theological impulse culminated in fourth-century sacerdotalism, which, in contrast to the Letter to the Hebrews, depicted bishops especially as the Christian equivalent of a Levitical, priestly caste. Tridentine teaching extended sacerdotalists' patterns of thinking to the presbyterate but left the sacramental character of the episcopacy vague.

The Protestant reformers, by contrast, quite correctly found no biblical evidence for the existence of a Levitical priesthood in first-century Christianity. Calvin denied that the ordained should be regarded as priests.

Vatican II called into question not the truth but the theological adequacy of a Tridentine theology of priesthood by setting aside the substance of a hierarchicalist interpretation of ordained ministry and by juxtaposing in its theology of priesthood both biblical and sacerdotalist terminology. Vatican II, however, continued to insist on the priestly character of ordained ministry and on its qualitative difference from the priesthood of the faithful. At the same time, however, Catholic theology seems hard pressed to justify its position without using the dubious language and assumptions of fourth-century sacerdotalism.

The proclamation of the sacramentality of episcopal orders in the documents of Vatican II illustrates the tendency of which I speak. *Lumen gentium* asserts:

> This sacred synod teaches that by episcopal consecration is conferred the fullness of the sacrament of orders, that fullness which in the Church's liturgical practice and in the language of the holy Fathers of the Church is undoubtedly called the high priesthood, the apex of the sacred ministry (*Lumen gentium,* 21).

In proclaiming bishops the high priests of the Church, Vatican II did not cite the authority of the New Testament, for the very good reason that the New Testament does not sanction such a portrayal of episcopal office. Instead, the council cited the authority of the Fathers of the Church. In other words, it appealed to the sacerdotalist tradition. In my own opinion, the council would have done better to (1) distinguish between a hieratic priesthood and presbyterial oversight, (2) to reserve the former to Jesus alone, as the Letter to the Hebrews does, and (3) attribute to the bishop the fullness of presbyterial oversight.

The Woes of Sacerdotalism

The council's appeal to a sacerdotalist theology labors under a certain number of theological difficulties. It stands at the very least in tension with the doctrine of the Letter to the Hebrews, which asserts that Jesus and Jesus alone deserves the title of the high priest of the new covenant in virtue of his incarnation, atoning, death, and glorification at the right hand of the Father.

A second difficulty attends a sacerdotalist interpretation of ordained ministry: it holds up the wrong ideal to Christian leaders. A Christian understanding of religious leadership contrasts with the Levitical priesthood at every point but one.

(1) The members of the Levitical priesthood belonged, as we have seen, to an elite, professional caste. The first leaders of the Christian community, however, saw themselves as following a servant Messiah. Leadership in the Christian community demanded, therefore, the willingness to act as the least of all, the servant of all (Mark 20:24-28; Matt 10:41-45; Luke 22:24-27; John 13:1-16).

(2) Membership in the Levitical priesthood depended on ancestry; it did not flow from a sense of personal vocation. Leadership in the Christian community, however, flowed directly from a sense of one's charismatic call to serve the community and from the confirmation of that call through the laying on of hands (2 Tim 1:6).

(3) The Levitical priesthood transformed one into a man of the sanctuary. As Church leadership evolved historically, conflicts within the community eventually motivated the concentration of cultic authority in the hands of the ordained. Nevertheless, Church leadership did not initially imply exclusive control of Christian cult. Nor should ordained leaders today cling to exclusive control of cult if that possessiveness fails to serve the common good of the community.

(4) The Levitical priesthood sought through the mediation of cult and oracular pronouncements to make a transcendent God present to his people. The first Christians by contrast had a vivid sense of the immanent presence of the Father and of Jesus in the Holy Breath's action and inspiration.

(5) In one respect, however, leadership in the apostolic Church and the Levitical priesthood did coincide. Both consecrated one to a ministry of teaching. Levitical priests explained the Law to the faithful. Church leaders during the apostolic age proclaimed the gospel. That single similarity, however, scarcely justifies calling the ordained the Levites of the new covenant.

The Difference Between Ordained Priesthood and the Priesthood of the Faithful

In other words, if Catholic theology hopes to defend theologically a qualitative difference between the priesthood of the ordained and that of the faithful, it needs to find a better defense of its position than fourth-century sacerdotalism affords. It also needs to coordinate its position better with the biblical witness by making three theological moves.

First, a Catholic theology of ordained ministry needs to root itself solidly on the biblical principle that Jesus and Jesus alone functions as the great hieratic high priest of the new covenant. He does so in virtue of his incarnation, atoning death, and glorification at the right hand of the Father, where he now pleads for the sinners for whom he died.

Second, a Catholic theology also needs to assert that all Christians participate in the priesthood of Jesus by actively sharing in the service of atonement that he accomplished: by identifying as he did with humanity in its direst need and deepest suffering and by ministering actively to those whose needs and sufferings outstrip all others.

Third, Catholic theology needs to assert that different members of the Church participate in qualitatively different ways in the priesthood of Jesus in virtue of the different kinds of charismatic ministry they exercise.

The New Testament offers theological foundations for understanding the ministry of the ordained as priestly when it characterizes the Church as the priestly people of God. If the ministry of the Church can legitimately be called priestly, the ministry of its leaders must qualify as priestly as well. That ministry differs qualitatively from the ministry of the baptized because ordination confirms a charism of Church leadership and because charisms differ among themselves qualitatively. Hence, the charism of Church leadership together with the ministry it inspires differs qualitatively from the priestly ministry of the laity.

In other words, bishops, priests, deacons, and lay people all participate in the one priesthood of Christ; but they do so differently because they serve others in Jesus' name with different sets of priestly responsibilities. Bishops care for the unity of the Church, for its fidelity to the apostolic witness, and for the pastoral needs of the dioceses they administer. Priests represent and assist the bishops, bring the concerns of both the diocese and the universal Church to the people of God, and pastor the flocks entrusted to them. Deacons assist priests and bishops in their ministry. The ordained, moreover, serve the people of God in the image of Christ and measure the effectiveness of their own ministry by the success with which they promote the apostolate of the laity. The laity, for their part, follow the divine Mother's inspirations as she anoints them to worship the triune God, to perform different kinds of Church ministry, and to proclaim the gospel to unbelievers.

All the Churches agree that ordination commits one to a ministry of proclamation and of cultic leadership. In the past Protestants have emphasized a ministry of proclamation over cultic ministry, while Catholics emphasized cultic ministry over a ministry of proclamation. Vatican II offers, I believe, a helpful formula for reconciling the two positions. We need to look upon cultic worship as a form of proclamation. Indeed, sacramental worship qualifies as the most efficacious form of gospel proclamation, because it evokes from people either an initial conversion to Christ or the ongoing renewal and deepening of their initial conversion commitment. Moreover, if people engage in sacramental worship with unconverted hearts, then the Word proclaimed in the sacrament stands in efficacious judgment over their hypocrisy (1 Cor 11:28-32).

The Right to Ordination and the Common Good of the Church

The history of ordained leadership in the Church teaches us, however, that the right of the ordained to lead worship should not be interpreted as an exclusive right if such exclusivity fails to serve the common good of the Christian community. The concentration of cultic responsibility in the hands of the ordained sought initially to ensure that the Church would be served by competent sacramental ministers. The principle of competence rather than exclusive clerical control of worship ought, then, to regulate the Church's sacramental discipline.

Here again the documents of Vatican II illumine the responsibilities of the Church's ordained leaders. They recognize three fundamental ecclesial rights of all baptized Christians: the right to Christian instruction, the right to ready access to the sacraments, and the right and duty to exercise their charisms in service to others (*Lumen gentium,* 37; *Apostolicam actuositatem,* 3). When the lack of ordained ministers deprives the people of God of ready access to the sacraments, Church leaders, especially the bishops, stand under the serious responsibility of seeing to it either that competent lay sacramental ministers are trained in sufficient numbers to meet the Church's needs or that the Church's laws be revised to allow the ordination of competent people whom canon law excludes from Church leadership.

Beyond Clericalism

These insights into the purpose of ordained ministry illumine another facet of sacerdotalist theology, its elitism. In a sense, the common good of the Church requires that its leaders comprise an elite group within the community. One would scarcely want the Church led by cretins and incompetents, although it has been on occasion. Clericalism, however, misconceives the character of elite leadership. The ordained ought to lead God's people in the service of atonement. They ought to do so in the image of a humble, crucified Christ. Clericalism, by contrast, transforms the clergy into a power elite. Power elites use positions of authority for self-aggrandizement or in order to oppress rather than to serve those they govern. In other words, in addition to the forces of concupiscence that plague all believers, the ordained have to deal with the concupiscent power of clericalism.

A sacerdotalist and hierarchicalist theology of priesthood fosters clericalism to the extent that it portrays the ordained as standing above the laity and apart from them instead of standing among them and in solidarity with them. Moreover, in sacerdotalist theology, only the ordained participate directly in the priesthood of Christ.

One need not, however, think of Christian priesthood in sacerdotalist terms. The New Testament doctrine of the priesthood of all believers suggests that the entire Christian community participates in the priesthood of Jesus in virtue of its common call to mediate Christ to the world. If, as I have suggested, one's particular charismatic calling in the Church specifies the way in which each Christian exercises his or her priesthood, then, one can legitimately speak of the priesthood of the Church as mediating between the priesthood of Christ, on the one hand, and the priesthood both of the laity and of ordained priests, on the other. In such a theological construct of priesthood, ordained priests exercise a different kind of priesthood from the laity but they function within the Church and among the laity not over the laity and apart from them. In other words, if we see the priestly vocation of the Church as a whole as mediating between the priesthood of Christ, on the one hand, and the charismatically specified priestly ministry of both ordained priests and the laity, we can avoid the clericalistic elitism implicit in sacerdotalist modes of thinking.

c. Have Sacred Orders a Hierarchical Structure? Bishops, priests, and deacons certainly exercise different ministries in the Church.

Moreover, until modern times the structures of Church leadership evolved in a culture that conceived in hierarchical terms both society and reality as a whole. Should, however, contemporary Christians continue to conceive Church leadership as hierarchical?

The Second Vatican Council certainly calls the ordained leadership a hierarchy, and the term has justification in so far as it suggests subsidiarity in the structures of Church governance. The college of bishops governs the Church and functionally succeeds the apostles. Priests serve collegially under the bishops, represent them, and assist them in serving and governing the Church. Deacons assist both priests and bishops by ministering pastorally to the people of God and by helping administer the affairs of the Church.

Subsidiarity vs. Hierarchy

The term "hierarchy," however, implies more than subsidiarity. In its original formulation it connotes, as we have seen, a trickle-down theory of grace that reduces lay Christians to a position of passivity within the Church. As we have also seen, the ecclesiology of Vatican II set aside these negative connotations of the term "hierarchical," even though it continued to use the term itself. Nevertheless, in the popular mind the term "hierarchy" continues to connote clericalism.

For my part, I believe that we would be better advised, given the misleading connotations of the term "hierarchy," to stop using it altogether. Why not speak instead of a community governed according to subsidiarity of authority and responsibility? Moreover, properly understood subsidiarity implies not autocracy but genuine sensitivity to the needs of all. Indeed, the Catholic Church needs to generate new Church structures that better guarantee the rights of all persons affected by official Church actions. We need for example to address the following questions: Should the synod of bishops evolve into a senate of bishops with universal legislative authority? Should the senate of bishops take over many of the functions now handled by the Vatican curia? Can we enact an adequate bill of ecclesial rights for all baptized Christians? How can we further democratize Church structures? How can we better ensure due process in doctrinal disputes? How can we make sure that the laity have a more effective voice in the selection of their bishops and priests? How can we prevent the use of episcopal appointments to impose a particular theological ideology on the Church as a whole?

d. Do Orders Confer a Character; And, If So, In What Does It Consist? As we saw in considering the rites of initiation, when Augustine compared unrepeatable sacraments to a brand or tatoo, he laid the foundations for transforming a disciplinary practice into a metaphysical reality. His metaphor inspired medieval theologians to teach that rituals whose repetition Church discipline forbids cannot be repeated *because* they leave a mark on the soul.

The Meaning of "Character" Recalled

We should, as we have seen, find nothing mysterious about an act that marks the emerging human self; for every decision we take marks us by either creating a new habit or reinforcing an old one. A decision to perform an unrepeatable ritual act that confers permanent (but morally conditioned) ecclesial rights and responsibilities differs, however, from other acts precisely in that it confers permanent rights and responsibilities on the one to whom the ritual is administered. The rite of baptism, as we saw, confers the morally conditioned right to participate in Church's life and worship. The rite of confirmation confers the morally conditioned right and responsibility to minister charismatically as a Christian lay apostle. The different rites of ordination confer the morally conditioned right and responsibility to lead the Christian community as a deacon, priest, or bishop.

The Character of Ordained Leadership

In what does the morally conditioned character of that right consist? Ever since the Donatist controversy, the Church has taught, quite correctly, that a worshipper's relationship to God within an act of sacramental worship does not depend on the merits of the minister but on the action of divine grace and on the dispositions of the worshipper. Nevertheless, ordained ministry does bring with it the responsibility of giving the Christian community an example of dedicated, Christlike service. Those among the ordained who abuse a position of leadership for self-aggradizement should be disciplined and, if necessary, either temporarily or permanently disbarred from public ministry. In this sense, then, the rights and responsibilities conferred by the character of orders remain morally conditioned. Even defrocked ministers retain a virtual right to lead the people of God in the sense that repentance and reconciliation (not reordination) suffice to restore them to active ministry. Moreover, at the time of the Donatist controversy the Church decided to sanction the baptisms conferred by heretical and schismatic ministers on the condition that in baptizing they intend to do what the Church does in initiating neophytes. In those cases, therefore, the Church mitigated the moral conditions to function sacramentally by reducing them to the mere intention to baptize.

Does the character conform the ordained to Christ? To answer this question, one need only examine the kind of commitment made in ordination. The ordained commit themselves to serve the community in the image of Jesus Christ, the great high priest who suffered and died to take away the sins of the world. Ritual incorporation into the ranks of the ordained conforms one, then, to Christ in the sense that it commits one morally to living in his image. That moral commitment defines one's subsequent reality as a person. Moreover, that commitment stands in public judgment of the conduct of the ordained. As in the case of the characters conferred by the rite of initiation, however, the profound conformity of the ordained to Christ derives more from active response to the graces of ordination than it does from the character; for in the case of the justly defrocked and unrepentant minister, the character of ordination alone, when unaccompanied by the grace of ordination, confers only the virtual right to exercise ordained ministry. Moreover, because the character conforms the ordained to Christ by virtually assimilating them to him morally, it does so irrespective of the sex of the ordained, as it did in the case of women deacons.

Service vs. Power

Does the character give priests power over the Body and Blood of Christ, as some medieval theologians claimed? In the present discipline of the Church priestly ordination certainly gives one the right and responsibility to celebrate the Eucharist. One may, however, question whether the phrase "power over the Body and Blood of Christ" adequately describes the consequences of ordination. It focuses too narrowly on the Eucharistic ministry of the ordained, and within the Eucharist it focuses too narrowly on the moment of consecration. The character, the unchangeable fact that one has been incorporated once and for all into the priestly ministry of the Church, entails much more than the right to pronounce the words of consecration at the Eucharist. It entails all the rights and responsibilities of diaconal, presbyterial, and episcopal leadership. The belief that the character confers power over the Body and Blood of Christ also labors under a second speculative disadvantage, for it interprets ordained leadership under the morally ambiguous rubric of power rather than portraying it as humble service in the image of Christ.

Does the character advance one up the hierarchical ladder of the Church? Ordination to the priesthood certainly entails more rights and responsibilities than ordination to the diaconate, and ordination to the episcopacy certainly entails more rights and responsibilities than ordination to the priesthood. If, however, as we have seen, we are better advised to avoid the term "hierarchy" in describing the responsibilities of church leaders, we are also better advised to avoid it in speaking of the character of ordination.

e. Should Clerical Celibacy Be Imposed by Law? Most Catholics take the celibacy of the clergy for granted. Nevertheless, not until the late Middle Ages did the Latin Church effectively impose celibacy through canonical legislation. The Oriental Churches never required celibacy of their priests. The Protestant Churches abandoned clerical celibacy in the sixteenth century. Should the Catholic Church revoke its legislation requiring celibacy of its priests, it would realign itself with the rest of the Christian world. It would also remove a major obstacle to reuniting the Christian Churches.

The Legislation of Clerical Celibacy

As we have seen, the original impulse to impose celibacy on Church leaders sprang in part from a questionable kind of clericalism. Celibacy was supposed to dramatize the Christian priest's spiritual superiority to Jewish priests. One can also find in patristic arguments favoring celibacy hints of an unhealthy suspicion of matter and sexuality: celibacy supposedly endowed the clergy with a quasi-angelic status.

When, however, push came to shove, none of these theological rationalizations decided the matter canonically. The canonical legislation of clerical celibacy seems to have happened primarily for financial reasons, in order to prevent the loss of priestly benefices to the Church through inheritance. With the collapse of the benefice system, the original economic motives for the legislation disappeared. One cannot, then, study the history of clerical celibacy without facing the inevitable question: does the canonical legislation of celibacy really serve the common good of the Church?

Married Love and Celibate Love

Paul the Apostle argued that celibacy frees one from the responsibilities of married life and therefore allows one to serve the kingdom with greater pastoral freedom than married clergy enjoy. The argument still has validity. Even though married people can fulfill the duties of official Church leadership as efficiently as celibates, ordained ministry and celibate love exhibit a kind of conaturality. Let us try to understand why.

For the Christian both married and celibate love embody four fundamental traits: concreteness, reciprocity, universality, and gratuity. Love's concreteness flows from the fact that it always seeks out specific individuals or communities. Love's reciprocity results from the fact that humans need to receive as well as to give love. Christian love's universality means that it excludes no one in principle and in any given situation seeks out first those in greatest need. Christian love's gratuity results from the fact that it suffers sin and rejection with the same loving forgiveness as Jesus.

Because a husband and a wife commit themselves personally to one another for life, married love manifests more clearly than celibate love the concreteness and reciprocity of Christian love. At least it does so to the extent that spouses live faithful to their marriage promises. Human frailty ensures, of course, that married life will have need for atoning love. Moreover, as we have seen, married couples and even families can witness to the gratuity and universality of Christian love by reaching out to those in greatest need.

At the same time, celibate Christian love witnesses more dramatically to the universality and gratuity of Christian love than to its concreteness and reciprocity. Those vowed to celibacy renounce marriage for the sake of the kingdom in order to have freedom to minister to those in greatest need. Celibates like married people need to love and be loved and therefore need through friendship to know the concreteness and reciprocity of love. Nevertheless, the renunication of marriage for the sake of ministerial availability to the poor and the needy calls more visible attention to the universality and gratuity of Christian love than to its concreteness and reciprocity. Those in greatest need often find it hard to respond adequately to the love they receive.

Celibacy and Ordination

Since the ordained leaders of the Church have as one of their apostolic responsibilities to care especially for the least and neediest in both the Church and the human community, celibacy and ordained ministry do, as Paul the Apostle saw, have a certain affinity for one another. Paul, however, would never have dreamed of imposing celibacy on the other apostles by law. Moreover, even if one concede that the charism of celibacy can enhance a ministry of ordained leadership, the fact remains that the charism of ordained leadership differs from the charism of celibacy. Married people can function very effectively as ministers of the Church.

The Church recruits its ordained leaders from the ranks of the laity. Moreover, the Second Vatican Council lists among the fundamental rights and duties of lay Christians the right and duty to exercise within the Church any charism the divine Mother might bestow on them (*Apostolicam actuositatem*, 3). The ordained have the responsibility of discerning the divine Mother's charismatic inspirations, but they exceed the limits of their authority when they suppress those inspirations (*Lumen gentium*, 12).

The Need for Canonical Reform

We have, then, serious reason to question whether the legal imposition of clerical celibacy really serves the common good of the Church. The law of clerical celibacy arbitrarily excludes competent married persons from the ranks of the Church leadership. Does it not, then, do what Church leaders must never do: suppress the divine Mother's charismatic inspirations? Moreover, as the number of priests dwindles in this country, the right of all baptized Christians to ready access to the sacraments, and especially to the Eucharist, ought to take precedence over the inertia of clerical institutions. We shall see whether the episcopacy as a whole will choose to respect or to violate those rights by giving those currently excluded by canon law from Church leadership free access to ordination.

I am not arguing that only married persons should have access to ordination. For the reasons just given, the Church will always have place for celibate priests. I am arguing that canonical legislation that does not leave the divine Mother free to decide whom she wants to lead the Church fails to promote its common good.

f. Should the Church Ordain Women? These reflections also throw light on the question of women's ordination. Those who oppose women's ordination ordinarily object that since Jesus ordained only men, the Church must also. They also argue that since the character of ordination conforms one to Jesus the great high priest and since he was male, all those ordained to the priesthood must belong to the same sex as he.

The State of the Question

The theological community as a whole has found both arguments specious, and correctly so. True enough, Jesus chose only men when he called the Twelve. The apostolic leadership of the Church did not, however, devolve on the Twelve alone. Women certainly saw the risen Christ, and the Gospel of John gives us reason to think that Mary of Magdala numbered among the apostles (John 20:10-18). Moreover, as we have seen, the New Testament testifies that women numbered among the local Church leaders that succeeded the apostles.[2]

Moreover, as we have seen, the character of ordination conforms ordinands to Christ the high priest by giving them the morally conditioned right to lead the Christian community publicly and officially. Of itself the character confers only a virtual right to exercise such leadership, since delinquent, unreconciled ministers who have been justly defrocked lack the actual right to minister publicly, except in those circumstances in which Church discipline allows them to do so. Hence, actual response to the graces of ordination conforms one more profoundly to Christ the crucified high priest than does the character. Moreover, nowhere in the New Testament do we find likeness to Christ predicated on sex. Rather we resemble Christ when we live in his image, whatever our sex happens to be.

In addition, the history of ordained ministry suggests that when in the fourth century the clergy, largely for political reasons, began to transform itself into the Levites of the new covenant, they also adopted the sexist structure of the Levitical priesthood. Certainly, the fourth century brought the expulsion of women from the ranks of the clergy.

2. For a fuller discussion of these issues, see Leonard Swidler and Arlene Swidler, eds., *Women Priests: A Catholic Commentary on the Vatican Declaration* (New York: Paulist, 1977) and Elisabeth Meier Tetlow, *Women and Ministry in the New Testament: Called to Serve* (New York: University Press of America, 1980).

Vatican II on Sexism

Vatican II condemned sexism as sinful. It defended the right of women "to choose a husband, to embrace a state of life, or to acquire an education or cultural benefits equal to those recognized for men" (*Gaudium et spes,* 10). Vatican II also called for a greater participation of women in human culture and in the Church's apostolate (*Gaudium et spes,* 30, 60). The council correctly saw sexism as an ethical issue. If God condemns sexism in secular society, it seems unlikely that he will condone it in the Church. As a consequence, historical arguments that appeal to the Church's constant tradition of excluding women from the ranks of the priesthood only document centuries of bigotry and oppression.

Moreover, the same principles that justify the abrogation of the legal imposition of clerical celibacy, also entail that charismatically competent women enjoy access to ordained Church leadership. The divine Mother must be allowed to dispense her charisms freely (*Ad Gentes,* 23). The ordained leaders of the Church must never suppress her charismatic activity (*Lumen gentium,* 12). When in the fourth century the clergy expelled women from their ranks, they did precisely that.

Marriage and orders both seal and sanction specific ministerial vocations within the Church. The other rituals of the Church also foster ongoing conversion, but they do so differently from the vocational sacraments. In the chapters that follow, we shall examine how the rites of reconciliation and anointing and how the Eucharist itself advance the ongong conversion of baptized Christians.

PART II

Three Rites of Ongoing Conversion

CHAPTER V

The Rite of Reconciliation

We have reflected on adult conversion and on the Christian rituals of initiation that seal that experience. We have also examined the two vocational sacraments of marriage and orders and the experiences of ongoing conversion that they ritualize. As we have seen, in each of the vocational sacraments one responds to the divine Mother's charismatic anointing and undertakes a form of ecclesial service in the name and image of Jesus.

The first stage of adult initiation, baptism, commits Christians to the lifelong process of putting on the mind of Christ. The second stage, confirmation, commits one to lifelong openness to the divine Mother's charismatic call, whatever form that may take. One cannot, then, ritually confirm a specific charism of service and respond to it in a Christlike manner without implicitly renewing one's Christian covenant of initiation; for in so acting, one does what one promised to do on becoming a Christian.

Moreover, by the same ritual act one undertakes publicly new ecclesial responsibilities. In matrimony, Christian couples reaffirm their covenant of initiation in the context of taking on the responsibilities of founding a family and transforming it under God into a realm of saving grace. Ordinands renew their covenant of initiation by accepting incorporation into the ranks of public Church leadership. Once ordained, they must embody the Word they proclaim and serve the Christian community in the image of a servant Messiah. In committing themselves to follow the gift-giving Breath in the ministry of Christian leadership, the ordained reaffirm their original commitment to Christ in the context of assuming new ecclesial responsibilities. Because both marriage and orders impose responsibilities that go beyond those assumed in the rites of initiation, responsible consent to either vocation demands a measure of ongoing conversion proportionate to the new responsibilities assumed.

Reconciliation and Anointing

In the rites of reconciliation and anointing, one also reaffirms one's original covenant of initiation. Christian initiation forgives sins committed prior to one's ritual incorporation into the family of God. In the rite of reconciliation one reaffirms one's baptismal covenant in the repentant renunciation of sins one has committed after initiation. In the rite of anointing one reaffirms one's Christian covenant in the context of a prayer for healing.

In the present chapter we will examine the rite of reconciliation, and in the chapter that follows, the rite of anointing.

This chapter divides into five parts. The first part reflects on the forces of concupiscence that cause Christians to sin personally after entering the Church. The second examines Jesus' own ministry of forgiveness and reviews New Testament foundations for a theology of reconciliation. The third part surveys the historical development of the rite of reconciliation. Part four notes some of the principal controversies that this sacrament has occasioned. Part five focuses on the revised ritual of reconciliation and the experience of ongoing conversion that it seals. In this final section of the chapter, I shall also attempt to respond to the principal controversies occasioned by the rite of reconciliation.

Let us, then, begin to understand the significance of the rite of reconciliation by reflecting on the forces that conspire to betray baptized Christians into sin.

1. The Forces of Concupiscence and the Sins of Christians. In order to understand better the relationship between the forces of concupiscence and personal sin, we need first to examine the concrete shape that those forces take in our society. Then we shall reflect on the ways in which they help motivate personal sin. Finally, we shall focus on the challenge of ongoing personal conversion.

a. The Forces of Concupiscence. In reflecting on the rites of initiation, we saw that Christian baptism takes away original sin by transforming it into concupiscence. Remember that the term "original sin" designates the sinful situation of the unbaptized. Institutionalized sin and the bad example of others corrupt those who lack faith even more readily than they corrupt believers.

The Social Shape of Concupiscence

The situations that nurture or corrupt us do not lie outside of personal experience; they enter into it and shape it in conscious and unconscious ways. As a consequence, those raised in racist, sexist, anti-Semitic cultures tend to imbibe bigotry with the air they breathe. Worship of the almighty dollar breeds materialism, consumerism, and greed. Lying ideologies lull us into accepting gross injustice as part of the natural scheme of things. Group pressure and the exigencies of survival can also drug the conscience with false prudence and slogans of national or group security.

After initiation into the Christian community the forces of original sin do not evaporate. They continue to exert pressure on the hearts, minds, and consciences of Christians. Repentance and conversion teach the baptized to name those forces as sinful; for faith changes the way one perceives them. Prior to conversion, they poison one's personality in subtle and often unconscious, unacknowledged ways. Repentant commitment to Christ unmasks that pernicious influence.

Moreover, sacramental initiation introduces converts into an ecclesial realm of grace that counteracts to some extent the influence that environmental evil exerts on the conduct of the baptized. Prior to baptism one knows situational sin as original sin (i.e., as the corrupting lot of anyone born into the world without the remedy of grace), after baptism one experiences those same sinful forces, not as personal sin, but as the effect and cause of sin in the baptized. In other words, one experiences them as concupiscence.

Life-Giving Forces in American Culture

Not every force in our culture qualifies as concupiscent. Most Americans I have met display an enormous amount of good will and personal concern for others. Many live committed lives and long for a more just world. In business, government, and family, people work hard, share liberally, cultivate fairness, and lend a helping hand. Faith in God motivates worship and mutual forgiveness.

We must also resist the self-righteous temptation to scapegoat all of our national institutions as inherently evil and unjust. Americans take legitimate pride in the rights and freedoms that our constitution guarantees. We look with satisfaction on the imagination and enterprise that created our economic system. Immigrants still look to this nation as a land of opportunity, and many find social advancement on our shores. Most of our people detest war and desire peace. As individuals and sometimes as a nation, we respond generously to extraordinary appeals to help the starving. Many Americans labor to improve the lot of the people of the Third World. Some have given their lives to that end.

Concupiscence American Style

The fact remains, however, that sinful forces do corrupt our culture and can corrupt our lives. Moreover, an essay on American concupiscence must focus exclusively on the powers that threaten to corrupt us and must close its eyes to our national virtues. Can we begin, then, to name some of the forces in North American culture that come from sin and lead to sin?

The converting Christian who resists the forces of concupiscence judges them with the mind of Christ. Initiation, as we have seen, draws us into Jesus' own baptismal experience. In the process it sets believers in conflict with the same evil powers that put him to the test. His temptations become our own, while the same Holy Breath that inspired his sinless rejection of Satan's wiles empowers us to do the same.

As we have seen, Jesus summoned his disciples to a morality of faith. He invited them to trust absolutely in the Father's providential care for each of them. Those who refuse to trust God absolutely place their trust in something else. Many prefer to trust themselves.

The Sin of Individualistic Self-Reliance

This nation has in fact for two centuries transformed individualistic self-reliance into a seeming virtue. We idealize the self-made achiever, the rugged individualist who through grit and aggressive initiative achieves success, power, and wealth. Our national myths transform the self-reliant individualist into a lonely hero. What American has not cheered the solitary gunslinger who rides out of the hills to defend innocent sod-busters against the gunmen whom powerful ranchers have hired to drive them from their farms? Who has not empathized with the courageous loner battling the system: the tough private investigator who fights police corruption, the mob, and city hall in order to prove the innocence of a client framed for a crime his client never committed? Who has not cheered the intrepid reporter who doggedly pursues the front-page story that exposes corruption in high places?

Pragmatic American individualists claim the right to say or do whatever they must in order to get ahead. Expressive individualists claim the right to say or do whatever expresses their inviolable inner selves. Both forms of individualism thrive in the world of the up-wardly mobile.

A Culture of Individualism

Individualistic self-reliance teaches Americans to discover the meaning and purpose of life within themselves. In less industrialized cultures adolescents come of age by rites of passage that introduce them collectively to the responsibilities of adult living. In industrial-ized, bourgeois America adolescents come of age by declaring their independence: typically, they leave home to find themselves as indi-viduals. In the process, they may also leave the Church with its com-mon creed and community of shared memories, hopes, and lives in order to formulate a personal creed, whether religious or not. Instead of committing themselves to genuine communities that make claims upon them, young Americans frequently settle for relatively super-ficial companionship among those with a similar life-style.

Self-reliant individualism cuts people off from the sources of ethical discourse. It replaces both the language of moral obligation and the religious narratives that make ultimate sense of human life and death with the language of pragmatic utility or of aesthetic prefer-ence. The pragmatic individualist believes that getting ahead takes precedence over anything else. The expressive individualist justifies personal choices by an idiosyncratic appeal to subjective feeling: "I do what feels right to me, you do what feels right to you. Don't in-terfere with my freedom of expression, and I won't interfere with yours." For both forms of individualism questions of the common good, of shared moral obligation, or of the rights of others never arise in any serious or challenging way.[1]

Technological, bourgeois culture idolizes the rugged, self-reliant individualist; but what contemporary, secular culture calls an ideal, the gospel calls idolatry. The commitment of faith to which Jesus calls his disciples contradicts the vicious egocentrism that individualism palms off as virtue. Instead of isolating individuals in themselves and

---

1. For a lucid study of the impact of individualism on North American cul-ture, see Robert N. Bellah, Richard Madsen, William M. Sullivan, Ann Swidler, and Steven M. Tipton, *Habits of the Heart: Individualism and Commitment in Ameri-can Life* (Berkeley and Los Angeles, CA: University of California Press, 1985).

instead of condemning them like spiders to spin their webs of value out of their own innards, Christian faith looks to God as the ultimate source of moral value. The Christian lives God-centered, not self-centered.

Individualism vs. the Gospel

Moreover, instead of committing one to single-minded self-advancement, Christian trust in God's personal, providential care for each individual frees one to reach out in concrete, practical ways to others. Believing Christians share their bread, the physical supports of life, with those in greatest need. They also dedicate themselves to bringing into existence a religious community whose memories endow life with shared meaning and whose hopes orient it to the future God has promised. In other words, the converting Christian recognizes in the pragmatic and expressive strains of individualism that infect North American culture major forces of concupiscence.

Greed and Capitalism

Other forces in contemporary culture conspire to corrupt the Christian conscience. Christian faith comes to concrete expression in care and concern for those in greatest need. In a capitalist economy like our own, however, those in greatest need often must fend for themselves in an aggressive open market largely indifferent to their survival.

Money becomes capital when one uses it to make more money. In classical capitalist theory free and open competition supposedly curbs the cupidity of self-interested entrepreneurs. The capitalist who greedily overprices goods will supposedly soon find himself without buyers. Self-interest did not, however, prevent sweatshops, child labor, and the other horrors of *laissez-faire* capitalism. Nor has it prevented in more recent times the concentration of massive amounts of wealth in the hands of a few, the erosion of the middle class, and the spread of poverty.

Robert Heilbroner and Lester Thurow, drawing on the work of Jan Pen, illustrate graphically this tendency within capitalism. They correlate income with personal physical height and then imagine a parade of people stretching from the west to the east coast of the United States. Each individual stands as tall as his or her income. They describe the parade in the following terms:

Assume the height of the middle class family to be 6 feet, representing a median income of $23,000 in 1980. This will be our height as observers. What would our parade look like?

It would begin with a few families *below* the ground, for there are some households with negative incomes; that is, they report losses for the year. Mainly these are families with business losses, and their negative incomes are not matched by general poverty. Following close on their heels comes a long line of grotesque dwarfs who comprise about one fifth of all families, people less than three feet tall. Some are shorter than one foot.

Only after the parade is half over do we reach people whose faces are at our level. Then come the giants. When we reach the last 5 percent of the parade—incomes around $56,000—people are fifteen feet tall. At the end of the parade, people tower six hundred to six thousand feet in the air—one hundred to one thousand times taller than the middle height. What is the largest income in the country? We do not know: Probably our one or two billionaires have incomes of over $100 million.[2]

The Christian View of Wealth

Some people are born to wealth; and some wealthy people attempt to manage their fortunes in ways that benefit those less advantaged. Other members of the wealthy classes show less responsibility and generosity. The Letter of James expresses in vivid rhetoric the spontaneous response of the early Christian conscience to the ruthless and selfish amassing of enormous fortunes.

> Next a word to you who have great possessions. Weep and wail over the miserable fate descending on you. Your riches have rotted; your fine clothes are moth-eaten; your silver and gold have rusted away, and their very rust will be evidence against you and consume your flesh with fire. You have piled up wealth in an age that is near its close. The wages you never paid to the men who mowed your fields are loud against you, and the outcry of the reapers has reached the ears of the Lord of Hosts. You have lived on earth in wanton luxury, fattening yourselves like cattle—and the day of slaughter has come. You have condemned the innocent and murdered him; he offers you no resistance (Jas 5:1-6).

Moreover, an important strain in patristic moral teaching echoes James's rhetoric. The Christian tradition defends the right of all persons to the possessions they need in order to live a humane life. Those

2. Robert Heilbroner and Lester Thurow, *Economics Explained* (Englewood Cliffs, NJ: Prentice-Hall, 1980) 42.

who heap up wealth at the expense of the poor plunder them and owe them restitution.[3]

International Greed

One can observe the inequities of capitalism writ large in the international economy. In their aggressive drive to maximize profits, the industrial nations have arranged world trade to their own economic advantage. Tariff restrictions and other trade barriers favor First-World economies. Loans to economically ailing countries effected through the International Monetary Fund, the World Bank, and the International Finance Corporation must meet conditions set by the rich, industrial nations. All too frequently those conditions yield to economically developing nations short-term benefits but long-term headaches, as higher interest rates, inflation, and currency devaluation combine to drive the borrowing nations ever deeper into debt. Often, too, aid from the First World to the Third serves the national interests of the economically developed nations rather than the real needs of developing ones. The bulk of foreign aid flowing from the United States, for example, goes to its military allies and increasingly serves military rather than humanitarian purposes.[4]

The growing power of multinational corporations dramatizes the cupidity that unbridled capitalism can instill in human hearts. The multinationals like to portray themselves as the harbingers of world peace. Their managers speak of the obsolescence of the warring nation state and aspire to world domination through economics. They dream of transforming this planet into a global shopping center.

In point of fact, the policies of the multinationals often show them more concerned with political stability than with the establishment of a just peace, more greedy for profits than worried about the economic improvement of the nations that host their factories and plants.

By transferring their centers of production to countries without labor unions, the multinationals dole out what by Western standards amounts to sweatshop wages. In the process, they have also

3. Cf. Charles Avila, *Ownership: Early Christian Teaching* (London: Sheed and Ward, 1983).

4. Cf. Susanne Toton, *World Hunger: The Responsibility of Christian Education* (New York: Orbis, 1982) and The Brandt Commission 1983, *Common Crisis North-South: Co-operation for World Recovery* (London: Pan Books, 1983).

effectively undercut the bargaining power of organized labor in unionized nations. They have manipulated the media in Third World countries to create artificial markets, thus persuading people already living economically marginal lives to waste their money on junk food. Unhindered by environmental laws they have polluted the Third World with impunity.[5]

Even multinationals that attempt to abide by self-imposed moral codes can in the end subvert the economies of the Third-World nations that host their plants and factories. The multinationals do so by paying higher wages that siphon off the best business talent from local industries and by maintaining an oligopolistic control of the home market that ends by lowering employment in less developed nations. Multinationals buy from their own sources and thus hurt local suppliers. They modernize production in ways that lower the demand for human employment. Finally, they employ advanced technologies that effectively prevent local industries from competing.[6]

The Corruption of Consumerism

Needless to say, few people in a capitalist economy such as ours rise to the power, wealth, and position of a captain of industry. The majority of people experience the corrupting influence of capitalism in succumbing to the consumerist propaganda of large corporations. In pandering to one's own artificially engendered needs one easily loses concern for the real needs of others.

We are considering the forces of concupiscence present in our society. The ethics of discipleship that Jesus lived and inculcated enable us to identify those forces; for they contradict his moral vision. Self-reliant individualism, capitalistic greed, and consumerism all run counter to the moral demands of gospel living.

5. Richard J. Barnett and Ronald E. Mueller, *Global Reach: The Power of the Multinational Corporations* (New York: Simon and Schuster, 1974); Robert Ledogar, *Hungry for Profits: U.S. Food and Drug Multinationals in Latin America* (New York: IDOC/North America, 1975); Peter J. Henriot, S.J., "Restructuring the International Economic Order," in *Multinational Managers and Poverty in the Third World,* edited by Lee A. Tavis (Notre Dame, IN: University of Notre Dame Press, 1982) 34–50.

6. Cf. Michael Francis and Cecelia S. Manrique, "Clarifying the Debate" in *Multinational Managers and Poverty in the Third World,* edited by Lee A. Tavis (Notre Dame: University of Notre Dame Press, 1982) 74–76.

The Lust for Power

Other forces in our culture, however, also contradict a Christian morality of faith. Jesus came to establish the reign of God on earth as in heaven, but he refused to found the kingdom on the coercive use of power. Indeed, the Gospels tell us that he rejected secular messianism as a form of idolatry. Contemporary Christians can, however, bow down before the idol of power often in subtle and unconscious ways.

This nation has known all too intimately the coercive uses of power. Born of a bloody revolution, the United States used guile, disease, and superior weaponry to solve "the Indian problem." While Northern slavers grew fat on the triangular trade, Southern planters grew rich on the sweat and misery of black people. Capitalists hired hooligans to club and shoot strikers into submission. Racists terrorized the black community with hideous, sadistic lynchings. Organized crime and illegal drug traffic claim their regular victims. Terror haunts our city streets: we need only open the morning paper or listen to the evening news in order to hear the latest catalogue of rape, murder, and violence.

As a nation we also practice violence in other ways. We entered the Second World War as crusaders against Nazi tyranny and Japanese expansionism, but we emerged from that contest morally tainted. We first developed and then twice dropped the atomic bomb, the only nation ever not only to use it but to use it against civilian populations. Today, the military-industrial complex gobbles up billions of dollars annually for the development, production, and deployment of nuclear weapons. Military strategists have begun to dream of waging limited nuclear war.

Deterrence and the Arms Race

The Catholic bishops of the United States have rejected nuclear deterrence as a long-term solution to the threat of nuclear war; but they did give a strictly conditioned, short-term moral toleration to a policy of deterrence. They predicated such tolerance, however, on the aggressive pursuit of peace, of nuclear disarmament, and of the eventual destruction of existing stockpiles of nuclear weapons.[7] Until

7. National Conference of Catholic Bishops, *The Challenge of Peace: God's Promise and Our Response* (Washington, D.C.: United States Catholic Conference, 1983).

the accession of Mikhail Gorbachev to political power in Russia, the Reagan administration committed itself instead to the development and installation of first-strike weapons like the MX and kept up steady pressure to extend the arms race into space.

The nuclear arms race corrupts the national conscience in other ways as well. We can parallel the development and proliferation of nuclear arms with the growth of world hunger. Some dispute any causal connection between these two events. This, however, we know for certain: the billions currently being spent on nuclear weapons are not being used in order to feed the hungry or clothe the naked. Americans like to think of themselves as a generous people. The record shows, however, that at present the bulk of our foreign aid serves military rather than humanitarian ends. Under the Reagan administration Americans have taken national pride in "walking tall," even though walking tall involves soft-pedaling concern for human rights, immoral acts of aggressive war, and illegal meddling in the internal affairs of other nations.

The Sin of Social Fragmentation

The moral exigencies of gospel living spotlight other forces of concupiscence in North American culture. Commitment to Christ dedicates the converting Christian to break down the social barriers that divide people from one another. Nevertheless, the degrading poverty to which generations of blacks and native Americans have been subjected, economic and political discrimination against women, and jingoistic suspicion of Latinos and of all people of color testify all too eloquently to the fact that white, middle-class values rather than the obedience of faith rule the consciences of many North American Christians.

We have drawn upon a theology of Christian conversion in order to identify some of the forces of concupiscence in North American culture. In the section that follows we shall attempt to understand how those same forces conspire to motivate personal sin in the baptized.

b. The Passage from Concupiscence to Personal Sin. It takes little imagination to see that the forces of concupiscence that distort North American culture can easily transform themselves into a school for all the vices.

Covetousness

Pragmatic individualism inculcates habits of arrogance and of greed. An absolute commitment to self-advancement takes its toll of the conscience. It teaches one not to rock the boat by questioning shady business practices and to value cost-effectiveness more than a quality product. The absolute determination to rise within the existing power structures of human society almost certainly demands the willingness to sacrifice other responsibilities to one's family or colleagues. At the very least, pragmatic individualism inculcates a radical kind of human selfishness.

Take Dan, for example, an up-and-coming young executive entrusted with the task of filing a report on one of his company's foreign subsidiaries. He found the subsidiary paying little more than sweatshop wages, juggling their books, and polluting the land. When warned by a friend, however, that a moralizing report would not sit well with his superiors and would be remembered the next time Dan came up for promotion, he knew what he had to do. He gave the subsidiary a clean bill of health.

Lust

Expressive individualism provides ready rationalizations for human lust. For the expressive individualist sexual morality degenerates into the aesthetic choice of a personally appealing sexual lifestyle. Any sexual activity becomes permissible to which sexual partners consent personally even though it results in the irresponsible creation of human life, teaches one to use other people for the sake of one's own egotistical self-indulgence, or spreads an incurable and fatal disease.

Take Sue and Joe, for instance. By their fourth year in college they had seen through the artificiality of conventional morality. They decided to be themselves and began sleeping together. They found beauty in sex until Sue missed her period. Then Joe moved out, and she contacted the abortion clinic.

Gluttony and Envy

Consumerism breeds its own kind of gluttony. Gluttony involves more than overeating, although the battle of the bulge obsesses middle-class Americans. Gluttons cultivate and pander to their own artificial needs while neglecting the real needs of others. In class-conscious, capitalistic America staying ahead of the Joneses and moving in the right social circles can begin to take on the character of a corrupting moral absolute. Moreover, in a world divided between affluent and underdeveloped countries, the overconsumption that capitalism and consumerist propaganda encourage in the First World begins to take on the characteristics of institutionalized gluttony.

Sloth

It has been said that capitalism has transformed every one of the capital sins except sloth into seeming virtues. Sins of omission, however, express a kind of moral sloth, an endemic reluctance to lift a finger to oppose discrimination and injustice. The ideologies that a capitalist economic system spawns in order to mask the injustices it perpetrates breed just such a lethargy of conscience.

Take Ron and Vivian, for instance, an affluent, suburban, couple, regular church-goers too, until the new pastor started talking politics and economics in the pulpit. Ron got so mad he stopped Sunday worship altogether. He renewed his membership in the White Citizens' Council and donated the money he used to give to church to support the Contras. Vivian still goes to church; but when the pastor starts talking social justice, she just tunes him out. She thinks of her garden or of the folks at the country club.

Bigotry and Pride

Similarly, racism, sexism, and ethnic discrimination teach the socially advantaged conscience to acquiesce in every form of legal, distributive, and commutative injustice and even to connive in their perpetuation.

Take Alex, for example. He runs a tidy little business. He will tell you frankly that he has nothing personally against "niggers" and "wetbacks." Nevertheless, the fact remains that he wouldn't dream of hiring one. The idea of a woman executive just makes him laugh.

Anger

Violence breeds violence, injustice breeds injustice. Personal misery and victimization by a corrupt social system can easily harden people into rugged individualists determined above all to survive personally. Repressed rage and desperation explode in crimes of violence.

Take Andy, for instance. Born and raised in an urban ghetto, he swore he would not die there. When the chance came to make some money pushing drugs he took it. Once he himself got hooked on cocaine, he found the habit hard to support. He stole what he could till the vice squad caught him.

Clericalism

Although the Church seeks to provide for its members a realm of grace that protects them from the forces of concupiscence, no Christian should naively imagine that those forces fail to function within the Church itself. As we have seen, clericalism tempts Church leaders to walk the paths of power rather than of humble service, to suppress the divine Mother's charismatic inspirations rather than to encourage them. The arrogance or insensitivity of the ordained has caused more than one Christian to abandon the sacraments. Dogmatic rigidity in the official pastoral magisterium, the illegitimate exclusion of the married and of women from the ranks of Church leadership, the rigidity of divorce legislation, and the arbitrary suppression of legitimate theological pluralism offer other stumbling blocks to the baptized. Nor do clerics alone scandalize believers. Clericalism works hand in glove with apathy and absence of conversion in lay Christians.

Take Fr. Tom, for example. He knew from the first that Vatican II was a mistake. Forced by his bishop to establish a parish council, he let them know right away who ran things. He told them that they could advise him all they wanted but that he would decide how to organize his parish. When a bunch of kookie charismatics wanted to get a prayer group started, he laughed them out the room. Some parishioners protested his high-handedness and then voted with their feet. They either stopped coming to Mass or went to another parish. Most of the parish, however, didn't seem to care one way or another.

Pride, covetousness, lust, anger, gluttony, envy, sloth—from these sins all others flow as they themselves flow from the forces of concupiscence.

The absence of ongoing sociopolitical conversion in the baptized conspires with the forces of concupiscence to betray them into sin. Other forces, however, motivate sinful lapses from grace. To these other forces we turn in the section that follows.

c. The Challenge of Ongoing Personal Conversion. The sins of the baptized can flow from the absence of sociopolitical conversion and from culpable acquiescence in the forces of concupiscence. They can also flow from a failure to meet the challenge of ongoing personal conversion.

Resistance to Affective Conversion

Ongoing affective conversion demands an enduring willingness to face one's own unconscious capacity for violent and destructive acts. Those who refuse to do so can suffer from ego inflation. Inflated egos tend to exhibit a blinding form of self-infatuation. Self-reliantly convinced of their own mastery of themselves and of the challenges that confront them, they ignore the unhealed anger, anxiety, and guilt that fester in the unconscious. Then comes the day when the inflated ego oversteps itself, undertakes too much, or succumbs to its unacknowledged capacity for violence.

Confronted with the destructive consequences of its former self-infatuation, the ego passes from inflation to deflation. Guilt and self-doubt now torment it. It desperately needs to experience forgiveness in order that it can bring to conscious healing the unconscious rage, fear, and guilt that have betrayed it into acting destructively.

Forgiveness inaugurates a period of emotional convalescence during which the deflated, disintegrated ego gradually moves to a new level of conscious integration. Soon the reconstructed ego is riding high again; and if it again neglects the exigencies of ongoing affective conversion, it is heading for another fall. The converting Christian recognizes in the self-infatuation of ego inflation and in the destructive conduct it motivates the fact of personal sin.[8]

Take Ed, for instance. If anyone ever suggests to him that he flies off the handle and may need therapy, he first tells the individual where to go and then a few minutes later flies off the handle. Moreover, every now and then, for reasons he can't explain, he puts away too many beers. If his wife nags him about it when he comes home, he blackens her eyes. He feels bad about it afterwards and goes to confession, because deep down he loves his wife; but he just can't seem to break the pattern.

Resistance to Intellectual Conversion

Failure to take ongoing responsibility for the consequences of intellectual conversion can also betray one into personally sinful con-

8. Edward F. Edinger, *Ego and Archetype* (Baltimore: Penguin, 1973) 37–61.

duct. Intellectual conversion commits one to the relentless pursuit of truth. It demands the critical rejection of corrupting ideologies and of personal prejudices that rationalize sinful conduct. Self-righteousness, ego inertia, and social pressure can, however, combine to betray the baptized Christian into self-deception and lies.

Take Rita, for example. When she heard the new teacher at the Bible school was indoctrinating her children with theories about evolution, she raised a ruckus with the principal. She said she would not have her children's minds stuffed with pseudo-scientific garbage that contradicted the Word of God. She made enough of a stink to get the man transferred. In the meantime, her husband was using his connections on the church school board to get the "heretic" blackballed.

Resistance to Moral Conversion

The spontaneous egocentrism of the human psyche can also motivate immoral, selfish conduct in the baptized: acts of deceit; violations of legal, commutative, or distributive justice; sins of omission; spiteful, destructive behavior. Needless to say, all such lapses of conscience point to the absence of ongoing moral conversion.

Take George, for instance. He knew that the gas tank on his company's newest model in sports cars was positioned in such a way that it would explode easily in a serious collision. When, however, an analysis showed that redesigning the car would cost a lot more than the company would spend on the lawsuits brought by the accident victims or their families, he approved the design for manufacture.

Resistance to Socio-Political Conversion

The same spontaneous egocentrism resists the obedience of faith and ongoing sanctification in the name and image of Jesus. The gospel demands the willingness to die to everything that does not lead to union with God. Anxiety, however, betrays the baptized into finding their security in the things of this world: in wealth, honor, and prestige. Fear of the Cross betrays the Christian conscience into sinful compromises. Love of convenience and personal luxury render believers insensitive to the needs of the poor and leave them reluctant to identify with them. Resentment hardens the heart in embittered unforgiving hatred of persons and groups. Social pressure lulls the baptized into passive acquiescence in class distinctions. Shallow ritualism supplants authentic Christian worship.

Take Walter, for example. He had made a bundle building atomic weapons for the government. He thought himself a loyal Catholic, but then he read about *The Challenge of Peace* and the bishops' pastoral on the economy. The next time he saw the archbishop he told him that the Church was making a bad mistake meddling in politics and economics and ought to stick to preaching the gospel. He also canceled his contribution to the archdiocesan drive.

We have been considering the forces of antichrist that betray the baptized into sin and religious hypocrisy. The time has come to reflect on Jesus' proclamation of divine forgiveness and on the ways in which the paschal mystery extends the experience of divine forgiveness to those who believe.

2. Divine Forgiveness. In the New Testament the revelation of divine forgiveness advances in two stages. Jesus first proclaims the Father's desire to forgive sinners. He then effects that forgiveness by his atoning death and glorification and by the mission of the sanctifying Breath of God.

a. Jesus' Ministry of Forgiveness. The Gospels tell us that Jesus preferred the company of sinners because he had come especially for them, to summon them to repentance and reconciliation with God (Mark 2:17). The renunciation of sin and acceptance of God's reign certainly lay at the heart of his message (Mark 1:15). Jesus, however, seemed to prefer the company of public sinners for other reasons as well: He found them more open to his message than smug, self-righteous hypocrites (Mark 3:29; Luke 18:9-14).

Jesus, Sin, and Divine Forgiveness

In the face of sin Jesus exhibited no moral compromise. He insisted that the sinful heart defiles its possessor (Mark 7:21ff.). His disciples must cultivate a personal justice that transforms them more totally than the superficial legalism practiced by the Pharisees (Matt 5:20).

Jesus abhorred sin, but he proclaimed ceaselessly God's compassion for the sinner. He taught as well that one can never earn divine forgiveness; it comes to us as pure gift. In the parable of the two sons, both err in imagining that they can earn the father's love. Instead that love reaches out to them whether they commit acts of sinful profligacy or lapse into works righteousness. In the same way God's love reaches out to each of us (Luke 15:11-32). Jesus also required his disciples to forgive one another with the same relentlessness as that with which God forgives them (Matt 18:22; 5:43-48).

Jesus also linked his proclamation of divine forgiveness to his ministry of healing. The obedience of faith that he demanded heals the paralysis of sin and restores fullness of life (Mark 2:1-12; Matt 9:1-8; Luke 5:17-26).

b. The Victory over Sin. Jesus' proclamation of the kingdom brought him into open conflict with the forces of sin. The Gospels of Mark and of John insist most explicitly on this facet of his ministry, but all the Gospels make the point clearly. Jesus encountered personally the intransigence of sin: a hardness of heart in others that resisted repentance and refused the divine forgiveness he has come to proclaim (John 3:19-20; 9:40). That same religious intransigence bred murderous hatred of his person and ministry in the hearts of his adversaries (Mark 3:6; Matt 12:14; John 8:39-47; 11:45-54).

The Conflict with Sin

In his passion, then, Jesus encountered the naked power of sin embodied in the religious and political establishments of his day. Together they conspired with the treachery of Judas to nail the innocent Son of God to the cross. Confronted by that same power, most of his disciples abandoned him in cowardice and dismay. Jesus for his part atoned for sin in his passion by suffering its consequences without retaliating in kind. Instead he prayed for his persecutors and extended to the good thief the promise of paradise (Luke 23:33-34; 39-43).

The Victory over Sin

Jesus' resurrection sanctions his message and ministry with divine authority and reveals that the power of God encompasses and transcends the sinful powers that conspired to destroy him. Moreover, the risen Christ triumphs over the sinfulness of his own disciples by sending them in their weakness and vascillation the sanctifying Breath of God to effect in them repentance and the obedience of faith. The sanctification she inspires conforms them to his image and emboldens them to confront fearlessly the principalities and powers that crucified the Lord of Life (Acts 2:42-47; 4:1-31).

We have so far reflected on the forces that betray the baptized into sin and on the historical revelation of divine forgiveness in

Christ. In the section that follows we shall examine the development of the ritual that mediates God's forgiveness to Christian backsliders.

3. The Development of the Christian Rite of Reconciliation. The first Christians believed that by baptism they had died to sin and risen to new life in the power of God's Holy Breath (Rom 8:1-39). Nevertheless, they also had to deal pastorally with serious backsliders, with those whose conduct so contradicted the obedience of faith as to amount to a renunciation of the gospel. They did so by adapting to Christian purposes the Jewish practice of expelling sinners and heretics from the synagogue. The apostolic Church excommunicated serious backsliders and barred them from active participation in Eucharistic worship.

Binding and Loosing in the Apostolic Church

The First Letter to the Corinthians reveals the pastoral purpose of Christian excommunication: it sought to bring stubborn sinners to their senses so that they could be reconciled once again to God and readmitted to Eucharistic Communion. First Corinthians also gives some indication of the kinds of sins the first Christians regarded as worthy of excommunication: serious sexual immorality, usury and swindle (in other words, the serious economic exploitation of others), and idolatry (1 Cor 5:9-13). The Johannine tradition characterized sins that merit excommunication as "deadly" (1 John 5:16).

In excommunicating backsliders from the community and in reconciling them after verifiable signs of repentance, the apostles exercised the power of binding and loosing that Jesus had conferred on the Twelve in constituting them judges in the new Israel. Since the Church constitutes a liberating realm of divine grace, those excluded from it were considered bound since they had forfeited the liberty of living as daughters and sons of God in Jesus' image. They were loosed, or liberated from slavery to sin, when they repented and were reincorporated into the Eucharistic community (Matt 16:19; 18:15-18).

The Emergence of Ritual Reconciliation

We cannot say at this historical distance whether the apostolic Church made use of formal rituals of excommunication and reconciliation. Local churches seem to have developed their own rites of reconciliation, but by the third century the readmission of backsliders to Eucharistic Communion had developed rituals that parallelled the catechumenate. Readmission into the Church after serious sin had come to be regarded as a "second and more laborious baptism." It made sense, therefore, that the process of reconciliation parallel in some sense the rites of initiation.

The ritual reconciliation of backsliders was preceded by a period of preparation analogous to the catechumenate. Unlike the catechumens, however, backsliders were expected to perform acts of penitence that gave evidence of the sincerity of their return to gospel living. Not uncommonly, the rite of reconciliation consisted in the bishop's imposing hands and invoking the Holy Breath on the penitent in a manner reminiscent of the second moment in the rite of initiation, but the reconciled sinners did not undergo a second rite of initiation. Rather, the rite of reconciliation itself restored participation in the sanctifying, gift-giving Breath of Christ that deadly sin had forfeited.

The Struggle with Rigorism

During the first three centuries backsliders could not expect the luxury of frequent reconciliation. We find some evidence that initially straying Christians could anticipate at most only a single opportunity for ritual reincorporation into the Church after apostasy or serious sin (Hermas, *The Shepherd,* Mandate 4, 1). Rigorists regarded apostasy, adultery, murder, and idolatry as "unforgiveable sins" and sought to exclude those who committed them from any possibility of ever being readmitted to Eucharistic Communion. The cult of the martyrs, however, attenuated somewhat the rigors of early penitential practice. "Letters of peace" written by Christian martyrs prior to their execution in which they promised to pray for this or that backslider facilitated the process of readmission into the Church after serious sin.

Gradually, Church leaders relaxed somewhat the severity of the Church's penitential discipline; more sinners were admitted to the rite of reconciliation, even though they could be required to perform as much as thirty years of penance prior to readmission to the Eucharistic banquet. The severity of discipline differed somewhat from one region to the next. As the rigorists lost ground, however, theologians came to perceive public penance as an assured prelude to forgiveness and public reconciliation (Athanasius, *On the Gospel of Luke,* 19; Ambrose of Milan, *On Penitence,* I, 8; John Chrysostom, *On the Priesthood,* III, 5). After the fourth century, priests as well as bishops functioned as ordinary ministers of the rite of reconciliation.

Churches in Asia Minor developed ritual stages of readmission to Eucharistic Communion. "Weepers" remained outside the church during the Eucharistic celebration and besought Christians in good standing to pray for them. "Hearers" stood in the rear of the church during the Liturgy of the Word. "Kneelers" received the bishop's blessing and were dismissed before the Eucharistic liturgy began. "Standers" could remain for the entire Eucharist but could not receive Eucharistic Communion.

The Emergence of Auricular Confession

During the early Middle Ages, the Irish Church revolutionized the rite of reconciliation. Isolated from the rest of Christian Europe, the monks of Ireland developed their own penitential discipline. They introduced the practice of private auricular confession. They allowed frequent confession and assigned penances to be performed after absolution instead of requiring them as a condition for absolution. Instead of absolving penitents by imposing hands in the manner of bishops, the Irish monks absolved with a simple blessing.

In the sixth century they exported this practice to Europe together with the penitentiaries they had developed for proportioning assigned penances to the gravity of different sins. Predictably, these innovations drew initial condemnation from traditionalists. More conventional Church leaders felt that the easy access to absolution that the Irish monks offered sinners cheapened the grace that the older penitential discipline conferred.

Abuses developed around the new penitential practice. Sometimes poorly educated priests dispensed absolution far too liberally and automatically. Eventually, however, despite several episcopal attempts to defend the older, more rigorous discipline, the popularity of auricular confession won out. After the eighth century bishops and canonists contented themselves with regulating the practice of auricular confession canonically.

The Impact of Auricular Confession

The eventual official acceptance of private, auricular confession supplied the rite of reconciliation with a new purpose. During the patristic era it had served the exclusive purpose of readmitting excommunicated Christians to Eucharistic Communion. The ready access to ritual reconciliation that the practice of auricular confession provided now made possible confessions of devotion. One need not have committed a sin worthy of excommunication in order to receive the sacrament. Instead, Christians began to use the rite of reconciliation as a way of nurturing ongoing conversion and spiritual growth.

To this day the rite continues to perform both functions in the life of the Church. Moreover, official acceptance of auricular confession effected something like a division of labor in the administration of the rite of reconciliation. Priests administered the rite with much greater frequency than bishops, who now chiefly absolved those formally excommunicated from the Church.

Nevertheless, the Christian community also lost something in turning from its earlier penitential discipline to private, auricular confession. The performance of public penance prior to reacceptance into Eucharistic Communion together with the rituals that had accompanied it had communicated vividly both to lapsed Christians and to the Church as a whole the social, ecclesial dimensions of sin and reconciliation. Auricular confession, by contrast, dispensed with shared, public penance and sought above all to nurture personal repentance and ongoing conversion.

By the twelfth century, except for canonical legislation regulating formal excommunication, the elaborate process of reconciliation developed during the patristic era had been replaced for all practical purposes by the scholastic distinction between mortal and venial sin. Mortal sins excluded one from access to Eucharistic Communion and required sacramental absolution before penitents could receive the body and blood of Christ. Venial sins did not require confession prior to Eucharistic Communion but could receive absolution in confessions of devotion.

Other theological distinctions emerged to fit the new penitential discipline. In auricular confession, acts of penitence followed sacramental absolution. This occasioned the scholastic distinction between the temporal and eternal punishment due to sin. Sacramental absolution took away the eternal punishment due to sin: in other words, it saved serious sinners from damnation for their misdeeds; but absolution did not take away the temporal punishment due to sin, for absolved sinners had still to perform acts of penance required in atonement for their sins. Moreover, those who failed to expiate their sins fully in this life would do so in purgatory.

The Debate over Sacramentality

As we shall see, the Protestant reformers rejected the sacramentality of ritual reconciliation. As a consequence, it disappeared as an independent ritual in both the Lutheran and Calvinist traditions. The Council of Trent, of course, defended the sacramentality of ritual reconciliation; but in reforming this sacrament Trent focused on the individual sinner and on the proper dispositions he or she needed to bring to the sacrament. In post-Tridentine Catholicism the structure of the ritual remained unchanged until the Second Vatican Council. The newly revised rite absolves in the vernacular, includes Scripture readings, encourages the communal celebration of reconciliation, and allows for either anonymous or face-to-face confession. We shall reflect on the significance of the new rite later.

As in the case of the other sacraments, the development of the rite of reconciliation helps put the controversies about this ritual into historical perspective. To these controversies we turn in the section that follows.

4. Issues in the Development of the Rite of Reconciliation. As we have seen, during the patristic era, rigorists opposed the gradual relaxation of Church discipline. Nevertheless, official Church leaders moved gradually to mitigate the harshness of the Christian community's earliest penitential practices. Indeed, one can only imagine how flinty, patristic rigorists like Novatian and Montanus would have reacted to the laxity of auricular confession.

Over the centuries, three sets of issues have exercised theologians of this sacrament. First, medieval theologians disagreed about the way in which this ritual forgives sins. Second, during the Reformation, the Protestant reformers attacked the practice of auricular confession and denied its sacramentality. They also differed in other ways from the Council of Trent in their interpretation of its significance. Third, within official Catholic teaching we discover significant contrasts between the way in which the Council of Trent treated this sacrament and its handling in the documents of Vatican II. Let us reflect on each of these speculative developments in turn.

a. How Does Reconciliation Effect Forgiveness? The eleventh century produced no treatises on the rite of reconciliation; but twelfth century theologians made it the subject of heated debate.

The Acts of the Penitant

Peter Abelard taught that reconciliation with God requires penance, confession, and satisfaction (*Ethica,* 17). Contrition, he held, removes sin from the heart; for God forgives the sinner the moment he or she turns from sin in genuine sorrow. Ritual confession simply communicates to the repentant sinner in a sensible way the fact that divine forgiveness has occurred. The ritual also helps the penitent deal with the punishment due to sin by imposing a penance (*On the Letter to the Romans,* L II, p. 211).

Peter Lombard defended a similar position. He included the rite of reconciliation in the canon of the sacraments. In his discussion of the forgiveness of sin he underscored the importance of the acts of the penitent: personal remorse for sin and the determination not to sin again. He also taught that God and the Church forgive sins differently. God alone forgives and retains sins, for he alone removes sin's stain from the soul and remits the eternal punishment that serious sin entails. The Church for its part imposes penances on sinners and readmits serious sinners to sacramental communion. Sacramental absolution does not, then, forgive sin as such. Instead it declares to the penitent the fact of God's forgiveness (Peter Lombard, *Sentences,* IV, d.18, c.6).

The Efficacy of Absolution

Hugh and Richard of St. Victor found fault with such a muted account of the efficacy of sacramental absolution. They recognized the need for lapsed Christians to repent of their sins, but they both insisted that ritual absolution does more than assure penitents that God has forgiven them. Rather absolution invokes the divine authority given by Christ to his apostles either to forgive or retain sins. God therefore acts through sacramental absolution to forgive the sins of repentant Christians (Hugh of St. Victor, *De Sacramentis,* II, xiv, 8; Richard of St. Victor, *De Potestate Ligandi et Solvendi,* XII–XVIII).

Despite the protests of the Victorine theologians, however, by the end of the twelfth century theological opinion had swung behind Abelard and the Lombard, a shift partly motivated, no doubt, by the popularity of the Lombard's *Sentences* as a theological text.

The Thomistic Compromise

During the thirteenth century Thomas Aquinas reconciled the two positions by nuancing the position taken by the Victorines. He argued that the acts of the penitent—sorrow, the confession of one's sins, and appropriate acts of penitence—provided the sacrament with its matter. The absolution provided the form, for it gave formal and official expression to the divine forgiveness that the sacrament effects. In other words, both the acts of the penitent and the rite of absolution contribute something essential to the sacrament. The penitent renounces sin, and God acts through his minister to forgive the sin renounced.

Reconciliation in the Late Middle Ages

In the fourteenth century John Duns Scotus portrayed ritual absolution as a definitive judgment that remits the guilt of penitents (*Oxford Commentary,* IV, d. xiv, q. 4). Moreover, in the twilight of the Middle Ages, theologians tended to place so much stress on the efficacy of sacramental absolution that they created the misleading impression that it eliminated sin automatically. Both the Protestant reformers and the Council of Trent would react negatively to such legalism.

In the fifteenth century, the Council of Florence included the rite of reconciliation in the canon of the sacraments. This council also approved a Thomistic theology of the sacrament, describing the acts of the penitent as the ritual's matter and absolution as its form. Both contribute something essential to the sacrament. Together they effect the forgiveness of sin (DS 1323).

We shall return to these questions in reflecting on the significance of the revised ritual of reconciliation. Before doing so, however, let us examine some of the other controversies that this sacrament has occasioned.

b. Is Reconciliation a Sacrament? In the sixteenth century Martin Luther reacted negatively to a number of the abuses that had come to surround the medieval rite of reconciliation. He encouraged private confession. His position on the use of the power to bind and loose in ritual absolution shifted in the course of his life but tended to resemble that of Peter Lombard. He believed that repentant trust in the forgiveness of God forgives sin. The word of absolution brings to sinners the assurance of divine forgiveness. If they believe that word they are absolved (Luther, *The Sacrament of Penance* 1-20).

Luther also condemned any approach to confession that smacked of works righteousness: sinners do not earn the forgiveness of God by their acts of penitence. Rather, the redemptive death of Christ, which forgave sin once and for all, effects in the penitent the "grace of forgiveness," which consists in a sense of peace and joy born of faith in God's saving mercy. (Catholic theology by contrast interpreted the "grace of forgiveness" as a real cleansing of the soul from its former sin.) Luther, moreover, denied that only priests can absolve from sin and questioned the right of bishops to reserve particular sins to themselves for absolution. (Luther, *Works,* 14:81-91; 36:84-86).

While Luther favored the practice of confession, he could find no scriptural justification for it (Luther, *Works,* 36:86). Because he did not require his followers to submit their sins to ritual absolution, this sacrament was eventually replaced in the Lutheran church by a general confession of sins at the beginning of Sunday worship.

Calvin on Reconciliation

Calvin denied the sacramentality of auricular confession. He held that the New Testament presents only baptism as effecting the forgiveness of sins (Calvin, *Institutes,* IV, 19, 16). He knew the Fathers of the Church well enough to realize that the patristic Church had excommunicated backsliders and then readmitted them to Eucharistic Communion through rites of reconciliation, but he saw little resemblance between patristic practice and the auricular confession of his day. Indeed, Reformation debates about the sacraments took place largely in ignorance of the historical evolution of Christian ritual. Like Luther, Calvin believed that Christians should feel free to unburden themselves of guilt by confessing their sins to one another; but he denied the need for officially absolving the baptized (*Ibid.,* III, 4, 12).

Anglican Reconciliation

The Anglican tradition at first took a more moderate stand on the sacrament of reconciliation than either Luther or Calvin. It recognized in the rite of reconciliation a sacrament of the Church rather than one instituted by Christ. After the seventeenth century, however, the practice of private confession declined in the Church of England, although it still functions in contemporary Anglican piety.

The Tridentine Response

The Council of Trent responded to the Protestant challenge with a forthright defense of the sacramentality of auricular confession. It refused to confine the sacramental forgiveness of sins to baptism alone and traced the institution of the rite of reconciliation to the words of the risen Christ in John 20:22-23: "Whose sins you shall forgive, they are forgiven them; whose sins you shall retain they are retained" (DS 1701–1703).

Like the Protestant reformers, however, Trent rejected the legalism that characterized a late medieval theology of the rite of reconciliation and, like the Council of Florence, confirmed instead the doctrine of Aquinas. Trent held that both the acts of penitent and the absolution of the minister contribute something essential to the sacrament (DS 1671–1672).

Trent devoted considerable attention to the contrition required of penitents who seek absolution, but the council failed to develop an adequate theology of conversion. As a consequence, in describing the contrition of the baptized it focused rhetorically on the heinousness of sin (DS 1669, 1672, 1676).

Trent also treated the rite of reconciliation itself somewhat narrowly by portraying it primarily as a judicial act: in it the minister of the sacrament functions as an ecclesiastical judge who passes judgment on the guilt of penitents and on the sincerity of their repentance. Penitents must confess all mortal sins by number and species. They must perform the penance imposed by the minister. Tridentine theology insisted as well that in absolving sinners, the minister exercises the power to bind and loose that Jesus gave to his apostles (DS 1679–1693, 1706–1711).

Trent also defended the legitimacy of penitents performing acts that seek to satisfy for their past misdeeds. Such acts, the council held, in no way derogated from the satisfaction for sin accomplished by Jesus' atoning death (DS 1712–1715).

We shall return to the question of sacramentality later. Before we do so, however, we need to examine the ways in which a Catholic understanding of this ritual has evolved since the sixteenth century.

c. Contemporary Issues in the Theology of Reconciliation. As we have seen, Reformation debates about the sacraments largely ignored the historical evolution of Church ritual. Moreover, the historical research into the rite of reconciliation that preceded Vatican II uncovered some important oversights in Trent's handling of this sacrament. As a consequence, the theology of ritual reconciliation promulgated by the Second Vatican Council contrasts notably with Tridentine teaching on this subject.

The Council of Trent, as we have seen, concerned itself primarily with the defense and reform of auricular confession. It therefore focused somewhat narrowly on the individual penitent and portrayed the absolving minister as an ecclesiastical judge of the penitent's personal worthiness to receive absolution. Vatican II, by contrast, insisted on reconciliation as an ecclesial act that undoes both the personal and the social consequences of sin.

Restoring the Ecclesial Dimensions of Reconciliation

This new insistence on the social dimensions of reconciliation in the Church's conciliar teaching echoed the concerns of the liturgical movement, whose reforms Vatican II sanctioned. Those who pushed for liturgical reform prior to the Second Vatican Council had studied the history of Christian ritual and had discovered the strong emphasis on the communal dimensions of worship present in the first centuries of the Christian era. They criticized the individualism that had come to characterize twentieth-century sacramental devotion. They called for greater communal participation in sacramental worship and for a conscious retrieval of its ecclesial dimensions.

Vatican II insisted that human sin has ecclesial as well as personal consequences. It affects not only the sinner's personal relationship with God but inflicts a wound on the Christian community as well. It gives scandal and sullies the Church's collective witness to the gospel (*Lumen gentium,* 11). As a consequence, baptized sinners need reconciliation not only with God but with the Christian community as well (*Lumen gentium,* 11, *Presbyterorum Ordinis,* 5). Moreover, in addition to reconciling baptized sinners to God and to the Church, the rite of reconciliation performs another function: it nurtures ongoing repentance and conversion in the baptized (*Christus Dominus,* 30).

The liturgical reforms of Vatican II sought to recover a sense of the communal dimensions of sin and reconciliation that the Church's early penitential practice vividly communicated. The council did not, however, repudiate the practice of auricular confession. Instead, postconciliar liturgical reforms encouraged communal penance services that supplement individual confessions. These services seek to communicate to the faithful that the rite of reconciliation not only rectifies the relationship of baptized, repentant sinners to God but also restores the integrity of the Christian community's shared life and collective witness to Christ that sin destroys (Roman Catholic Rite of Penance, 5; hereafter this ritual will be abbreviated RCRP).

We have examined some of the major controversies that have surrounded the rite of reconciliation. In the section that follows we shall try to understand the structure and significance of the ritual itself.

5. The Significance of Sacramental Reconciliation. Our survey of the theological debate about this rite has raised a number of questions that we shall attempt to answer. We shall first examine the structure and significance of the revised ritual itself and then reflect on its sacramentality.

a. The Structure and Significance of the Revised Rite. The revised rite of reconciliation advances in four stages.

The Dispositions of the Penitent

First, penitents need to experience contrition for any sins they have committed. Instead, however, of focusing narrowly on the personal renunciation of sin as the Council of Trent did, the revised rite of reconciliation calls lapsed Christians to a transforming experience of integral conversion before God.

The situation of the penitent differs from that of the catechumen. Catechumens seek to deepen an initial conversion as they prepare to commit themselves publicly to lifelong sanctification and mutual service of others in the Church of Jesus Christ. Penitents reaffirm the commitment made during Christian initiation after some significant lapse from grace. By rededicating lapsed Christians to gospel living, reconciliation advances the process of ongoing conversion.

A theology of conversion throws light on the dispositions that penitents need to bring to this sacrament. Penitents need to probe the affective, intellectual, and moral roots of sin in their lives. Christians measure the sinfulness of human acts and attitudes not merely against the Ten Commandments but also against Jesus' vision of the kingdom. Anything counts as sin that prevents one from endorsing that vision wholeheartedly and from growing in the quality of hope, faith, love, and service to which he summoned his followers. Penitents also need to understand the concupiscent forces in their environment that have led them to sin so that they can defend themselves against their influence in the future or eliminate them.

The Rite of Reconciliation

The rite of individual reconciliation itself begins with the confessor's welcoming the penitent. Together they read some appropriate passage from the Bible. The Scripture reading sets the tone for the second moment in the rite of reconciliation: the confession of sins.

In confessing their sins, penitents should open their hearts to their confessors, acknowledging candidly the motives and consequence of their sinful acts. The Church requires penitents to confess every serious sin they have committed, for serious sin bars one from Eucharistic Communion. Moreover, only the authority that originally imposed a formal excommunication can lift it. The absolution of such sins is then reserved to the bishop or to the pope.

This arrangement makes sense given present Church discipline. In using the rite of reconciliation, one renounces sin in the context of renewing publicly and officially one's sacramental covenant of initiation. It makes sense, therefore, that the one who celebrates the ritual have the authority to speak officially in the name of Christ and of the Church. Bishops and priests enjoy such authority in virtue of ordination.

The revised rite also requires, however, that the ordained should in fact possess the charisms that confessors need in order to administer this ritual effectively: discernment, a sound knowledge of sinful disorders, and an understanding of the means of remedying them. Confessors must also understand the movement of divine grace and the dynamics of initial and ongoing conversion. Conscious of their own weakness, confessors should welcome sinners with the readiness and compassion of Jesus and preserve the secrecy of the confessional absolutely (RCRP, 10).

In the third moment of reconciliation, penitents determine to amend their lives and to undo as far as possible the consequences of their sins. Together, penitent and confessor need to decide how best to counteract the impact of sin upon the penitent's own life and upon the lives of those against whom he or she has sinned.

The Meaning of Satisfaction for Sin

As we have seen, auricular confession reversed the order of penitential discipline in the Church. Instead of requiring penitential acts as proof of the sincerity of one's conversion before absolving penitents of sin, auricular confession assigned acts of penitence to be performed after absolution in "satisfaction for one's sins." How should one understand these acts of "satisfaction"?

Since God takes the initiative in forgiving us freely and gratuitously in Christ, acts of satisfaction in no way earn divine forgiveness, nor should they be undertaken in a spirit of self-hatred. Rather, one seeks to satisfy for one's sins by attempting as far as possible to undo their consequences in oneself, in the lives of others, and in human society.

We also need to purify the notion of satisfaction from any hint of divine vindictiveness. God takes no pleasure in human suffering, nor does he require it of us as a condition for forgiving us. If the paschal mystery discloses anything about God, it reveals the unconditioned character of God's will to forgive sinners. If God requires repentance as a condition for forgiveness, he does so because the unrepentant refuse to recognize their need to be forgiven and therefore cannot claim the reconciliation with God that he freely offers. Satisfaction for sin does not, then, mean paying a debt of suffering to an angry and vengeful God. Satisfaction means atonement, at-one-ment, reconciliation with a God who has loved us first, even in our sinfulness, and who bears the consequences of our sins freely in love and forgiveness. One satisfies for sins, then, by entering into the atonement of Christ, by forgiving oneself and others with Christlike love and by doing what lies in one's power to undo the consequences of sin.

More concretely, one satisfies for one's past sins by deepening in an ongoing personal conversion and by suffering without sinning the consequences of one's own and others' moral viciousness. One satisfies for sin by serving as God's instrument in opposing the forces of sin and concupiscence and in mitigating their impact on oneself and on others. One satisfies for one's own sins by mitigating the evil and suffering they cause insofar as it lies within one's power.

Sacramental Absolution

In the fourth and final stage of the rite of reconciliation, the confessor absolves the penitent's sins. Absolution reincorporates serious sinners into Eucharistic Communion and fosters ongoing conversion in those guilty of less grave offenses (RCRP, 5–6). Moreover, the rite of reconciliation undoes the sins of Christians and their consequences by treating them in the way that God does: by encompassing them with the atoning love of Christ. The Christian community suffers the sins of its members and, in imitation of its crucified Lord, refuses to counter sin with the sin of spite. Atoning love also endows the emptiness of sin with saving significance.

As we have seen, two councils of the Church, Florence and Trent, endorsed Thomas Aquinas's explanation of how this sacrament forgives sin, and correctly so. Aquinas saw that the rite of reconciliation forgives sin in two ways. The graced repentance of the Christian backslider restores the commitment to an integral fivefold conversion that serious sin withdraws and that minor sins undermine. At the same time, however, those who absolve fallen Christians publicly and officially from their sins speak with the authority of the risen Christ who sanctions efficaciously the divine forgiveness that they proclaim.

Absolution serves important human needs, as the following incident illustrates. Not long ago a Presbyterian friend of mine was lamenting the absence of the rite of reconciliation from his tradition. He and his wife had just divorced. As he looked back over the painful experience of separation, he regretted deeply many things he had said, done, or left undone. He had repented personally of the hurt and suffering he had helped to cause. He had experienced the forgiveness of other human beings; but he felt keenly the need for someone to assure him of God's forgiveness. His ritual tradition, however, lacked the means to minister to his needs.

As we have seen, humans need healing when confronted with the destructive consequences of personal acts of moral viciousness. For psychic healing to occur, the deflated human ego needs to experience from another some formal assurance of forgiveness in order to deal emotionally with the evil consequences of its destructive, inflated choices. The sinful Christian ego needs more. Specifically, it needs the assurance of both the divine and the human forgiveness that the rite of reconciliation mediates.

Moreover, personal repentance alone cannot undo the ecclesial consequences of sin. Public confession of postbaptismal sin and its official sacramental absolution accomplish that. In the case of serious sinners sacramental absolution reestablishes their original baptismal covenant with God by readmitting them to full Eucharistic Communion.

Absolution has other ecclesial consequences as well. As we have already seen in chapter six, the baptismal character confers the morally conditioned right to participate in the shared worship and life of the Church. The character of confirmation confers the morally conditioned right and duty to minister charismatically to others as a member of the Christian community. The serious sinner forfeits the exercise of both rights by failing to fulfill the moral conditions that their exercise presupposes. Absolution entitles one formerly excommunicated to exercise responsibly the rights that flow from two characters conferred by the rites of initiation.

The Efficacy of Absolution

In reflecting on the debates about the rite of reconciliation, we saw that Catholic theology speaks of the grace of forgiveness as a real change, as a cleansing from sin. Protestant theology speaks more experientially than metaphysically: it describes the grace of reconciliation as the experience of peace and joy that comes with claiming the forgiveness of Christ. Can one reconcile these two understandings of forgiveness?

In the theology of grace developed in these pages, one need not choose between an experiential and a real change. Nor can one adequately understand experience as a purely subjective event. Every experience has both personal and social dimensions. Moreover, every real change reshapes experience in some way; and every new experience embodies a new reality.

The ritual decision made under grace to repent of one's sinfulness and recommit oneself to fully converted gospel living effects a real personal change in the penitent. Absolution changes one further by mediating the efficacious forgiveness of Christ and by reincorporating one into the family of God. By restoring one to Eucharistic Communion, it draws one anew into the paschal mystery. It reconsecrates one to ongoing growth in hope, faith, and love and to the charismatic service of others in Jesus' name and image. In all these ways the rite changes one both really and experientially.

The Communal Celebration of Reconciliation

The ritual of reconciliation closes with praise to God for his mercy and with the dismissal of the penitent.

The communal celebration of the rite of reconciliation has roughly the same structural pattern as the reconciliation of individuals.[9] Communal celebration, however, seeks to evoke a shared

9. Communal reconciliation begins with a suitable hymn and with the celebrant's greeting to the community. A Liturgy of the Word follows which consists of scriptural readings, responses to the readings, and a homily in which the celebrant exhorts those present to examine their consciences while reminding them both of the mercy of God and of the need to repent sincerely of all sin. The homily should also reflect on the social character of sin: how it sullies the Church's witness and ministry and corrupts secular society. Finally, the homilist should remind the faithful that true repentance requires one to seek as far as possible to undo the consequences of one's sins. Then, the penitents confess their

sense of the ecclesial dimensions of reconciliation. The sins of the baptized call into question the sincerity of the Church's shared witness to Christ. They betray the Church's common mission. They harm those whom God loves and would have us love.

Moreover, the ritual recovery of the ecclesial dimensions of the rite of reconciliation points to a broader fact: the Church's total ministry of reconciliation extends far beyond the celebration of ritual reconciliation itself. That ministry involves every Christian. As committed peacemakers, the disciples of Jesus must not only forgive their enemies; but they must also live reconciled to one another. As a consequence, the rite of reconciliation derives its full sacramental significance from the Church's total ministry of reconciliation; for in the last analysis we experience reconciliation to God most profoundly through reconciliation to a community of reconcilers.

Catholics who return to the sacraments after a prolonged period of alienation from the Church probably have pastoral needs that a perfunctory absolution alone will not meet. Pastoral experimentation in this country suggests that such individuals profit from a more prolonged process of reconciliation which could occur appropriately during Lent. In the course of such a process penitents benefit from theological updating; but more importantly, with the help of other penitents and of the pastoral team that ministers to them those seeking reconciliation to the Church come to terms not only with their need for forgiveness but also with their need to forgive the past hurts that alienated them from the Church. Sharing one's story with others who also seek reconciliation can facilitate the healing needed. When such an extended process of reconciliation occurs during Lent, the washing of the feet on Holy Thursday provides an appropriate liturgical context for a ceremony of public readmission into Eucharistic Communion.

In the course of reflecting on the significance of the rite of reconciliation, we have attempted to respond to some of the issues that debate about this sacrament has raised. Disagreement over the sacramentality of this ritual has particularly divided Catholic and Protestant theologians. To this issue we turn in the section that follows.

---

sins and express their repentance, sorrow, and commitment to amend their lives. After determining with the penitent an appropriate way to satisfy for the specific wrong he or she has done, the celebrant pronounces the absolution. When appropriate, he may give general absolution. The rite concludes with a prayer of praise to God for his mercy and with the dismissal of the penitents (RCRP, 15–35).

b. The Sacramentality of the Rite of Reconciliation. The rite of reconciliation restores the covenant of grace that the rites of initiation sealed. It therefore qualifies as an act of new covenant worship distinct in purpose from the rites of initiation, for it reconciles the lapsed rather than incorporates neophytes for the first time. Because reconciling lapsed Christians publicly and officially to God and to the Church engages the common good of the Christian community as a whole, only those whom the Church has appointed to do so may absolve in God's name from sin.

The rite of reconciliation derives directly from the ministry of Jesus. It derives ultimately from his proclamation of God's will to forgive repentant sinners and from his appointment of the Twelve as judges in the new Israel. It derives proximately from the paschal mystery; for his death, his resurrection; and his mission of the divine Mother to sanctify his followers and to build them up charismatically into a prophetic community transformed the judicial authority of his apostles into the authority to bind and loose, to admit people into the Church or to exclude them from participation in the Eucharistic banquet.

The New Testament narrates all these developments. It makes no sense, therefore, to speak of ritual reconciliation as a sacrament of the Church rather than of Christ. The ritual roots itself ultimately in the ministry of Jesus even though the Church gave reconciliation its present ritual shape, just as it did to all the other sacraments, including baptism and Eucharist.

The rites of initiation draw one into the paschal mystery by inaugurating the believer's graced transformation in the image of the risen Christ. The rite of reconciliation draws serious sinners into the paschal mystery by sealing their repentant renunciation of sin after a fall from grace. Reconciliation also deepens the initial conversion of those guilty of minor offenses and so deepens their participation in the death and resurrection of the Lord. Through repentance and reconciliation backsliders die anew to sin and reopen their hearts to receive the life-giving Breath of the risen Christ.

In renouncing postbaptismal sin, Christians profess their faith publicly and officially in the Lordship of Jesus, in the Father he proclaimed, and in the sanctifying, gift-giving Breath they send into the world. They submit their lives anew to the obedience of faith by following the divine Mother's guidance in living as a child of the Father in Jesus' image. Moreover, they do so in the hope that by allowing the divine Mother to conform them to him, they will also share in his resurrection.

Finally, the rite of reconciliation effects the grace it signifies—namely, the forgiveness of postbaptismal sin—to the extent that it expresses faith in the triune God and deepens that faith. The rite expresses not only personal faith in the forgiveness of God but also the Church's shared belief in its divine mission to proclaim that forgiveness sacramentally to sinners.

We may, then, conclude that the rite of reconciliation reproduces all the fundamental traits of a ritual sacrament.

The Social Context of Reconciliation

The rite itself, however, does not exhaust the graced significance of reconciliation; for reconciliation comes to full sacramental expression in the graced transformation of Christian lives. The rite celebrates the mutual forgiveness of Christians. Hence, the living reality of that forgiveness endows the rite of reconciliation with its full sacramentality.

In the course of this chapter, we have reflected on the history and significance of only one of the sacraments of healing: the rite of reconciliation. In the chapter that follows we shall consider a second rite of healing: the anointing of the sick. As we shall see, it too seeks to effect the ongoing conversion of baptized Christians.

CHAPTER VI

The Rite of Anointing

In the last chapter we considered the first of the Church's rituals of healing. In this chapter we shall ponder the second: the rite of anointing. Our considerations divide into five parts.

The first part reflects briefly on the relationship between sickness and conversion. That reflection will provide an experiential context for understanding the Christian ministry of faith healing. The second part of our argument provides a biblical background for understanding Christian ministry to the sick. In it we examine Jesus' ministry of faith healing and its prolongation in the apostolic Church. The third stage of our argument traces the historical development of the rite of anointing itself. That history helps contextualize the theological debates which this ritual has occasioned. In the fourth part of this chapter we will survey the three principal controversies that surround this sacrament. Finally, we will reflect on the significance of the revised rite of anointing and of its place within the healing ministry of the Church as a whole. In the course of doing so, we shall attempt to resolve the unresolved theological questions concerning Christian ministry to the sick.

1. Illness and Conversion. People seem to have an almost endless capacity for projecting human vindictiveness onto God. As a consequence, when illness strikes, not infrequently the afflicted fallaciously perceives the disease as a divine punishment. As we have already seen, however, the ministry, death, and glorification of Jesus gives the lie to the belief that God harbors vindictive enmity toward sinners. Those same events reveal that God desires our healing and salvation, not our misery.

The Experience of Illness

All organic life sickens and dies. Nevertheless, the human experience of sickness, even the experience of a fatal illness, when it transpires in faith, can itself become a source of healing and of life. That happens when illness occasions conversion.

Sickness does more than debilitate us physically. It engages us as persons. Illness in any form reminds us of the fragility and vulnerability of human life. Life-threatening illnesses tend in addition to raise the religious question: in the face of possible death, one can hardly avoid wondering about the ultimate purpose of human existence.

All serious illness, however, raises questions about the quality and therefore ultimately about the purpose of life. Diseases of the nervous system leave one literally paralyzed. Every debilitating disease, however, effects a kind of paralysis. The experience of physical diminishment and the prospect either of its prolongation or of one's own eventual demise forces reflection on the use one has made of the gift of life heretofore.

Some illnesses have identifiable physical causes. Microbes invade our bodies and impair vital functions. Other forms of illness, however, spring from emotional disorder. Depression, neurosis, and psychosis can have physical side effects. Moreover, even biologically caused diseases affect one emotionally; and emotional attitudes can either promote or hinder convalescence.

Illness and Conversion

The emotional impact of illness links sickness to conversion, for their cure forces initial and ongoing affective conversion. Illness forces one to face one's human limitations and mortality. As a consequence, the sick often have to confront themselves emotionally in new and potentially healing ways. The depressions that sometime accompany a disease or that follow upon total anesthesia may surface deep-seated feelings of resentment, anxiety, or self-hatred very much in need of healing.

Any illness can, moreover, cause or occasion an experience of either initial or ongoing religious conversion. Ignatius of Loyola traced his own initial conversion to idle fantasies that occurred during a period of prolonged convalescence. Similarly, diseases that threaten life itself or the quality of life challenge one to a deeper faith and trust in God. They invite the Christian to enter personally into the passion of Christ.

Illness can also bring its own moral crises as well. Invalids, for example, need to resist the temptation to lapse into destructive attitudes of resentment and counterdependency toward those who care for them.

Illness can even bring new intellectual insights into the meaning and purpose of human life and existence. Suffering can teach a kind of compassionate wisdom. It can give new insight into the human condition. I have known more than one workaholic who discovered through the inactivity forced by illness the importance and value of interpersonal relationships.

Sickness can, then, shape character and advance the process of personal conversion. When it does so, physical diminishment occasions responsible liberation and new life.

Moreover, some diseases have important social consequences. Some forms of illness ostracize one socially. A leprosarium stands in Carville, Louisiana, not because the climate of that state advances treatment of the disease (it does not) but because at the time of the hospital's construction only the state of Louisiana was willing to allow lepers treatment within its borders. Indeed, any illness that strikes terror into the human heart transforms the sick into social pariahs, as some AIDS victims have discovered.

How, then, does the gospel respond to the human experience of sickness?

2. Jesus' Ministry of Healing. Jesus certainly engaged in a ministry of faith healing. All four evangelists describe that ministry but do so in ways that emphasize different dimensions of its significance for the postresurrection Church.

Exorcism in Mark

Mark, for example, portrays Jesus' healing ministry as an integral part of his eschatological conflict with the powers of evil. Mark's Jesus inaugurates his healings with an exorcism. Mark locates the exorcism at the very beginning of Jesus' public ministry. Jesus confronts a demoniac in a synagogue in Capernaum, silences the demon who proclaims him Messiah, and with a simple command drives the devil from the demoniac's body. The event underscores the pneumatic authority that inspires Jesus' mission and calls attention to the novelty of his doctrine.

In describing the exorcism Mark portrays two forces in conflict: 1) the Holy Breath who has just descended on Jesus at the moment of his baptism in order to inaugurate the last age of salvation and 2) the forces of evil personified in the demon Jesus casts out. The baptismal Breath had first driven Jesus into the desert in order to confront the demonic forces of evil (Mark 1:9-13). She also inspires Jesus' new religious vision and endows his proclamation of the kingdom with authority. Now she empowers him to vanquish the devil with a simple command. Moreover, Jesus rebukes the departing demon for revealing his messianic identity (Mark 1:21-28).

Mark punctuates his account of Jesus' ministry of healing with other references to demonic conflict. As in his account of Jesus' first exorcism, Mark describes how the demons seek to betray Jesus' messianic secret, a literary device that the evangelist uses to remind the reader of that first miracle and of the eschatological conflict it inaugurated (Mark 1:32-34; 3:10-12; 5:1-20; 9:14-29).

In Mark's Gospel, perhaps the most dramatic confrontation between Jesus and the demonic powers that enslave humans occurs in the cure of the Gerasene demoniac. This exorcism follows Jesus' calming of a storm, a miracle that recalls the victory of God's creative Word over the powers of chaos at the dawn of creation (Mark 4:35-41; Gen 1:1-2). Jesus casts the dem is tormenting the demoniac into a herd of swine, and they rush headlong into the very waters whose chaos Jesus has just tamed by the naked power of his own Word. Clearly, the divine creative authority residing in Jesus empowers him not only to triumph over the devil but to do so decisively (Mark 5:1-20).

Sin and Healing in Mark

In Mark, moreover, Jesus' ministry of healing quickly brings him into conflict with human sinfulness as well. When Jesus heals a man with a withered hand on the Sabbath, he so enrages the Pharisees who observe the miracle and regard it as a violation of the Sabbath rest that they immediately begin to plot with the Herodians to accomplish Jesus' murder (Mark 3:1-6). The incident clearly foreshadows Jesus' crucifixion. Moreover, in their enduring hardness of heart, Jesus' enemies will eventually sin against the Holy Breath by attributing his exorcisms to the power of Beelzebul (Mark 3:22). That same intransigence will send Jesus to the cross.

In Mark's account, Jesus' healing ministry also reveals his power to forgive sins. When friends lower a paralytic through the roof so that Jesus can cure him, Jesus first forgives his sins and then cures him as a proof of the fact that as the Son of Man he enjoys power on earth to do so (Mark 2:1-12).

Jesus' Power over Death in Mark

In raising the daughter of Jairus Jesus reveals his power over death itself. The fact that only Peter, James, and John witness the miracle links it to Jesus' final eschatological confrontation with the forces of evil in his passion and glorification; for these same disciples will be chosen to witness both his transfiguration and his agony in the garden (Mark 9:2-8; 14:26-52). The miracle foreshadows, then, Jesus' own resurrection and the full revelation of his eschatological authority over the powers of death. As a consequence, it also portends the full scope of Jesus' healing power, which includes the power to raise from the dead (Mark 5:35-43; 14:33).

The cure of the woman with a bloody flux precedes the raising of Jairus's daughter. Moreover, Mark links the two events literarily. Jairus's daughter died at the age of twelve, and the women had been suffering her ostracizing physical affliction for twelve years. The two healings reveal Jesus' relationship to the old and the new covenants. Not only has he the power to free people from the bondage of the Law, as he does in the case of the older woman; but he himself will inaugurate the new covenant by rising from the dead (Mark 4:21-43).

The connection between Jesus' ministry of healing and the risen life he will communicate to his disciples causes Mark to find symbolic significance in the cures Jesus' effects: they foreshadow the healing he will accomplish when in the power of his resurrection he will baptize his followers with a Holy Breath. For example, the healing of blind Bartimaeus has clear symbolic meaning. Having gained the power to see, Bartimaeus now follows Jesus on "the way." The first Christians called their movement "the way." The healing of blind Bartimaeus foreshadows, then, the risen Christ's power to heal the blindness of unbelief and to enable those he enlightens to follow him faithfully along "the way" even to Jerusalem and death (Mark 10:46-52).

Other Symbolic Healings in Mark

One suspects similar symbolic intent in the cure of the blind man of Jerico and of the deaf man who after his cure testifies publicly to what Jesus has done for him. Those who hear the deaf man testify further to the fact that Jesus "has done all things well. . . . He makes the deaf hear and the dumb speak." As Breath-baptizer the risen Christ will also empower humans to hear the Word of the gospel and to proclaim it to others (Mark 7:31-37; 8:22-26). So too, when Jesus cures Peter's mother-in-law, she immediately sets herself to serve him and his disciples. Moreover, when Jesus raises the sick woman from her bed, Mark says that he "lifted her up." The verb "to lift up" (*egerein*) connotes resurrection. The story suggests that those whom Jesus heals by sharing with them his own risen life serve him and one another faithfully in his image (Mark 1:29-31).

Mark also uses the verb *egerein* in his account of the cure of the epileptic demoniac. After Jesus casts out the demon, the bystanders pronounce the epileptic boy dead; but Jesus reaches out his hand and lifts the boy up (*egeiren auton*). Here the verb underscores the eschatological significance of the miracle: Jesus frees from the bondage of sickness and of Satan by raising others up, by giving them a share in his own risen life (Mark 9:14-28).

Finally, Mark makes it clear that Jesus' ministry of healing has not only personal but public, social consequences. Twice Jesus cures two ostracizing illnesses: the man with leprosy (Mark 1:29-31) and the woman with a flux of blood (Mark 5:21-34). Both illnesses rendered those who possessed them unclean. Clearly, the healing that Jesus brings reaches out to social outcasts in order to reincorporate them into the fabric of ordinary public and private life.

Moreover, Mark narrates the cure of the leper with profound irony. The leper confronts Jesus as an outsider, as a social outcast whom the Law constrained from frequenting the places other people did. In curing the leper Jesus transforms him from an outsider into an insider, into one who can once again enjoy a normal social life. Because, however, the leper disobeys Jesus' command to keep the cure a secret, he unwittingly transforms Jesus himself into an outsider: the notariety forces Jesus to dwell in the same desert places the leper once occupied. Nevertheless, the crowds flock to Jesus. Mark seems to be asserting that Jesus came to make the outsiders insiders, to create the new Israel that excludes no one in principle from its care and concern. In the process of accomplishing this, Jesus, the Suffering Servant of God, himself became an outsider, rejected by his people and executed on a cross. Nevertheless, Jesus the outsider continues to draw people to himself because he redefines the meaning of outside and inside. Those who flock to Jesus the outsider are really insiders, because they have been included in the kingdom he proclaimed (Mark 1:40-44).

Finally, in healing the daughter of the Syro-Phonecian woman, Mark's Jesus makes it clear that his ministry of healing encompasses the Gentiles as well (Mark 7:24-30).

Matthew's Adaptation of Mark's Healing Stories

Matthew reproduces the main lines of Mark's account of Jesus' healing ministry, but he deemphasizes the theme of demonic conflict that Mark highlights and emphasizes other theological themes instead. For example, while both evangelists find in Jesus' Sabbath healings and the enmity they aroused a foreshadowing of his atoning death, Matthew twice portrays Jesus the healer as the servant of Yahweh who freely takes upon himself human sinfulness and brokenness (Matt 8:17; 12:9-21; Isa 43:1-4; 53:4). Matthew thus asserts even more explicitly than Mark that the miracles Jesus performs anticipate the healing he will accomplish by his atoning death and resurrection.

Moreover, instead of portraying Jesus' healing ministry primarily as an eschatological conflict, as Mark had, Matthew prefers to view it as a sign of the arrival of God's kingdom. He precedes the inaugural proclamation of the kingdom in the Sermon on the Mount with an abundant outpouring of miraculous cures that seem to embrace both Jew and Gentile. Matthew also clusters most of Jesus' miracles in the narrative section that immediately follows the Sermon on the Mount. He thus creates the impression that Jesus' inaugural proclamation of the kingdom was followed at once by a flood of divine healing (Matt 4:23-25; 8:1-17, 23-27; 9:1-8, 15-22, 27-31, 32-35).

We find in Matthew's account of the cure of the leper (Matt 8:1-4) none of the ironic twists that Mark gives to the story. Matthew, however, shows a concern to make a different theological point. He follows the cure of the leper with a second inclusive miracle: Jesus heals the centurion's servant and predicts that the Gentiles will by their faith supplant the chosen people in the kingdom he is proclaiming (Matt 8:5-13). In the process, Matthew underscores the fact that the healing power of the kingdom reaches out not only to the outcast Jew but to the alien Gentiles as well.

Moreover, Matthew's Jesus interprets the significance of his own ministry of healing more explicitly than Mark's. From prison the Baptist sends some disciples to ask Jesus whether or not he is "the mightier one" whom John had prophesied would come after him and who would baptize with a sanctifying Breath. Jesus instructs John's disciples to return and tell the Baptist what they have seen Jesus doing: proclaiming the good news of the kingdom amidst abundant signs of healing that manifest his possession of the divine Breath in eschatological abundance. In other words, Jesus' ministry of healing lends divine, pneumatic sanction to his proclamation of the kingdom and inaugurates the end time (Matt 11:2-6).

In other respects, however, Matthew's account of Jesus' ministry of healing reproduces the same theological concerns as Mark. Both portray Jesus the healer vanquishing the devil (Matt 8:23-27; 9:32-34), forgiving human sins with eschatological authority (Matt 9:1-8), and conquering death itself (Matt 9:15-22). Moreover, Matthew's Jesus performs the same kind of symbolic and socially inclusive miracles as Mark's (Matt 8:1-15; 9:27-34). Moreover, Matthew like Mark uses the verb *egerein* to connote the gift of risen life; but he does so on different occasions: when Jesus raises the daughter of Jairus (Matt 9:25) and in the cure of the paralytic (Matt 9:1-7). In the latter instance, the story suggests that the divine forgiveness of sinners that Jesus proclaims communicates a share in risen life.

Luke's Account of Jesus' Healing Ministry

Luke situates Jesus' healing ministry in a slightly different theological context. He portrays Jesus as the joyful prophet of a season of jubilee whose coming Isaiah had foretold. He therefore situates Jesus' miracles in the context of that prophetic ministry.

Luke begins his account of Jesus' public ministry with the story of his rejection by the townspeople of Nazareth. Having astonished the whole of Galilee by his Breath-filled preaching, Jesus returns to preach in the synagogue of the town where he grew up. He is handed the scroll of the Scriptures and reads the words of the prophet Isaiah:

> The Breath of the Lord is upon me because he has anointed me to preach good news to the poor. He has sent me to proclaim release to the captives and recovering of sight to the blind, to set at liberty those who are oppressed and to proclaim the acceptable year of the Lord (Isa 61:1-2; 58:6).

Jesus' rejection at Nazareth foreshadows his rejection by his own people and their inability to comprehend that they had been chosen by God to mediate his salvation to the Gentiles. At the same time, the citation from Isaiah sets the context for Jesus' public ministry. He announces a divinely appointed season of salvation, of liberation from oppression, and of healing (Luke 4:14-30).

Because Luke desires to portray Jesus as the joyful, Breath-filled prophet of the kingdom, he deemphasizes the conflict that Mark discovers in Jesus' healing ministry. Although Luke's Jesus performs three exorcisms (Luke 4:11-37; 8:26-39; 10:37-43), Luke omits Mark's repeated references to demonic conflict. Similarly, after Jesus cures the man with a withered hand on the Sabbath, Luke notes that the miracle caused Jesus' enemies to discuss what they would do about him; but he refrains from portraying them as immediately plotting his death, as Mark does (Luke 6:6-11). Luke also portrays the exorcism of the epileptic demoniac boy primarily as an astonishing manifestation of the divine majesty (Luke 9:37-43). Matthew, in narrating the same incident, focuses on the transcendent character of Jesus' power and on his disciples' participation in it (Matt 9:14-20), while Mark, as we have seen, underscores its eschatological significance (Mark 9:14-29).

Moreover, at the same time that Luke underplays the link between Jesus' ministry of healing and his passion, he also underscores the fact that Jesus' miracles foreshadow the ultimate miracle of the resurrection. Luke supplements Mark's account of the raising of Jairus's daughter with the story of Jesus raising from the dead the son of the widow of Nain. Only he of all the evangelists records this event (Luke 7:1-10).

Like Matthew, Luke precedes Jesus' inaugural discourse with an outpouring of healings (Luke 6:17-19). Moreover, in his account of Jesus' reply to the Baptist's question, Luke underscores even more than Matthew the abundance of cures that Jesus had just performed (Luke 7:18-23).

Although Luke omits the story of the cure of the daughter of the Syro-Phonecian woman, he nevertheless emphasizes in his own way the universal scope of the salvation that Jesus' healing ministry portends. As we have already seen, he does so in his account of Jesus preaching at Nazareth. Moreover, in his account of the cure of the centurion's servant he expands in sympathetic terms his portrait of the centurion whose faith foreshadows the inclusion of the Gentiles in the kingdom (Luke 7:1-10).

In other respects, however, Luke like Matthew endorses the main lines of Mark's theological interpretation of Jesus' ministry of healing. It reveals his power over the demonic forces of evil (Luke 4:11-37; 8:22-39; 10:37-43). Like Mark, Luke finds in Jesus' healing ministry a revelation of his authority as Son of Man to forgive sin (Luke 4:17-26) and of his power over death itself (Luke 7:11-17; 8:40-56). Luke's Jesus, like Mark's, performs cures that symbolize the

grace that will flow from his resurrection: His power to heal the blindness of unbelief and to empower the proclamation of the good news
(Luke 4:38-39; 14:1-6; 18:35-43), even though Luke does not emphasize the symbolic significance of these cures as much as Mark. Finally,
Luke's Jesus also performs inclusive miracles that break down social
barriers (Luke 4:12-14; 7:1-10).

Jesus' Ministry of Healing in John

The Gospel of John gives an account of only three cures performed by Jesus: the healing of the nobleman's son at Cana, the cure
of the cripple at the pool of Bethsaida, and the healing of the man
born blind. John also narrates the raising of Lazarus. Nevertheless,
the Fourth Gospel insists even more explicitly than the Synoptics on
the symbolic character of Jesus' miracles. They function in the Fourth
Gospel as "signs," as anticipatory revelations of the glory of the risen
Christ.

The Synoptics portray the miracles of Jesus as acts of power
(*dynamis*) that manifest the pneumatic authority (*exousia*) with which
he conducts his ministry. John makes an analogous point somewhat more forensically. The Fourth Gospel begins with the cross-
examination of the Baptist by emissaries from Jerusalem and ends
with Jesus' trial and execution. Moreover, as the conflict between the
forces of light and darkness waxes more and more violent, Jesus encounters repeated cross-questioning by his enemies. In this context,
the fourth evangelist portrays Jesus' miracles as acts of testimony by
the Father on behalf of his Son (John 5:36; 10:25-26).

Despite the importance that the Johannine tradition places on
the miracles of Jesus, however, the story of the cure of the nobleman's
son at Cana warns against making physical healing a condition for
faith and insists that authentic faith transcends such immediate visible
signs. Jesus at first laments that people require cures before they will
believe and then demands faith of the nobleman before he has pal-
pable proof of his son's cure (John 4:43-54).

In curing the cripple at the pool of Bethsaida on the Sabbath
Jesus claims as much right to work on the Sabbath as the Father does.
In rabbinic teaching, God ceased from his creative activity on the Sab-
bath but continued to perform acts of divine judgment on that day.
In the Fourth Gospel, therefore, Jesus' Sabbath miracles reveal that
he possesses divine authority to judge the world in the Father's name.
As a consequence, his ministry of healing fulfills the religious sig-
nificance of the Jewish Sabbath celebration (John 5:1-47).

The cure of the man born blind reveals Jesus as the light of the world (John 9:3-5). The blind man's washing at the pool of Siloam (which means "sent") foreshadows Christian baptism and the commissioning enlightenment it will bring (John 9:7). Moreover, as the cured beggar bears public witness to Jesus, he is drawn into conflict with the same powers of darkness as will seek to destroy Jesus himself. Like Mark, then, John looks upon Jesus' ministry of healing as an integral part of his eschatological battle against the powers of evil and of darkness. Moreover, John, like Mark, insists that those who experience Jesus' healing enlightenment can expect to be drawn into his passion (John 9:1-41).

The raising of Lazarus reveals Jesus as "the resurrection and the life," as possessing the power to raise from the dead and to give eternal life to anyone who believes in him (John 11:9-26). Moreover, as in the case of the man born blind, Lazarus suffers the hatred of Jesus' enemies (John 12:11).

The Gospel Witness to Faith Healing

In all four Gospels, then, Jesus' ministry of healing endows his proclamation of the kingdom with sacramental significance by transforming it into a manifestation of divine authority and power. On the one hand, his ministry of proclamation establishes the context of faith for interpreting the cures he performs; and, on the other hand, the miraculous cures manifest the divine, pneumatic authority with which he announces God's reign. Only faith, however, perceives the full significance of Jesus' power to heal, a faith that roots itself ultimately in his resurrection.

Moreover, because the resurrection of Jesus reveals the full scope of his divine authority, Jesus' miracles foreshadow the full scope of the salvation the risen Christ will accomplish. His power to heal physically reveals his authority to heal the paralysis of sin, not only personally but through the mission of his sanctifying Breath. His exorcisms reveal that he has come to break the power of Satan over humankind. His power to mend broken bodies and raise from the dead manifests his power to communicate risen life to those who believe in him and to transform them graciously in his image. His inclusive miracles reveal the universal, inclusive scope of the reign of God he proclaims.

In reflecting on the experience of illness, we noted its connection with conversion. In describing Jesus' healing ministry, the Gospels also link healing and conversion. The physical cures Jesus performs symbolize the salvation he has come to bring. They fore-shadow the risen life he will bestow on those who repent and be-lieve in him. In giving sight to the blind, Jesus manifests his power to enlighten the converted heart through faith.

Healing in the Apostolic Church

Moreover, the New Testament makes it clear that the Church prolongs with the divine Breath's sanctioning authority Jesus' own ministry of healing. Matthew asserts that Jesus communicated his own healing power to the Twelve (Matt 10:1). John's Jesus promises his followers that they will perform even greater signs than he (John 14:12). Moreover, Luke describes the healing ministry that the apostles conducted in the early Church. The same miraculous signs that sanctioned Jesus' proclamation of the kingdom accompany the apostles' proclamation of the risen Christ (Acts 2:43; 5:12-16). Both exorcisms and miraculous cures accompany the deacon Philip's evan-gelization of the Samaritans (Acts 8:7-8). The Holy Breath who in-spires Peter to cure cripples and raise from the dead, empowers Paul to perform similar miracles in his ministry to the Gentiles (Acts 3:1-10; 9:12-43; 14:8-10; 20:7-12).

Healing in James

In the Letter of James we also find evidence that the leaders of local communities whom the apostles appointed not only carried on a similar ministry of healing but recognized its connection with con-version and the forgiveness of sin. In his final exhortation, James writes:

> Is one of you ill? He should send for the elders of the congrega-tion to pray over him and anoint him with oil in the name of the Lord. The prayer offered in faith will save the sick man and the Lord will raise him up, and any sins he may have committed will be forgiven. Therefore confess your sins to one another and pray for one another and you will be healed (Jas 5:14-16).

The passage indicates that already within the first generation of Chris-tians, public prayer for healing had begun to take the form of a ritual anointing. That anointing was perceived as effecting the forgiveness of sins. James speaks of those anointed as members of the commu-nity. Their sins do not merit excommunication, but they nevertheless constitute failings of sufficient note to warrant confession. The anointing, therefore, expresses a reaffirmation of one's original converted commitment to Christ after minor lapses.

The anointing, however, also seeks to effect physical healing. The experience of serious illness confronts one with one's own mortality and invites a repentant reassessment of one's life. Nevertheless, the anointing that James recommends promises no automatic restoration to health. It promises only that the Lord will "raise up (*egerei*)" the sick person. The verb could refer to an actual physical cure; or it could express the certainty of sharing in Christ's resurrection, presumably in the event that the anointed patient actually died rather than recovered physically.

The passage in James also gives evidence that in the apostolic Church the ministry of healing was not exercised exclusively by Church leaders. James's final exhortation, "Therefore confess your sins to one another and pray for one another, and you will be healed," suggests that other members of the community besides the elders practiced a ministry of healing that was accompanied by prayer for the forgiveness of minor offenses. The First Letter of John leaves an analogous impression, although in the Johannine community the prayer for forgiveness does not clearly occur in the context of faith healing (1 John 5:16-17).

We have reflected on New Testament foundations for a theology of sacramental anointing. In order to understand not only the purpose of this sacrament but also the theological controversies it has occasioned, we need to understand how the rite of anointing evolved. To this problem we turn in the section that follows.

3. The Development of the Rite of Anointing. The evolution of the rite of anointing divides roughly into four historical periods. The first extends from the first to the ninth centuries. During this period Christian faith healing enjoyed a certain charismatic spontaneity. During the second period, from the ninth to the fourteenth centuries, the ritual underwent standardization and clericalization. This same period saw it increasingly assimilated to the rite of reconciliation and transformed from a prayer in faith for healing and forgiveness into a rite of the dying. During the third period, the sixteenth century, Protestant reformers repudiated the ritual and denied its sacramentality. In the fourth period, from the sixteenth century to the present, one witnesses repeated attempts to reform and restore the ritual.

The Early Christian Ministry of Healing

The *Didache* provides the oldest Christian liturgical formula for blessing oil (*Didache,* 10). The blessing occurs in a Eucharistic context and apparently consecrates the oil for use in anointing the sick. In the third century, *The Canons of Hyppolytus* allude to two different contexts in which anointing with blessed oil occurred. First, in the case of less serious illnesses blessed oils were distributed in church for the use of the sick within their homes. Second, the ordained leaders of the community visited those suffering from serious illnesses in order to anoint them and pray for healing (*Canons* 219, 199–200, *Apostolic Constitutions,* VIII, 29). The prayer for healing also involved the laying on of hands.

The prayers consecrating the oil during the first five centuries included both prayers of thanksgiving and of blessing. Ordinarily, the bishop blessed the oil, which was then treated with great reverence. As one would expect, with the passage of time Church leaders turned their attention to the pastoral regulation of the rite of anointing. Nevertheless, one continues to find evidence until the ninth century that in addition to the healing ministry of the ordained, lay Christians used blessed oils in the home in praying for the sick (DS 216). In the first five centuries we find no evidence whatever that the dying were anointed.

Anointing played a clearly defined role in the Church's early penitential discipline. Only serious sinners excommunicated from the Church received the rite of reconciliation. Two other Church rituals dealt with minor, postbaptismal offenses: the Eucharist and the anointing of the sick. The Eucharist provided the ordinary means for forgiving the minor failings of baptized Christians. Understandably enough, however, in times of serious illness, Christians found it helpful to seek absolution for minor faults while praying for healing.

The Clericalization of the Healing Ministry

Between the sixth and eighth centuries the Frankish Church developed a variety of blessings and formal rituals of anointing to be used by the ordained. By the ninth century these diverse rituals had become consolidated into a fairly elaborate and unified liturgical ceremony. When Charlemagne imposed the Latin Rite on the French Church, Alcuin, his chief theological adviser, appended to the Roman sacramentary a rite of anointing for use by the clergy of the Gallican Church. At this point, while the Church of Rome practiced both public and private anointing, by the ninth century it had not yet canonized any ritual for use by the clergy, although it would eventually canonize the Gallican rite of anointing.

The ninth century saw the disappearance of lay anointing. The promulgation of an official priestly ritual for anointing the sick not only helped standardize anointings administered by the ordained but also enhanced their public status within the community. Some historians also see in the eclipse of lay anointing a disciplinary reaction against superstitious uses of the consecrated oil. Whatever the explanation, from the late ninth century on only priests can anoint.

The clericalization of the Church's healing ministry changed it in dramatic ways. It drastically reduced the number of competent healers. Moreover, traditionally, the ordained had visited only the most seriously ill; but by the late ninth and early tenth centuries the ritual had come to be administered only to those at the point of death.

Medieval Abuses

The severity of medieval penitential discipline also helped transform the practice of anointing from a rite of healing into ministry to the dying. Only Christians in good standing could be anointed. Not infrequently, however, serious sinners opted to avoid the burden of performing onerous public penances by postponing the rite of reconciliation until they lay on their deathbeds. Having confessed, the dying Christian would then undergo sacramental anointing.

As the practice of deathbed anointing spread, it changed first popular, then theological perceptions of the ritual's purpose. People assumed that anointing sought to prepare one for the final ordeal of death. Eventually, among theologians the rite acquired a new name: *extrema unctio,* or last anointing. Once the medieval Church forgot the healing purpose of anointing, theologians increasingly emphasized the spiritual effects of the ritual. They equated its effects with those of the rite of reconciliation: it effected the forgiveness of sins and thus prepared the dying for entry into future glory (Albert the Great, *On the Sacraments,* Tr. VII, q. 4; Bonaventure, *Commentary on the Book of Sentences,* IV, d. xxxiii, a. 1, q. 1; Thomas Aquinas, *Commentary on the Book of Sentences,* IV, d. xxxiii, q. 3, a. 2; John Duns Scotus, *Oxford Commentary on the Book of Sentences,* IV, d. xxxiii, qu.un).

Eventually, these shifts in belief transformed the ritual itself: instead of a single anointing to effect healing, each of the five senses

186 Three Rites of Ongoing Conversion

were now anointed in order to forgive the sins committed with it. By the thirteenth century anointing had replaced *viaticum,* or final communion, as the ritual of the dying.

Conciliar Teaching about Healing

The Council of Florence endorsed both the medieval notion that the rite of anointing should be administered only to dying and the late medieval practice of anointing all five senses for the forgiveness of the sins committed through them. The council's decree managed, however, to preserve some sense of the original purpose of the rite of anointing when it asserts that it seeks to effect the healing of both soul and body (DS 1324).

The Council of Trent rejected the late medieval belief that anointing only forgives sin in order to introduce one into future glory. It included physical healing in its list of the graces that sacramental anointing seeks to effect. The council conceded, however, that the rite also takes away sin and the remnants of sin, brings spiritual healing, and evokes faith in God's mercy (DS 1696, 1717).

In the wake of Trent, however, few Christians took the healing purpose of the sacrament seriously. In the popular imagination of Christians who practiced this ritual, it effected not so much the grace of healing as ritual preparation for death.

The Second Vatican Council acted decisively to complete the theological retrieval of the true purpose of anointing that the Council of Trent had initiated. Vatican II called for a renewal of the Church's entire ministry of healing. The revised rite of anointing anticipated that in addition to the clergy's sacramental anointing of those most seriously ill, lay Christians would minister to the sick, not only by tending to their physical needs but also by exercising a ministry of faith healing. In effect, then, Vatican II rejected decisively as both false and misleading the notion that ritual anointing seeks to prepare one for death. It reaffirmed officially the original understanding of anointing as a prayer for integral healing in faith, and it attempted to restore lay participation in the Church's healing ministry (*Sacrosanctum Concilium,* 73-75; *Lumen gentium,* 11, 28; *Presbyterorum Ordinis,* 5; Roman Catholic Anointing and Care of the Sick, 1-37; hereafter references to the revised ritual will be abbreviated RCACS).

We have reflected on the way in which the rite of anointing has evolved. That evolution contextualizes the theological debates that attend this ritual. Let us, then, examine in the section that follows some of the major theological controversies that anointing has occasioned.

4. Issues in the Development of the Rite of Anointing. In the course of its long and somewhat checkered history, the rite of anointing has occasioned three major controversies. Theologians and Church leaders have disagreed about its purpose, its sacramentality, and the frequency with which it ought to be repeated.

a. The Purpose of Anointing. As we have just seen, by the twelfth century many theologians had come to assimilate anointing to reconciliation and to portray it as a sacrament of the dying. In the twelfth century, Hugh of St. Victor offered an important exception to that pattern. He found a double purpose in the sacrament: the forgiveness of sin and the alleviation of physical illness. It always heals in the sense that it always forgives sins if received with contrition. The rite may be repeated at the sick person's request (Hugh of St. Victor, *De Sacramentis,* II, 15).

Hugh's understanding of anointing reproduced faithfully a patristic understanding of this ritual. Moreover, other twelfth century theologians defended a similar position; but they could not agree concerning the rite's primary purpose. Did it seek primarily to forgive sin, to heal, or to protect one from the devil's wiles at the moment of death? In the end as medieval theology of anointing evolved, other minds and other teachers than Hugh were destined to carry the day.

Extreme Unction

One of Hugh's contemporaries, Peter Lombard, included anointing in his canon of the sacraments. He spoke of two purposes embodied in this ritual: the forgiveness of sin and healing, but he anticipated that the rite would be administered only to the dying. He named the rite "last anointing" or "extreme unction" (Peter Lombard, *Sentences,* IV, d. 23).

Thomas Aquinas and Bonaventure misunderstood anointing as ritual preparation for death and for the enjoyment of the beatific vision (Thomas Aquinas, *Summa Contra Gentiles,* IV, 73; Bonaventure, *In Librum Sententiarum,* IV, d. xxiii, a. 2, q. 2). John Duns Scotus emphasized the ritual's capacity to forgive venial sin (John Duns Scotus, *Oxford Commentary,* I, d. 23, n. 3). These great theological lights did not err in associating anointing with the forgiveness of sin, for the ritual had from the beginning absolved minor postbaptismal offenses. They erred rather in failing to recognize its healing purpose and in portraying it as a sacrament of the dying.

As we have seen, both the Council of Trent and Vatican II set aside as false the notion that the rite of anointing prepares one for death. Vatican II reasserted the original purpose of the ritual even more clearly than Trent: anointing seeks to effect both physical and personal healing. Nevertheless, while the official pastoral magisterium has resolved this particular debate among sacramental theologians, many Christians still need reeducation and preparation in the proper use of this ritual.

Besides disagreeing over the purpose of anointing, theologians have also disputed its sacramentality. Moreover, as we shall see in the following section, the first debate helped motivate the second.

b. The Sacramentality of Anointing. Theological misunderstanding about the purpose of anointing in the late middle ages set the stage for disagreement concerning its sacramentality at the time of the Reformation.

Protestant Anointing

Martin Luther saw no connection between the text in the Letter of James describing the healing ministry of the first presbyters and the sacramental practice of the Renaissance Church. James described a rite of healing. The Roman Church he knew anointed the dying for the forgiveness of their sins. Luther permitted anointing but considered it a human invention. He therefore eliminated the rite of anointing from his list of official Church sacraments (Luther, *Works,* 36, 117–123).

Moreover, in accord with the Platonic cast of his thought, Luther understood sickness in highly spiritualized categories. Since only God exemplifies genuine reality, sickness belongs to the deceitful world of sensory appearances. As a consequence, while God may intend sickness as a grace, we might perceive it as a bane. Luther also stressed that all divine healing must proceed from the indwelling of God, whose presence in the soul transforms it into his sanctuary (Luther, *Works,* 26:508, 36:570).

John Calvin also saw no connection between the passage in James and the sacramental practice of the Roman priests of his day. He questioned (incorrectly) whether James in referring to "elders" might not refer to older members of the community rather than to official Church leaders. Since, in addition, he did not believe that living Christians possessed the charism of healing described in the New Testament, he dismissed the rite of anointing as so much sham and denied it sacramental status (Calvin, *Institutes,* IV, xix, 18).

In 1549 the Anglican Church anointed its sick ritually and prayed for the forgiveness of their sins and restoration to health. By 1552 *The Book of Common Prayer* had, however, dropped the ritual. Not until the late nineteenth and twentieth centuries were attempts made to restore it.

The Tridentine Response

As we have seen, the Council of Trent responded to Protestant criticism of ritual anointing by reinstating somewhat hesitantly the original purpose of the ritual. Trent also defended the ritual's sacramentality and its institution by Christ. The council denied Protestant allegations that one should dismiss the ritual as a mere human figment (DS 1716). Trent also insisted correctly against Calvin that the elders who did the anointing in the Letter of James should be understood as official church leaders (DS 1719).

c. The Frequency of Anointing. We find considerable disagreement among medieval theologians concerning the frequency with which the sick should be anointed. The disagreement reflected the ritual diversity with which different dioceses went about the care of the sick and dying. Some theologians denied the rite could be repeated, others held it could be repeated on request. The revised rite of anointing stresses the pastoral purpose of the sacrament and allows its repetition within the same illness should the patient take a turn for the worse (RCACS, 9).

We have considered biblical foundations for the rite of anointing, the ritual's historical evolution, and some of the major controversies that have surrounded this rite. In the section that follows we shall reflect on the significance of this ritual. Our reflections will analyze the way in which anointing fosters ongoing conversion. They will also lay foundations for resolving the unresolved theological debates about this sacrament.

5. The Significance of the Rite of Anointing. One cannot understand the purpose of the Christian rite of anointing without situating it within the Church's healing ministry as a whole. We shall, therefore, begin these reflections on the significance of ritual anointing by examining the scope of a Christian ministry of healing. Second, our analysis will focus on the rites of healing themselves. In the course of doing so, our argument shall attempt to clarify the purpose of this ritual and the frequency with which it should be administered. Finally, we shall attempt to resolve the debate over its sacramentality.

a. The Scope of Christian Healing. The rites of initiation seal a conversion that commits Christians individually and collectively to reach out in Jesus' name to those in greatest need. Among the needy, the sick, the aged, and the dying hold a special place. If, moreover, the Church intends to prolong historically Jesus' own ministry of healing, it must do so in ways that express his vision of the kingdom. The Church cannot, as a consequence, confine its healing ministry to elderly, sick, and dying Christians. Any person struck down by serious mental or physical illness or mutilation, anyone passing through the ordeal of old age or the stages of dying has a claim upon Christian compassion and charity.

The Healing of Persons

Christian healing concerns itself not with bodies alone but with persons. Christian healers must respect the integrity and dignity of each individual to whom they minister. Nevertheless, healing begins most fundamentally with concern for the physical needs of those suffering. The Church attempts to provide the sick with a healing realm of grace that frees them to advance through illness to a deeper conversion and dependence in faith upon God. Such healing communities provide the Church's rites of healing with a sacramental context that makes sense of what they celebrate and seek to effect; for, just as the full sacramentality of the rites of reconciliation presupposes a community in which Christians forgive one another in the name and image of Jesus, so too the rites of healing presuppose a community of hope, faith, and love whose confident expectation of God's healing disposes the suffering to experience it. The sick for their part minister to the rest of the community by their prayer and by entering into the atonement of the suffering Christ who endured pain and affliction without sinning.

Those personally called by God to a ministry of healing need, of course, to make use of the best medical and psychological remedies available in order to alleviate human misery. Christian hospitals need to provide patients with the best possible therapies and maintain the highest professional standards in their hospital staffs.

Christian physicians and therapists need to practice a similar professionalism.

The Charismatic Ministry of Healing

In confronting sickness, old age, and death, the Church does not, however, confine itself to employing the best scientific or human remedies available. In ministering to believers the Church, like Jesus, exercises a ministry of faith healing. That ministry includes the sacramental ministry to the sick, but it also includes the faith healing practiced by lay Christians.

Despite the serious aberrations that distorted the rite of anointing during the late Middle Ages and despite lapsed faith in the contemporary availability of the divine Mother's charisms, popular Catholic piety during both medieval and modern times never lost its confidence in the healing power of faith. Until Vatican II, however, Catholics tended to attribute healing in response to prayer to the intercession of Mary or of one of the saints in heaven rather than to the charismatic giftedness of some living Christian. The charismatic renewal has, however, taught innumerable Catholics to take seriously the present availability of all the divine Mother's gifts, including the gift of healing. Moreover, restored charismatic consciousness has led a number of lay Catholics to undertake a personal ministry of faith healing in response to the divine Mother's call. In that enterprise they deserve the support and encouragement of the rest of the Church. Moreover, the full restoration of the rite of anointing for which Vatican II called will not occur until all Catholics learn to approach prayer for healing with the same concrete, expectant faith as one encounters in charismatic prayer groups.

Here, moreover, we should note that even those professionally trained as doctors, nurses, psychiatrists, and psychologists can and, when the occasion offers, should practice a ministry of faith healing. In addition to employing the best medical and psychological therapies available, Christian doctors, nurses, and therapists can also pray with their patients for healing. The Society of Christian Therapists has, for example, successfully encouraged many who minister to the emotionally disturbed to incorporate prayer for healing into the therapeutic process with no diminishment of professional psychological standards. If one takes the divine Mother's charisms seriously, such an approach to therapy should come as no surprise; for a charism often changes, not what one does in ministering to others, but the way in which one does it. The charismatic healer may employ human remedies in ministering to the suffering but will look ultimately to God both to guide the therapy and effect healing.

As we have seen, the involvement of lay Christians in the Church's ministry of faith healing enjoys the abundant sanction of tradition. Until the ninth century lay Christians employed oils blessed by the bishop in order to anoint the sick and pray for their conversion and physical restoration. Moreover, while the clericalization of ministry to the sick that occurred during the ninth century may have found partial pastoral justification at the time because of ignorance and superstition among the laity, history suggests that the decision to allow clerics only to pray with others for healing probably contributed to the decadence into which the rite of anointing fell during the late Middle Ages. It certainly reduced the number of available faith healers and very likely encouraged the postponement of anointing until those suffering lay close to death.

Sacramental Healing Ministry

A sacramental ministry of faith healing needs, then, to be situated within the entire spectrum of the Church's healing ministry. A sacramental ministry of faith healing addresses the same illnesses as do the members of the healing professions and lay charismatic healers. How, then, does sacramental healing differ from these other forms of faith healing? In order to answer that question, we need to examine the significant structure of the rite of healing itself.

b. The Rites of Healing. Sacramental ministry to the sick includes both the rite of anointing and bringing them Holy Communion. Let us focus first on the rite of anointing.

The Scope of Christian Healing

The rite of anointing like the healing ministry of the Church as a whole seeks to extend historically Jesus' own ministry of healing. In that sense Jesus instituted sacramental ministry to the sick, for the sacraments of the sick simply ritualize the ministry he inaugurated. One cannot, then, understand the purpose of sacramental ministry to the sick without a sound insight into the purpose of Jesus' own healing ministry.

As we have seen, the New Testament situates Jesus' ministry of healing in an eschatological context. His exorcisms and miracles signal the arrival of the end time, of God's decisive victory over sin,

Satan, and suffering. An eschatological understanding of Jesus' ministry to the sick and possessed demands as well that one interpret that ministry in the light of Jesus' passion and resurrection. When one does so, one is forced to distinguish theologically between ultimate and provisional healing. Moreover, within provisional healing one must distinguish dimensions of cure. Let us reflect on the implications of these distinctions.

Ultimate and Provisional Healing

God heals us ultimately by raising us from death in the image of the risen Christ. Our mortal bodies must be transformed after the pattern of his glorified body. By comparison every other human experience of healing counts as only provisional. Moreover, genuine provisional healing advances one toward ultimate healing.

I distinguish three dimensions within provisional healing: conversion, the transformation of suffering into grace, and physical healing, which may or may not occur miraculously.

Both initial and ongoing conversion effect healing. Affective conversion heals neurosis and psychosis. Intellectual conversion heals the mind of blindness, rigidity, dogmatism, and prejudice. Moral conversion heals human egocentrism. Sociopolitical conversion seeks to heal sinful institutions and the suffering born of human oppression and exploitation.

Christian conversion perfects the healing that the other forms of conversion effect by teaching them the healing power of faith. Christian conversion elevates the other forms of conversion by orienting them toward ultimate healing in Christ. A Christian ministry of faith healing must not, then, focus narrowly on the cure of physical illness. Faith healing seeks more fundamentally to help the sick and suffering to grow in personal sanctification by deepening in hope, faith, love, and the desire to serve others in Jesus' name.

A kind of healing occurs in faith when the sick discover in their very illness the means for growing in union with God. When that occurs, faith transforms the suffering that illness causes into a participation in the atoning suffering of Christ. Then the suffering itself begins to take on meaning because it conforms one to Christ and so advances one's ultimate healing. Indeed, faith and trust in God in the midst of suffering constitutes an important part of the ministry of the sick to the rest of the Christian community.

Prayer for healing may, however, engage a third dimension of cure when it restores the sick person to health. Moreover, cures that have no apparent natural cause count as miraculous. Like Peter's mother-in-law, such healing frees one to minister to others in Jesus' name and in the power of his gift-giving Breath. Indeed, pastoral experience suggests that those who have experienced healing in faith tend to make the best faith healers.

Sacramental Prayer for Healing

The revised rite of anointing takes into account all the forms of healing discussed above. It looks for ultimate healing in personal resurrection and seeks to deepen in the sick the kind of conversion that advances one toward risen glory. It encourages the sick to expect the healing power of God to transform them personally without predetermining the precise form that healing will take. The minister of anointing should then make sure that those who are anointed approach the sacrament with the proper dispositions and faith expectations (RCACS, 1–4). As a way of ensuring that the sick have the proper dispositions, the revised ritual recommends that the rite of reconciliation precede that of anointing (RCACS, 64). Because, however, the sacramental rite of anointing, in addition to begging God's physical healing, also constitutes repentant commitment to the triune God in faith, it has the capacity to forgive minor sins in its own right.

Ideally, the rite of anointing should be celebrated in a communal context, with the minister's prayers supported by the prayers of the infirm and of their family, friends, and other Christians. Such communal celebrations remind those who minister to the sick and, indeed, the Church as a whole of their responsibility to provide therapeutic communities that foster healing in faith.

The ritual opens with a greeting of peace and a blessing with water that reminds the sick of their covenant of initiation and of the share in the passion and resurrection of Christ that it guarantees (RCACS, 68–70). That reminder underscores the fact that through the rite of anointing, the sick renew their covenant of initiation in repentant faith.

An appropriate reading from sacred Scripture then follows. It should recall God's healing power and encourage the sick to approach the sacrament with the confidence of experiencing that power (RCACS, 72). When it seems appropriate, the Scripture reading is followed by a short litany that invokes divine healing on those about to be anointed. The minister may add other appropriate intercessory prayers that encourage the faith of the sick (RCACS, 73). The minister of the sacrament then imposes hands on the sick person and prays for healing (RCACS, 74).

After the imposition of hands, the minister blesses the oil with a prayer that invokes the Holy Breath who inspired Jesus' healing ministry. If the minister uses blessed oil, a prayer of thanksgiving to God for the healing he effects through the twofold mission of his Son and Breath replaces the prayer of blessing (RCACS, 75–75b). The minister then anoints the sick person on the forehead and hands saying, "Through this holy anointing may the Lord in his love and mercy help you with the grace of the Holy Spirit. May the Lord who frees you from sin save you and raise you up." To each prayer the anointed replies, "Amen" (RCACS, 76). The second prayer alludes to the Letter of James and reproduces its ambiguities: the phrase "raise you up" could refer to the restoration of health, to final resurrection, or to both.

A prayer that God will heal the sick person follows. All present then recite the Lord's Prayer as an expression of committed rededication to the kingdom in the obedience of faith. After the Our Father, the sick person receives Holy Communion, if he or she desires. The ritual closes with a final blessing (RCACS, 77–79).

As we have seen, the revised rite of anointing allows the repetition of the sacrament only if the patient takes a marked turn for the worse; but it recommends ongoing prayer with the sick for their recovery. That prayer can, of course, occur at any time; or it could precede Communion of the sick (RCACS, 49–58).

Communion of the sick proceeds simply and straightforwardly. After the greeting of peace and blessing with holy water, those to receive Communion confess their sins and receive an absolution. An appropriate passage from sacred Scripture is read. All recite the Lord's prayer. The sick then receive Communion. The ceremony concludes with a final prayer and blessing (RCACS, 46–58).

An insight into the genuine purpose of anointing provides the means for resolving the debate over its sacramentality. To this theological problem we turn in the following section.

c. The Sacramentality of the Rite of Anointing. Should anointing rank among the sacraments of the Church? As we have seen, disagreement over its sacramentality at the time of the Reformation sprang largely from the abuses and misunderstandings that marred ministry to the sick during the late Middle Ages. If, however, one examines the commitment required of those anointed, the act of worship they perform, when properly understood, fulfills all the conditions for inclusion in the canon of the sacraments.

A Sacrament of Healing

The anointed pray for healing: for the ultimate healing that comes with risen glory, for a deepening of their conversion to Christ which the rites of initiation originally sealed, for the repentant forgiveness of minor sins and failings, and, if God wills, for physical healing as well. One cannot pray such a prayer publicly and officially without renewing ritually one's Christian covenant of initiation. Anointing, then, qualifies as a ritual act of new covenant worship.

The rite of anointing engages the Church's shared faith in the healing power of God revealed in the eschatological mission of his Son and Breath. The anointed reaffirm publicly and officially their sacramental covenant of initiation. Hence, only those can celebrate it whom the Christian community authorizes to do so. I see no reason in principle, however, why competent lay healers could not receive official authorization to anoint sacramentally and also to administer when pastorally appropriate the rite of reconciliation. Such authorization would in fact enhance the ministry of lay healers engaged full-time in the healing profession.

Anointing ritualizes the ministry of faith healing that Jesus began and that the Church prolongs historically. It therefore traces its origin to his ministry.

One prays for healing with expectant faith in the power of the risen Christ and with a willingness to share, if God wills it, in his atoning suffering and death. That faith and commitment together with the ongoing conversion they express draws the sick person more deeply into the paschal mystery. At the same time, anointing proclaims the victory over sin and suffering that the Father accomplished in Jesus' ministry, death, and resurrection and that the Church proclaims in the power of his Breath.

Finally, the rite of anointing effects the healing it signifies. It deepens conversion and reaffirms one's covenant of initiation, and it may effect physical healing as well.

Healing in the Context of Covenant Renewal

How, then, does the rite of anointing differ from other forms of faith healing? It differs both in its context and in its consequences. Sacramental prayer for healing occurs in the context of a public reaffirmation of one's covenant of initiation. It differs in its consequences in that, like confessions of devotion, it forgives minor offenses committed after baptism.

We may, then, conclude that in reacting to the distortions that marred ritual anointing during the late Middle Ages, the Protestant reformers overreacted. Protestants, of course, experience healing in faith, although outside of a ritual sacramental context. One would hope, however, that Protestant Christians would also one day rediscover the grace of sacramental healing and have the opportunity to experience the consolation it brings to those with illness.

The rite of reconciliation, as we have seen, derives its full sacramental significance from the reconciling ministry of the Church as a whole. Something similar can be said of the rite of anointing: it extends the Church's ministry of faith healing to those most seriously ill. At the same time, it celebrates the healing ministry of the Church as a whole as it extends in space and time Jesus' own compassionate ministry to the sick.

6. Conclusion. We have examined the commitment of faith embodied in Christian initiation, in the two vocational sacraments of marriage and orders, and in two other sacraments of ongoing conversion: reconciliation and anointing. We have, however, still to consider that sacrament that more than any other seeks to deepen committed conversion to Christ and draw one ever deeper into the paschal mystery. I refer, of course, to the Church's ongoing Eucharistic worship. To this, the greatest of the sacraments, we turn in the chapter that follows.

CHAPTER VII

The Lord's Supper

In the first chapter of this study we saw that Catholic theology has traditionally associated the rites of initiation and of reconciliation with the experience of conversion. Our analysis of the moral demands of committed sacramental worship in subsequent chapters concedes the truth of that position but calls into question its adequacy. That subsequent analysis portrays all the sacraments of the Church as converting rituals. The rites of initiation seal an initial adult conversion to Christ. The other sacraments foster ongoing conversion.

Marriage and orders, the vocational sacraments, foster conversion by confirming specific charismatic calls to public service in the Christian community. They deepen conversion because in both rituals adult Christians reaffirm their covenant of initiation while undertaking new ecclesial responsibilities that nevertheless flow from their original covenant of initiation.

The rite of reconciliation forgives sins committed after baptism and seals a repentant recommitment to converted Christian living. In the rite of anointing the Church prays with its sick in the context of a public reaffirmation of the Christian covenant of initiation. Anointing, then, embodies a deeper commitment to Christ in the face of sickness and possible death.

All the Church's sacramental rituals, therefore, either seal an initial conversion to Christ or deepen in some significant fashion the experience of ongoing conversion. In the present chapter we turn our attention to that ritual which more than any other seeks to effect ongoing conversion to Christ: the Eucharist. Our reflections divide into five major sections. In the first we shall reflect on the biblical foundations for a theology of Eucharistic worship. The second section examines the historical development of Eucharistic ritual. The third section considers differing theological interpretations of Eucharistic worship. The fourth section examines the structure and significance

198

of Eucharistic celebrations. The fifth section reflects on the relationship that unites the following elements of Eucharistic worship: anamnesis, the sacrificial character of the Eucharist, its eschatological character, and Christ's real Eucharistic presence.

1. Biblical Foundations for Eucharistic Worship. All four Gospels inform us that Jesus, on the night he was betrayed, gathered with his disciples for a final meal. Sensing his own impending death, Jesus on that occasion performed a prophetic gesture in order to interpret to his followers the significance of what he was about to suffer. He took bread, blessed it, broke it, and, calling it his body, gave it to them to eat. He thus assured them that in dying he gave himself totally to them as the source of their life. He then took a cup of wine, called it his blood, said it would seal a new covenant, and gave it to them to drink. For the Jews the blood of the covenant signified the bond of life linking God to his people. Jesus thus prophesied that his death would seal a covenant that would bind his disciples to God in a new and life-giving way. Jesus also told his followers to repeat his actions in his memory.

It took, however, not only Jesus' death but also his resurrection and his mission of the Pentecostal Breath into the Church for his disciples to comprehend the full significance of the prophetic gesture which he performed at that final supper. How, then, did they express this new comprehension? In order to answer this question, let us examine in turn the principal New Testament witnesses who address it.

The Eucharist in Paul

We find the first Christian account of the Lord's Supper and the earliest interpretation of its significance in the letters of the Apostle Paul. Writing approximately twenty years after the death and resurrection of Jesus, Paul compared the bread and wine of the Eucharist to the pneumatic food, the manna, which God provided for the Hebrews during their desert wanderings (1 Cor 10:1-4). By the term "pneumatic" Paul probably meant "God-given," although we can probably also find in the word an allusion to the Breath-inspired character of Christian worship. In comparing the Eucharistic bread and wine to manna, Paul proclaimed them the "way-bread" of Christians, the food divinely given to sustain believers in their journey through life to glory with the risen Christ. He warned, however, that those who eat it need to show greater fidelity to God than that exhibited by those who ate manna in the desert.

The Eucharist in Paul's mind creates Christian fellowship. It unites Christians to the risen Lord and to one another in a manner analogous to the religious communion created by Jewish and pagan sacrifices. Sharing in the Blood of Christ binds the baptized to him; eating his Body unites them in the one body of Christ. For Paul, then, participation in the sacred fellowship which the Christian sacrifice effects excludes the baptized from participation in the idolatrous worship of the pagans (1 Cor 10:15-22).

In his account of the institution of the Eucharist, Paul underscores the eschatological character of Eucharistic worship by describing it as a proclamation of the Lord's death "until he comes" (1 Cor 11:23-26). For Paul, then, Eucharistic worship expresses Christian longing for the fulfillment of the redemption and salvation begun in Christ.

The Last Supper in Mark

In Mark's account of the Last Supper, Jesus performs his prophetic gesture during the Passover meal which he celebrates with his disciples (Mark 14:12-16). As Jesus approaches death he offers himself in sacrifice, providing the blood for a new covenant between God and the new Israel he has already begun. The new Israel includes "the many" for whom he will die, all those who will come to believe in him. In Mark's Gospel, then, Jesus' prophetic gesture interprets the events of the passion which it introduces.

In order, however, to understand the full scope of Mark's Eucharistic theology, one must look beyond his institution narrative and the events of Jesus' passion which that narrative introduces. In addition, one must take into account earlier events in Mark's account of the life of Jesus which foreshadow the Eucharist. More specifically, Mark narrates both multiplications of loaves and fishes in a manner that clearly parallels these miracles with his institution narrative. In both miracle stories Jesus takes the food, blesses it, breaks it, and gives it to his disciples, just as he will do in instituting the Eucharist (Mark 6:41; 8:6).

The Miracles of Multiplication in Mark

In his account of the feeding of the four thousand, Mark portrays Jesus as the shepherd of Israel moved with concern and compassion for his flock. He expresses that compassion initially by teaching them, by imparting to them the wisdom he has come to bring (Mark 6:34). Moreover, Mark sees in the bread that Jesus distributes a symbol of the wisdom he imparts, for those who understand the full significance of the miracle of the loaves grasp the deeper implications of Jesus' teaching and of the miracles he performs (Mark 8:17-20). What deeper revelation does Mark discover in the miracle of the loaves and fishes?

After the first miracle of multiplication, Jesus sends the disciples across the Sea of Galilee while he retires to a mountain to pray. The disciples encounter strong headwinds. As they toil against wave and storm, Jesus comes to them walking on the water. They mistake him for a ghost; but Jesus corrects them by saying: "Take heart! I am. Have no fear!" As Jesus joins them in the boat, the winds drop. This miracle leaves the disciples utterly astounded and confused, because, Mark notes, "they did not understand about the loaves" (Mark 6:47-52).

In the Synoptic Gospels, Jesus' cosmological miracles help focus the central Christological question, the question that Jesus puts to all his disciples: "Who do you say I am?" As Jesus walks upon the water and symbolically subdues the forces of chaos, he identifies himself by invoking the divine name: "I am." For Mark, then, the participation in Eucharistic worship that the miracle of the loaves foreshadows includes faith in the divinity of Jesus.

It also includes belief in God's universal saving will, as the second miracle also cryptically suggests. Jesus performs the first miracle of the loaves on Jewish soil; he performs the second in Gentile territory as a foreshadowing that the Gentiles will also gather around the Eucharistic table in the new Israel that he founds (Mark 8:1-10).

As in the case of the first multiplication, Mark follows the second with an allusion to its deeper symbolic significance. Immediately after the second multiplication, the obtuse Pharisees demand that Jesus perform some sign to validate his mission. Having refused to give a sign, Jesus immediately warns his disciples against "the leaven of the Pharisees and the leaven of Herod." By the leaven of the Pharisees Jesus probably means their hard-hearted refusal to believe in him. By the leaven of Herod he probably means all of those attitudes opposed to the gospel that that violent and sensuous monarch symbolized. When the disciples misunderstand his warning, Jesus points their attention to the two miracles of the loaves for them to discover there the meaning of his admonition.

For Mark, then, those who participate in the Eucharist partake of the bread of wisdom that Jesus comes to impart. That wisdom allows them to recognize both Jesus' divinity and the universality of the salvation he brings. Those who feed on Jesus' wisdom discover it in the act of sharing in the Eucharist. Eucharistic wisdom purifies the heart of unbelief, violence, and carnality. The disciples of Jesus, however, can understand neither the miracles of multiplication nor the Eucharist that they foreshadow until Jesus dies on the cross, rises again, and baptizes his followers with the divine Breath; for ultimately the paschal mystery endows the Eucharist with its full meaning.

The Last Supper in Matthew

Matthew's institution narrative closely parallels Mark's with minor verbal variations. Like Mark, Matthew portrays the supper as a Passover celebration (Matt 26:17). Matthew, however, insists explicitly that the covenant sacrifice that Jesus' Eucharistic actions prophesy will effect the forgiveness of sins (Matt 26:26-29). In others words, his self-sacrifice on the cross not only creates the new covenant but also atones for sin.

The Miracles of Multiplication in Matthew

In his account of the first miracle of the loaves and fishes, Matthew omits Mark's references to Jesus as the shepherd of Israel. Instead, he portrays the miracle as an expression of the same compassion as Jesus shows to the sick and the suffering. Like Mark, however, Matthew portrays both miracles of multiplication as foreshadowings of the Eucharist (Matt 14:13-21; 15:32-39).

Moreover, while Matthew follows the first miracle of multiplication with the account of Jesus' walking on the water, unlike Mark he fails to link with Eucharistic faith Jesus' implicit proclamation of his divinity through his use of the divine name. Instead, Matthew embellishes the story with an account of how Peter at Jesus' command also walked on the water only to sink through lack of faith. This embellishment shifts the dramatic focus of Mark's original story from Jesus' divinity to the disciples' faith in him. Matthew also shows little patience with the obtuseness exhibited by the disciples in Mark's account. In Matthew, the disciples, confronted with the miracle immediately worship Jesus and confess: "Truly your are the Son of God" (Matt 14:22-33).

In his account of the second miracle of multiplication, Matthew once again embellishes the Markan narrative. In Matthew as in Mark the second multiplication anticipates the inclusion of the Gentiles in the new Israel's Eucharistic worship. Matthew, however, adds Sadducees, who denied the resurrection, to the group of Pharisees who ignore the miracle of multiplication and demand of Jesus a validating sign. Like Mark's Jesus, Matthew's refuses to perform a miracle; but then, unlike Mark's, he promises a sign, the sign of his own resurrection, to which he refers cryptically as "the sign of Jonah" (Matt 16:1-4; 12:38-42).

Like Mark's, Matthew's Jesus warns, not against "the leaven of the Pharisees and the leaven of Herod," but against "the leaven of the Pharisees and the leaven of the Sadducees." Instead of reacting with puzzlement, however, the disciples in Matthew's account immediately recognize that by "leaven" Jesus means the doctrine of the Pharisees and Sadducees. As does Mark, however, Matthew links the rejection of this false leaven to Eucharistic faith by alluding to the two miracles of multiplication.

Clearly, then, while Matthew confesses the divinity of Jesus, whom his gospel proclaims as "God-with-us" (Matt 1:23; 28:20), he does not associate the confession of Jesus' divinity as closely as Mark does with Eucharistic belief. He does, however, link it even more explicitly than Mark does to belief in Jesus' resurrection. Mark contrasts Eucharistic faith with the unbelief of the Pharisees and with the violence of heart of self-indulgent rulers like Herod who murder God's witnesses. Matthew contrasts Eucharistic faith with the pharisaical unbelief and with the refusal to acknowledge the resurrection.

The Last Supper in Luke

Like Matthew, Luke regarded the Last Supper as a paschal meal (Luke 22:7-8); but Luke diverged at certain points from the other Synoptic accounts of the Last Supper. We find two cups mentioned in Luke's narrative of the meal. At the beginning of the supper Jesus assures his disciples of his longing to share this meal with them. He then passes a cup among them (not the Eucharistic cup) as he assures them that he will not drink wine again until the kingdom arrives (Luke 22:15-18). (The extra cup in Luke's narrative may reflect the evolution of Eucharistic ritual in the evangelist's community.)

In the other Synoptics a similar assurance from Jesus occurs after the institution of the Eucharist but with no mention of a separate cup (Matt 26:29; Mark 14:25). These Synoptic allusions to the fulfillment of Eucharistic worship in the final establishment of God's kingdom underscore its eschatological character. The Eucharistic meal foreshadows the final messianic banquet in heaven.

Before the meal Luke's Jesus also shares the bread as his Body and tells his disciples to repeat the gesture in his memory. After the meal he gives them wine to drink assuring them that it is the new covenant in his Blood (Luke 22:19-20). Luke's institution narrative omits Matthew's reference to the atoning character of Jesus' death.

The Miracle of Multiplication in Luke

Luke's Gospel contains only one miracle of multiplication. As in the other two Synoptics, the multiplication foreshadows the Eucharist (Luke 9:12-17; 22:19). In addition, Luke, like Matthew, links Eucharistic faith to belief in the risen one (Luke 24:30). Nevertheless, even though Lukan theology insists on the universality of the salvation revealed in Christ, he omits the multiplication of the loaves in Gentile territory, the account of how Jesus walked on the water, and the warning against false leaven.

The Last Supper in John

John's account of the Last Supper lacks an institution narrative altogether, although a later editor may have incorporated elements of such a narrative into the bread of life discourse (John 6:51-58), which contains the substance of the Fourth Gospel's Eucharistic doctrine. Members of the Johannine community seem to have called into question Jesus' real Eucharistic presence; and that fact colors the Fourth Gospel's theology of the Eucharist, which makes faith in the real presence a condition for sharing in Jesus' resurrection.

The Bread of Life Discourse

The bread of life discourse meditates at some length on a single verse from Exodus: "He gave them bread from heaven to eat" (Exod 16:4). In the first half of the bread of life discourse, Jesus portrays himself as the new manna, as the living bread come down from heaven in order to give life to the world. As the living bread, he satisfies every human hunger and thirst because he imparts risen life to those who believe in him. The bread he gives also imparts the divine wisdom born of faith. Receiving the living bread means accepting Jesus as the one whom the Father has sent, for only those will share the gift of life whom the Father draws to him in faith (John 6:20-50).

John 6:51 marks the transition to the second section of the bread of life discourse. In it Jesus equates the bread that he has come to give with his own flesh. He insists that only those who consent to eat his flesh and drink his blood will enjoy the eternal life he promises, for sharing in Jesus' body and blood causes him to dwell in his disciples and they in him (John 6:51-58).

The discourse ends with Jesus assuring his incredulous disciples that they should not interpret his words according to the flesh but in the life-giving illumination of the divine Breath. John, then, insists explicitly on the pneumatic inspiration of Eucharistic worship. Moreover, belief in Jesus' real Eucharistic presence constitutes a condition for discipleship. Indeed, those who reject his real presence in the Eucharist align themselves with Judas, the traitor, and with the powers of darkness (John 6:59-71).

Hints of Eucharistic Worship in the New Testament

The New Testament may contain other cryptic references to Christian Eucharistic worship. The First Letter of Peter, for example, describes the Christian community as a house of the divine Breath's building, as a holy priesthood offering in the power of the divine Breath sacrifices acceptable to God (1 Pet 2:5). The hint of Temple imagery and the reference to priesthood could allude to community celebrations of the Eucharistic sacrifice. In the course of reflecting on the sacrament of orders, we examined the theology of priesthood contained in the Letter to the Hebrews. One can interpret those reflections as having no sacramental significance. Some exegetes have even interpreted them as antisacramental. Nevertheless, one can also read them as providing a clue to the theological presuppositions that New Testament Christians brought to Eucharistic worship. Similarly, the visions of the heavenly court in the Book of Revelation contain descriptive details derived from early Eucharistic worship (Revelation 5–6). These vague allusions, however, add nothing significant to New Testament Eucharistic theology.

New Testament Eucharistic Theology

The New Testament, then, uses a variety of rich and suggestive images to interpret the significance of Eucharistic worship. The first Christians looked upon the Eucharist as the Christian sacrifice and compared it both to a covenant sacrifice and to a sacrifice of atonement. Comparisons between the Eucharist and manna point to the Eucharistic as a celebration of the Christian Exodus and therefore implicitly portray it as an expression of the conversion experience that grounds Christian freedom. The New Testament also assimilates the Eucharistic bread to the bread of divine wisdom: those who partake of that bread share an enlightenment inspired by the Breath of the risen Christ. Eucharistic wisdom frees the heart to confess Jesus' resurrection, his divinity, and his living presence in pneumatic worship. Eucharistic worship unites those who share in it with the risen Lord and with one another. It creates the body of Christ. In the Fourth Gospel, belief in Christ's real Eucharistic presence functions as a test of authentic Eucharistic faith.

The New Testament also employs a variety of images in order to highlight the eschatological dimensions of Eucharistic prayer. Those who eat the Body of Christ and drink his Blood proclaim his death in expectant longing for his second coming. The Eucharistic banquet anticipates the final messianic banquet that will celebrate the final and complete establishment of God's reign. Finally, those who share in the Eucharistic meal already participate in the risen life of Christ through his indwelling and that of his Breath. They therefore number among the first fruits of the kingdom.

We have reflected on New Testament foundations for Eucharistic theology. In order to understand the theological controversies that have also shaped contemporary Eucharistic faith, we need next to examine the development of Eucharistic worship, for that development contributed significantly to Christian disagreements about its significance.

2. The Development of Eucharistic Ritual. We lack detailed information concerning the manner in which first-century Christians celebrated the Eucharist. We do know, however, that this ritual lay at the heart of their worship. They gathered every week on the Lord's Day to break Eucharistic bread and share the cup.

a. Early Developments. In his account of the institution of the Eucharist, Paul the Apostle cites the prophetic actions of Jesus at the Last Supper not only as the foundation of Christian communal worship but also as its pattern. The ritual repetition of Jesus' words and actions proclaims his death over and over in confident expectation of his second coming (1 Cor 11:23-26).

Eucharistic Worship at Corinth

Moreover, the First Letter to the Corinthians opens a window on how one of the Pauline communities celebrated the Eucharist. At

Corinth the Eucharist seems to have functioned as a plenary session of the entire community. It could not begin until all the members had arrived. The meal opened with a blessing over the bread, which was then broken and distributed to all, probably in words and gestures imitating those of Jesus at the Last Supper. A meal followed that celebrated the ecclesial gathering of the body of Christ. In accord with Jewish custom at the meal's close the cup of blessing was produced, blessed, and shared in proclamation of the death and second coming of the Lord (1 Cor 11:17-26). Very likely after this ritual meal there followed a charismatically inspired prayer service that included prophecy and teaching.

The Early Patristic Eucharist

The *Didache* describes the Eucharist as a pure sacrifice and requires Christians to confess their sins in mutual reconciliation before taking part in it (*Didache*, 14). We also find evidence in the *Didache* that very early Christians had dissociated the Eucharist from the context of a shared meal (*Didache*, 9–10).

In the middle of the second century, Justin Martyr wrote the earliest reasonably detailed patristic account of Eucharistic ritual we possess. He made no mention of a meal. The one who presides over the shared worship pronounces the Eucharistic Prayer, which the community sanctions with a solemn "Amen." This prayer lies at the heart of the ritual and transforms the bread and wine into the Body and Blood of Christ (*1 Apology*, 66). By participating in the Eucharist, Christians offer a pure sacrifice to God and remember the incarnation and passion of God's Son (*Dialogue with Trypho*, 41, 70, 117).

By the second century, Eucharistic worship had acquired a rudimentary structure. A lector read from the Old Testament and from the Gospels. The president of the Eucharist delivered a homily. After the homily common prayers of petition followed, including prayers for the emperor and secular authorities. The kiss of peace sealed these prayers. Bread and a cup containing wine mixed with water were then brought to the president who pronounced over them the Eucharistic Prayer. The community sanctioned the prayer with a solemn "Amen." Deacons distributed Communion to those present and carried it to the sick.

The earliest descriptions of the Eucharist make it clear that the ceremony divided into two parts, with each part sometimes celebrated in two different places. The first part, the Liturgy of the Word, derived from Jewish synagogue worship and contained readings, hymns, and a homily. The second part, the Eucharistic Liturgy, reproduced the actions of Jesus at the Last Supper: taking bread and wine, blessing them, breaking the bread, distributing the consecrated elements to those present.

Early Ritual Embellishments

Gradually the first part of the ceremony, the Liturgy of the Word, underwent embellishment through the introduction of rites intended to dispose the congregation to prayer. The singing of a psalm accompanied the entrance of the Eucharistic ministers. Then either the presiding bishop or a deacon greeted the community and called it to worship.

Probably in the fifth century Pope Gelasius introduced a litany into the Roman Rite that custom subsequently abbreviated to the ninefold petition for mercy in the *Kyrie eleison* (*Lord have mercy*). By the eighth century this prayer had acquired general usage.

The *Gloria in excelsis Deo* (*Glory to God in the highest*) originated as a popular hymn. The oldest Latin text dates to the seventh century. In the East monks chanted the *Gloria* during the Liturgy of the Hours. In the West the *Gloria* entered the Liturgy of the Hours in the fourth century. According to a not improbable tradition, the hymn first entered Eucharistic ritual at a midnight Christmas liturgy celebrated by the pope. Its use was extended to Sundays and feasts by Pope Symmachus (A.D. 498–514), who initially restricted its use to liturgies where bishops presided. By the seventh century priests could also intone the *Gloria* but only at Easter.

The collect, an opening prayer pronounced by the celebrant, ended the introductory rite of the Roman Eucharist in the fifth century. Either Pope Leo I or his immediate predecessor introduced the prayer. While liturgists offer different interpretations of its purpose, its literary structure followed a distinctive Roman formula. It began by invoking the divine name under the rubric of some attribute or saving action performed by the deity. A petition followed together with an explanation of the reason for asking. A concluding formula then invited the congregation's "Amen."

The Liturgy of the Word

The Liturgy of the Word also evolved with time. The first Christians adapted Jewish synagogue worship to their own needs. Readings were taken from the Old Testament and from Christian sources.

Occasionally, readings from nonscriptural books like the Acts of the Martyrs were used to commemorate a special feast. Very likely, liturgical usage first canonized the Eastertide readings. During the fourth century, however, the readings for Sunday worship and for important feasts like Christmas, Epiphany, and Ascension also underwent canonization.

As early as the second century we have evidence of the chanting of psalms between the readings. Not until the fourth century, however, do we find responsorial chants led by a cantor with the congregation repeating the refrain. In all rites except the Ethiopian and Gallican, the Alleluia accompanied the gospel reading.

The homily, a borrowing from the synagogue service, dates to the earliest celebrations of the Eucharist. It explained and meditated on the significance of the readings, applying them to the lives of those gathered in worship.

The recitation of the creed entered the Liturgy of the Word in the East during the great Christological controversies of the fourth century. In the sixth century, the custom spread to the West where the creed was chanted.

During the heyday of the catechumenate in the third century, the nonbaptized were dismissed toward the end of the Liturgy of the Word, before the common prayers of petition and the kiss of peace; but with the disappearance of the catechumenate the rite of dismissal was either omitted or abbreviated.

Fourth and Fifth Century Developments

By the fourth and early fifth centuries, the Latin Eucharistic Liturgy had undergone ritual elaboration as well. The kiss of peace, which had terminated the common prayers of petition and had preceded the preparation of gifts, shifted to the Communion rite. The Eucharistic Liturgy contained an offertory ritual in which the presiding bishop presented the offerings of the faithful; but we have no clear evidence that a formal prayer accompanied the offering.

The Eucharistic Prayer itself began with a dialogue between the celebrant and the congregation, followed by the preface, an introductory prayer of praise. About the year 400 the Western Church began to appropriate the Eastern practice of concluding the preface with the "Holy, holy, holy." The Eucharistic Prayer expanded to include the commemoration of specific individuals. The Epiclesis, or invocation of the Holy Breath over the offerings, preceded the institution narrative. The Anamnesis, a prayer calling to mind the Lord's passion, resurrection, and ascension, as well as a prayer of offering followed the institution narrative.

The Communion rite also evolved. It began with the kiss of peace and with the breaking of the bread. In Rome a fragment of the bread consecrated at the pope's Eucharist was taken round on Sundays to each of the other local liturgies as a gesture of unity and solidarity. As early as the third century a fragment of bread was mixed with the wine. The earliest Communion rites did not include the Lord's Prayer. (The liturgical use of the Lord's Prayer dates to the beginning of the fourth century in Africa, but the ceremony in question may not have been Eucharistic.) At Communion time worshippers received the consecrated bread with joined hands. A blessing pronounced over the people as they bowed their heads and a postcommunion prayer concluded the worship.

We have examined the early development of Eucharistic ritual. We need now to reflect on how contemporary forms of worship underwent canonization in both the East and the West.

b. The Formation of the Byzantine Eucharist. The prestige that the see of Constantinople enjoyed enabled the Byzantine Rite to supersede other rites in the East, just as the Roman Rite eventually replaced other Western rituals. In the seventh century, the Byzantine Eucharist began with the procession of both bishop and people into the church. The bishop took his place in the sanctuary to the chanting of the hymn *Trisagion* (Thrice Holy). After the bishop's greeting, "Peace be with you," three Scripture readings ensued: a lesson from the Old Testament, followed by a responsorial psalm; an epistle, followed by the Alleluia; and the gospel, followed by a homily. After the homily those forbidden to attend the Eucharistic Liturgy were dismissed and the doors of the church closed, even though the catechumenate had by this time effectively disappeared.

The Liturgy of the Faithful

In the seventh century the Byzantine "liturgy of the faithful" probably began with a litany led by one of the deacons. The bread and wine were then brought to the altar. In the Byzantine Rite we find no offertory procession of the people like the one that developed in the West; instead people turned in their gifts as they entered the church. Eventually, the transfer of gifts developed into the "Great Entrance," a solemn procession symbolizing Christ going to his passion. The kiss of peace and the recitation of the Nicene Creed followed the Great Entrance. The creed had been introduced by the Patriarch Timothy at the beginning of the sixth century. The anaphora, or Eucharistic Prayer, which had begun as a prayer of the entire congregation had, with the clericalization of Christian worship, evolved into a prayer silently recited by the priest alone.

The Lord's Prayer followed the anaphora. In rites other than the Byzantine, the Lord's Prayer followed the fraction rite as an immediate preparation for communion. Under Gregory the Great, however, the Latin Church adopted the Byzantine placement of the Lord's Prayer at the beginning of the Communion service, with the result that both ritual traditions separated the Lord's Prayer from the distribution of Communion itself. After the Lord's Prayer in the Byzantine liturgy the celebrant first elevated the consecrated elements, then distributed them to the people, although theological stress on their holy, even terrifying character, discouraged most communicants. A hymn followed Communion, and the liturgy ended with a blessing of the people probably preceded by a prayer of invocation.

Ninth Century Developments

The ninth century saw other modifications of the Byzantine Eucharist. Now the gifts were prepared before the liturgy as a whole, instead of at the Great Entrance. The prayers that accompanied the preparation of the bread and wine, called the *Proskomidia,* anticipated petitions that would later find inclusion in the anaphora: for example, in the liturgy of St. Basil, the petition that the bread be blessed and received at the heavenly altar, or, in the liturgy of St. John Chrysostom, the invocation of the Holy Breath on the sacred elements. A psalm with a refrain replaced the *Trisagion* as the entrance hymn. Instead of beginning with the entry of clergy and people into the church, the liturgy now began with the entry of the clergy into the sanctuary. In this procession, called the "Little Entrance," the Book of the Gospels was carried. The great *Synapte,* or litany, and the chanting of the displaced *Trisagion* followed. During the Liturgy of the Word, the Old Testament reading disappeared; but the responsorial psalm that had followed it remained. A litany followed the sermon.

In the Byzantine Rite of the ninth century, the liturgy of the faithful began with the dismissal of the catechumens and with two prayers of the faithful. The prepared elements were brought in. The kiss of peace and the creed preceded the anaphora; a litany followed it, while the priest prayed silently. The conclusion of the priest's silent prayer led into the Our Father, a prayer of blessing, the elevation of the sacred elements, and Communion. The priest distributed Communion under both species with a spoon. A prayer of blessing and a litany of thanksgiving followed Communion. The deacon dismissed the people, and the priest's "Prayer behind the Ambo"[1] ended the liturgy.

By the ninth century the Byzantine Eucharist had, then, achieved the basic ritual structure it presently enjoys. In the eleventh century prayers for the use of priest and deacon during the entrance rite were introduced. The fourteenth century also brought some new complexity to the preparation of the elements.

How, then, did the canonization of Eucharistic worship develop in the West?

c. The Eucharist in the West. Meanwhile, in the West a different kind of ritual development was transforming the Roman Eucharist. By the beginning of the fifth century the Roman anaphora had achieved fixity, even though other parts of the Eucharistic Liturgy continued to show local variations. By the beginning of the sixth century, however, the overall framework of the Roman Eucharist had taken shape.

The production of liturgical books facilitated this standardization of worship; but in the West the French kings, not the papacy, first imposed legal uniformity on Eucharistic piety: first Pepin and then more effectively Charlemagne between 785 and 790. The legal imposition of the Roman Rite upon the Frankish kingdom ensured that the West would celebrate its liturgy in the popularly unintelligible Latin tongue.

Medieval Ritual Pluralism

The Roman liturgy in Italy, the Gallican in France, and the Mozarabic in Spain evolved separately. By the end of the tenth century, however, the Gallican version of the Roman Rite had officially replaced Roman ritual in the city of Rome itself.

The eleventh century saw the emergence of several unfortunate changes in Latin Eucharistic worship. Instead of facing the congregation in a communal celebration, the altar faced the rear wall of the church. Instead of leading a community celebration, priests now said, or read, Mass with their backs to the people.

1. The ambo was a raised desk from which the gospel or epistle was either read or chanted.

The tendency to look upon the celebration of the Eucharist as exclusively a priestly function found further reinforcement in the emergence of the private Mass. The practice developed in the monasteries, which celebrated the Eucharist daily, rather than weekly. In monasteries with several priests, each priest-monk would celebrate his own private, daily Mass.

The extreme clericalization of Eucharistic worship during the high Middle Ages reduced the laity to the role of spectators in some sacred drama rather than active participants in an act of shared prayer and praise. Moreover, medieval concern with the real presence of Christ in the Eucharist led to popular devotional obsession with the moment of consecration. In urban centers people would rush from church to church on Sunday in order to be present at the consecration and elevation of the host and chalice. Abuses such as these sowed the seeds of dissension that would flourish during the Protestant Reformation.

We shall consider later the Eucharistic controversies that split Protestant and Catholic during the Reformation. For the moment, however, let us examine how the Protestant reformers transformed Eucharistic ritual.

d. Protestant Reforms of Eucharistic Ritual. In 1523 Martin Luther issued his *Formula Missae et Communionis,* an initial revision of the Roman Eucharist. The *Formula* followed closely the structure of the Roman Mass, although it excised the offertory prayers and most of the canon. The *Formula* prescribed that the Eucharistic Liturgy be celebrated in Latin. The institution narrative, however, preceded the *Sanctus* and *Benedictus.* During the *Benedictus* the celebrant elevated the consecrated elements. The Lord's Prayer followed; but the embolism, the traditional prayer developing the final petition of the Our Father, was dropped. The *Agnus Dei* accompanied the administration of communion. Two collects, a *Benedicamus Domino* with an Alleluia and a biblical blessing concluded the service.

In his *Deutsche Messe* of 1526, however, Luther proposed more radical revisions in the Eucharistic rite. In contrast to the *Formula* of 1523, the vernacular replaced Latin as the language of prayer. The *Deutsche Messe* omitted the *Gloria in excelsis* and adopted versified forms of the creed and of the *Sanctus.* The celebrant read the institution narrative and as in the rite of 1523 elevated the consecrated elements as a memorial and proclamation. The faithful could receive Communion under both species.

Radical Protestant Eucharistic Reforms

Zwingli, who regarded the Eucharist as simply a memorial service, called for even more radical Eucharistic reforms. He transformed
Sunday worship into a preaching service. He allowed the celebration
of the Eucharist only four times a year, four times as often as the
medieval laity had been obliged to communicate. He replaced the
canon of the mass by four prayers: a recapitulation of redemption
that included the Our Father; prayers for feeding on the Bread of
Heaven, for the grace to imitate Jesus' sacrificial dedication, for unity
with him; and the institution narrative. After an exhortation to a devout Communion, the Our Father and a precommunion prayer followed. The elements were carried silently to the people in their seats.
The service concluded with a brief thanksgiving and dismissal.

In Strasbourg Bucer adopted a rite similar to Zwingli's but with
modifications. He introduced into the rite an authoritative declaration of pardon and the reading of all four (!) biblical versions of the
institution narrative. The Eucharistic exhortation muted the tone of
thanksgiving. The institution narratives preceded Communion and
combined intercession with prayer for a devout Communion.

The Strasbourg ritual provided the basis for Calvin's revision
of Eucharistic worship. He pushed unsuccessfully for a weekly Eucharist, but the Geneva city council overrode his suggestion and imposed instead a quarterly celebration. John Knox experienced the
Geneva ritual at Frankfurt and transported it to Scotland.

At the basis of these radical Protestant transformations of Christian worship lay the Eucharistic controversies that divided Catholic
and Protestant at the time of the Reformation. We shall examine the
more important of those controversies presently. First, however, let
us consider the Eucharistic reforms instituted by the Council of Trent
and their subsequent transformation in the liturgical revolution
authorized by the Second Vatican Council.

e. Tridentine Reforms of Eucharistic Ritual. In its liturgical reforms
Trent responded to the Protestant challenge by revising the Roman
Missal and, with the help of the printing press, by imposing on Roman
Catholics everywhere a uniform Eucharistic rite. The Eucharistic reforms undertaken by the Council of Trent reflect, however, the liturgical myopia of late medieval piety, which regarded the celebration
of the Eucharist as an exclusively clerical activity, as a sacrosanct ritual performed by priests and their trained assistants.

The council retained Latin as the Church's official liturgical language. It allowed lay Communion only under one species. It also

canonized the "Low Mass" as normative for the ordinary celebration of the Eucharist. In the rite of "Low Mass," liturgical functions previously performed by the deacon, lector, choir, and people all belonged to the priest. In a "High Mass," by contrast, a choir sang the legislated liturgical texts, which could, moreover, be sung in any appropriate musical setting. Composers of genius, like Bach, Mozart, Beethoven, and others, would take liturgical advantage of that liberty and compose High Masses of great sublimity.

The revised Roman missal gave new order and uniformity to the Eucharistic service, but Trent's liturgical reforms failed finally to meet two fundamental Protestant objections to late medieval liturgical worship: its unintelligibility and the exclusion of the laity from active participation. In point of fact, the majority of the bishops at Trent favored a vernacular liturgy in principle; but, given the chaotic times in which they had undertaken liturgical reform, they decided conservatively that the time to change from Latin to the vernacular as the Church's official liturgical language lay somewhere in the future. Fear of heresy seems to have motivated their reluctance to encourage active lay participation in the Church's worship.

f. From the Liturgical Movement to Vatican II. The Catholic liturgical movement developed largely in response to the inadequacy of the Tridentine reform of worship. Until 1897 Rome placed vernacular translations of the liturgy on the Index of Forbidden Books. In the early part of the twentieth century, however, vernacular missals for lay use began to enjoy popularity. The celebrating priest still exercised a monopoly over liturgical functions, but the laity could now read simultaneously in the vernacular the prayers he recited in Latin.

The Liturgical Movement

In 1903 Pius X encouraged the laity to participate in liturgical singing. The liturgical movement subsequently introduced the dialogue Mass, in which the entire congregation recited in Latin the liturgical responses to the priest's prayers. Offertory processions and the introduction of lectors who read the epistle and gospel in English from the pulpit after or during the priest's reading of them in Latin also increased lay participation in Eucharistic prayer.

As the liturgical movement gained impetus, however, it chafed under the inadequacy of even these innovations. Studies of the history of Eucharistic worship alerted liturgists to the communal character of early Church worship, to the diversity of liturgical functions, to the eschatological context of early sacramental prayer. Liturgists began pushing for sacramental worship in the vernacular and for its structural overhaul, including the Eucharist.

The Reforms of Vatican II

The Second Vatican Council sanctioned the revolution in worship for which the liturgical movement called. It rejected the notion that the Eucharist is a "one-man sacrifice" and rediversified the liturgical roles within Eucharistic worship: the choir, community, lectors, Eucharistic ministers, and liturgical assistants all make a distinctive contribution along with the celebrant to the Church's shared Eucharistic worship. Diversification dramatized the shared, communal character of Eucharistic prayer.

Vatican II turned the altar around and diversified the place of worship as well: it took the Liturgy of the Word away from the altar and in the process differentiated it more clearly from the Liturgy of the Eucharist. The council called for the simplification of the rites of the Church, for a revision of the lectionary that would make the riches of the Bible liturgically available, and for a reform of the liturgical year. Full and active participation of the laity in the Eucharistic celebration became the norm of sound Eucharistic piety. The council also allowed the celebration of the Eucharist in the vernacular (*Sacrosanctum Concilium; Lumen gentium,* 12).

The historical development of Eucharistic worship allows one to understand the origins of contemporary worship. It also provides a context for understanding the principal theological controversies that have surrounded the Eucharist. In the section that follows we shall call attention to three of those controversies.

3. Controversies Concerning the Eucharist. The Fathers of the Church reflected deeply and at length on the significance of Eucharistic worship. In their writings we find cumulative meditations on different facets of this, the greatest of the sacraments.

The Eucharist in the Fathers of the Church

The Fathers of the Church looked upon Eucharistic worship as a corporate act of the Church, as a sign of Christian unity, as the visible manifestation of the Church's very reality (Ignatius of Antioch, *Eph.,* 13.1; *Phil.,* 1.4; *Smyrn.,* 8.20; *Didache,* 9.1; Augustine of Hippo,

Sermon 262; Gregory of Nyssa, *Ep. 3 ad Eustathium*). In Eucharistic worship the Church gives thanks for the redemption accomplished in Christ (Justin Martyr, *1 Apology*, 65; *Dialogue with Trypho*, 14.1; Ignatius of Antioch, *Eph.*, 13.1; *Smyrn.*, 7.1; *Philad.*, 4.1; Irenaeus of Lyons, *Against the Heresies*, 4.18; Basil of Caesarea, *On the Holy Spirit*, 66). In thanking God, the Christian community also invokes his continued blessing and prays for his continued redemption of sinful humanity. The Fathers also recognized that in the Eucharist the Church remembers the paschal mystery in the power of the divine Breath. More than any ordinary act of human remembering, the Eucharistic *anamnesis* makes that mystery a living, present reality (Justin Martyr, *Dialogue with Trypho*, 41.1, 70.4, 117.3; John Chrysostom, *Homily on Matt* 25:4).

As theological consensus concerning the Eucharist unraveled, it divided into three principal debates. Theologians argued over the real presence of Christ in the Eucharist. They debated the sacrificial character of Eucharistic worship. Finally, as Eucharistic theology evolved, we find an eclipse and reemergence of an awareness of the eschatological dimensions of Eucharistic prayer. In chapter six of volume one we have already reflected on the issues that surfaced in the course of theological debates over the real presence. Readers may review those issues now, if they feel the need to do so. In the present chapter, we shall examine the two other areas of controversy that have exercised Eucharistic theologians: the sacrificial and the eschatological dimensions of Eucharistic worship.

a. The Eucharistic Sacrifice. The Fathers of the Church speak consistently of the Eucharist as a sacrifice. Participation in Eucharistic worship draws the Church into the atoning sacrifice of Christ by recalling with the consent of faith Jesus' death and glorification (Augustine, *City of God*, 10.6). By the end of the fourth century, however, we find a significant shift in theological understanding of the Eucharistic sacrifice. One discovers a strong sense in some writers that the Eucharistic worshipper stands in the very presence of Christ sacrificed (John Chrysostom, *On the Priesthood*, 6.4; Cyril of Jerusalem, *Mystagogic Catechesis*, 5.10; Gregory of Nyssa, *Letter 171*). This shift in Eucharistic rhetoric parallels the rise of fourth-century sacerdotalism and reflects the ways in which it transformed theological perceptions of the liturgical function of the ordained within the Eucharist. Besides leading the shared worship of the community, as high priests of the new covenant the ordained in each Eucharistic celebration performed an act analogous to the sacrifices of the Levitical priesthood. Rhetorical emphasis on the role of the celebrant in effecting the Eucharistic sacrifice encouraged, then, a rhetorical "objectification" of the sacrifice itself. The Fathers, however, explain Christ's sacrifice in each act of Eucharistic worship by appealing to the eternal and transtemporal character of the Eucharist. We find, then, in patristic literature no hint of the temporal repetition of Christ's original sacrifice; nor do we find any suggestion that the Eucharistic sacrifice adds anything to the sacrifice of Calvary, although both issues would one day preoccupy Reformation theologians.

The Eucharist as Sacrifice in the Medieval Church

As medieval debate over the presence of Jesus in the Eucharistic species developed, we find a parallel tendency in the high Middle Ages for theologians not only to emphasize the sacrificial character of the Eucharist (often to the neglect of its eschatological dimensions) but also to portray the Eucharist as a sacrificial act that applies the merits of Christ to the souls of Christians (Bonaventure, *Commentary on the Book of Sentences,* IV, d.xii, a.1, qq.1-3; Thomas Aquinas, *Summa Theologiae,* III, lxxix and lxxxiii, 1; John Duns Scotus, *Oxford Commentary on the Book of Sentences, Quaestiones Additae de Sacrificio,* I–IX).

These theological tendencies helped motivate popular aberrations in Eucharistic piety and were to a certain extent influenced by them. As we have already seen, emphasis on the real presence of Christ in the Eucharist produced in late medieval piety a distorted popular obsession with the moment of consecration. The Middle Ages also witnessed the extreme clericalization of Eucharistic worship. Once private Masses had emerged in the monasteries, well-to-do Christians began paying priests stipends to offer Mass privately for their intentions. The practice fostered the popular illusion that in every Eucharist priests function as the principal, if not the sole, agents of worship, in that they say the Mass for the intentions of absent people. The patristic sense of the Eucharist as an act of the Christian community as a whole faded from the popular imagination.

Luther on the Eucharist as Sacrifice

Martin Luther could find no scriptural justification for the medieval belief that in celebrating the Mass Christian priests offered sacrifice on behalf of others. He conceded that the Eucharist could be considered a sacrifice in the sense that in it the priestly people of God offered themselves anew to the deity in union with Christ, but he saw no need for priestly mediators between God and the Christian community. Luther interpreted the institution of the Eucharist as Christ's last will and testament and its celebration in the community as that testament's seal. The Eucharistic celebration assures Christians of their salvation in Christ, for in the Eucharist Christians know by faith the sacrament's significance and experience God's forgiveness despite their sinfulness (Luther, *Works*, 14:35-52). Other Protestant reformers agreed with Luther that the New Testament nowhere speaks of the Lord's Supper as a cultic sacrifice (Zwingli, *Commentary on True and False Religion*, 18; Calvin, *Institutes*, IV, xvii–xviii).

Trent on the Eucharist as Sacrifice

The Council of Trent in response to these objections insisted on the sacrificial character of Eucharistic worship, defining it as "a true and actual sacrifice" (DS 1751). Trent looked upon the Eucharist as the one true sacrifice of Christ and appealed to the Letter to the Hebrews (7:24-27) in justification of its position. The Eucharist makes present the bloody sacrifice that Jesus offered on the cross, preserves its memory until the end of time, and applies its healing power to effect the forgiveness of sins (DS 1740).

As we have seen, the text of the Letter to the Hebrews leaves its Eucharistic intent somewhat vague. Trent would, then, have found stronger scriptural justification for the sacrificial character of the Eucharist in the words that Jesus used in instituting the ritual. At the Last Supper he certainly used sacrificial language in order to declare the bread his Body and the wine his covenant Blood. Moreover, he ordered his followers to repeat these sacrificial actions and words in his memory. Instead, however, Trent opted to portray the Eucharist as a representation, recall, and application of the saving death of Christ.

The language that this council used in order to describe the role of the celebrant in the Eucharist had, moreover, sacerdotalist overtones. It spoke of the apostles and their successors as priests of the new covenant who in the Eucharist perform a sacrificial act analogous to the sacrifices of the Levitical priesthood (DS 1743–1754).

Post-Tridentine Developments

The terms in which Trent chose to defend the sacrificial character of the Eucharist helped motivate some of the theological excesses that developed in post-Tridentine Catholic Eucharistic theology. That theology tended to locate the sacrificial character of the Eucharist in the destruction or alteration of the bread and wine on the altar or in the mystical slaughtering of Christ through the separate consecration of his Body and Blood.

Contemporary Catholic theology has abandoned these post-Tridentine aberrations largely in consequence of a rediscovery of facets of the Eucharist that the authors of these misleading theories ignored. Contemporary Catholic theology insists with the Fathers of the Church on the communal character of Christian worship. It portrays the Eucharist as the sacrament that symbolizes and effects the union of Christians with one another in the mystical body and with Christ, its head. Moreover, in its Eucharistic worship the sacramentality of the Church reaches its fullest expression.

Vatican II on the Eucharist as Sacrifice

Concerns such as these led the Second Vatican Council to qualify the sacerdotalist language employed by the Council of Trent in its defense of the sacrificial character of the Eucharist. Vatican II calls the Eucharist a sacrifice; but the council discovered the Eucharistic presence of Christ in the proclamation of the sacred Scripture, in the Eucharistic species, and in the Christian community as a whole. Moreover, instead of portraying the Eucharist as a sacrifice offered to God by a quasi-Levitical priest, Vatican II spoke of it as the sacrifice of the Church as a whole.

> Rightly, then, the liturgy is considered as an exercise of the priestly office of Jesus Christ. In the liturgy the sanctification of humanity is manifested by signs perceptible to the senses, and is effected in a way which is proper to each of these signs; in the liturgy full public worship is performed by the Mystical Body of Jesus Christ, that is, by the Head and His members. From this it follows that every liturgical celebration, because it is an action of Christ the priest and of His Body the Church, is a sacred action surpassing all others. No other action of the Church can match its claim to efficacy, nor equal the degree of it (*Sacrosanctum Concilium,* 7).

While the liturgy does not exhaust the Church's action, it remains

> . . . the summit toward which the activity of the Church is directed; at the same time it is the fountain from which all her power flows. For the goal of apostolic works is that all who are made sons of God by faith and baptism should come together

to praise God in the midst of His Church, to take part in her sacrifice, and to eat the Lord's supper (*Sacrosanctum Concilium,* 9–10).

In every Eucharistic celebration the Church renews its covenant with God. Hence, more than any other action of the Church, Eucharistic worship sanctifies humanity and glorifies God (*Sacrosanctum Concilium,* 10).

If, then, one compares Vatican II's discussion of the Eucharistic sacrifice with Trent's, one observes important shifts in theological emphasis. While Vatican II spoke of the sacrificial character of the Eucharist, it located the Christian sacrifice not primarily or exclusively in the activity of the Eucharistic celebrant but in that of the entire Church united with Jesus Christ, its head and great high priest. Moreover, the council discovered the priestly ministry of Christ in all the liturgical worship of the Church.

We shall return to these themes in discussing the significance of Eucharistic worship. Before we do so, however, let us reflect on a third controverted area of Eucharistic theology: the eclipse and reemergence of eschatological awareness.

b. The Eclipse and Reemergence of Eschatological Eucharistic Awareness. As we have seen, New Testament Eucharistic piety used a variety of images to express eschatological longing. In the New Testament we find the Eucharist described as a proclamation of the Lord's death "until he comes." New Testament writers portray the Eucharist as a foretaste of the final messianic banquet. Finally, they discover in those assembled to worship the first fruits of the kingdom. All three themes underwent embellishment in the writings of the Fathers of the Church.

The Fathers on Eucharistic Eschatology

Maximus the Confessor held that Eucharistic worship signifies, prefigures, resembles, and typifies the preaching of the gospel that marks the beginning of the end (Matt 24:14) (*Mystagogy,* 14–21). Theodore of Mopsuestia assured his congregation that those who communicate in the Eucharist receive in hope the incorruptible, risen life of Christ that he will impart in its fullness on the last day. Christians celebrated the Eucharist on Sunday as the day on which Christ rose from the dead, the day that foreshadowed their own final resurrection (Ignatius of Antioch, *Magn.,* 9; *Ep. Barn.,* 15, 8ff.; Justin Martyr, *1 Apology,* 67; *Dialogue with Trypho,* 41 and 138; Basil of Caesarea, *On* the Holy Spirit, 27, 66; Augustine, *Epistles 55, 23*). The orientation of Christian churches toward the east expressed a similar eschatological longing, since popular belief held that Jesus, the sun of justice, would return for the final judgment from the east (*Apostolic Constitutions*, II, 57).

In describing the Eucharist as a foretaste of the heavenly messianic banquet we find three different emphases in the writings of the Fathers. Some emphasize the future fulfillment of the present act of worship (Irenaeus of Lyons, *Against the Heresies*, IV, 18, 5, V, 33, 1ff. and 36, 3; Augustine, *Quaestiones Evangeliorum*, I, 43). Other Fathers stress that those who share in the Eucharist participate here and now in the banquet of the Lamb (Jerome, *Letter*, 120, 2; Eucherius of Lyons, *Instruction*, I, 2). Other Fathers still try to strike a balance between the present and the future, between the salvation achieved and that which is coming (Origen, *Exhortation to Martyrdom*, 40; Cyprian of Carthage, *Letter*, 63, 9). This third line of interpretation better accords not only with New Testament eschatology but also with the religious vision of Jesus himself, who saw in his teaching, healings, and exorcisms the very presence of the kingdom he proclaimed, even though its full realization lay somewhere in the future (Matt 10:38; 11:2-6; Luke 7:18-23; 12:50).

Finally we find that the Fathers of the Church frequently portray Eucharistic worshippers as the first fruits of the kingdom. That portrayal roots itself in two New Testament beliefs: the Breath of Christ inspires Eucharistic worship; and pneumatic life, which the Eucharist communicates, yields a present participation in the risen life of Christ. The Fathers embellish these New Testament doctrines by portraying the Eucharist as medicinal, as curing human corruptibility by transforming those who communicate into the likeness of the risen Christ (Gregory of Nyssa, *Cat. Or.*, 37; Augustine, *Sermon*, 57, 7; Cyril of Alexandria, *On Adoration in Spirit and Truth*, XII; Theodore of Mopsuestia, *Homily XXI;* Cyril of Jerusalem, *Mystagogic Catechesis*, 4, 1 and 3).

The Eclipse of Eschatological Eucharistic Awareness

The first Christians realized very early that Jesus would not return soon. Nevertheless, throughout the patristic period Eucharistic piety preserved healthy eschatological awareness. Why did it disappear in the Latin Church? Three forces combined to bring about the eclipse of eschatological awareness in Eucharistic worship: (1) Medieval debates about the real presence narrowly focused both popular piety and theological concern upon the present transformation of the bread and wine at the time of consecration. Obsession with the real presence of Christ in the Eucharist obscured the orientation of Eucharistic piety toward the future. (2) During the Middle Ages, Eucharistic theology, partly in response to aberrations in popular Eucharistic devotion, depicted the sacrificial dimension of Eucharistic worship as the application of the past merits of Christ to the present salvific needs of Christians. A lopsided concern with the sacrificial aspect of the Eucharist to the exclusion of its eschatological dimension set the tone for Reformation debates about the Eucharist. (3) The embittered polemics of the Reformation over the meaning of the real presence and the sacrificial character of the Eucharist caused both Catholics and Protestants alike to neglect its eschatological dimension both in theological discourse on the Eucharist and in popular Eucharistic devotion.

The Retrieval of Eschatological Eucharistic Awareness

As we have seen, the liturgical movement with its concern to retrieve forgotten forms of Eucharistic piety effected a scholarly retrieval of the eschatological dimensions of Eucharistic worship. Nevertheless, the effective communication of these scholarly insights to the average Eucharistic worshipper still lies somewhere in the future.

We have reflected on the major Eucharistic controversies and on the ways in which they both reflected and helped shape the evolution of popular Eucharistic piety. The time has come to attempt to reach a normative insight into the purpose of Eucharistic prayer. In order to reach such an insight, we need to reflect on the significant structure of Eucharistic worship; for it embodies a specific kind of converted religious commitment.

4. The Structure of Eucharistic Prayer. As we have seen, the Second Vatican Council described Eucharistic worship in the most exalted terms as both the summit of the Church's activity and the source of its power. This description sounds inflated until one contextualizes it in an adequate theology of conversion. Authentic Eucharistic worship demands, expresses, and fosters an integral, fivefold conversion to Christ. It gathers the Christian community as a community in order to celebrate and further its graced transformation in the Holy Breath of Christ. Authentic Eucharistic worship embodies, therefore, the shared hope of Christians, their shared faith, and their shared love. It recommits them to the search for a just social order in a charismatic community of public witness and of mutual service.

The Centrality of Eucharistic Communion

As we shall see, the entire movement of Eucharistic worship culminates in the moment of Communion. As we have also seen, first Holy Communion completes the process of sacramental incorporation into the Christian community. Moreover, Eucharistic Communion constitutes the only repeatable part of the rite of initiation. As a consequence, one cannot engage in Eucharistic worship without reaffirming one's original covenant of initiation. As a consequence, Eucharistic worship commits Christians both personally and collectively to the process of ongoing conversion.

Moreover, the relationship between the Church's Eucharistic worship and the process of ongoing conversion establishes a relationship between the Eucharist and the other sacraments as well. As we have seen, marriage, orders, reconciliation, and anointing also foster ongoing conversion. Hence, one cannot worship Eucharistically without reaffirming the covenant commitment that those sacraments ritualize. In recommitting themselves to Christ in the Eucharist, married Christians implicitly reaffirm their marriage covenant, just as the ordained in worshipping Eucharistically recommit themselves publicly to leading the Christian community in the service of atonement. Eucharistic worship also opposes Christians anew to the corrupting influences of concupiscence and absolves those who participate in it of minor, repented, postbaptismal faults. Eucharistic worship reaffirms therefore the renunciation of postbaptismal sin that both reconciliation and anointing absolve.

How, then, does Eucharistic prayer unfold, and how does it summon the Christians to ongoing conversion and foster it within them?

a. Introductory Rites. Because the Eucharist celebrates and fosters the Christian community's ongoing repentance and conversion to Christ, it begins appropriately with a penitential rite and with the invocation of God's mercy. An appropriate hymn or song should accompany the entrance of the celebrant. After venerating the altar and greeting the community, either the celebrant or some other appropriate minister immediately invites the assembled worshippers to a communal confession of personal sinfulness.

Only Christians in good standing can participate fully in Eucharistic worship. Serious sinners need to seek absolution in the rite of reconciliation before returning to the table of the Lord. The penitential rite that begins Eucharistic worship envisages, therefore, not serious sin but minor failings. It reminds the community of its baptismal renunciation of sin and of Satan and forgives minor, postbaptismal faults.

The Lord Have Mercy

The *Lord have mercy,* unless already included in the penitential rite, follows it. The revised Roman Rite has restored the original form of this prayer by transforming it into a litany. The litany celebrates the mercy of God revealed to us in Christ and provides a transition from the penitential rite to the *Glory to God,* on those occasions when this prayer is either recited or sung.[2] The hymn adds a note of solemnity and of joy to the Eucharists in which it is used. Predominantly Christocentric, the *Glory to God* also honors the Father and the Holy Breath. As a joyful profession of faith, it parallels liturgically the confession of Trinitarian faith that follows the renunciation of Satan in the baptism of adults.

Clearly, the penitential rite and the prayers that follow it seek to give ritual expression to the Eucharistic community's ongoing repentance and recommitment to gospel living.

The introductory rite concludes as the celebrant leads the community in the opening prayer, or collect. The collect introduces themes that the day's Scripture readings will develop. It also provides, therefore, a ritual transition from the introductory rites to the first major portion of the Eucharist: the Liturgy of the Word.

b. The Liturgy of the Word. In each Eucharist the Liturgy of the Word consists of readings from the Bible and responses to those readings. On Sundays and major feasts three readings are proclaimed: one from the Old Testament, a selection from some New Testament book other than the Gospels, and a passage from one of the four Gospels. During the week, the Liturgy of the Word consists of two readings: the semiconsecutive reading one of the books of either testament and the semiconsecutive reading of one of the Gospels.

2. This ancient Christian hymn is sung or recited on Sundays outside the seasons of Advent and Lent, on solemnities and feast days, and at special local celebrations.

The liturgical structure of the Liturgy of the Word makes it clear that the good news demands a response from those who hear it. The community responds to the first reading with a responsorial psalm and greets the proclamation of the good news with a joyful alleluia or other prayer of praise. The celebrant responds to the gospel and to the other readings with a homily. On Sundays and special feast days, the community responds to the homily by professing its shared faith in the Nicene Creed. Finally, the Liturgy of the Word closes with general intercessions. These prayers of petition not only lift up to God special needs but also remind the community of its responsiblity to do something about those needs.

Annually during the thematic seasons of Advent, Christmas, Lent, and Easter, the revised lectionary invites the Eucharistic community to meditate on the central mysteries of Christian faith. During the rest of the liturgical year, called ordinary time, it attempts to introduce worshippers to the Bible as a whole. How, then, does Eucharistic meditation on the Word of God seek to advance ongoing conversion?

The Liturgy of the Word and Ongoing Conversion

As we saw in reflecting on the social dynamics of Christian conversion, both initial and ongoing conversion ordinarily presuppose a social context, a matrix of divine grace that both challenges and encourages converts to ever deeper commitment to Christ. We also saw that the sharing of all the divine Mother's charismatic inspirations helps create such a matrix of grace. The sharing of the gifts transforms the Church into a community of shared memories, shared hopes, and shared lives. Through shared memories the Christian community consciously reappropriates the historical events that found it. That act of recollection endows the Church with its present sense of identity. The authentic hopes of the Christian community flow from just such a shared self-understanding in faith. For the Christian community to reach the fullness of shared faith consciousness, however, it must transform shared hopes into shared deeds and shared lives.

The structure of the lectionary invites the worshipping Church to ponder over the course of the liturgical year its shared origin and destiny in Christ. It seeks therefore to evoke the kind of shared faith consciousness that will bear fruit in charismatically inspired acts of service to the Church and to humanity, acts that express and deepen converted commitment to Christ.

The Homily

Moreover, the Liturgy of the Word culminates in the homily that seeks to explain the meaning of God's Word in a way that relates it to the lives of the assembled community and challenges them to ongoing conversion in Christ.

Those who preach need to show sensitivity both to the ethnic, social, and economic backgrounds of the members of the community they serve and to their human diversity as well. Homilists should ambition an inculturated proclamation of God's Word, one that not only interprets the good news in terms intelligible within a particular cultural context but also challenges those who live in that culture to repentance and authentic gospel living. The homily should celebrate as well the common hope, faith, and love that unites the assembled community to one another and to the Church as a whole. It should express the common concerns of Christians and challenge the worshipping community to ongoing conversion at every level.

Effective preachers proclaim God's Word with sensitivity to the cares and concerns, the needs and fortunes of the people they serve. The homily should flow from a personal meditation on the sacred Scripture and on its relevance to the lives of contemporary Christians. It should break open the text in ways that respect its significance and render it comprehensible to God's people.

Because liturgical preaching seeks to effect ongoing conversion at every level, homilists should in the course of the liturgical year address all of the different kinds of issues that foster such conversion. Homilists should challenge the community to grow in Christian hope by confronting the disordered affections that stifle healthy emotional growth in individuals and in the congregation as a whole. They should feed the minds of contemporary Christians by contextualizing historically the main tenets of the Christian faith and by challenging Christians to advance beyond fundamentalism to a sound theological grasp of the creed they profess. Homilists must also seek to help contemporary Christians to form their consciences responsibly, and they should summon believers in season and out to commit themselves to one another in love. Homilists also need to understand the basic principles of Christian spirituality: how to pray, the moral conditions for growth in sanctity, the scope and challenge of Christian, hope, faith, and love.

Contemporary Christians also need to hear in season and out the Church's social gospel proclaimed from the pulpit. Such prophetic preaching will unmask the enslaving ideologies and false myths that pervade any given culture. In this country it will challenge North American Christians to advance beyond the social fragmentation, greed, and indifference to human suffering that individualism inculcates. A prophetic proclamation of the gospel will denounce racism, sexism, and classism together with the bigotry, social ostracism, and violence they inspire. Such preaching will unmask the exploitative potential of uncurbed capitalism and summon North American Christians to transcend narrow individual and national interests by creating an economic and social order grounded in a shared commitment to the common good of all people. Prophetic preaching will denounce the global evils of poverty and oppression that result from neo-colonialism at the same time that it defends human and religious rights from dictatorial suppression. Prophetic preaching will challenge injustice within the Church and condemn its pious rationalization as pharisaical hypocrisy and oppressive ideology. Prophetic preaching will, in a word, seek to mobilize local Christian communities to confront as a community the social ills of our time in the light of the ethical demands of gospel living. It will summon Eucharistic communities not only to avoid evil but to oppose it collectively.

Finally, because Christian conversion demands responsiveness not only to the divine Mother's sanctifying enlightenment but also to her charismatic inspirations, prophetic preaching will challenge Eucharistic communities to live in openness to all of her gifts. Prophetic preaching will, then, demonstrate its full effectiveness by bringing into existence self-ministering, charismatic communities. Their mutual service and witness to the world create a matrix of divine grace that contextualizes Eucharistic worship and endows it with revelatory, sacramental significance.

The Liturgy of the Word seeks, then, to heighten both personal and shared faith consciousness through an ongoing, communal meditation on God's Word. Through seasonal readings, the Liturgy of the Word recalls the major mysteries of the life of Christ and the founding of the Church. Through consecutive readings it reviews the whole of salvation history. The Liturgy of the Word culminates in the homily, which elucidates the meaning of God's Word and relates it in challenging and practical ways to the lives of contemporary Christians. Effective preaching both encourages and challenges those gathered in worship to cultivate all the dynamics of an integral, five-fold conversion. The Liturgy of the Word also seeks to evoke from the worshipping community a new openness to the divine Mother's charismatic inspirations. It challenges initiated Christians to recommit themselves to living as a self-ministering Christian community, eager to grow in hope, faith, love, and just living through deeds of charismatic service to both the Church and humanity. The Liturgy of the Word thus prepares the worshipping community for the solemn renewal of the Christian covenant that occurs during the second part of Eucharist.

c. The Eucharistic Liturgy. Jesus' prophetic action at the Last Supper provides the Eucharistic Liturgy with its ritual structure. On that occasion Jesus took bread, blessed it, broke it, and gave it to his disciples. The Eucharistic rite divides accordingly into four parts. During the preparation of the gifts the celebrant assisted by the community takes bread and wine. During the Eucharistic Prayer the celebrant pronounces a prayer of blessing. During the Communion rite the celebrant first breaks the bread and then gives it together with the wine to those gathered in Eucharistic worship. This basic ritual structure is embellished with other enhancing gestures and prayers. Nevertheless, the four actions of taking, blessing, breaking, and giving define the fundamental shape of the Eucharistic action.

The Preparation of Gifts

The taking, or preparation of the gifts, prepares the blessing, or Eucharistic prayer. The breaking of the bread, or fraction rite, prepares it to be given at the moment of Communion. As preparatory rituals, the taking and breaking perform a subsidiary function within the Eucharistic Liturgy. As a consequence the prayer of blessing and Eucharistic Communion stand out as the two principal acts within the Eucharistic action as a whole. Moreover, the prayer of blessing consecrates the gifts and prepares them for the moment of Communion. It therefore stands in a subsidiary place with respect to the Communion rite. In other words, the dynamic movement of the Eucharistic Liturgy culminates in Eucharistic Communion, i.e., in the only repeatable part of the rite of Christian initiation. Let us reflect on the significance of each stage in the act of Eucharistic worship.

The ritual preparation of the gifts begins with the preparation of the altar. The corporal, a square cloth, is spread on the altar; and the chalice and the purificator, the cloth used for cleaning the chalice, are placed upon it. Members of the community then bring forward the bread and wine as an expression of the community's free self-donation in faith to God. The simultaneous collection of money to support the Church's diverse ministries confirms the community's solidarity with those who present the bread and wine in their name at the altar. So too does the offertory hymn that accompanies these actions. It inaugurates the Liturgy of the Eucharist in the same way that the entrance song inaugurates the liturgy as a whole. The offertory song also provides a communal meditation on the principal themes of the feast being celebrated and thus ties the preparation of the gifts to the Liturgy of the Word. The incensation of the gifts and of the altar adds special solemnity to the ritual, the rising smoke symbolizing the shared prayer of the community.

The prayers that accompany the offering of the gifts underscore the preparatory character of the ritual. The prayers of blessing that accompany the elevation of the bread and wine foreshadow the Eucharistic blessing that will transform them into the Body and Blood of the Lord. A prayer of intercession follows the blessing of the bread and wine and beseeches God to be pleased with the community's offering. The celebrant then prepares himself for his own part in the Eucharistic Liturgy to follow by washing his hands. The act signifies his desire for personal purity of heart and is accompanied by a prayer of contrition for sin. The rite concludes as the celebrant invites the community to echo his prayer that their offering be acceptable to God. After they respond, he pronounces a prayer over the gifts. Just as the collect terminates the entrance rite, so too the prayer over the gifts brings to a close the preparation of the gifts.

The very structure of the ritual preparation of the gifts engages the entire community. All participate actively in it. All contribute something fundamental to it. The celebrant's actions at the altar simply focus the entire community's act of self-offering to God.

The Eucharistic Prayer

The dialogue that introduces the Eucharistic Prayer performs a similar function. It reminds the community that the celebrant pronounces the Eucharistic Prayer in solidarity with them and in their name. Moreover, by chanting or saying the *Holy, Holy, Holy,* the profession of faith after the institution narrative, and the solemn Amen after the entire Eucharistic Prayer, the community gives voice to its conscious solidarity with the celebrant as he pronounces the Eucharistic blessing.

The prayer of blessing itself contains eight elements: (1) In the preface the celebrant praises and thanks God the Father for his saving mercy by underscoring some specific aspect of his creative and redemptive love. At the close of the preface, the celebrant invites the congregation to ratify his prayer by joining in (2) the *Holy, Holy, Holy.*

(3) In the epiclesis the celebrant, speaking in the name of the Church as a whole, invokes the divine power of the Holy Breath, beseeching God that the bread and wine be transformed into the Body of Blood of Christ. (4) The institution narrative follows. In it the celebrant recalls Jesus' prophetic actions at the Last Supper which his death, resurrection, exaltation, and mission of the divine Mother fulfill. The two prayers that follow underscore that fulfillment. (5) The anamnesis reminds the community that it performs this memorial of the Lord in obedience to his command and makes specific reference to his death, resurrection and ascension. (6) The prayer of offering that follows the anamnesis reminds the community that it worships Eucharistically in the power of the divine Breath who proceeds from the risen Lord. The prayer joins the self-offering of the community to Jesus' own self-immolation on the cross and beseeches God that those assembled in worship be daily drawn more and more into Jesus' atoning sacrifice until all people know perfect union with the Father, through the Son, and in the Holy Breath. (7) Other petitions follow the prayer of offering and join the prayers of the assembled community to those of the Church as a whole. They invoke the divine blessing on all Christians, living and dead, and on all people, who are called to share in the salvation effected in the mission of God's Son and Breath. (8) The Eucharistic Prayer closes with a doxology and with the great Amen by which the assembled community solemnly ratifies in faith the blessing that the celebrant has just pronounced in their name.

The Anaphora as Blessing

The Eucharistic Prayer derives its basic literary structure from the Jewish prayer of blessing. Like the Jewish blessings it praises God for his saving deeds in history, but unlike the Jewish blessings it celebrates the death and resurrection of Jesus and his sending of the Holy Breath as the culmination and fulfillment of every other saving act that God has ever performed.

In addition to blessing God, however, the Eucharistic Prayer also consecrates the bread and wine for use in the Communion rite. The recall of God's saving deeds culminates in the epiclesis and institution narrative. The epiclesis invokes the transforming power of the divine Breath upon the gifts of bread and wine. The institution narrative calls to mind Jesus' prophetic words and actions at the Last Supper. All prophetic words and gestures enjoy divine authority and efficacy, but the prophetic words and deeds of the incarnate Word possess an authority and efficacy that transcend any other word pronounced in God's name.

Moreover, Jesus' Eucharistic words and deeds foretold the paschal mystery itself. They prophesied that by dying Jesus would become a source of life for his disciples. He did so by rising and by sending them the divine Mother to conceive in them the risen life he already possesses. At the Last Supper Jesus also prophesied that his Blood would seal a new covenant between God and humanity. In his resurrection he stands revealed as Lord and God, as the perfect union of the divine and human, as the divine pattern of all human transformation in God, as the new covenant that the prophets foretold. Both by invoking the Holy Breath and by pronouncing over the bread and wine the efficacious, prophetic words of God's own Son, the celebrant consecrates them for use in the Communion rite.

In blessing God, one renews one's covenant with him; for in the prayer of blessing one recalls God's saving acts, his prior redemptive commitment to us, as a way of reaffirming one's own commitment in faith to him. Appropriately, then, the Eucharistic prayer of blessing introduces the solemn renewal of the Christian covenant in the Communion rite.

The Fraction Rite

The Communion rite divides basically into the fraction rite and the actual distribution of Communion. The Lord's Prayer and the rite of peace precede the fraction rite and seek to dispose the community for the reception of Communion.

The Lord's Prayer, as we have seen, expresses Jesus' own best hopes for his disciples: that they reverence the divine name wholeheartedly, that they submit to the moral demands for membership in the kingdom, that they look to God in trust and share their bread with others, that they forgive one another with God's own forgiving love, that they live in fidelity to God until the very end. In either reciting or singing the Our Father, the Eucharistic community professes its willingness to obey the new covenant in imitation of God's sinless Son whom they seek to imitate. The prayer called the embolism develops the final petition of the Our Father and closes with a communal doxology.

The celebrant then prays for the gift of peace and invites the congregation to share the kiss of peace. The ritual symbolizes the community's desire to live the mutual forgiveness and reconciliation to which they assented in the Our Father.

The recitation or chanting of the *Lamb of God* accompanies the fraction rite. The prayer that accompanies the mingling of a particle of the consecrated bread with the consecrated wine reminds the community of the ultimate purpose of their communion in the Body and Blood of Christ: participation in the life of the triune God.

Eucharistic Communion

The celebrant first prepares himself for Communion with a silent prayer while the people pray silently. He then shows them the Eucharistic bread and invites them to partake in a spirit of humility. The congregation responds by reciting the *Lord I Am Not Worthy.*

The celebrant first communicates himself and then the community. When appropriate, Eucharistic ministers assist in the distribution of Communion. During Communion the community joins in a hymn that expresses its solidarity in faith as it solemnly renews its baptismal covenant. A period of silent prayer follows Communion, and a meditation hymn may be sung.

The prayer accompanying the reception of Communion harkens back to the institution narrative. As the celebrant gives the consecrated bread to the communicant, he says, "The Body of Christ." As he gives the cup, he says, "The Blood of Christ." Both times the communicant responds "Amen" before eating and drinking the consecrated species. The "Amen" together with the act of eating and drinking expresses the communicant's personal assent to the fulfillment of Jesus' Eucharistic prophecy in his death, glorification, and sending of the divine Mother. The reception of Holy Communion thus seals anew the Christian covenant of initiation and recommits the communicant to living its consequences.

Moreover, the Liturgy of the Word contextualizes each Eucharistic covenant renewal. Having pondered the Word of God and the ways in which it challenges one both to deeper conversion and to more generous charismatic service, the worshipping community in every Communion service renews its covenant with the triune God in the expectation that the divine Mother will transform them in the power of the Word that they have heard.

Like the entrance rite and the Liturgy of the Word, the Communion rite closes with a prayer by the celebrant. This time, however, he prays appropriately that the mystery that the community has just celebrated will indeed bear practical fruit in their lives. The entire service concludes with a final blessing, with the dismissal of the community, and when appropriate with a recessional hymn.

The Unity of Eucharistic Worship

Taken together, then, the Liturgy of the Word and the Eucharistic Liturgy form a dynamic unity. The Liturgy of the Word reminds the assembled community of its shared Christian identity and challenges them to live personally and collectively in ways that express that identity. The Eucharistic Liturgy then challenges them to recommit themselves actively to gospel living by renewing their Christian covenant with God. That covenant includes not only their covenant of initiation but also all the subsequent sacramental covenant commitments they have made, for those commitments deepen and extend one's covenant of initiation.

What then does Eucharistic worship signify? In the section that follows I shall attempt to summarize the conclusions of the preceding analysis in order to provide a theological frame of reference for addressing and resolving the principal controversies that have surrounded this supreme Christian sacrament.

5. The Significance of Eucharistic Worship. Events signify. By that I mean that they possess an emerging relational structure that the mind can grasp evaluatively. When through processes of evaluation we grasp the significant structure of events, we endow them with meaning. What, then, does the Eucharist signify, and how ought we to grasp its significance?

The Eucharist as an Ecclesial Act

As we have seen, during the late Middle Ages the extreme clericalization of Eucharistic worship led to the popular misunderstanding that "priests say Mass for the intentions of the people." Vatican II rejected this misleading notion and returned to an earlier and sounder Church discipline in which presiding celebrants lead the Christian community in a shared act of worship. Accordingly, the revised Eucharistic ritual structures worship in such a way that it embodies the corporate act of the entire assembled community. The act of Eucharistic worship engages the entire worshipping community both collectively and personally. The presiding celebrant focuses the worship and acts as the community's leader and representative. When, therefore, Christians gather for worship they come to do something *together.* The diversification of roles and functions within the Eucharist underscores the communal character of the Eucharistic action. The celebrant presides, lectors read, the choir leads communal singing, ushers keep order, members of the community present the gifts, the prayer itself advances as dialogue between the celebrant and the community, the congregation as a whole confirms the actions that the celebrant performs in its name, and all personally renew the Christian covenant at the moment of Communion.

In worshipping Eucharistically the Christian community *does* what Jesus *did* at the Last Supper. Because that same act of recall constitutes the third, culminating moment of Christian initiation, every time Christians gather to worship Eucharistically, they renew their original covenant commitment to live and die in Jesus' image in the hope of sharing actively in his risen glory. They do so after pondering anew the Word of God and the way it ought to shape their lives. They recommit themselves to living according to the mind of Christ whose vision transvalues natural human attitudes, beliefs, consciences, and institutional commitments.

Eucharistic Remembering

In Eucharistic worship, the Christian community remembers its origins. It does so in each act of Eucharistic worship through shared meditation on the Word of God and by recalling in the Eucharistic prayer the central mysteries of Christian faith. The Eucharistic community meditates comprehensively on its origins in the course of the liturgical year as it celebrates the different mysteries in the life of Christ and follows the cycles of readings in the lectionary. The homily supplements and focuses the community's personal reflections on the meaning of God's Word. Moreover, meditation on the Word of God culminates in a collective reaffirmation of faith and recommitment to the Christian covenant. Clearly, the Eucharistic recall of Christian origins seeks to deepen hope, faith, love, and commitment to social justice and make it practical. The Eucharist thus seeks to advance the Christian community along the path of integral conversion to Christ.

Moreover, in remembering Jesus' death, resurrection, and ongoing mission of the divine Mother to and in the Church, the assembled community makes the paschal mystery a living, present reality. Christians gather to worship in the power of the same Holy Breath who inspired Jesus' life and ministry and whom he in his risen glory breathes into his Church. The divine Mother acts within the Eucharist to conform the assembled community more perfectly to Jesus in his atoning sacrifice and to advance them on the path to final resurrection. She comes to make them into other Christs, living as sons and daughters of God in his image. She inspires the community to renew its covenant to live as the body of Christ united in mutual charismatic service. She thus comes to effect the real presence of the risen Lord in the worship of his people. She makes him really present in the assembled community, in the good news Eucharistically proclaimed and assented to, and in the sacred elements consumed in covenant renewal.

Eucharistic Hope

The shared faith that Eucharistic worship embodies motivates the assembled community's common hopes as well. Human hope, as we have seen, is born of repentant confrontation with the dark side of the psyche. The Eucharist invites and expresses the Christian community's renunciation of minor sinful lapses committed after sacramental initiation and functions as the ordinary ritual means of forgiving lesser sins. From the ongoing healing in faith of disordered and sinful affections springs the Christian community's hope to share in the risen life of Christ. Moreover, that hope roots itself in the present experience of personal and collective transformation in the image of the risen Lord; for by teaching us to live as daughters and sons of God in Jesus' image, the divine Mother conceives within us the risen life of Christ.

While the Eucharist shapes the ultimate hopes of worshipping Christians, it also provides the means for sharpening and articulating the worshipping community's short-term projects and aspirations. Eucharistic worship provides an important forum for interaction between the ordained leaders of the community and its members. The homily gives Church leaders an important occasion to elicit support for the different Christian ministries that the community undertakes. Parish announcements perform a similar, subordinate function. Moreover, the funds collected at the offertory supply concrete, financial backing for the community's charitable undertakings.

Eucharist as Covenant Renewal

By publicly renewing the Christian covenant, the Eucharist also recommits the Christian community to gospel living. It renews their determination to respond to the divine Mother's sanctifying inspirations as she teaches her children to put on the mind of Jesus. It recommits them personally and collectively to the task of realizing God's kingdom in the sinful world in which we live. It rededicates Christians personally and collectively to do the deeds of charity and justice. It consecrates them to serve one another and the society in which they live in openness to the divine Mother's charismatic inspirations. The homily also provides an opportunity, too seldom taken, for instructing the faithful in the Church's social gospel and for alerting them to the structural injustices of the society in which they live. Such instruction uncovers to the faithful the forces of concupiscence that seek to erode their commitment to Christ. It seeks to mobilize the worshipping community to take a collective stand against injustice and oppression whether in the Church or in society as a whole.

Clearly, then, the Eucharist also manifests the presence and action of God in the Christian community. It recommits the Church to live as the family of God bound together in a common love that imitates the free self-donation of the divine persons to one another in the unity of the divine family. It celebrates the visible signs of divine grace in the lives of those assembled to worship: their shared hope, faith, love, mutual service, and dedication in God's name to the works of justice. The Eucharist, when actually lived, thus brings the sacramental presence of the triune God within the Church to its fullest ritual expression. Moreover, it summons the Christian community to ongoing repentance of those sinful lapses that obscure the presence of God within its midst and that transform it from a sacramental sign of grace into a school for scandal.

These reflections on the significance of Eucharistic worship provide a theological context for resolving the major controversies that have surrounded this central and supreme Christian ritual. In the section that follows, we shall attempt to understand one way of effecting such a resolution.

6. Anamnesis, Sacrifice, and Eschatology. No Christian community calls into question the sacramental character of Eucharistic worship, and correctly so. As we saw in the course of reflecting on the rites of initiation, when viewed in the context of ecumenical consensus, adult baptism and the Eucharist define the very meaning of the term "sacrament."

As we have seen, Eucharistic worship has, however, occasioned three important theological debates: medieval and Reformation controversies concerning the real presence, Reformation debates concerning the sacrificial character of the Eucharist, and the eclipse and retrieval of eschatological awareness in Eucharistic worship. In chapter six we saw that one cannot understand adequately Christ's presence in the Eucharist if, in the manner of medieval theologians, one focuses narrowly on his presence in the sacred elements. An adequate theology of the real presence needs to attend to all the different forms of Christ's presence in Eucharistic worship: his presence in the worshipping community itself, in its faith-filled act of worship, in the inspired Scriptures that mediate its shared sense of identity in faith, in the proclamation and assimilation of God's Word, in the entire Eucharistic Liturgy which includes the bread and wine that perform a central symbolic, sacramental function in the Christian community's shared covenant renewal.

Anamnesis and Real Presence

In chapter six of volume one we also reflected on the relationship between anamnesis and real presence. As we saw, the Breath-inspired act of anamnesis mediates the real presence of Christ in the Eucharist and in the Eucharistic elements. We also reflected on one possible way of updating Tridentine teaching concerning the real presence of Christ in the Eucharistic elements. As we saw, in discussing this aspect of the doctrine of the real presence Trent invoked a distinction between reality and appearance. I suggested that we need to amplify Tridentine teaching on this point by distinguishing three different senses of reality and appearance. Let us recall these distinctions here, for they relate ɔ what follows.

First, prior to their consecration by the epiclesis and institution narrative, the bread and wine appear to be ordinary bread and wine. Here appearing means becoming evident, and the reality coincides completely with the appearance. When something appears in this first sense, the reality itself becomes obvious to our senses. Prior to their Eucharistic consecration the bread and wine we see, smell, taste, and touch are, as they appear, just bread and wine and nothing else. Second, after their Eucharistic consecration, however, the bread and wine only appear to be bread and wine. By that I mean that one would err were one to state that the consecrated elements are just ordinary bread and wine. Why so? A thing's reality results from its history, not from some reified, abstract essence. Whenever we use bread and wine we change them in some way. When we use them Eucharistically, we change them sacramentally into the Body and Blood of Christ. In this second sense of reality and appearance (the mere reality), reality and appearance differ. The bread and wine we see, smell, taste, and touch has ceased to be what it was, just bread and wine. In the third sense of reality and appearance, the two partially coincide; for in the third meaning of these two terms, the things that appear to us by becoming directly and efficaciously manifest to our senses disclose a deeper reality that can be grasped only indirectly through a process of intuitive or inferential evaluation. In Eucharistic worship we grasp that reality either intuitively or inferentially only in faith. Thus we can say truly that we would err were we to judge the consecrated bread and wine just bread and wine. Why? Because, when they have been really changed through use in Eucharistic worship, the total reality that appears to the eyes of faith is the reality of the risen Christ efficaciously transforming the entire act of Eucharistic worship through the power and illumination of his Breath.

The act of shared anamnesis apprehends the active, efficacious presence of Christ in the act of Eucharistic worship. It does not therefore make Christ efficaciously present. If it did, Christ's action in the Eucharist would depend on the faith of the worshipping community. Instead, the faith of the community perceives and responds to the efficacious presence of the risen Christ. In every Eucharist the risen Christ holds the efficacious initiative. Within Eucharistic worship he acts efficaciously in obedience to the Father and in collaboration with the divine Mother in order to transform his community according to his saving intentions. He acts through the celebrant, in and with the worshipping community. Hence, in worshipping the risen Lord the assembled community collaborates with its redeemer, and through the divine Mother's illumination it consciously acknowledges his action in their midst. Christ's saving, efficacious presence within each Eucharist precedes and makes the community's anamnesis possible. By that I mean that the efficacious presence of Christ within the Eucharist creates the possibility for its apprehension in conscious Eucharistic faith.

The risen Lord sends the Holy Breath to the Church in obedience to the Father's saving will. Her coming makes the Christian community consciously present in faith to its Lord and savior. Through her Christ dwells in the worshipping community and in its act of worship. She inspired the Scriptures. She empowers the Eucharistic proclamation of the Word and the response of faith it evokes. She inspires the faith of the Eucharistic celebrant to transform sacramentally ordinary bread and wine into the Body and Blood of Christ, and she inspires the worshipping community to recognize the presence of the Eucharistic Christ.

Traditionally, the term *anamnesis* designates the worshipping community's conscious response within worship to the divine Mother's illumination. As we shall soon see, taken together, Christ's Eucharistic presence and the act of anamnesis hold the key to resolving theological arguments about the sacrificial and eschatological character of the Eucharist. They also illumine the profound interrelationship that unites anamnesis and real presence, on the one hand, with the sacrificial and eschatological dimensions of Eucharistic worship, on the other.

Anamnesis and Sacrifice

Research into the historical development of Eucharistic worship convinced Catholic theologians that Reformation debates about the Eucharist as sacrifice rooted themselves to no small degree in the aberrations of late medieval piety: the extreme clericalization of Eucharistic worship that medieval devotion fostered and the theological rationalization of those ritual aberrations.

Catholic rediscovery of the communal character of Eucharistic worship led in the deliberations of Vatican II to an abandonment of a clericalized understanding of the Eucharistic celebrant. Instead of viewing the Eucharistic celebrant as the principal or even sole agent in the act of Eucharistic worship, Catholic theology now looks upon the celebrant as one who presides over a collective act of worship performed by the Christian community. Moreover, as we have seen in reflecting on the sacrament of orders, Catholic theology has also managed to assimilate most of the insights of Lutheran belief in the priesthood of the faithful. Accordingly, Catholic theologians no longer imagine the Eucharistic celebrant as sacrificing Christ on the altar for the sake of the community. Instead, they speak of the Eucharist as the sacrificial worship of the Christian community as a whole.

Atonement as At-One-ment

At the same time Catholic theology rediscovered a New Testament theology of atonement. In the New Testament Jesus atones for sin by suffering its consequences without sinning. Moreover, baptism in his Breath inevitably draws his followers into his own atoning sacrifice by pitting them in forgiving and prophetic love against the same forces of evil that conspired to nail him to the cross. Breath-baptism comes to full ritual expression in Christian initiation, and Eucharistic worship renews formally and sacramentally the covenant sealed with God at the time of initiation. Inevitably, then, the Eucharistic anamnesis draws the worshipping community into the one atoning sacrifice of Christ.

Originally, Luther's reluctance to speak of the Eucharist as a sacrifice stemmed from a fear of derogating from the sacrifice of Christ on the cross. Once it became clear to both Lutherans and Catholics that they could speak of the Eucharistic sacrifice in theological terms that avoided Luther's difficulty, they were able to agree on its sacrificial character while sidestepping some of the principal misunderstandings that divided them at the time of the Reformation.

Moreover, both the Catholic and the Lutheran traditions acknowledge the legitimacy of petitionary prayer and allow prayer for the dead. That fact provides the two Churches with a common point of departure for discussing the sense in which the Eucharistic sacrifice might be offered "for the living and the dead." The Eucharist draws the living Church into the one sacrifice of Christ who died for us all. In uniting itself in prayer to Christ, the great high priest, the Christian community legitimately lifts up to God in prayer those for whom he died. In the Eucharist, moreover, the Church prays not only for the living but also for those who died unprepared for perfect union with God in heaven.[3]

Remembrance and Presentational Immediacy

Every act of remembrance makes the past present, for every human evaluative response enjoys presentational immediacy. Presentational immediacy grounds not only our presence to ourselves and to our world but also the human experience of the present moment. Whenever I remember something, therefore, that past event enters into the present evaluative texture of experience and colors the way I respond to myself and to my world. As we have seen, however, anamnesis differs from ordinary, natural acts of remembrance by making the recalled reality really and sacramentally present; for in recalling the paschal mystery, the worshipping Eucharistic community enters more deeply into and in the process embodies the very reality it recalls.

Jesus' sacrifice of atonement culminated in his resurrection, glorification, and historical revelation as Savior and Lord. When the Christian community recalls the death and resurrection of Jesus, the community's shared commitment of faith, which the Breath of Christ empowers and inspires, draws the worshipping community really and

---

3. Lutherans and Catholics in Dialogue, *The Eucharist as Sacrifice* (New York: U.S.A. National Committee of the Lutheran World Federation and the Bishops Committee for Ecumenical and Interreligious Dialogue, 1967).

actively into the mystery of Christ's dying and rising. Eucharistic anamnesis thus makes the Eucharistic community present to Jesus' original atoning sacrifice in more than just remembrance, for Eucharistic worship transforms the worshiping community itself into a participatory reembodiment of that sacrifice.

The sacrificial character of Eucharistic worship orients anamnesis to the past but not exclusively so. Anamnesis recalls what has already happened: the ministry, death, and glorification of Jesus. The conscious recall of those same events creates the worshipping community's present sense of religious identity; but anamnesis also grounds ultimate Christian hope in the final resurrection of the just as well as proximate hope for the establishment of God's kingdom on earth as in heaven. Hence, every recall of the paschal mystery also looks forward to Jesus' coming again in glory, to that moment when all the redeemed will share fully in the risen life of Christ. At the same time, the act of anamnesis rededicates those who worship to the service of the kingdom. Clearly, then, the sacramental recall of the resurrection of Jesus both embraces and anticipates the future. Let us reflect in more detail on this second temporal dimension of Eucharistic recall.

Prediction and Hope

The human mind perceives the future in two ways: through prediction and in hope. When we predict the future we do so rationally, inferentially, and dispassionately. When we make a prediction we infer on the basis of facts that we have categorized hypothetically that other facts not presently in evidence, will, under specified conditions, become manifest. When we grasp the future in hope we perceive it intuitively and affectively. Christian hope perceives the future intuitively in the light of God's self-revelation in Jesus and in his Breath. It does so with the faith that that revelation inspires.

Intuition perceives reality through the mediation of images. As we saw at the beginning of this chapter, three clusters of religious images have traditionally colored Eucharistic hope. Christians remember the death of Christ with a longing for his return in glory. They therefore perceive Eucharistic worship in hope as a foretaste of the heavenly banquet. They also perceive those gathered in worship as part of the first fruits of the kingdom. When these images function within Eucharistic anamnesis, they make the future present with the same sacramental efficacy as the past events that anamnesis recalls; for at the same time that the act of anamnesis draws one sacrificially into the paschal mystery, it also advances one toward resurrection and future glory. Through the action of God's Breath in their lives, Christians already share in the risen glory of Christ. Indeed, bodily resurrection means the total pneumatic transformation of the human person in God in a manner that reproduces Jesus' own resurrection. Our resurrection does not, then, lie only in the future. It is being accomplished in us even now, incrementally, every time we recommit ourselves to God in faith; for that recommitment conforms us more perfectly to the image of Jesus and advances us on the path to final resurrection.

Moreover, Christians do not advance toward an empty future that they themselves must create with promethean self-reliance. The very reality of the triune God constitutes the future to which we advance. That God reaches out actively to us to draw us toward the future to which he has promised by progressively incorporating us into the divine family. Indeed, God holds the initiative in creating that future, while we advance toward it in response to that divine initiative. Through Eucharistic anamnesis we encounter in shared, conscious faith the God who creates our future by drawing us patiently, gradually toward himself.

The Temporal Structure of Anamnesis

Anamnesis, therefore, has a complex temporal structure. Through anamnesis the Eucharistic community appropriates its past by recalling the death of the Lord. That act of recall endows the Eucharist with a sacrificial character. Because, however, in recalling the paschal mystery the worshipping community also remembers the resurrection of the Lord, anamnesis simultaneously orients that community to the future promised it in God. The hope that remembrance of the resurrection grounds creates the eschatological character of Eucharistic worship and orients it to the future. Finally, because conscious human evaluative responses ground our experience of the present moment, in making the saving past and future present, anamnesis creates the Christian community's present sense of identity and mediates its presence in worship to its Eucharistic Lord. It therefore expresses the Christian community's shared consciousness in faith of the real presence of Christ in the Eucharist. In other words, not only do both the sacrificial and the eschatological character of Eucharistic worship give evaluative texture to the worshipping community's perception in faith of Christ's real Eucharistic presence; but, since Christ's Eucharistic presence includes not only his efficacious presence to the worshipping Eucharistic community but also that community's presence to him in the power of the Breath he sends, the sacrificial and eschatological dimensions of the Eucharist also contribute something constitutive to the total presence of Christ in every committed act of Eucharistic worship.

Not only does anamnesis unite the sacrificial and eschatological dimensions of Eucharistic worship to the real presence, but anamnesis also links all three to the experience of conversion. In every act of Eucharistic worship, we become present to the Father and to the Son of God—who died, who rose again, and for whose second coming we yearn—only to the extent that our worship expresses a genuine commitment to deepen in an integral, fivefold conversion and to live in generous openness to the divine Mother's sanctifying, charismatic inspirations. In other words, while anamnesis unites the sacrificial and eschatological dimensions of Eucharistic worship, conversion authenticates anamnesis. The inauthentic Eucharistic recall of Christ's death until he comes expresses, not living faith, but ritual hypocrisy and transforms what ought to be and experience of lifegiving grace into an experience of divine judgment. We shall reflect on this last point in greater detail in the section that follows.

The Modalities of Real Presence

As we have seen, Vatican II expanded a Catholic interpretation of Christ's real Eucharistic presence by calling attention to the different modalities of that presence. The preceding account of the real presence builds on the foundations laid by that council by suggesting that within its broadened understanding of the real presence one must distinguish two ways in which Christ becomes present within Eucharist worship. First, he transforms the act of worship efficaciously according to his saving intentions. Second, he sends the divine Mother to the community to inspire its prayerful awareness of his efficacious presence in their midst. The second form of presence, which takes the form of Eucharistic anamnesis, perceives the first, responds to it, and mediates the worshipping community's present awareness of its Eucharistic Lord in both memory and hope. Memory of God's saving action in Christ makes Eucharistic anamnesis sacrificial, while longing for the fullness of salvation in Christ makes it eschatological.

These reflections on the relationship that obtains among conversion, anamnesis, real presence, sacrifice, and eschatological hope call attention to the mysterious complexity of Eucharistic worship and challenge contemporary theologians to do justice to the many facets of that complex religious experience. In that task liturgical theology has not always succeeded. The Eucharist recalls the death of Jesus, but it also celebrates his victory: His glorification and his mission of the divine Mother in and to the Christian community as a downpayment on its own share in risen life. When Christians gather to worship God, they bless God for his saving deeds, but they also enter more deeply into the atoning sacrifice of Christ. In Eucharistic worship Christians celebrate their salvation in Christ, but they also acknowledge their continuing sinfulness and need for repentance and forgiveness. While they acknowledge the immanent presence of God in the Church assembled for worship, that worship also orients them toward the transcendent reality of the triune God who encompasses this world even as he becomes its transcendent future.

Eucharistic Consecration

Finally, contemporary theology needs to avoid portraying the entire Eucharistic action as consecratory as an alternative to affirming the consecratory character of the epiclesis and institution narrative. Both affirmations point to a truth about Eucharistic worship. An analysis of the structure of Eucharistic Prayer reveals that it possesses a coherent unity and integrity. Because of that unity and integrity one may speak of the entire Eucharistic action as consecratory. That fact, however, should not obscure the diverse purposes of different moments within the Eucharistic act of worship. Each part of the Eucharist prepares for the parts that follow it, and the different moments within Eucharistic worship serve diverse ends. The introductory rites prepare the community for the celebration of the Liturgy of the Word. The Liturgy of the Word prepares the community to renew the Christian covenant in the Liturgy of the Eucharist. The preparation of gifts prepares them for use in the Eucharistic Prayer. The fraction rite prepares the consecrated bread for distribution in the Communion rite. The Eucharistic Prayer consecrates the bread and wine and transforms them sacramentally into the Body and Blood of Christ. Moreover, within the Eucharistic Prayer, the invocation of the Holy Breath upon the gifts and the reproduction of Jesus' prophetic words and gestures at the Last Supper perform a special consecratory function. Indeed, as an integral part of a unified act of worship, they endow the entire Eucharistic action with consecratory intent.

Historians debate the universal use of the institution narrative in early Eucharistic worship. Some have even suggested that some of the earliest Eucharists may not have contained a Eucharistic narrative. The evidence we possess points, however, to the fact that very early the institution narrative did in fact enjoy universal usage. Moreover, once it entered the anaphora it performed a consecratory function. So too did the invocation of the divine Breath upon the gifts. In a contemporary context, we may then legitimately regard both prayers as effecting the consecration of the bread and wine and as causing Christ's real presence in the sacred elements.

We have reflected on the ways in which a sound insight into the structure of Eucharistic worship points to the resolution of important debates about its meaning. In the following concluding reflections, we shall attempt to render the preceding speculative insights practical by probing some of their pastoral implications.

7. Some Pastoral Observations on Contemporary Liturgical Malaise. In the first chapter of this study I suggested that contemporary sacramental theology needs to address the malaise that often surrounds contemporary ritual worship. That malaise centers most often on Eucharistic worship, primarily because the Eucharist lies at the heart of Christian sacramental prayer. Do the preceding reflections suggest strategies for responding to that malaise? I believe that they do.

A sound liturgical and sacramental theology attempts to understand the meaning of sacramental worship by pondering the significant structure of Christian ritual. When, however, one reflects on the rites of Christian worship in the light of an adequate and updated theology of conversion, one must conclude that, because all the sacraments seek either to inaugurate or deepen converted commitment to Christ, their celebration in the serious absence of conversion transforms them into an act of religious hypocrisy. The unconverted Christian who worships sacramentally professes publicly and solemnly a commitment to Christ that he or she either rejects or resists.

The Centrality of Conversion

I am not suggesting that only the totally converted have the right to approach to the sacraments. Because the entire process of conversion takes a lifetime, everyone needs more of it. Sacramental worship does not, therefore, presuppose a community of the perfect. It does, however, presuppose a community committed in a heartfelt way to advancing in all five forms of conversion. When communities experience liturgical worship as hollow or meaningless, that experience suggests the strong possibility of some serious absence of conversion on the part of those gathered in worship. Moreover, the gospel summons not just individuals but communities to conversion. Communities of faith share a common experience of conversion when the social structures that mediate their corporate action and interaction embody and foster integral conversion to Christ. Eucharistic communities that prefer cultural Catholicism and middle-class morality to gospel living, communities that ignore or resist the divine Mother's charismatic call to service have good reason to experience sacramental worship as bland and uninspired. Eucharistic communities divided by unhealed enmity and violence of heart, fundamentalistic communities, pietistic communities without a care for the plight of the poor and oppressed, communities blinded by individualism, classism, sexism, racism, and by other ideologies of division, exploitation, and oppression might well sense a certain hollowness when they gather to profess publicly and officially their determination to live in the image of Christ.

The sacramental theology I have developed in these pages suggests one possible strategy for diagnosing the causes of contemporary liturgical malaise, for it grounds sacramental worship in a comprehensive insight into the forms and dynamics of conversion. The construct of conversion developed in these pages offers, then, a diagnostic tool for measuring the degree of authenticity (or the lack of it) that characterizes the personal and shared lives of worshipping Christians; for in the last analysis, a sound insight into the forms and dynamics of conversion and the use of such insight in order to discern the inauthenticities that mar the lives of worshipping Christians provides a sounder pastoral key to genuine liturgical renewal that does the superficial use of liturgical gimmicks.

In the present chapter we have reflected on the development and significance of Eucharistic worship. In the brief epilogue that follows we shall ponder the sacramental system as a whole as well as the challenge that committed sacramental worship poses to the contemporary Church.

EPILOGUE:

The Sacramental System and Committed Worship

Catholic theologians have traditionally described the rites of the Church as a system, but they have not always offered a clear explanation of the principle that unites and systematizes sacramental worship. The reflections of the preceding chapters, however, allow us to name that principle: the dynamics of initial and ongoing conversion.

The Sacramental System

The rites of adult initiation seal an initial conversion to Christ. The commitment they embody inaugurates the process of ongoing conversion.

In the course of ongoing conversion Christians mature into a sense of how they are called to serve the Christian community. Two Christian vocations require sacramental confirmation: marriage and ordained Church leadership.

In the rite of reconciliation either Christians reconvert to Christ after serious sin or they reaffirm their covenant of initiation while renouncing minor faults. In either case they deepen in the experience of repentance and of ongoing conversion.

The rite of anointing also transforms the experience of serious illness into an opportunity for converting more deeply to God. In the face of physical diminishment and possible death, ailing Christians recommit themselves in faith to the God who has power to raise them up. They pray for healing while publicly reaffirming their baptismal covenant.

Finally, the shared Eucharistic worship of the Church provides Christians with the opportunity to renew again and again in repentant faith the covenant that they sealed with God in the rites of initiation. Participation in the Lord's Supper thus advances baptized Christians on the path of ongoing conversion.

One cannot, therefore, comprehend adequately the dynamics of initial and ongoing conversion without also understanding how the sacraments serve to advance the total process of conversion. Traditionally, Catholics have showed only a limited interest in conversion, partly because they associated it with only two sacraments: baptism and reconciliation. A theology of conversion that probes in greater depth the complexity and dynamics of initial and ongoing conversion discovers, however, serious inadequacies in such a theological approach to the conversion process. Conversion in fact encompasses a lifetime and involves all seven of the sacraments.

The Challenge of the Restored Catechumenate Revisited

In chapter five, I alluded to the challenge that the restored catechumenate poses for the rest of the Church; for it confronts the community of the already baptized with the need to exhibit in their own lives at least that measure of conversion that the Church demands of neophytes.

Subsequent chapters have enabled us to explore in greater depth the scope of that challenge. Authentic, committed, sacramental worship demands the renewal and sanctification of married life and its recognition as one of the most basic charismatic ministries in the Church. It requires Christian spouses to challenge and support one another to ever deeper conversion to Christ. It requires the charismatic transformation of Christian homes into realms of grace capable of nurturing children to an integral, adult conversion to Christ. It invites Christian families to function whenever possible as ministerial teams concerned with the needs of the larger Church and of the world.

When viewed in the light of the scope and dynamics of Christian conversion, the restoration of the catechumenate also requires the ordained to model in their ministry of service the meaning of integral conversion to Christ. More specifically, it requires the clergy to resist and reject the concupiscent forces of clericalism with its idolatrous worship of power. It demands that the clergy distance themselves critically from inadequate theological interpretations of their role within the Church: from unhealthy elitism, from the inadequacies of sacerdotalism and of hierarchicalism. The exigencies of conversion challenge the ordained to espouse instead a priesthood that imitates Jesus' own priestly ministry: a priesthood of identification with the poor, the suffering, the outcast, and the marginal.

Because the restoration of the catechumenate implicitly summons the entire Church to converted living, it also requires that the Church as a whole reinterpret its healing ministry in the light of the moral demands of an integral, fivefold conversion. The restored rite of reconciliation invites the baptized not only to renounce the institutional forces of concupiscence that corrupt them affectively, intellectually, morally, and religiously but also to seek in the rite of reconciliation healing of the deeper causes of sin: the disordered emotional attitudes, the distorted beliefs, the irresponsible personal and social commitments that betray them into violating the Christian covenant. An updated theology of conversion also provides, as we have seen, useful diagnostic tools for analyzing the deeper causes of sin. Similarly, the restored right of anointing challenges the baptized to an expectant faith in God's power to heal them in whatever way they need healing.

Finally, when one understands Eucharistic worship in the light of the moral exigencies of converted living, one recognizes the need for all the baptized to exhibit in their daily lives the practical signs of the divine Mother's sanctifying, gift-giving presence. Christians can legitimately celebrate the victory of the risen Christ in their midst only when they live committed to challenge themselves and one another to advance in all five forms of conversion, only when they live in openness to all the divine Mother's charismatic calls, only when such openness visibly transforms their lives together into a matrix of divine grace that nurtures each and every member of the Eucharistic community to full maturity in Christ.

Sacraments and the Limits of Therapy

In the preface to this study I suggested that the experiential, foundational approach to the sacraments that I have proposed finds some truth in most of the constructs that theologians have used to understand Christian sacramental worship. I did not, however, include in that list of constructs a "therapeutic" approach to liturgical worship. A therapeutic theology of sacramental worship claims to describe the experience of Christian worship, but it does so by endowing psychological categories with "saving" significance. Moreover, it interprets salvation naturalistically as the process of humanization: holiness means simply becoming a better human being. Within worship, for example, one allegedly experiences salvation by getting in touch with one's body, senses, imagination, and sexuality. Moreover, a therapeutic approach to the sacraments discovers God's saving, therapeutic presence diffused throughout creation. Therapeutic worship uses the story of Jesus in order to facilitate human communication. It encourages the cultivation of listening and giving human relationships. A therapeutic approach to the sacraments refuses to speak of God in either objective or personal terms. It reduces Trinitarian theology to a description of the different ways God becomes present to humanity and, somewhat in the manner of William James, equates the reality of God with a vague "more" allegedly experienced in all human knowing and loving. The transcendence of God for the therapeutic theologian means the saving dimensions of personal and communal self-analysis. Therapeutic theology teaches that in order to speak about God one must always speak about oneself.[1]

In developing a foundational theology of the sacraments I did not draw upon a therapeutic account of the sacraments because I regard it not as a legitimate theology of sacramental worship but as a wholesale sellout to the most banal aspects of the culture of narcissism spawned by a decadent, therapeutic, captalistic society. The sacraments do, of course, have the capacity to heal us in faith; but while a therapeutic sacramental theology claims to describe religious experience, instead it substitutes for a sound insight into the forms and dynamics of Christian conversion a secularized account of worship that effectively deprives it of any genuine religious significance. It replaces the language of grace and of the supernatural with psychobabble, reduces the infinitely rich social reality of the triune God to a vague aura surrounding natural human growth processes, and grounds worship in individual and collective self-analysis that remains obtuse both to the action of God's Breath and to the rigors of the Christian search for social justice.

In naming this study, I fully intended the pun in its subtitle. I have tried to write an inculturated theology of the sacraments that addresses the pastoral needs of adult converts. Inculturated theology draws its symbols from the culture in which the Christian community roots itself, but it also uses the Gospel to challenge those who live in that culture to repentance and integral conversion to Christ. It avoids, therefore, the trap into which therapeutic theology falls

---

1. For a fuller description of a therapeutic approach to the sacraments together with some critical comments on it, see James Empereur, S.J., *Exploring the Sacred* (Washington, D.C.: The Pastoral Press, 1987).

when the latter endorses uncritically the shallow secularism of American culture. I have written a book for converts, but I have also tried to write a theology that encourages the ongoing conversion of baptized Christians, myself included. Perhaps, then, I can end this study in no more appropriate way than by citing the words of an old, traditional hymn:

> Let it breathe on us,
> Let it breathe on us,
> Let the Breath of God now breathe on us.

Glossary

ABBA: the Hebrew word for Papa; Jesus' name for God.

ABDUCTION: hypothetical inference; the initial classification of data in need of explanation on the basis of a principle assumed to govern reality.

ACCIDENT: that which exists in another as in a subject of inhesion.

ACTUAL GRACE: a concrete impulse to respond in faith.

AFFECTION: the vague initial emotive perception of experienced tendencies, a perception that when clarified by imagination can then judge imaginative perceptions of the real.

AFFECTIVE CONVERSION: the decision to turn from an irresponsible resistance to facing one's disordered affectivity to the responsible cultivation of a healthy, balanced, aesthetically sensitive emotional life.

AMBO: an elevated desk from which the epistle and gospel are proclaimed in Eucharistic worship.

ANAMNESIS: the act of Eucharistic recall that transforms the committed Eucharistic community into a re-embodiment of the very realities it recalls.

ANAPHORA: the central prayer of Eucharistic blessing proclaimed by the celebrant after the *Holy, Holy, Holy.*

ANOINTING: in sacramental theology, the sacramental prayer for the healing of serious illness that absolves minor sins committed after baptism and thus renews the Christian covenant.

ANNULMENT: the legal separation of Christian spouses involved in a failed marriage on the basis of the fact that their original marriage commitment fell short of what a Christian marriage covenant requires.

ANTI-SEMITISM: unjust discrimination against and persecution of Jews because of their Jewishness.

APOCALYPTIC: revelatory of the "end time" (the last age of salvation).

APPEARANCE: either what becomes immediately manifest to the senses or that hidden reality whose manifestation results from the correct interpretation of that which is sensibly and immediately manifest (see MERE APPEARANCE).

ATONEMENT: reconciliation; at-one-ment.

ATTITUDE: as a technical, psycho-therapeutic term, the tendency toward either introversion or extraversion.

AURICULAR CONFESSION: the secret acknowledgement of postbaptismal sins to one competent to absolve them.

AUTHENTIC: genuine; as a characteristic of conversion, endowed with that degree of responsibility that a genuine conversion demands.

AUTONOMY: the capacity to inaugurate activity.

BAPTISM: the ritual washing and invocation of the triune name that constitutes the first stage in the rite of adult Christian initiation.

BELIEF IN: trust in another person.

BELIEF THAT: a proposition asserted with the determination to take responsibility for its consequences.

BISHOP: one ordained to the episcopacy.

BREATH-BAPTISM: transformation in the image of Jesus in response to the illumination of the third person of the Trinity.

CATECHUMEN: one preparing for adult Christian initiation.

CATECHUMENATE: the period of religious preparation that precedes adult Christian initiation.

CERTITUDE: complete confidence of the truth of one's beliefs.

CHARACTER: the indelible "mark," distinct from the grace of a sacrament, left on a person by those sacraments administered only once, a "mark" that confers permanent, morally conditioned ecclesial rights and duties.

CHARISM: a particular manifestation of the grace (*charis*) of God; a gift of the Holy Breath of Christ empowering acts of service of others.

CHRISTIAN CONVERSION: that form of religious conversion that discovers God definitively and normatively revealed in Jesus Christ, the incarnate Son of God the Father, and in the Holy Breath they send into the world.

CLASSISM: an ideology that rationalizes the unjust concentration of wealth and power in the hands of one segment of society to the exclusion of others.

CLERGY: the ordained leaders of the Church viewed as set apart by ordination from the rest of the Church.

CLERICALISM: the sinful transformation of ordained Church leadership from a service elite dedicated to securing the Church's common good into a self-serving, oppressive power elite.

COLLECT: the prayer of the Eucharistic celebrant that closes the sacrament's introductory rites.

COLLEGE OF BISHOPS: all the bishops in communion with the pope in their collective pastoral function as supreme governing body in the Church.

COLLEGIALITY: in the strict sense, the sharing of the burdens and responsibilities of pastoral leadership on the part of the college of bishops; in the broad sense, the shared exercise of official pastoral leadership in the Church.

COMMON GRACE: gratuitous grace.

COMMUNICATION: an act that symbolizes meaning through social behavior.

COMMUNION: union with something other than oneself.

CONCEPTUAL RELATION: the intentional ordering of one quality to another.

CONCUPISCENCE: those forces in the experience of baptized Christians other than their own personal sins that come from sin and lead to sin.

CONFIRMATION: the imposition of hands and invocation of the Holy Breath of Christ that constitutes the second stage of adult Christian initiation.

CONSCIENCE: the ability to make decisions in the light of moral ideals and norms.

CONSCIOUSNESS: the ability to distinguish evaluatively between oneself and others.

CONTRITION: sorrow for sin with the determination to avoid it in the future.

CONVERSION: the passage from childish irresponsibility to the assumption of adult responsibility for some realm of experience.

COOPERATIVE GRACE: the personal human response to operative grace.

CREATED GRACE: the healing, elevation, and perfection of sinful human nature that the gratuitous, historical self-revelation and self-communication of God produces in the person who responds to that revelation in faith.

CREED: a set of personal and/or shared beliefs.

DEACON: one ordained to assist priests and bishops in the pastoral leadership of the Church.

DECISION: a concrete act, which in the higher forms of experience terminates and expresses a prior evaluative response.

DEDUCTION: predictive inference; the prediction of the emergence of factual data not yet in evidence made on the basis of an abduction.

DEPRIVATIZATION: the act of rendering human responses sociopolitically responsible.

DISCERNMENT: natural prudence charismatically transformed.

DIVORCE: the legal dissolution of a marriage bond.

DYNAMIC OF CONVERSION: the way one form of conversion conditions and transforms another.

ECCLESIAL: pertaining to the Church.

ELECT: those engaged in the period of intensive preparation for Christian initiation that occurs during Lent and culminates in their reception into the Church at the Easter Vigil.

ESCHATOLOGICAL: pertaining to the last age of salvation that the events of Easter and Pentecost begin.

EUCHARIST: the sacrament of the Lord's Supper.

EXCEPTIVE CLAUSE: the phrase "except for uncleanness (*porneia*)" that Matthew's Gospel inserts into Jesus' repudiation of Mosaic divorce practices.

EXORCISM: a prayer for deliverance from subjection to the powers of evil or from possession by them.

EXPERIENCE: a process composed of relational elements called feelings; reality in general.

EXPRESSIVE INDIVIDUALISM: an ideology that rationalizes economic, political, and social irresponsibility as the defense of one's core self from communal and institutional encroachment.

EXPRESSIVE SYMBOL: a physical event capable of interpretation.

EXTREME UNCTION: a medieval term for the rite of anointing that erroneously portrayed it as the sacrament of the dying rather than as a sacrament of healing.

EXTRAVERSION: the tendency to give shape to one's evaluative responses in the course of interacting with others.

FACT: a concrete decision; as a feeling, social relationship through reaction, collaboration, or coercion.

FACTUAL RELATION: the social ordering of selves to one another through activity.

FAITH: (most broadly) global assent to the free and gratuitous historical self-revelation and self-communication of God on the terms that a self-revealing God requires; (more narrowly) the theological virtue that consents to reality on terms divinely revealed; (most narrowly) a charism that endows the religious witness of a particular individual with social visibility.

FALLIBILISM: the logical doctrine that finite, human minds capable of error have a better chance of reaching the truth if they admit they can err than if they do not.

FIRST HOLY COMMUNION: the Christian neophyte's first reception of the Body and Blood of Christ at the Lord's Supper, which constitutes the third stage in the rite of adult initiation.

FEELING: a relational element within experience.

FOUNDATIONAL THEOLOGY: a strictly normative account of the forms and dynamics of conversion.

FREEDOM: the ability to choose either to act or not to act, to do one thing rather than another.

FUNCTION: as a technical, psycho-therapeutic term, the tendency to develop an ego biased toward sensation, feeling, intuition, or rational thinking.

FUNCTIONAL THEOLOGICAL SPECIALTY: an area of scholarly investigation that poses a specific kind of theological question whose resolution requires a correspondingly appropriate method.

FUNDAMENTALISM: the misguided attempt to preserve "fundamentals" through the uncritical reification of truth in fixed propositions.

GLOSSOLALIA: the charismatic gift of speaking in tongues.

GOD: that reality than which none greater can be conceived.

GRACE: the historical self-revelation and gratuitous, redemptive self-communication of God to a sinful world over and above the gift of creation.

GRATUITOUS GRACE: the charisms of the Holy Breath.

HABITUAL GRACE: the virtuous tendency to respond in global faith to the historical self-revelation and self-communication of God.

HABITUAL RELATION: the ordering of a general tendency to the kind of activity—whether decisive or evaluative—that it grounds.

HIERARCHICALISM: a account of the Church that models it after the alleged subordination of different orders of angels to one another in such a way that grace flows from the highest angelic and Church structures to the lowest.

HOLY COMMUNION: the reception of the Eucharist.

HOMILY: the explanation of the sacred texts read at a liturgy and their application to the lives of the worshippers.

HOPE: intuitive perception of the future; as a theological virtue, confidence that God will fulfill the promises he has made in Jesus Christ and in the gift of his Breath.

HUMAN PERSON: an autonomous, finite self capable of conversion.

IDEAL: an attractive possibility.

IDEOLOGY: a rationalization of a situation of injustice that falsely claims not only truth but self-evidence.

IMAGINATION: the ability to perceive reality appreciatively through the evaluative and interpretative use of images.

INDIVIDUALISM: an ideology of isolation that rationalizes the selfish cultivation of sociopolitical irresponsibility.

INDIVIDUALITY: unique selfhood.

INDUCTION: logical validation; either the verification (often within a range of probability) through the emergence of deductively predicted behavior that an abductively assumed principle governs reality or the disproof of that same abductive principle through the failure of the predicted behavior to emerge.

INEXISTENCE: the existence of one thing in another.

INFANT BAPTISM: the practice dating to the apostles of initiating neonates sacramentally into the Church.

INFERENCE: a logical argument that interrelates facts, defined categories, and general rules.

INITIAL CONVERSION: the decision when first made to pass from childish irresponsibility to adult responsibility in some realm of experience.

INTELLECTUAL CONVERSION: the decision to turn from an irresponsible and supine acquiescence in accepted beliefs to a commitment to validating one's personal beliefs within adequate frames of reference and in ongoing dialogue with other truth-seekers.

INTENTIONAL: conceptually related to.

INTERPRETATION: an evaluative account of significance.

INTERPRETATIVE SYMBOL: the evaluative grasp of meaningful relationship.

INTROVERSION: the tendency to give decisive shape to one's evaluative responses before acting.

INTUITION: appreciative, affective, imaginative thinking.

JUSTICE: the virtue that gives others their due; ultimately, that order in human society willed by God.

JUSTIFICATION: the initial transition from a state of sin and unbelief to the obedience of faith.

LAW: a general tendency to react or respond either evaluatively or decisively; as a feeling, an habitual relationship.

LECTIONARY: a book of liturgical readings.

LEVITICAL PRIESTHOOD: the office of cultic leadership, of teaching, and (until the time of David) of delivering oracles exercised by the members of the tribe of Levi under Mosaic Law.

LIFE: the capacity to grow organically and to engender realities like oneself.

LITANY: a communal dialogic prayer consisting of a series of petitions.

LOGICAL ADEQUACY: the ability of a theory to interpret all the realities it seeks to interpret.

LOGICAL APPLICABILITY: the capacity of a theory to interpret some realities.

LOGICAL COHERENCE: the characteristic of a theory whose key terms so imply one another that they remain unintelligible apart from one another.

LOGICAL CONSISTENCY: the absence of internal contradiction in some account of reality.

LOVE: felt, committed benevolence toward another person; as a theological virtue, felt, committed benevolence toward God and toward those to whom God stands benevolently committed.

MARRIAGE: the ritual commitment of a man and a woman to one another as husband and wife; the institution that results from such a commitment.

MERE APPEARANCE: an erroneous interpretation of reality rhetorically attributed not to the erroneous interpreter but to the reality erroneously interpreted, for example: "The stick I thrust into the water only appeared bent."

METHOD: a set of recurrent and related operations yielding cumulative and progressive results.

METAPHYSICS: a fallible account of the nature of reality as a whole that aspires to logical consistency, coherence, applicability and adequacy.

MIRACLE: an event that lacks any natural explanation and that summons one to faith in God's saving power.

MISSION: in Trinitarian theology, the historical sending of one divine person by another that reveals how they proceed from one another within the Trinity.

MONEPISKOPOS: a single bishop presiding over and administering a local Church as its chief pastor.

MORAL: that which makes ultimate and absolute claims.

MORAL ABSOLUTE: that which claims one's commitment in all circumstances.

MORAL CONVERSION: the decision to turn from irresponsible selfishness to a commitment to measure the motives and consequences of personal choices against ethical norms and ideals that both lure the conscience to responsible choices and judge its relapses into irresponsible selfishness.

MORAL EVIL: that which contradicts realities and values that make ultimate and absolute claims.

MORAL ULTIMATE: that to which one must cling beyond all else, even to the point of dying for it if necessary.

MYSTAGOGY: the period of religious formation that follows adult Christian initiation.

NATURE: those spatio-temporal processes that advance independently of the historical self-revelation and self-communication of God.

NATURAL CONVERSION: the transition from irresponsible to fully responsible conduct made in abstraction from the historical self-revelation and self-communication of God.

NEOPHYTE: one recently accepted into a community.

NORM: a principle of judgment or of conduct.

NORMATIVE THINKING: explanation; an insight into the way things ought to behave.

OBEDIENTIAL POTENCY: the ability to receive a supernatural gift provided God chooses gratuitously to give it.

ONGOING CONVERSION: the practical acceptance of the consequences of the initial transition from irresponsible to responsible behavior.

OPERATIVE GRACE: an action of God that inaugurates personal transformation in faith.

ORDINATION: ritual, sacramental incorporation into the ranks of public Church leadership.

ORGANISM: a living reality.

ORIGINAL SIN: the personal and institutional sins of others that constitute the morally corrupting environment into which each human person is born.

PASCHAL MYSTERY: the death and resurrection of Jesus and the Pentecostal sending of the Holy Breath into the Church.

PERSON: an autonomous center of evaluation and decision endowed with vital continuity, self-awareness, and the capacity to enter into responsible social relationships with realities like itself.

PERSONAL SANCTIFICATION: the process of being set aside for the service of God through transformation in the image of Jesus.

PERSONAL SIN: one's own decision taken in violation of the will of God.

PRECATECHUMENATE: the period of inquiry that precedes the catechumenate.

PRESENTATIONAL IMMEDIACY: the presence to reality together with the sense of the present moment that evaluative response contributes to conscious experience.

PRIEST: one ordained to the presbyterate or episcopacy.

PRIESTHOOD: the office of mediating God to humanity.

PRINCIPLE OF ALTERNATION: as a logical term, the methodological precept that the mind in its attempt to understand reality should oscillate between close studies of a limited range of the real and the construction of a metaphysics.

PRIVATIZATION: the irresponsible ignoring of sociopolitical responsibilities.

PROCESSION: within Trinitarian theology, the eternal origin of one divine person from another.

PROSKOMIDIA: in the Byzantine Eucharistic Rite, preparatory prayers pronounced over the Eucharistic bread and wine.

PRUDENCE: the virtue of making correct moral judgments.

QUALITY: an instance of particular suchness; as a feeling, an intentional value.

RACISM: unjust racial discrimination and persecution on the basis of race.

RATIONAL: inferential.

REAL EUCHARISTIC PRESENCE: the reality of the risen Christ—body, blood, soul, and divinity—as it efficaciously informs and transforms the entire act of Eucharistic worship including the sacred elements of bread and wine consecrated and consumed in Eucharistic worship.

REALM OF EXPERIENCE: a distinguishable domain within a process composed of relational elements called feelings.

RECONCILIATION: the sacrament that forgives the sins Christians commit after their sacramental incorporation into the Church.

RELATION: the ordering of one reality to another.

RELATIONS OF DISTINCTION: the negative ordering of one reality to another that justifies saying that the one is not the other.

RELIGIOUS: making ultimate and absolute claims.

RELIGIOUS CONVERSION: the recognition of God as the ultimate ground of absoluteness and ultimacy; the decision to stop ignoring or opposing God and to begin to respond in faith to some historical, revelatory, self-communication of God.

REPENTANCE: the rejection of all sinful obstacles to faith in a self-revealing, self-communicating God.

RESPONSIBILITY: accountability to oneself, to others, and ultimately to God.

RESURRECTION: total personal transformation in God after death.

RITE OF ELECTION: the ceremony that welcomes catechumens into the period of intensive Lenten preparation for their sacramental initiation into the Church at the Easter Vigil.

RUBRIC: a directive, normally printed in red, for how to celebrate an official Church ritual.

SACERDOTALISM: a theological interpretation of the role of bishops and of priests in the Church that assimilates their functions to those of the Levitical priesthood.

SACRAMENT: in the broad sense, an event that both reveals and conceals the reality of God; in the strict sense, a symbolic, ritual act of new covenant worship 1) that expresses shared faith of the Church universal, 2) that is therefore celebrated by a person authorized to speak in the name of the Christian community and of the God it worships, 3) that, by challenging one prophetically to faith in Jesus' Lordship, in the Father he proclaimed, and in the Holy Breath they send, gives access in faith to the paschal mystery of Jesus' death, glorification, and sending of the Holy Breath, and 4) that effects what it signifies to the extent that it expresses faith and deepens faith.

SACRAMENTALITY: in the broad sense, having the character of both revealing and concealing God; in the strict sense, inclusion in the official canon of the Church's ritual sacraments.

SACRAMENTARY: a collection of prayers and rubrics for the Eucharist.

SALVATION: the experience of standing in a life-giving relationship to God that delivers one from sin, death, and bondage of the Law.

SANCTIFICATION: the act of being consecrated to the service of God.

SANCTIFYING GRACE: moral transformation in supernatural faith, hope and love through docility to the Holy Breath's enlightenment.

SATAN: the angelic prosecuting attorney in the court of Yahweh who evolves in Hebrew and Christian angelology into the personification of the forces of anti-God and of antichrist.

SCRUTINIES: rituals celebrated during the Eucharist on the third, fourth, and fifth Sundays of Lent designed to support the self-examination in which the elect engage during the intensive period of preparation that precedes their sacramental initiation into the Church.

SELF: an autonomously functioning reality.

SENSATION: a vague evaluative perception of environmental impact upon an organism; sensation includes seeing, hearing, tasting, touching, smelling, and perceptions of one's own bodily processes.

SEXISM: unjust discrimination and persecution on the basis of sex.

SIGNIFICANCE: the relational structure of reality which renders it capable of evaluative interpretation.

SIN: violation of the will of God.

SOCIOPOLITICAL CONVERSION: the decision to turn from unreflective acceptance of the institutional violations of human rights to a commitment to collaborate with others in the reform of unjust social, economic, and political structures by empowering the

oppressed to demand and obtain their rights from their op-
pressors.

STAGES OF FAITH: discernible levels of cognitive awareness within faith
distinct from conversion.

STRICTLY NORMATIVE: pertaining to an account of the way one ought
to behave in the light of norms and ideals appropriated by the
one acting as personally binding.

SUBSTANCE: that which exists in itself and not in another as in a subject of inhesion.

SUPERNATURAL: that which transcends what nature can accomplish on
its own.

SUPREME: that than which none greater can be conceived.

SYMBOL: that which mediates the evaluative grasp of significance; symbols divide initially into expressive symbols, interpretative symbols, and communications.

SYNOPTICS: the Gospels of Matthew, Mark, and Luke, called Synoptic
(viewed together) from the habit of reproducing all three
Gospels in parallel columns on the same page for the purpose
of studying their similarities and differences.

THEISM: a religion that discovers absoluteness and ultimacy in some
reality that transcends space and time and enjoys all conceiv-
able perfection.

TRANSFINALIZATION: a theological explanation of transubstantiation
that explains the real change it effects as a transformation of
purpose and therefore in reality.

TRANSIGNIFICATION: a theological explanation of transubstantiation
that explains the real change it effects as a change in meaning
and therefore in reality.

TRANSUBSTANTIATION: a technical theological term for the real change
that sacramental consecration effects in the Eucharistic bread
and wine.

TRANSVALUATION: the reevaluation of a conception of reality that occurs when that conception is used in a novel frame of reference
that endows it with new connotations.

TRISHAGION: in the Byzantine liturgy, a hymn of praise to triune God
as thrice holy.

UNCONSCIOUS: lacking the ability to distinguish between oneself and
others.

UNCREATED GRACE: reality of God viewed as gratuitously revealing and
communicating himself to his sinful creatures in a way that goes
beyond the gift of creation.

UNITIVE RELATIONS: relations that effect shared reality, for example, shared ideals, shared purposes, shared lives.

UTILITARIAN INDIVIDUALISM: an ideology that fallaciously justifies doing anything that leads to one's economic, political, or social advancement.

VIATICUM: the reception of Holy Communion in preparation for death.

VICE: a morally evil habit.

A Partial Bibliography of Secondary Sources[1]

I. Conversion and Catechumenate:

Anderson, William A. *In His Light: A Path into Catholic Belief.* Dubuque, IA: William C. Brown, 1985.

Archer, Anthony, O.P. "Theology and Sociology: Two Approaches to Religious Conversion." *New Blackfriars* (April 1981) 62:180-90.

Aubin, Paul, S.J. *Le probléme de la "conversion": étude sur un term commun a l'hellenisme et au christianisme des trois premiers siècles.* Paris: Peauchesne et Fils, 1962.

Balducelli, R. "A Phenomenology of Conversion." *Ligourian* (November 1977) 10:545-57.

von Balthasar, Hans-Urs. "Conversion in the New Testament." *Communio* (Spring 1974) 1:47-59.

Bardy, Gustave. *Le conversion au christianisme durant les premiers siècles.* Paris: Aubier, 1947.

Christian Initiation of Adults: A Commentary. Washington, DC: United States Catholic Conference, 1985.

Butler, John T. "The RCIA Today." *Today's Parish* (April–May 1988) 20:33-4.

Conn, Walter. *Christian Conversion: A Developmental Interpretation of Autonomy and Surrender.* New York: Paulist, 1986.

_____. *Conscience: Development and Self-Transcendence.* Birmingham, AL: Religious Education Press, 1981.

_____. "Conversion." *New Catholic World* (March–April, 1986) 229:52-88.

_____. "Conversion: A Developmental Perspective." *Cross Currents* (Fall 1982) 32:323-8.

1. An exhaustive discussion of the secondary sources for this study would have expanded the footnotes beyond all reasonable proportion. I therefore offer without comment this selective bibliography in the hope that those who use this study will find these suggestions for further reading both enlightening and pastorally useful.

_____. *Conversion: Perspectives on Personal and Social Transformation.* Staten Island, NY: Alba House, 1978.

_____. "Jesus' Invitation to Paradox." *Contemplative Review* (Fall 1984) 17:1-5.

_____. "Moral Conversion: Development Toward Critical Self-Possession." *Thought* (June 1983) 170–87.

_____. "Passionate Commitment: The Dynamics of Affective Conversion." *Cross Currents* (Fall 1984) 34:329-36.

"Conversion." *Lumen Vitae* (1987) 42:369-427.

Crespo, Joaquin. "Conversion." *Christus* (December 1984) 49:9-11.

Doran, Robert M., S.J. *Subject and Psyche: Ricoeur, June, and the Search for Foundations.* Washington, DC: University Press of America, 1977.

_____. *Psychic Conversion and Theological Foundations: Toward a Reorientation of the Human Sciences.* Chico, CA: Scholars Press, 1981.

Duffy, Regis A. *On Becoming a Catholic: The Challenge of Christian Initiation.* San Francisco, CA: Harper & Row, 1984.

Duggan, Robert P., ed. *Conversion and the Catechumenate.* New York: Paulist, 1984.

_____. "Conversion, the Catechumenate, and Cultural Adaptation." *New Catholic World* (July–August 1979) 222:169-72.

Dujarier, Michel. *A History of the Catechumenate.* New York: Sadlier, 1952.

_____. *The Rites of Christian Initiation: Historical and Pastoral Reflections.* New York: Sadlier, 1977.

_____. *A History of the Catechumenate: The First Six Centuries.* Trans. Edward J. Hassel. New York: Sadlier, 1979.

Dulles, Avery R., S.J. "Fundamental Theology and the Dynamics of Conversion." *Thomist* (April 1981) 45:175-93.

Dunning, James B. *New Wine, New Wineskins: Exploring the RCIA.* Chicago: Sadlier, 1981.

_____. "The Rite of Christian Initiation of Adults: Model of Adult Growth." *Worship* (March 1979) 53:142-56.

Eigo, Francis E., O.S.A. *The Human Experience of Conversion.* Villanova, PA: Villanova University Press, 1987.

Fowler, James W. *Stages of Faith: The Psychology of Human Development and the Quest for Meaning.* San Francisco, CA: Harper & Row, 1981.

Freburger, William J. "The Problems of Conversion." *Priest* (April 1985) 41:37.

Giblet, Jean. "The Christian Dimension of Conversion." *Lumen Vitae* (1982) 37:165-75.

Gelpi, Donald L., S.J. *Experiencing God: A Theology of Human Emergence.* Lanham, MD: University Press of America, 1987.

_____. *The Divine Mother: A Trinitarian Theology of the Holy Spirit.* Lanham, MD: University Press of America, 1984.

_____. *God Breathes: The Spirit in the World.* Wilmington, DE: Michael Glazier, 1988.

_____. *Grace as Transmuted Experience and Social Process: and Other Essays in North American Theology.* Lanham, MD: University Press of America, 1988.

_____. *Inculturating North American Theology: An Experiment in Foundational Method.* Atlanta, GA: Scholars Press, 1988.

de Gidio, Sandra, O.S.M. *RCIA: The Rites Revisited.* Minneapolis, MN: Winston, 1984.

Gergory, Wilton D. "The Challenge of Parish Conversion." *Chicago Studies* (August 1984) 23:197-208.

Griffen, Emilie. *Turning: Reflections on the Experience of Conversion.* Garden City, NY: Doubleday, 1980.

Happle, Stephen, and James J. Walter. *Conversion and Discipleship: A Christian Foundation for Ethics and Discipleship.* Philadelphia, PA: Fortress, 1986.

Häring, Bernard. *The Law of Christ: Moral Theology for Priests and Laity.* Trans. Edwin G. Kaiser. 3 vols.; Westminster, MD: Newman, 1961, 1:387-562.

Hellwig, Monika K. "The Call of the King: Conversion to Justice and Peace." *The Way* (Spring 1985) 52:43-52.

Kavanagh, Aiden. "Unfinished and Unbegun Revisited: The Rite of Christian Initiation of Adults." *Worship* (July 1979) 53:27-40.

Kemp, Raymond B. *A Journey in Faith: An Experience of the Catechumenate.* New York: Sadlier, 1979.

Leggio-Agate, Grace. "Conversion Toward Martyrdom." *Sisters* (May 1985) 56:546-9.

Maertens, Thierry. *Histoire et pastorale du rituel de catechumenat et du batème.* Bruges: Publications de Saint-Andre, 1962.

McBrien, Richard P. "Models of Conversion: An Ecclesiological Reflection." *Living Light* (Spring 1981) 18:7-17.

Navone, John, S.J. "Bipolarities in Conversion." *Review for Religious* (May–June 1981) 40:436-50.

_____. "Conversion Expressed in Dialogue and Story." *Review for Religious* (September–October 1982) 41:738-43.

_____. "Four Complementary Forms of Conversion." *Studies in Formative Spirituality* (February 1989) 10:27-35.

Nedoncelle, M. "La phenomenologie d'une conversion." *Nouvelle Revue Théologique* (June 1973) 95:548-66.

O'Rourke, David K. *A Process Called Conversion.* Garden City, NY: Doubleday, 1985.

O'Shea, John. "RCIA: Conversion, Lent, and Eastertide." *Music and Liturgy* (1986) 12:11-23.

Rahner, Karl, S.J. "On Conversions to the Church." *Theological Investigations.* Trans. Karl-H. and Boniface Kruger. 21 vols.; Baltimore, MD: Helicon, 1967, 3:373-384.

_____. "Some Remarks on the Question of Conversions" *Theological Investigations.* Trans. Karl-H. Kruger. 21 vols.; Baltimore, MD: Helicon, 1966, 5:315-335.

Saint-Laurent, George E. "Pre-Baptismal Rites in the Baptismal Catechesis of Theodore of Mopsuestia." *Diakonia* (1981) 16:118-26.

Searle, Mark. "Issues in Christian Initiation: Uses and Abuses in the RCIA." *Living Light* (March 1986) 22:199-214.

_____. "The Journey of Conversion." *Worship* (January 1980) 54:35-55.

Smith, Marc E. "Can Moral and Religious Conversion Be Separated?" *Thought* (June 1981) 56:178-84.

Stuhlmueller, Carol. "The Minister's Conversion in Ministering." *Ministries* (March 1980) 1:22-4.

Thurston, Bonnie Bowman. "Repentance." *Living Light* (August 1988) 21:3-6.

Tyrrell, Bernard J., S.J. *Christotherapy: Healing through Enlightenment.* New York: Seabury, 1975.

_____. *Christotherapy II: A New Horizon for Counselors, Spiritual Directors, and Seekers of Healing and Growth in Christ.* Ramsey, NJ: Paulist, 1982.

Reedy, William J., ed. *Becoming a Christian.* New York: Sadlier, 1979.

Wallis, Jim. *The Call to Conversion.* San Francisco, CA: Harper & Row, 1981.

Watson, D. "Towards an Understanding of Christian Conversion." *Clergy Review* (March 1980) 65:79-86; (April 1980) 65:121-8; (June 1980) 65:204-9.

II. Sacraments and Sacramentality:

Alfaro, Juan, S.J. "Cristo, Sacramento de Dios Padre: La Iglesia Sacramento de Cristo Glorificado." *Gregorianum* (1967) 48:190-200.

Allen, Diogenes. "The Restoration of Sacramentality in a Post-Modern World." *Liturgical Music* (Spring 1985) 19:85-88.

Arceneaux, Louis A., C. M. "Sacraments: Encounters with Other Persons as Well as with God." *Priest* (March 1984) 40:40-43.

Arturi, B. "The Sacraments to Non-Catholics?" *Priest* (September 1977) 33:22-5.

Barth, Marcus. "Baptism, Eucharist, and Ministry: Questions and Considerations." *Theology Today* (January 1986) 42:490-498.

Baum, Gregory. "Word and Sacrament." *Thought* (June 1963) 38:190-200.

Bausch, William J. *A New Look at the Sacraments.* Mystic, CT: Twenty-Third Publications, 1983.

Botte, Dom Bernard, O.S.B. "Vatican II et le renouveau liturgique." *Questions Liturgiques* (1981) 62:3-134.

Blackburn, Terence. "Sacraments and Social Action." *Liturgy* (1987) 6:66-71.

Boff, Leonardo. *Sacraments of Life and Life of the Sacraments: Story Theology.* Trans. John Drury. Washington, DC: Pastoral Press, 1987.

Bouyer, Louis. *Rite and Man: Natural Sacredness and Christian Liturgy.* Trans. M. Joseph Costelloe. Lanham, MD: University Press of America, 1985.

Brand, Eugene L. "The Lima Text as a Standard for Current Understandings and Practice." *Studia Liturgica* (1986) 16:40-63.

Brinkman, B. R. "On Sacramental Man: I." *Heythrop Journal* (1972) 13:371-401.

_____. "On Sacramental Man: II: The Way of Intimacy." *Heythrop Journal* (1973) 14:5-34.

_____. "On Sacramental Man: III: The Socially Operational Way." *Heythrop Journal* (1973) 14:162-189.

_____. "On Sacramental Man: IV: The Way of Interiorization." *Heythrop Journal* (1973) 14:280-306.

_____. "On Sacramental Man: V: The Way of Sacramental Operationalism." *Heythrop Journal* (1973) 14:396-416.

Calivas, Alkiviviadis. "The Lima Text as a Pointer to the Future: An Orthodox Perspective." *Studia Liturgica* (1986) 16:80-91.

Callahan, Annice C. "Karl Rahner's Theology of Symbol: Basis for His Theology of the Church and the Sacraments." *Irish Theological Quarterly* (1982) 49:195-205.

Casel, Odo. *The Mystery of Christian Worship and Other Writings.* Ed. Burkhard Neuheuser, O.S.B. Westminster, MD: Newman, 1962.

Challancin, James. "Human Experience and Sacramental Theology." *Chicago Studies* (August 1987) 26:196-215.

Chauvat, L. M., *et al. Sacraments de Jesus-Christ.* Paris: Desclee, 1983.

Christopher, Michael. "Are Sacraments on the Way Out?" *U.S. Catholic* (November 1983) 48:48-50.

Christopherson, Kenneth E. "Putting Humpty Dumpty Together Again: The Baptism, Eucharist, and Ministry Document." *Southern American Baptist Quarterly* (December 1985) 364–382.

Cooke, Bernard. *Christian Sacraments and Christian Personality.* New York: Doubleday, 1965.

_____. *Ministry to Word and Sacrament: History and Theology.* Philadelphia, PA: Fortress, 1976.

_____. *Sacraments and Sacramentality.* Mystic, CT: Twenty-Third Publications, 1983.

_____. "Presidential Address: Death and Resurrection of Sacraments." *Catholic Theological Society of America Proceedings* (1983) 38:45-57.

Crow, Paul A., Jr. "BEM: Challenge and Promise." *Theology Today* (January 1986) 42:478-489.

Congar, Yves, O.P. *Lay People in the Church: A Study for a Theology of the Laity.* Trans. Donald Attwater. Westminster, MD: Newman, 1965.

Crichton, J. D. "Signs, Symbols, Mysteries." *Worship* (May 1964) 38:469-74.

Cullman, Oscar. *Les sacrements dans l'évangile johannique.* Paris: Presses Universitaires de France, 1951.

Davies, John Gordon. *The Spirit, The Church, and the Sacraments.* London: Faith, 1954.

Diekmann, Godfrey, O.S.B. "Sacramental Life—The Mystery Shared." *Worship* (October 1964) 38:589-598.

Dore, J., ed. *Sacraments de Jesus-Christ.* Paris: Desclee, 1983.

Downey, Michael. "Teaching Sacramental Theology." *Liturgy* (1985) 5:61-72.

_____. *Clothed in Christ: The Sacraments and Christian Living.* New York: Crossroad, 1987.

Doyle, Thomas P. "Sacramental Law in the New Code: Part One." *Priest* (November 1984) 40:34-38.

_____. "Sacramental Law in the New Code: Part Two." *Priest* (December 1984) 40:27-32.

Duffy, Regis A. "Of Reluctant Celebrants and Reliable Symbols." *Heythrop Journal* (1977) 18:165-177.

_____. *Real Presence: Worship, Sacraments, and Commitment.* San Francisco, CA: Harper & Row, 1982.

Duval, Andre. *Des sacrements au concile de Trente: rites et symbols.* Paris: Editions de Cerf, 1985.

"Eastern Orthodox-Roman Catholic Agreed Statement on BEM." *Ecumenical Trends* (May 1985) 14:73-76.

Eigo, Francis A., O.S.A., ed. *The Sacraments: God's Love and Mercy Actualized*. Villanova, PA: Villanova University Press, 1979.

Eastwood, Cyril. *The Royal Priesthood of the Faithful: An Investigation of the Doctrine from Biblical Times to the Reformation*. Minneapolis, MN: Augsburg, 1963.

Empereur, James, S.J. *Exploring the Sacred*. Washington, DC: Pastoral Press, 1987.

Fahey, Michael A., ed. *Catholic Perspectives on Baptism, Eucharist, and Ministry*. Lanham, MD: University Press of America, 1986.

Feidler, Paul A. *The Sacraments: Encountering the Risen Lord*. Notre Dame, IN: Ave Maria Press, 1986.

Fiedler, Ernest J. *The Sacraments: An Experiment in Ecumenical Honesty*. Nashville, TN: Abingdon, 1969.

Fink, Peter E., S.J. "Toward a Liturgical Theology." *Worship* (December 1973) 47:601-609.

Fransen, Piet. "The Church and the Trinity." *Thought* (March 1963) 38:68-88.

_____. "Sacraments as Celebrations." *International Theological Quarterly* (1976) 43:151-70.

_____. "Sacraments, Signs of Faith." *Worship* (December 1962) 36:31-50.

Gallagher, W. "Sacramentality of the Christian Life." *Cross and Crown* (March 1975) 27:39-50.

Ganoczy, Alexandre. *An Introduction to Catholic Sacramental Theology*. Trans. Rev. William Thomas and Rev. Anthony Sherman. New York: Paulist, 1984.

Garijo-Guembe, Miguel M. "Sakrament und Sakramentalitaet." *Catholica* (1986) 40:110-24.

Gelpi, Donald L., S.J. *Charism and Sacrament: A Theology of Christian Conversion*. New York: Paulist, 1976.

_____. "The Church: Sacramental and Charismatic: Avoiding False Dichotomies." *Church* (1987) 3:19-24.

Gilkey, Langdon B. "Symbols, Meaning, and the Divine Presence." *Theological Studies* (June 1974) 35:249-67.

Gillan, Garth. "Symbol: Word for the Other." *Worship* (April 1967) 41:275-283.

Granger, Roger. "The Sacraments as Passage Rites." *Worship* (May 1984) 58:214-22.

Greeley, Andrew M. "Stamp Out Sacramental Tyranny." *U.S. Catholic* (May 1985) 50:13-15.

_____. "Empirical Liturgy: The Search for Grace." *America* (1987) 157:379-83.

Green, Thomas J. "The Church's Sanctifying Office: Reflections on Selected Canons in the Revised Code." *Jurist* (1984) 44:357-411.

Gundyayev, Abp. Kirill. "The Significance and Status of BEM in the Ecumenical Movement." *Greek Orthodox Theological Review* (Summer 1985) 30:179-195.

Gurrieri, John A. "Sacramental Validity: Ecumenical Questions." *Ecumenical Trends* (May 1986) 15:69-73.

Grifiss, James E., Jr. "Sacramental Grace." *Worship* (October 1968) 42:487-494.

Gy, Pierre-M. "Problems de theologie sacramentaire." *Maison-Dieu* #110:129-42.

_____. "Sacraments and Liturgy in Latin Christianity." *Christian Spirituality* (1985) 365–381.

Guzie, Tad. *The Book of Sacramental Basics.* New York: Paulist, 1981.

Häring, Bernard. *The Sacraments and Your Everyday Life.* Ligouri, MO: Ligouri Publications, 1976).

Halligan, Nicholas, O.P. *The Mystery and the Celebration of the Sacraments.* 3 vols.; New York: Alba House, 1973.

_____. *The Sacraments and Their Celebration.* New York: Alba House, 1986.

Hellwig, Monika K. "Growth, Tension, and the Sacramental Life." *The Way* (April 1983) 23:108-14.

_____. *The Meaning of the Sacraments.* Dayton, OH: Phlaum Press, 1972.

Himes, Michael. "This Graced World: Trinity, Grace, and Sacraments." *Church* (Spring 1985) 1:3-12.

Hofmeister, Philipp. *Die heiligen Oele in der morgen- und abendlaendischen Kirche.* Wuertzburg: Augustinus Verlag, 1948.

Hovda, Robert. "The Amen Corner: Celebrating the Sacraments for the Life of the World." *Worship* (January 1988) 62:72-9.

Huels, John M., O.S.M. "The Use of Reason and Reception of Sacraments by the Mentally Handicapped." *Jurist* (1984) 44:209-19.

Irwin, Kevin W. "Recent Sacramental Theology." *Thomist* (October 1983) 47:592-608.

Jones, Cheslyn, Geoffrey Wainwright, Edward Yarnold, S.J. *The Study of Liturgy.* New York: Oxford University Press, 1978.

Kavanaugh, Aiden, O.S.B. "Sacraments as an Act of Service." *Worship* (January 1965) 39:89-96.

Kilmarten, Edward J. "Sacraments Revisited," *New Catholic World.* (May–July 1974) 217:126-9.

Kinast, Robert L. "Sacramental Vitality" *Chicago Studies* (April 1987) 26:63-74.

Küng, Hans. *The Sacraments: An Ecumenical Dilemma.* New York: Paulist, 1966.

Lacoste, Jean-Yves. "Sacraments, Ethique, Eucharistique." *Revue Thomiste* (April–June 1984) 84:212-42.

Lawler, Michael G. *Sacraments as Prophetic Symbols.* New York: Seabury, 1984.

_____. *Sacrament and Symbol: A Contemporary Sacramental Theology.* New York: Paulist, 1987.

Limouris, Gennadios, and Nomikos Michael Vaporis, eds. *Orthodox Perspectives on Baptism, Eucharist, and Ministry.* Brookline, MA: Holy Cross Orthodox Press, 1985.

Lynch, John J. "Sacramental Preparation: Six Principles." *Church* (1987) 3:9-18.

Martelet, G., S.J. "De la sacramentalité propre à l'Église ou d'un sense de l'Église inseparable du sens du Christ." *Nouvelle Révue Théologique* (January 1973) 95:25-42.

May, Rollo, ed. *Symbolism in Religion and Literature.* New York: Brazillier, 1960.

McNamara, B. "Christus Patiens in Mass and Sacraments: Higher Perspectives." *Irish Theological Quarterly* (January 1975) 42:17-35.

Martos, Joseph. *The Catholic Sacraments.* Wilmington, DL: Michael Glazier, 1983.

_____. *Doors to the Sacred: A Historical Introduction to Sacraments in the Catholic Church.* New York: Doubleday, 1981.

Morrisey, F. G. "Renewal of Sacramental Canon Law after the Second Vatican Council." *Église et Théologie* (October 1974) 5:347-73.

Muller, Denis. "Parole de Dieu, langage et symbole: éléments pour une reflexion sur le culte reformé." *Irenikon* (1985) 58:199-208.

Murion, Philip J. "A Sacramental Church." *America* (March 1983) 148:226-8.

Murphy, T. "Sacraments and Ministry." *Chicago Studies* (Spring 1975) 14:83-95.

Musurillo, Herbert, S.J. "Sacramental Symbolism and the Mysterion of the Early Church." *Worship* (April 1965) 39:265-74.

O'Connell, Matthew J., S.J. "New Perspectives in Sacramental Theology." *Thought* (March 1961) 36:40-58.

_____. "The Sacraments in Theology Today." *Thought* (March 1961) 36:40-58.

O'Neill, Colman E., O.P. *Sacramental Realism: A General Theory of the Sacraments.* Wilmington, DL: Michael Glazier, 1983.

Osborne, Kenan B., O.F.M. "Methodology and Christian Sacraments." *Worship* (November 1974) 48:536-49.

_____. *Sacramental Theology: A General Introduction.* New York: Paulist, 1988.

Palme, Paul. *Sacraments and Worship.* Westminster: Newman, 1963.

Powers, Joseph M., S.J. *Spirit and Sacrament: The Humanizing Experience.* New York: Seabury, 1973.

Rahner, Karl, S.J. *The Church and the Sacraments.* Freiberg: Herder, 1963.

_____. "The Concept of Mystery in Catholic Theology." *Theological Investigations.* Trans. Karl H. and Boniface Kruger. 21 vols.; Baltimore, MD: Helicon, 1967, 4:36-60.

_____. *Inquiries.* New York: Herder & Herder, 1964.

_____. "Personal and Sacramental Piety." *Theological Investigations.* Trans. Karl H. Kruger. 21 vols; Baltimore, MD: Helicon, 1963.

_____. "The Theology of Symbol." *Theologican Investigations.* Trans. Karl H. and Boniface Kruger. 21 vols.; Baltimore, MD: Helicon, 1967.

_____. "What is a Sacrament?" *Worship* (May 1973) 47:274-84.

_____. *Ueber die Sakramente der Kirche: Meditationen.* Freiburg in Breisgau: Herder, 1985.

Renear, Miles. "Gestalt Therapy and Sacramental Experience." *Journal of Pastoral Care* (March 1976) 30:3-15.

Robert, Paul. *The Atonement and the Sacraments.* New York: Abingdon, 1976, 30:3-15.

Roberts, William P. *Encounters with Christ: Introduction to the Sacraments.* New York: Paulist, 1985.

_____. "The Sacraments: Signs of Conversion." *New Catholic World* (March–April 1986) 229:78-82.

Ross, Susan A. "The Aesthetic and the Sacramental." *Worship* (January 1985) 59:2-17.

"Sacraments et Ministères." *Etudes* (January 1984) 360:89-103.

Schillebeeckx, Edward, O.P. *Christ the Sacrament of the Encounter with God.* Trans. Mark Schoof and Laurence Bright. New York: Sheed and Ward, 1963.

_____. ed. *The Sacraments in General.* New York: Paulist, 1968.

Shea, W. "Sacraments and Meaning." *American Ecclesiastical Review* (June 1975) 169:403-16.

Sheets, John R., S.J. "Symbol and Sacrament." *Worship* (February 1967) 42:194-210.

Sloyan, Gerard S. "Jewish Ritual of the First Century C.E. and Christian Sacramental Practice." *Biblical Theological Bulletin* (July 1985) 15:98-103.

Sullivan, C. Stephen, F.S.C. *Readings in Sacramental Theology.* New York: Prentice-Hall, 1964.

Sullivan, Walter Francis. "The Sacraments, Canon Law, and the Rights of Disabled Persons." *America* (April 1986) 154:321-4.

_____. "The Significance of Vatican II's Decision to Say of the Church of Christ Not That It 'Is' But That It 'Subsists In' The Roman Catholic Church" *Centro Pro Unione Bulletin* (Spring 1986) 29:3-8.

Tappeiner, Daniel A. "Sacramental Causality in Aquinas and Rahner: Some Critical Thoughts." *Scottish Journal of Theology* (1975) 28:243-57.

Taylor, Michael, S.J., ed. *The Sacraments: Readings in Contemporary Sacramental Theology.* New York: Alba House, 1981.

Thurien, Max, ed. *Church Response to BEM.* Geneva: World Council of Churches, 1986.

Tillard, J. M. R. "Koinonia—Sacrament." *Mid-Stream* (October 1986) 25:375-385.

Traets, C., S.J. "Rite et liturgie sacrementelle." *Questions Liturgique* (1974) 55:11-31.

Turner, Denys. "Sacrament and Ideology." *New Blackfriars* (April 1983) 64:425-41.

Van Roo, William, S.J. "Reflections on Karl Rahner's 'Kirche und Sakramente.'" *Gregorianum* (1962) 44:465-500.

Vaillancourt, Raymond. *Toward a Renewal of Sacramental Theology.* Trans. Matthew J. O'Connell. Collegeville, MN: The Liturgical Press, 1979.

Wainwright, Geoffrey. "Sacramental Theology and the World Church." *Catholic Theological Society of America Proceedings* (1984) 39:69-83.

_____. "The Lima Text in the History of Faith and Order." *Studia Liturgica* (1986) 16:1-2, 6-21.

_____. "Baptism, Eucharist, and Ministry: A Liturgical Appraisal of the Lima Text." *Studia Liturgica* (1986) 16:1-128.

Weber, Robert E. "Are Evangelicals Becoming Sacramental?" *Ecumenical Trends* (March 1985) 14:36-38.

White, James F. "The Missing Jewel of the Evangelical Church." *The Reformed Journal* (June 1986) 36:11-16.

Worden, T. *Sacraments in Scripture.* Springfield, IL: Templegate, 1966.

Worgul, Goerge S., Jr. *From Magic to Metaphor: A Validation of the Christian Sacraments.* New York: Paulist, 1980.

_____. "The Future of Sacraments." *Chicago Studies* (April 1985) 24:59-68.

_____. "What Is A Sacrament?" *U.S. Catholic.* (January 1977) 42:29-31.

World Council of Churches, *Baptism, Eucharist, and Ministry.* Geneva: World Council of Churches, 1982.

III. Christian Initiation:

Aland, K. *Did the Early Church Baptize Infants?* (London: SCM Press, 1963).

Antekeier, Charles, and Van and Janet Vandegriff. *Confirmation: The Power of the Spirit.* Notre Dame: Ave Maria, 1972.

Amedon, P. "Baptismal Spirituality for Adults." *Priest* (November 1975) 30:24-6.

Artz, Thomas R., C.SS.R. "Confirmation: The Sacrament of Spiritual Maturity." *Ligourian* (June 1981) 69:34-9.

Austin, Gerard, O.P. "The Rite of Initiation and Ecumenical Issues." *Ecumenical Trends* (March 1988) 47:44-7.

Balhoff, Michael J. "Age for Confirmation: Canonical Evidence." *Jurist* (1985) 44:549-87.

Barry, R. "Confirmation in a Modern Perspective." *Priest* (October 1976) 32:17-8.

Barth, Karl. *The Teaching of the Church Regarding Baptism.* Trans. Ernest A. Payne. London: S.C.M. Press, 1965.

Beach, M. "Confirmation Contract Demands Commitment." *Worship* (January 1964) 38:84-91.

Beasley-Murray, George. *Baptism in the New Testament.* London: Macmillan, 1963.

Bevenot, M. "Cyprian's Platform in the Rebaptism Controversy." *Heythrop Journal* (April 1978) 19:123-42.

Bohen, Marian, O.S.U. "Confirmation Catechesis." *Worship* (January 1975) 38:84-91.

Boudelle, Guy. "Reflection on the Place of the Child in the Church: 'Suffer the Little Children to Come to Me." *Communio* (Winter 1985) 12:349-67.

Bourgeois, Henri. *On Becoming Christian: Christian Initiation and Its Sacraments.* Mystic, CT: Twenty-Third Publications, 1985.

Brankin, A. "Confirmation: The Mystical Seal of the Holy Spirit." *Homiletic and Pastoral Review* (April 1980) 80:11-6.

Brimlow, T. "Confirmation: The Forgotten Sacrament." *Clergy Review* (March 1975) 60:147-51.

Brown, Raymond E. "We Confess One Baptism for the Forgiveness of Sins." *Worship* (May 1966) 40:260-271.

Bryce, Mary Charles, O.S.B. "Confirmation: Being and Becoming a Christian." *Worship* (May 1967) 41:284-298.

Buckley, F. "The Right to Sacraments of Initiation: The Individual and Community." *Origins* (November 1978) 8:329-36.

Brown, Schuyler. "Water-Baptism and Spirit-Baptism in Luke Acts." *Anglican Theological Review* (April 1977) 59:135-51.

Collins, A. "Sacramental Aspects of Paul's Thought on Baptism and the Lord's Supper." *Chicago Studies* (Spring 1977) 16:177-33.

Collins, R. "Luke 3:21-22, Baptism or Anointing." *Bible Today* 14 (April 1976) 821–831.

Courth, Franz. "Die Firmung Als Sakrament der Kirchlichen Sendung." *Mitverantwortung Aller in der Kirche.* F. Courth and A. Weiser, eds. (1985) 134–149.

Crehan, Joseph, S.J. *Early Christian Baptism and the Creed.* London: Burns, Oates, Washbourne, Ltd., 1948.

Crichton, James D. "A Debate Continued: The Purpose of Confirmation." *Clergy Review* (April 1983) 68:147-8.

Cullmann, Oscar. *Baptism in the New Testament.* Trans. J. K. S. Reid. Chicago: Regnery, 1950.

Cully, Kendig Brubaker, ed. *Confirmation Re-Examined.* Winton, CT: Morehouse-Barlow, Co., 1982.

Davis, Charles. *Sacraments of Initiation: Baptism and Confirmation.* New York: Sheed and Ward, 1964.

De Latte, R. "Saint Augustin et le baptême," *Questions Liturgiques* (1975) 56:177-223.

Delcuve, Georges, S.J. "Becoming Christians in Christ: The Dynamics of the Sacraments of Baptism, Confirmation, and the Eucharist." *Lumen Vitae* (1973) 28:76-96.

Dix, Dom Gregory. *The Theology of Confirmation in Relation to Baptism.* London: Dacre Press, 1946.

Dolan, P. "Second Thoughts on Delaying the Baptism of Infants: Salvation Is a Gift of God, Not a Human Accomplishment." *Priest* (June 1977) 33:31-3.

Eckstein, Joan. "Confirmation: A Problem Sacrament." *Catechist* (Fall 1986) 20:34-41.

Eliade, Mircea. *Rites and Symbols of Initiation.* New York: Harper, 1958.

Elkstrom, R. "A New Approach to Confirmation." *Religion Teacher's Journal* (January 1979) 12:48-50.

Eller, Vernand. *In Place of Sacraments: A Study of Baptism and the Lord's Supper*. Grand Rapids, MI: Eerdmans, 1972.

Emswiler, J. "High School Confirmation." *Religion Teacher's Journal* (January 1976) 9:16-17.

Fisher, B. "Baptism of the Spirit." *One in Christ* (November 1974) 9:127-33.

Feuillet, A. "Les 'sacrifices spirituels' du sacerdoce royale des baptises (1 P 2, 5)." *Nouvelle Révue Théologique* (1974) 94:704-28.

George, A., S.M. *Baptism in the New Testament*. Trans. David Askew. Baltimore, MD: Helicon, 1964.

Gusmer, C. "The Revised Adult Initiation and Its Challenge to Religious Education." *Living Light* (Spring 1976) 13:92-8.

Hall, Theodore, O.P. "Baptized but Never Converted." *Homiletic and Pastoral Review* (April 1987) 87:52-7.

Hallesby, O. *Infant Baptism and Adult Conversion*. Trans. Clarence J. Carlsen. Minneapolis, MN: Augsburg, 1964.

Haas, LaVerne. *Personal Pentecost: The Meaning of Confirmation*. St. Meinrad, IN: Abbey Press, 1973.

Hamman, Adalbert. *Le baptème et la confirmation*. Paris: Dsclee, 1969.

Holeton, David R. "Changing the Baptism Formula: Feminist Proposals and Liturgical Implications." *Ecumenical Trends* (May 1988) 17:69-72.

Holkema, Anthony. "The Holy Spirit in Christian Experience." *Reformed Review* (Spring 1975) 28:183-191.

Hoeslinger, Morbert. "Zum neuen Taufritus und tom Taufgespraech." *Bibel und Liturgie* (1972) 177–191.

Jensen, Robert W. "The Mandate and Promise of Baptism." *Interpretation* (1976) 30:271-87.

Jeremias, Joachim. *Infant Baptism in the First Four Centuries*. Philadelphia, PA: Westminster, 1960.

Kavanaugh, Aiden. *Confirmation: Origins and Reform*. New York: Pueblo, 1988.

_____. "Christian Initiation of Adults." *Worship* (June–July 1974) 48:381-35.

_____. "The Norm of Baptism: The New Rite of Initiation of Adults." *Worship* (March 1974) 48:143-52.

_____. "Confirmation: A Suggestion from Structure." *Worship* (September 1984) 58:386-95.

Keating, C. "Baptism Sets our Boundaries." *New Catholic World* (May–June 1974) 217:100-104.

Keifer, R. "Christian Initiation: The State of the Question." *Worship* (August–September 1974) 48:392-404.

Kelly, William J., S.J. "Reflections on the Status of a Theology of the Layman." *Theological Studies* (December 1967) 28:706-32.

Kiesling, C. "Confirmation and Full Life in the Spirit." *St. Anthony's Messenger* (January 1974) 18:12-17.

Küng, Hans. "Confirmation: What's the Fuss?" *U.S. Catholic* (July 1975) 40:19-22.

Laham, Lifti. "Der peneumatologische Aspekt der Sakramente der christlichen Mystagogie (oder Initiation)." *Kyrios* (1972) 97–106.

Landini, L. "Baptismal Practices in Catholic Hospitals." *Jurist* (Spring–Summer 1975) 35:296-309.

Larose, P. "The New Testament and Confirmation." *Catechist* (April 1979) 12:27-8.

Leclercq, Jean, O.S.B. "The Sacraments of the Easter Season." *Worship* (May 1960) 34:297-309.

Ligier, Louis, S.J. "La priere et l'imposition des mains: autour un nouveau Rituel romain de la confirmation." *Gregorianum* (1972) 23:407-486.

Losoncy, Lawrence James. "The Easter Sacraments." *Ligourian* (April 1988) 76:2-5.

Maas-Ewerd, Theodor. "Verdraengt der neue Taufritus den Taufbrunnen?" *Bibel und Liturgie* (1972) 180–185.

Mallia, Paul, S.J. "Baptized into Death and Life." *Worship* (June–July 1965) 39:425-430.

Marchal, Michael. "Pentecost and Baptismal Promises." *Modern Liturgy* (April 1988) 15:12-3.

Marsh, Thomas S. *A Gift of Community: Baptism and Confirmation.* Wilmington, DE: Michael Glazier, 1984.

_____. "The Theology of Confirmation." *Furrow* (November 1976) 27:606-16.

Martos, Joseph. "Confirmation Should Not Be Automatic." *U.S. Catholic* (July 1984) 49:11-12.

_____. "Let's Deny Baptism to the Babies of Fallen Away Catholics." *U.S. Catholic* (February 1984) 49:13-5.

McAlister, M. "A Parent Involvement Program for Confirmation." *Religion Teacher's Journal* (January 1975) 8:19-21.

McDonnell, Kilian, O.S.B., and Arnold Bittlinger, eds. *The Baptism in the Holy Spirit as an Ecumenical Problem.* Notre Dame, IN: Charismatic Renewal Services, 1972.

Miller, Randolph C., and John R. Whitney. "Response to 'Confirmation Today.'" *Anglican Theological Review* (1972) 360–363.

Murphy Center for Liturgical Research. *Made Not Born: New Perspectives on Christian Initiation.* Notre Dame, IN: University of Notre Dame Press, 1976.

Mulholland, K. "Are We Asking Too Much of Our Confirmation Students?" *Religion Teacher's Journal* (January 1976) 9:18-20.

Neumann, Don. "Unbaptized Children: What Can We Do?" *Today's Parish* (September 1988) 20:9-10.

Neunheuser, Burkhard. *Baptism and Confirmation.* Trans. John Jay Hughes. New York: Herder & Herder, 1964.

Nocent, Adrien. "Confirmation: The Difficult Catechesis." *Lumen Vitae* (1973) 28:97-109.

Nowakowski, J. "Celebrating Baptism." *Religion Teacher's Journal.* (September 1973) 7:46-47.

Osborne, Kenan B., O.F.M. *The Christian Sacraments of Initiation: Baptism, Confirmation, Eucharist.* New York: Paulist, 1987.

Pope Paul VI. "Address at a General Audience about Baptism." *L'Osservatore Romano* (May 20, 1976) No. 21 [425] 2.

Porter, H. Boone, Jr., "Baptism: Its Paschal and Ecumenical Setting," *Worship* (April 1968) 42:205-214.

Rahner, Karl, S.J. *A New Baptism in the Spirit: Confirmation Today.* Denville, NJ: Dimensions Books, 1974.

Reckinger, Franz. "'Accipe Signaculum': Die Firmung in neuer Gestalt." *Heiliger Dienst* (1972) 164–74.

"Rituel et pastorale de la confirmation." *Maison-Dieu.* 110:51-71.

Sawyer, Kieran, S.S.N.D. "Readiness for Confirmation." *Living Light* (June 1988) 24:331-9.

_____. "The Confirmation Dialogue Continues." *Living Light* (March 1986) 22:215-21.

Schnackenburg, Rudolf. *Baptism in the Thought of St Paul.* Trans. G. R. Beasley-Murray. New York: Herder & Herder, 1964.

_____. "Christian Adulthood According to the Apostle Paul." *Catholic Biblical Quarterly* (July 1963) 25:354-70.

Schwager, Raymond, S.J. "Wassertaufe, ein Gebet um die Geisttaufe." *Zeitschrift für Katholische Theologie* (1978) 100:36-61.

Searle, Mark. "Confirmation: The State of the Question." *Church* (1985) 1:15-22.

Smedt, Emile. *The Priesthood of the Faithful.* New York: Paulist, 1962.

Smith, K. "Confirmation Re-examined: An Evolving Theology and Practice." *Worship* (January 1974) 48:21-9.

Smith, Michael H. *Preparing for Confirmation.* South Bend, IN: Ave Maria, 1973.

Stendahl, Krister. "One Baptism for the Forgiveness of Sins." *Worship* (May 1966) 40:272-275.

Stevick, Daniel. "Types of Baptismal Spirituality." *Worship* (May 1966) 40:272-275.

Stuhlmueller, Carrol, C.P. "Baptism: New Life Through the Blood of Jesus Christ." *Worship* (January 1973) 47:11-26.

Sullivan, F. "Baptism in the Holy Spirit." *Catholic Mind* (April 1976) 74:10-23.

Thornton, Lionel. *Confirmation.* London: Westminster, 1954.

Thurien, Max. *Consecration of the Layman.* Trans. by W. J. Kerrigan. Baltimore, MD: Helicon, 1963.

Tillard, J. M. R., O.P. "La qualité sacerdotale du ministère chrétien." *Nouvelle Révue Théologique* (May 1973) 95:481-514.

Turner, Paul. *The Meaning and Practice of Confirmation.* New York: Lang, 1987.

Wild, R. "Baptism in the Holy Spirit." *Cross and Crown* (June 1973) 25:147-61.

Weger, Karl-Heinz, S.J. "Der Sinn der Kindertaufe." *Stimmen der Zeit.* (November 1980) 198:721-2.

Winkler, Gabriele. "Confirmation or Crismation? A Study of Comparative Liturgy." *Worship* (January 1984) 58:2-27.

_____. "The Original Meaning of Prebaptismal Anointing and Its Implications." *Worship* (January 1978) 52:24-45.

Yarnold, Edward, S.J. "Baptism and the Pagan Mysteries in the Fourth Century." *Heythrop Journal* (1972) 13:247-67.

IV. Marriage:

Alston, Jon P. "Evaluation of Church Officials' Attitudes Toward Making Divorce Easier and Toward Three Kinds of Intermarriage." *Journal for the Scientific Study of Religion* (1972) 282–286.

Ambrosiano, A. "Mariage et Eucharistie." *Nouvelle Révue Théologique* (April 1976) 98:289-305.

Ambrozic, Aloysius. "Indissolubility of Marriage in the New Testament: Law or Ideal?" *Studia Canonica* (1972) 269–88.

Ayvish, F. "Where Are You Going, My Pretty Wife: Marriage and Career." *U.S. Catholic* (October 1975) 40:38-39.

Barbeau, C. *Creative Marriage: The Middle Years.* New York: Seabury, 1976.

_____. "Fidelity." *Sign* (June 1976) 55:9-14.

_____. "Marriage Myths." *St. Anthony's Messenger* (April 1974) 81:10-15.

Bedouelle, Guy. "Reflection on the Place of the Child in the Church: 'Suffer the Little Children to Come to Me.'" *Communio* (Winter 1985) 12:349-67.

Baroody, E. "Love and Marriage Colonial Style." *Marriage* (November 1974) 56:12-15.

Barth, Karl. *On Marriage*. Philadelphia, PA: Fortress, 1968.

Bassett, W. *The Future of Christian Marriage*. New York: Herder & Herder, 1973.

Bird, Joseph and Lois. *The Freedom of Sexual Love*. New York: Image Books, 1967.

Bird, Otto. "The Complexity of Love." *Thought* (June 1964) 39:210-220.

Bishop, J. "Marriage: A Sign of the Kingdom." *New Blackfriars* (March 1975) 56:111-20.

Boivin, M. "On Dissolving Indissolubility." *New Blackfriars* (November 1975) 56:493-9.

Bouyer, Louis. "*Humanae Vitae* Ten Years After: Toward a Positive Theology of Marriage." *American Journal of Jurisprudence* (1980) 25:133-5.

Bromiley, Geoffrey W. *God and Marriage*. Grand Rapids, MI: Eerdmans, 1980.

Butler, S. "Breaking Dependency in Marriage." *Marriage* (August 1976) 58:22-5.

Carmody, Denise Lardner. "Marriage in Roman Catholicism." *Journal of Ecumenical Studies* (Winter 1985) 22:28-40.

Catholic Theological Society of America. *Human Sexuality: New Directions in American Catholic Thought*. New York: Paulist, 1977.

Chikopela, G. "Marriage Commitment." *African Ecclesiastical Review* (1972) 327–331.

Christiansen, Rita. "Beyond the Breaking Point." *Marriage* (August 1988) 70:8-10.

Coats, M. "A Kind Word for Marriage—Anyone?" *Marriage* (July 1974) 56:21-2.

Coleman, G. "Pastoral Theology and Divorce." *American Ecclesiastical Review* (April 1975) 169:256-69.

Concetti, G. "Christian Marriage Today." *L' Osservatore Romano* (July 1, 1976) No. 27 [43] 4.

Constantelos, Demetrios J. "Marriage in the Greek Orthodox Church." *Journal of Ecumenical Studies* (Winter 1985) 22:21-7.

Cosgrove, T. "Down the Aisle for One Last Gamble." *Ligourian* (October 1975) 63:39-43.

_____. "The Open House of the Happily Married." *Ligourian* (March 1974) 62:9-12.

Crespy, Georges, Paul Evdokimov, and Christian Duquoc. *Marriage and Christian Tradition*. Trans. Agnes Cunningham. Techny, IL: Divine Word, 1968.

Crouzel, Henri. "Le sens de *porneia* dans les incises mattheennes." *Nouvelle Révue Théologique* (November–December 1988) 96:28-34.

Cunningham, W. "Abstinence Compatible with Marriage?" *Homeletic and Pastoral Review* (October 1975) 76:23-8.

Curtin, William B. "The Dilemma of Second Marriages." *America* (August 18, 1973) 129:88-91.

Daly, Bernard M., and Kerans Patrick. "Christian Marriage: Is It Possible?" *America* (February 1973) 129:160-2.

Davidson, J. "Compatibility and One-fleshedness." *Marriage* (February 1975) 57:21-3.

Delbridge, John R. "Searching for Depth in a Shallow World." *Marriage* (April 1988) 70:8-10.

Delooz, P. "The Western Family, A Prospective Evaluation." *Cross Currents* (Winter 1974) 23:419-35.

Desdouits, M. "La dispense de marriage non consommé." *Esprit et Vie* (1972) 617–20.

Dillon, V. "Can the Family Survive?" *Columbia* (April 1976) 56:8-15.

Dinechin, Olivier de, S.J. "Fragilites conjugales." *Etudes* (June 1988) 368:747-58.

Dittrich, L. "The Politics of Marriage." *Marriage* (March 1974) 56:2-4.

Dominian, J. "Marital Breakdown." *Tablet* (October 4, 1975) 229:940-2.

Doms, Herbert. *The Meaning of Marriage.* London: Sheed and Ward, 1939.

Douglas, R. "Effects of *Machismo* On Marriage and Family." *Catholic Charities Review* (April 1974) 58:3-13.

Dues, Greg. "Hints for Parent Sacramental Preparation Programs." *Catechist* (January 1985) 40:207-9.

Dufresne, Edward R. *Partnership: Marriage and the Committed Life.* Paramus, NJ: Paulist-Newman, 1975.

Duncan, R. "Marriage and Family Living Forum." *Marriage* (November 1974) 56:10-11.

Dunn, Frank Gasque. *Building Faith in Families: Using the Sacraments in Pastoral Ministry.* Wilton, CT: Morehouse-Barlow, 1986.

Eisenstein, Victor W., ed. *Neurotic Interaction in Marriage.* New York: Basic Books, 1956.

Elwood, J. "Uncertain Togetherness." *Marriage* (August 1975) 57:22-6.

Everett, W. and J. "Childless Marriages: A New Vocation?" *U.S. Catholic* (May 1975) 40:38-9.

Fagan, Sean. "Divorce: A Possibility for Catholics." *Doctrine and Life* (1972) 625–635.

Finley, M. "Loving Sexually." *Marriage* (January 1976) 58:2-4.

Fitzgerald, G. "International Consultation on Mixed Marriages." *One in Christ* (November 4, 1974) 10:332-8.

Garrone, G. M. "Married Life and Charity." *L' Osservatore Romano* (May 2, 1974) No. 18 [318] 9.

Geaney, D. "Till Growth Do Us Part." *U.S. Catholic* (April 1975) 40:6-13.

"The German Bishops on *Humanae Vitae*." *Tablet* (December 3, 1967) 229:1229-31.

Gibert, Henri. *Love in Marriage.* Trans. Andre Humbert. New York: Hawthorne Books, 1964.

Gordon, Michael, ed. *The American Family in Social-Historical Perspective.* New York: St. Martin's Press, 1973.

Gosling, J. *Marriage and the Love of God.* London: Geoffrey Chapman, 1965.

Gray, Donald P. "Teilhard de Chardin's Vision of Love." *Thought* (December 1967) 42:519-42.

Griffin, Gerald G. *The Silent Misery—Why Marriages Fail.* Springfield, IL: Charles C. Thomas, 1974.

Gruenfelder, John. "The Unity of the Marital Act." *Worship* (October 1968) 42:498-501.

Guzie, Tad. "Developing a Theology of Marriage." *Way* (October 1974) 14:268-75.

Haines, A. "Making Marriages Last." *Family Digest* (October 1974) 30:40-43.

Hammer, M. "Premarital Counseling Equals Post Nuptial Happiness." *Marriage* (May 1976) 58:18-20.

Hanagan, J. *The Courage to Be Married.* St. Meinrad, IN: Abbey Press, 1974.

Häring, Bernard. "It's Wrong to Knowingly Beget Defective Children." *U.S. Catholic* (February 1976) 41:12-14.

_____. *Marriage in the Modern World.* Westminster, MD: Newman, 1965.

Haughton, R. *The Theology of Marriage.* Butler, WI: Clergy Book Service, 1971.

_____. "Marriage in the Future." *Sign* (June 1976) 55:33-7.

Hellman, Eugene, C.SS.P. *Polygamy Reconsidered: Plural Marriage and the Christian Churches.* Maryknoll, NY: Orbis, 1975.

Heffernan, V. "Teaching the Sacrament of Matrimony." *America* (February 22, 1975) 132:129-30.

Hettinger, C. "Psychic Incapacity for Marriage: Some Canonical and Medical Reasons for Uneasiness." *Priest* (June 1976) 32:32-3.

Hildebrand, Dietrich von. "Christian Marriage and Family." *Thought* (March 1961) 36:81-8.

_____. *Man and Woman*. Chicago: Franciscan Herald Press, 1965.

Higgins, J. "On Marriage and Preparation for Marriage." *Ligourian* (February 1975) 63:59-62.

Hillman, E. "Reconsidering Polygamy." *Communio* (November 1925) 102:560-2.

Huizing, Peter, S.J. "Bonum prolis ut elementum essentiale objecti formalis consensus matrimonialis." *Gregorianum* (1962) 44:657-722.

Hurst, Hugo. *A Search for Meaning in Love, Sex, and Marriage*. Winona, MN: St. Marys, 1970.

John Paul II. *The Theology of Marriage and Celibacy: Catechesis on Marriage and Celibacy in the Light of the Resurrection*. Boston: St. Paul Editions, 1986.

Joyce, George Hayward, S.J. *Christian Marriage: An Historical and Doctrinal Study*. London: Sheed and Ward, 1948.

Kasper, Walter. *Theology of Christian Marriage*. New York: Seabury, 1980.

Kavanagh, M. "What Today's Youth Expect of Marriage." *Ligourian* (March 1974) 62:34-9.

Kennedy, Eugene. *What a Modern Catholic Believes About Marriage*. Chicago: Thomas More Press, 1972.

Kenny, J. and M. "Should the New Family Be the Old Family." *Marriage* (February 1974) 56:2-6.

Ketteler, W. von. "Christian Marriage and Family." *Social Justice* (July–August 1975) 67:100-5.

Kilmarten, Edward J., S.J. "When Is Marriage a Sacrament?" *Theological Studies* (June 1973) 34:275-286.

Kindregan, Charles. *A Theology of Marriage*. Milwaukee, WI: Bruce, 1967.

Ladue, W. "The Age of Reason Re-examined: The Sacraments of Marriage and Confession." *Living Light* (Winter 1974) 11:564-71.

Laird, J. "How to Spend More Time with Your Husband and Make It Count." *Marriage* (April 1974) 56:2-5.

_____. "Speak Up and Strengthen Your Marriage." *Ligourian* (December 1975) 63:21-3.

Lauer, Eugene F. "The Holiness of Marriage: Some New Perspectives from Recent Sacramental Theology." *Studies in the Forms of Spirituality* (May 1985) 6:215-26.

L'Huiller, Bp. Pierre. "L'indissolubilité du mariage dans le droit et la practique orthodoxes." *Studia Canonica* (1987) 21:239-60.

Likoudis, J. "Morality and the Christian Family." *Social Justice* (May 1976) 69:49-54.

Lyons, A. J. and C. "How to Meet the Person You Married." *Ligourian* (December 1975) 63:15-17.

Mace, David. *Love and Anger in Marriage.* Grand Rapids, MI: Zondervan, 1982.

Mackin, Theodore, S.J. "Consummation: of Contract of Covenant?" *Jurist* (1972) 213–23.

_____. *Marriage in the Catholic Tradition: What is Marriage?* New York: Paulist, 1982.

_____. *Marriage in the Catholic Tradition: Divorce and Remarriage in the Catholic Church.* New York: Paulist, 1984.

_____. *Marriage in the Christian Tradition: The Marital Sacrament.* New York: Paulist, 1989.

McAdoo, Bp. H. "Marriage and Community." *One in Christ* (1974) 10:339-74.

McAndrew, David. "Pastoral Ministry to the Invalidly Married." *Catholic Lawyer* (1972) 237–42.

McAvoy, J. "Mariage et divorce: récherches contemporains de théologie." *Etudes* (August 1974) 341:269-89.

McCarthy, D. "From Contract to Covenant." *Marriage* (January 1977) 59:1-3.

McHugh, James T. *Marriage in the Light of Vatican II.* Washington, DC: Family Life Bureau of the U.S.C.C., 1968.

Mace, D. "New Hope for Better Marriages." *Marriage* (August 1975) 57:7-8.

Mahoney, Aiden, C.P. "A New Look at the Divorces Clauses in Matt 5, 32 and 19, 9." *Catholic Biblical Quarterly* (January 1968) 30:29-38.

Malone, Msgr. Richard, and John R. Connery, S.J. *Contemporary Perspectives on Christian Marriage: Position Papers from the International Theological Commission.* Chicago: Loyola University Press, 1984.

"Le mariage sacrement: Réponse de l'Église aux appels de la famille," *La Documentation Catholique* (November 2, 1975) 72:912-6.

"Marriage Jurisprudence." *Tablet* (September 13, 1975) 229:878.

Marshall, John, ed. *The Future of Christian Marriage.* London: Geoffrey Chapman, 1969.

_____. "The Pastoral Care of the Married." *Clergy Review* (April 1976) 61:149-51.

Mathon, Gerard. "Mariage-cérémonie ou mariage sacrement? À propos du mariage des mal-croyants; mariage par étapes ou étapes dans la préparation au mariage." *Questions Liturgiques* (1981) 62:21-42.

May, W. "What Does Marriage Mean?" *One in Christ* (1974) 10:339-57.

Meade, M. "An Unorthodox Marriage: A New Spirit of Ecumenism." *Sign* (September 1975) 55:20-3.

Mendonca, Augustin. "The Theological and Juridical Aspects of Marriage." *Studia Canonica* (1988) 22:265-304.

Mesolella, D. "Can You Spare Her Some Time?" *Sign* (December 1975–January 1976) 55:21-4.

Meyerdorff, John. *Marriage: An Orthodox Perspective.* St. Vladimir's Seminary Press, 1975.

Milhaven, J. "Church Neglects Physical Love." *National Catholic Reporter* (January 24, 1975) 11:7.

Murray, J. "Marriage Contracts for the Mentally Retarded." *Catholic Lawyer* (Summer 1975) 21:182-9.

Navone, John, S.J. "Love in the Message of St. Paul." *Worship* (August–September 1975) 40:437-44.

Nessel, William J. "The Catholic Divorcee—A Pastoral Approach." *Homiletic and Pastoral Review* (1973) 10–6.

Noonan, John T. *Power to Dissolve: Lawyers and Marriages in the Courts of the Roman Curia.* Cambridge, MA: Harvard University Press, 1972.

Norris, Thomas. "Why the Marriage of Christians Is One of the Seven Sacraments." *Irish Theological Quarterly* (1985) 51:37-51.

Olsen, M. "We Ourselves and Us." *Marriage* (November 1974) 56:2-6.

O'Neill, Coleman E. "Marriage as Sacrament." *Doctrine and Life* (April 1988) 38:172-8.

Otto, H. "How the Churches Are Making Good Marriages Better." *Marriage* (January 1976) 58:8-11.

Palmer, Paul. "Christian Marriage: Contract or Covenant?" *Theological Studies* (1972) 33:617-65.

_____. "Shall They Make A Covenant?" *Priest* (July & August 1975) 57:2-5.

_____. "When A Marriage Dies." *America* (February 22, 1975) 132:126-28.

_____. "Can the Church Condone Second Marriages?" *Priest* (January, 1976) 32:28-33.

Paul VI, *Humanae Vitae* (July 25, 1968).

Pelland, G. "Le dossier patristique relatif au divorce." *Science et Esprit* (1973) 99–120.

Phipps, William. "The Sensuousness of Agape." *Theology Today* (January 1973) 370–9.

Pitts, A. "Awakening: One's Husband's Liberation." *Marriage* (October 1975) 57:2-5.

Provost, J. "Marriage: Change in Pastoral Care and Canonical Practice." *Louvain Studies* (Fall 1974) 5:179-89.

Quere-Jaulmes, France, ed. *Le mariage dans l'Église ancienne.* Paris: Editions du Centurion, 1969.

Quesnell, J. *Marriage: A Discovery Together.* Fides, 1974.

Quesnell, Qentin. "They Made Themselves Eunuchs for the Kingdom of Heaven." *Catholic Biblical Quarterly* (July 1968) 30:335-58.

Quinn, J. "St. Bonaventure and the Sacrament of Matrimony." *Franciscan Studies* (1974) 34:101-43.

Ramaroson, Leonard. "Une nouvelle interprétation de la 'clasule' du Matt 19:9." *Science et Esprit* (May–September 1971) 23:246-51.

Ranieri, Ralph. "Marriage: Pathway to Holiness." *Ligourian* (June 1988) 76:34-8.

"Reforming Our Discipline: Second Marriages." *America* (December 1974) 131:362; Replies (January 11, 1974) 132:12-14.

Regnier, W. & M. "Building a Stronger Marriage." *Marriage* (November 1975) 57:10-2.

_____. "Don't Let Retirement Destroy Your Marriage." *Ligourian* (February 1974) 62:40-43.

Riga, Peter. "Divorce and Remarriage in the Catholic Church." *U.S. Catholic* (March 1973) 18–20.

_____. *Problems of Marriage and Sexuality Today.* Hicksville, NY: Exposition, 1973.

Robinson, Geoffrey. *Marriage, Divorce, and Nullity: A Guide to the Annulment Process in the Catholic Church.* Blackthorn, Victoria: Dove Communications, 1984.

_____. "Unresolved Questions in the Theology of Marriage." *Jurist* (1983) 43:69-102.

Roder, R., Jr. "Natural Law and the Marriage of Christians." *Jurist* (Fall 1975) 35:409-30.

Rolfe, David J. *Marriage Preparation Manual.* Paramus, NJ: Paulist-Newman, 1976.

Rosenbaum, V. "Troubled Marriages." *St. Anthony's Messenger* (November 1974) 82:34-8.

Rue, J. "All This Talk About Love." *Ligourian* (June 1976) 64:24-6.

_____. "Are Your Children Threatening Your Marriage?" *Ligourian* (June 1976) 64:24-6.

_____. "My Husband Wants to Make All the Decisions." *Ligourian* (August 1975) 63:48-51.

_____. *The Nine Most Common Marriage Problems and How to Overcome Them.* Ligouri, MO: Ligouri Publications, 1976.

_____. "The Other Man, the Other Woman." *Ligourian* (April 1976) 64:13-16.

_____. "Troubled Wines." *Ligourian* (August 1976) 64:26-9.

Salzman, L. "Commitment to and in Marriage." *Catholic Lawyer* (Summer 1975) 21:163-81.

Schillebeeckx, Edward, O.P. *Marriage: Human Reality and Saving Mystery.* 2 vols.; New York: Sheed and Ward, 1965.

Schreiber, A. *Marriage and the Family in a World of Change.* South Bend, IN: Ave Maria Press, 1975.

Shanahan, L. "Ecclesiastical Annulment." *Marriage* (May 1976) 58:2-6.

Schur, Edwin M., ed. *The Family and the Sexual Revolution.* Bloomington, IN: Indiana University Press, 1961.

Sequeira, John Baptist. *Tout mariage entre baptises est-il necessairement sacrement? étude historique, théologique, et canonique sur le lien entre baptême et mariage* Paris: Editions du Cerf, 1985.

Simon, Rene. "La fidelité conjugale" *Prètres Diocesains* (1972) 453–8.

Singleton, B. "Polygamy, and Tyre Pressures: The Sacramentality of Customary Marriages." *New Blackfriars* (October 1975) 56:436-48.

B. Smith, "Can Studying Your Dreams Help Your Marriage?" *Marriage* (April 1976) 58:1-12.

Steinmetz, U. and J. "How to Enrich Your Family Life." *Columbia* (April 1976) 56:16-23.

Stevenson, Kenneth. *Nuptial Blessing: A Study of Christian Marriage Rites.* London: S.P.C.K., 1982.

Sweeney, K. "The Bright Side of Marriage." *Marriage* (June 1976) 58:8-9.

Tetlow, Elisabeth Meier, and Louis Mulry Tetlow. *Partners in Service: Toward a Biblical Theology of Christian Marriage.* Lanham, MD: University Press of America, 1983.

Thomas, David M. *Christian Marriage: A Journey Together.* Wilmington, DE: Michael Glazier, 1983.

_____. "Promises to Keep." *Marriage* (June 1976) 58:2-5.

_____. "Will Christian Marriage Survive the Seventies?" *Ligourian* (March 1974) 62:13-17.

Thomas, J. "Demythologizing Marriage." *Marriage* (June 1976) 58:2-5.

Thompson, James J. "Out of the Briar Patch of Divorce, Remarriage, and Annulment." *New Oxford Review* (April 1988) 55:7-12.

Tierney, T. "Preparing Couples for Marriage: A New Perspective." *Homiletic and Pastoral Review* (January 1975) 65:24-30.

True, M., and J. Young. "Divorce and Remarriage." *Commonweal* (November 22, 1974) 101:185-90.

Vaillancourt, Raymond. "Théologie de l'indissolubilité du mariage dans l'Église catholique romain." *Studia Canonica* (1987) 21:261-4.

Versenyi, Laszlo. "Eros, Irony, and Ecstasy." *Thought* Winter, 1962, 37:598-612.

Walsh, E. and P. "Two in One Flesh." *Way* (October 1975) 15:278-84.

Wamboldt, William, S.J. "Canon Law on the Indissolubility of Marriage in the Roman Catholic Church." *Studia Canonica* (1987) 21:265-70.

Whelan, C. J., S.J. "Divorced Catholics: A Proposal." *America* (December 7, 1974) 131:363-65.

Whitehead, Evelyn Eaton, and James D. Whitehead. *Marrying Well: Possibilities in Christian Marriage Today.* New York: Doubleday, 1981.

Wilson, George B. "Reflections on the Order of Marriage." *Worship* (March 1968) 42:150-8.

"Work of the Ecumenical Commission on the Theology of Marriage." *L' Osservatore Romano* (May 20 1976) No. 21 [425] 11.

Wrenn, L. "A New Condition Limiting Marriage." *Jurist* (Summer–Fall 1974) 34:292-315.

Zwack, Joseph P. *Annulment: Your Chance to Remarry Within the Catholic Church: A Step-by-Step Guide Using the New Code of Canon Law.* New York: Harper & Row, 1983.

V. Orders:

Anciaux, Paul. *The Episcopate in the Church.* Trans. Thomas F. Murray. Dublin: Gill and Son, 1965.

Anderson, Bernard W. "Ordination to the Priestly Order." *Worship* (August–September 1968) 42:431-41.

Baker, Kenneth. "The Priest-Teacher and the Priest-Scholar." *Thought* (September 1967) 42:403-12.

Baldovin, John F., S.J. "Frustrating and Angering." *Commonweal* (September 1988) 115:462-3.

Begley, J. "Priesthood: A Relational Reality." *American Ecclesiastical Review* (January 1973) 167:3-10.

Bertrams, Wilhelm, S.J. "The Einheit von Papst und Bischofskollegium in der Ausuebung der Hirtengewalt durch den Traeger des Petrusamtes." *Gregorianum* (1967) 48:28-48.

Beyer, Jean. "The Ministry of Women in the Church: Current Questions." *The Way* (Autumn 1972) Supplement #17, 92–8.

Blenkinsopp, Joseph. "Presbyter and Priest: Ministry in the Early Church." *Worship* (August–September 1967) 41:428-38.

Botte, Dom B., *et al. The Sacrament of Holy Orders.* Collegeville, MN: Liturgical Press, 1957.

Bouyer, Louis, S.J. "Ministère ecclesiastique et succession apostolique." *Nouvelle Révue Théologique* (March 1973) 94:241-52.

Brown, Raymond. *Priest and Bishop: Biblical Reflections.* Paramus, NJ: Paulist, 1970.

_____. "Priestly Character and Sacramental Ordination." *Priest* (February 1975) 31:13-5.

_____. "The Challenge of the Three Biblical Priesthoods." *Catholic Mind* (March 1980) 78:11-20.

Bunnik, R. J. "The Question of Married Priests." *Cross Currents* (1965) 15:407-31; (1966) 16:81-122.

Catoir, J. "Suppose He Wants to Be a Priest." *Sign* (July–August 1975) 54:10-2.

Coleman, Gerald D. "The Homosexual Question in the Priesthood and Religious Life." *Priest* (December 1984) 40:12-9.

Colson, Jean. *Ministre de Jesus-Christ ou le sacerdoce de l'Evangile: étude sur la condition sacerdotale des ministres chrétiens dans l'église primitive.* Paris: Beauchensne et ses fils, 1966.

Clapsis, Emmanuel. "The Sacramentality of Ordination and Apostolic Succession: An Orthodox-Ecumenical View." *Greek Orthodox Theological Review* (1985) 4:421-32.

Cooke, Bernard. "Women and Catholic Priesthood." *Worship* (September 1977) 51:400-7.

Coppens, Joseph, ed. *Sacerdoce et celibat: études historique et théologique,* Louvain: Editions Peeters, 1971.

Crehan, Joseph, S.J. "The Typology of Episcopal Consecration." *Theological Studies* (June 1960) 21:250-5.

Curley E., and M. McIntyre, "Lovers and Leaders: Some Reflections on Matrimony and Orders: Sacraments of Service." *Religion Teacher's Journal* (January 1975) 8:26-9.

Davis, Charles. "Episcopate and Eucharist." *Worship* (October 1964) 38:502-15.

Dillenschneider, Clement. *Christ the One Priest and We His Priests.* Trans. Sr. M. Renelle. St. Louis, MO: Herder, 1964.

_____. *The Holy Spirit and the Priest: Toward an Interiorization of Our Priesthood.* Baltimore, MD: Helicon, 1964.

Dodd, William H. "Toward a Theology of Priesthood." *Theological Studies* (December 1967) 28:683-705.

Dominian, J. "The Wholeness-holiness Dimension of the Priesthood." *Clergy Review* (March 1975) 60:151-60.

Edwards, Denis. "The Ordination of Women and Anglican-Roman Catholic Dialogue." *Pacifica* (June 1988) 1:125-40.

Eissing, D. "Ordination und Amt des Presbyters." *Zeitschrift für Katolische Theologie* (1976) 98:35-51.

Feuillet, Andre *The Priesthood of Christ and His Ministers.* Trans. Matthew J. O'Connell. New York: Doubleday, 1975.

Fichter, Joseph, S.J., "Married Priests and Ecumenism." *Ecumenist* (January–February 1988) 26:26-30.

_____. "The Ordination of Episcopal Priests." *America* (September 17, 1988) 159:157-61.

Flahiff, George B., Cardinal, C.S.B. "Consecration and Ministry of Women: Synodal Observations." *The Way* (Autumn 1972) Supplement #17, 107–122.

Forrester, D. "The Priest as a Man Apart." *Tablet* (February 2, 1974) 228:103-4.

Galot, Jean, S.J. *Theology of the Priesthood.* Trans. Roger Balducelli. San Francisco, CA: Ignatius Press, 1984.

_____. "The Priesthood and Celibacy." *Review for Religious* (November 1965) 24:930-56.

Gibbons, P. "The Priesthood of the People of God: Survey." *Clergy Review* (January 1974) 59:14-32.

Gorman J., and J. Shea. "Seminary Training for Leadership." *Notre Dame Journal of Education* (Spring 1974) 59:14-32.

Grady, T. "The Priest Today." *Chicago Studies* (Summer 1974) 13:123-31.

Grindel, John A. "Different Expectations of Priests, Different Kinds of Training." *Origins* (August 18, 1983) 13:187-94.

_____. "The Old Testament and Christian Priesthood." *Communio* (Spring 1976) 3:16-38.

Guerrette, R. *The New Identity of the Priest.* Paramus, NJ: Paulist-Newman, 1973.

Gula, R. "A Model of Priesthood." *Priest* (November 1975) 31:14-16.

Hawkins, D. "Troubled Pastors." *Homiletic and Pastoral Review* (October 1974) 75:19-20.

Hinnebusch, P. "The Essence of Priestly Ministry." *Priest* (July–August 1974) 29:28-30.

Howard, Christian. "The Ordination of Women in the Anglican Communion and the Ecumenical Debate." *Ecumenical Review* (1977) 29:234-53.

Horvath, Tibor. "Who Presided at the Eucharist: A Comment on BEM." *Journal of Ecumenical Studies* (Summer 1985) 22:604-7.

Isusi, Begonia de. "Consecration and Ministry of Women in the Church: Personal Reflections." *The Way* (Autumn 1972) Supplement #17, 99–106.

Iraburu, Jose Maria. *Fundamentos Teologicos de la Figura del Sacerdote.* Burgos: Ediciones Aldecoa, 1972.

Kaczynski, Reiner. "Das Vorsteheamt im Gottesdiest nach dem Zeugnis der Ordinationsliturgie des Ostens und Westens." *Liturgische Jahrbuch* (1985) 35:69-84.

Kennedy, E. "Insufficient Guilt in the Room." *America* (March 27, 1976) 134:244-57.

Kilmarten, E. "Apostolic Office: Sacrament of Christ." *Theological Studies* (June 1976) 27:357-75.

Küng, Hans. *Why Priests?* Trans. John Cumming. New York: Collins, 1972.

Lane, T. "Life in the Spirit: Priesthood and Relationship." *Furrow* (June 1976) 27:357-75.

Large, J. "The Priest and the Ethnic Heritage." *Dimension* (Winter 1975) 7:145-8.

Larkin, Ernest E., O. Carm., and Gerard T. Bocollo, eds. *Spiritual Renewal of the American Priest.* Washington, DC: U.S. Catholic Conference, 1972.

Law, Bp. Bernard Francis. "The Episcopal Priests Who Seek Roman Catholic Priesthood." *Origins* (January 28, 1982) 11:517-8.

LeBlanc, Paul J. "A Survey of Recent Writings on Ministry and Orders." *Worship* (January 1975) 35–56.

Legardien, Leon. "Les assemblees liturgiques sans pretres." *Questions Liturgiques* (1981) 62:52-57.

Long, Steven A. "The Metaphysics of Gender and Sacramental Priesthood." *Louvain Studies* (Spring 1984) 20:41-59.

Lubac, Henri de, S.J. "Le Dialogue sur le Sacerdoce de saint Jean Chrysostom." *Nouvelle Révue Théologique* (1978) 100:821-831.

McBrien, R. "Mission and Priesthood in the Church." *Catholic Lawyer* (Fall 1972) 18:300-13.

McCloskey, P. "The New Rite of Ordination." *St. Anthony's Messenger* (June 1975) 83:16-22.

McDonagh, E. "Why Do They Leave?" *Furrow* (November 1975) 26:652-67.

Maly, Eugene. *The Priest and Sacred Scripture.* Washington, DC: U.S. Catholic Conference, 1972.

Martin, Dudly. "Is Ordination a Sacrament?" *Heythrop Journal* (April 1983) 24:149-58.

Meehan, J. "Changing Priest and Changing Parish . . ." *Dimension* (Winter 1975) 7:131-8.

Meyer, H. B., S.J. "Formulae Sacramentales Sacrorum Ordinum." *Zeitschrift für Katholische Theologie* (1978) 100:620-31.

Mitchell, Nathan, O.S.B. *Mission and Ministry: History and Theology in the Sacrament of Order.* Wilmington, DE: Michael Glazier, 1982.

Murphy, T. "Sacraments and Ministry" *Chicago Studies* (Spring 1975) 14:83-95.

O'Brien, J. "Ordaining Married Men: The Australian Experience." *Clergy Review* (November 1982) 67:406-11.

O'Brien, R. "Parish Leaderships: The Priest's Role." *Furrow* (August 1975) 25:445-8.

O'Byrne, S. "Thoughts on Priesthood." *Furrow* (August 1975) 25:445-8.

O'Donnell, J. "Reflections on Priesthood." *America* (June 21 1975) 132:480-1.

O'Hanlon, Daniel J., S.J. "A New Approach to the Validity of Church Orders." *Worship* (August–September 1967) 41:406-21.

Osborne, Kenan B., O.F.M. *Priesthood: A History of the Ordained Ministry in the Roman Catholic Church.* New York: Paulist, 1989.

Ott, Ludwig. *Le sacrement de l'ordre.* Paris: Editions du Cerf, 1971.

Palmer, Paul F. "A Case for Priestly Celibacy." *Thought* (September 1963) 42:348-64.

Paul VI *Priestly Celibacy.* Boston, MA: St. Paul Editions.

Payne, K. "Apprentice Priests." *Clergy Review* (June 1974) 59:421-3.

Perrin, Joseph Marie. *The Minister of Christ.* Trans. Thomas F. Murray. Dubuque, IA: Priory, 1964.

Polek, D. "The Priest Shortage—What Can We Do About It?" *Ligourian* (April 1975) 63:39-42.

Power, David Noel. *Ministers of Christ and His Church: The Theology of Priesthood.* London: G. Chapman, 1969.

Quinn, J. "Pastoral Problems in the American Church." *Catholic Theological Society of America Proceedings* (1973) 28:95-101.

Rahner, Karl, S.J. *Bishops: Their Status and Function.* London: Burns and Oates, 1964.

_____. "Priest and Poet." *Theological Investigations.* Trans. Karl-H. and Boniface Kruger. 21 vols.; Baltimore, MD: Helicon, 1967) 3:294-320.

_____. *The Priesthood.* Trans. Edward Quinn. New York: Seabury, 1973.

_____. "Priestly Existence." *Theological Investigations.* Trans. Karl-H. and Boniface Kruger. 21 vols.; Baltimore, MD: Helicon, 1967, 3:239-263.

_____. "The Renewal of Priestly Ordination." *Theological Investigations.* Trans. Karl-H. and Boniface Kruger. 21 vols.; Baltimore, MD: Helicon, 1969, 3:171-6.

_____. "The Theology of the Restoration of the Diaconate." *Theological Investigations.* Trans. Karl-H. Kruger. 21 vols.; Baltimore, MD: Helicon, 1966, 5:268-314.

_____. *Servants of the Lord.* New York: Herder and Herder, 1968.

Rambaldi, Giuseppi. "Docilita allo Spirito Santo, liberta dei figli di Dio, e obbedienza dei Presbiteri secondo il Decreto 'Presbyterorum Ordinins,'" *Gregorianum* (1967) 48:481-521.

Regan, D. "The Priest and Celibate Love." *Priest* (January 1976) 32:27-8.

Richard, M. "Beyond Priesthood: The Ministry of the Spirit." *Clergy Review* (May 1974) 59:313-20.

Rohls, Jan. "Das Geistliche Amt in de Reformatorischen Theologie." *Kerygma und Dogma* (April–June 1985) 31:135-61.

Rordorf, W. "L'ordination del évêque selon la Tradition Apostolique d'Hippolyte de Rome" *Questions Liturgiques* (1974) 55:135-50.

Ruther, George W. "A Consistent Theology of Clerical Celibacy." *Homiletic and Pastoral Review* (February 1989) 89:9-15.

Rynne, T. "After the New Breed—Ministry." *Priest* (July–August 1974) 30:13-6.

Sabourin, Leopold. *Priesthood: A Comparative Study.* Leiden: Brill, 1973.

Samo, R. "Questions Priests Are Afraid to Ask." *Clergy Review* (June 1974) 59:380-9.

Schillebeeckx, Edward, O.P. *Ministry: Leadership in the Community of Jesus Christ.* Trans. John Bowden. New York: Crossroad, 1981.

_____. "The Changing Meaning of Ministry; The Social Context of Historical Shifts in the Church." *Cross Currents* (Winter 1983–4) 33:432-54.

Shehan, L., Cardinal. "The Priest in the New Testament: Another Point of View." *Homiletic and Pastoral Review* (November 1975) 76:10-23.

Simons, T. "Revised Rites of Ministry." *Priest* (June 1973) 29:28-31.

Slesinski, R. "Priest as Icon." *Homiletic and Pastoral Review* (June 1976) 76:62-7.

Spiazzi, R. "The Main Lines of Priestly Spirituality." *L' Osservatore Romano* (January 29, 1976) No. 5 [409] 9–10.

Strovinskas, P. "The Prophetic Priest Today." *Priest* (October 1974) 30:24-8.

Suhard, Emmanuel Cardinal. *Priests Among Men.* Notre Dame, IN: Fides, 1960.

Sullivan, D. "Patterns of Priesthood." *Tablet* (June 7, 1975) 229:525-6.

Swidler, Arlene and Leonard, eds. *Women Priests: A Catholic Commentary on the Vatican Declaration.* New York: Paulist, 1977.

Tavard, George H., A.A. "The Ordained Ministry in Historical Ambiguity." *Doctrine and Life* (November 1988) 38:466-77.

_____. "The Ordained Ministry: Where Does It Fit?" *Doctrine and Life* (December 1988) 38:518-29.

Tetlow, Elizabeth Meier. *Women and Ministry in the New Testament: Called to Serve.* Lanham, MD: University Press of America, 1980.

Thottumkal, Thomas J. *Priesthood and Apostleship.* Scarborough, Ontario: Publication Services, 1973.

Tierney, T. "The Resignation of Priests." *Clergy Review* (November 1974) 30:24-8.

Tormey, John C. *Priests Are Only Human.* Canfield, OH: Alba Books, 1976.

Vanhoye, Albert, S.J. *Prêtres anciens, prêtre nouveau selon le Nouveau Testament.* Paris: Edition du Seuil, 1980.

_____. "Sacerdoce commun et sacerdoce ministeriel: Distinction et rapports." *Nouvelle Révue Théologique* (1975) 97:193-207.

Verhalen, P. "Priestly Ministry." *Priest* (February 1975) 31:21-4.

Wieh, Hermann. " 'Priester auf Zeit' conra *'character indelibilis'?'' Theologie und Glaube* (1975) 65:19-37.

Williams, M. "Professions: Life Style of the Clergy." *New Blackfriars* (December 1975) 56:559-61.

VI. Reconciliation:

Abeyasingha, N. "Pastoral Perspectives of the New Rite of Penance." *Priest* (November 1974) 30:27-9.

_____. "Penance and the Holy Spirit." *Review for Religious* (May 1974) 33:565-72.

Anciaux, Paul. *La théologie du sacrement de penitance au XIIe siècle.* Louvain: E. Vauwelaerts, 1949.

Artz, Thomas R. "Reconciliation: A New Look at Confession." *Ligourian* (September 1981) 69:47-52; (October 1982) 70:6-14.

Baggot, P. "The Sacrament of Forgiveness." *Furrow* (August 1974) 25:411-23.

Bandira, A. "Mary and the Sacrament of Penance." *Cross and Crown* (December 1975) 27:382-91.

Barry, David W. *Ministry of Reconciliation.* Canfield, OH: Alba, 1975.

Bartels, Lambert. "Reconciliation and Penance: A View from Ethiopia." *African Ecclesiastical Review* (August 1983) 25:220-25.

Barton, John. *Penance and Absolution.* New York: Hawthorne, 1961.

Baum, W. Cardinal. "New Rite of Penance." *L'Osservatore Romano* (April 15, 1976) No. 16 [420] 6-7.

Beraudy, Roger, P.S.S. "Reflexions sur le pardon et la culpabilité à propos du sacrement de penitence." *Nouvelle Révue Théologique* (1974) 96:20-31.

Bhaldraithe, E. de. "Another Look at General Absolution." *Clergy Review* (February 1987) 3:25-30.

Bostock, Michael S. *Penance Considered in the Light of Scripture.* London: Wickliffe, 1985.

Brusselmans, C. "Children and the Sacrament of Reconciliation." *Worship* (March 1975) 49:149-57.

Brusselmans C., and B. Haggerty. "Initiation into the Sacrament of Reconciliation." *Today's Catholic Teacher* (May 1976) 9:49-50.

Buckley, Francis J., S.J. *"I Confess": The Sacrament of Penance Today.* Notre Dame, IN: Ave Maria, 1972.

_____. "The Paschal Mystery and the Priest in the Sacrament of Penance." *Lumen Vitae* (1976) 31:223-33.

Bullen, Anthony. *My Book about Confession.* Slough: St. Paul Publications, 1987.

Cambell, J. "Reconciliation: New Rite, New Perspectives." *Priest* (March 1976) 32:14-15.

Champlin, Joseph M. *Together In Peace: Penitent's Edition and Priest's Edition.* South Bend, IN: Ave Maria, 1975.

Chenderlin, F. "Penance and Its Critics." *Homiletic and Pastoral Review* (December 1973) 74:55-65.

Coffy, Abp. R. "Pourquoi une reforme du Sacrement de Penitence?" *Documentation Catholique* (February 16, 1975) 72:168-72.

Coless, G. "The Sacrament of Penance: Creative Ferment." *Worship* (October 1973) 47:463-72.

Cooke, Bernard. *Reconciled Sinners: Healing Human Brokenness.* Mystic, CT: Twenty-Third Publications, 1986.

Cosgrove, W. "Reconciliation in Christian Life." *Furrow* (June 1974) 25:301-5.

Cothenet, E. "Sainteté de l'Eglise et pèches de chrétiens," *Nouvelle Révue Théologique* (1974) 96:447-70.

Cowgill, Carol. *Adult Confession: Conversion in Process.* W. C. Brown, 1984.

Crichton, J. "The New Order of Penance." *Music and Liturgy* (Fall 1974) 1:26-31.

Dallen, J. "Eucharist and Penance." *Worship* (July 1976) 50:324-8.

_____. "*Reconciliatio et Paenitentia:* The Postsynodal Apostolic Exhortation." *Worship* (March 1985) 59:98-116.

_____. "The Confession Crisis: Decline or Evolution?" *Church* (Summer 1988) 4:13-7.

_____. "What about the New Rite of Penance?" *Religion Teacher's Journal* (January 1976) 9:29-31.

Delobel, Joel. "L'onction par la pecheresse: La conformation littéraire de Lc 7:36-50." *Ephimerides Theologiae Lovaniensis* (1966) 42:415-75.

Di Giacomo, J. "Experiencing Reconciliation in a School." *America* (April 3, 1976) 134:284-6.

Donnelly, D. "The New Rite of Penance." *Sign* (April, 1976) 55:19-22.

Donovan, K. "The History of Penance in the West." *Music and Liturgy* (Fall 1974) 1:8-13.

_____. "The New *Ordo Paenitentialis*" *Clergy Review* (October 1974) 59:660-71.

Dougherty, M. "Preparation for the Sacrament of Penance." *Cross and Crown* (March 1976) 28:63-7.

Dutty, R. "Concelebration of Penance and a Therapeutic Model." *Worship* (May 1974) 48:258-69.

Edwards, John C. *Ways of Forgiveness.* London: Catholic Truth Society, 1984.

Eger, Josef. *Eneuerung des Busssakrament.* Freiburg: Seelsorge Verlag, 1965.

Fatula, Mary Ann, O.P. "The Ministry of Reconciliation." *Spirituality Today* (Summer 1988) 40:157-64.

Fink, Peter, S.J. "Investigating the Sacrament of Penance: An Experiment in Sacramental Theology." *Worship* (March 1980) 54:206-20.

Finnerty, V. "What Does the New Ritual of Penance Expect of the Priest?" *Review for Religious* (January 1976) 35:3-13.

Foley, L. *Your Confession: Using the New Ritual.* (Cincinnati, OH: St. Anthony's Messenger Press, 1975.

Gallen, John, S.J. "General Sacramental Absolution: Remarks on Pastoral Norms." *Theological Studies* (March 1972) 34:114-21.

Gramlich, M. "St. Paul on Reconciliation." *Sisters Today* (May 1975) 46:530-36.

Gula, Richard M. *To Walk Together: The Sacrament of Reconciliation.* New York: Paulist, 1984.

Guzie, Tad. *What a Modern Catholic Believes About Confession.* Chicago: Thomas More, 1974.

Gwinell, M. "Penance and Reconciliation: Human and Religious Approaches." *Clergy Review* (March 1976) 61:95-100.

Haggerty, B. "The Sacraments Today: The Sacrament of Reconciliation." *Today's Catholic Teacher* (February 1977) 10:22-3.

_____. "The New Rite of Reconciliation." *Catechist* (November 1975) 9:28-30.

Häring, Bernard. *Shalom: Peace.* New York: Farrar, Straus, Girous, 1968.

Hamelin, Leonce. *Reconciliation in the Church: A Theological and Pastoral Essay on the Sacrament of Penance.* Collegeville, MN: The Liturgical Press, 1980.

Hellwig, Monika K. *Sign of Reconciliation and Conversion: The Sacrament of Penance in Our Times.* Wilmington, DE: Michael Glazier, 1982.

Hinwood, B. "A Penance Service." *Review for Religious* (1974) 33:126-30.

Hollings, Michael. *Go in Peace: Reflections on the Use of Confession Yesterday, Today, and Tomorrow.* Great Wakering: Mayhew-McCrimmon, 1984.

Hugo, John H. "Health and Spiritual Renewal." *Pastoral Life* (January 1973) 2-9.

Hunter, Tom. *I Am God's Special Child: Preparing for My First Confession.* Middelsbrough: Arder, 1986.

Jicha, P. "A Plan for Penance." *Religion Teacher's Journal* (February 1973) 7:27-30.

Kelly, George A. *The Sacrament of Penance in Our Time.* Boston: Daughters of St. Paul, 1976.

Kirk, David. "Penance in the Eastern Churches." *Worship* (March 1966) 40:148-55.

McCarty, Shaun, S.T. "Pilgrim and Penitent: Direction and Sacramental Reconciliation." *Review for Religious* (November–December 1986) 45:819-30.

McNeill, John, and Helena M. Gamer. *Medieval Handbooks of Penance.* New York: Octagon Books, 1965.

Martin, Bernard. *The Healing Ministry in the Church.* Richmond, VA: John Knox, 1960.

McAuliff, Clarence, S.J. "Penance and Reconciliation with the Church." *Theological Studies* (March 1965) 26:1-39.

McCauley, George, S.J. "The Ecclesial Nature of the Sacrament of Penance." *Worship* (March 1962) 34:212-22.

McDonald, J. "Theological Premises of the New Rite of Penance." *L'Osservatore Romano* (January 29, 1976) No. 5 [409] 4.

Messie, Pierre, S.J. "Le Esprit nous reconcile." *Nouvelle Révue Théologique* (1980) 102:62-73.

Mick, Lawrence E. *Penance: The Once and Future Sacrament.* Collegeville, MN: The Liturgical Press, 1987.

Nefyodov, Gennadiy. "Sacrament of Penance: The Priest—Administrator of the Sacrament of Penance." *Journal of the Moscow Patriarchate* (1985) 2:77-78.

Nicolas, Adolfo, S.J. "The Sacrament of Reconciliation: Theological Considerations." *East Asian Pastoral Review* (1984) 21:303-29.

Opits, D. "Penance: A Sacrament of Friendship." *Religion Teacher's Journal* (January 1976) 9:28.

Orsy, Ladislas M., S.J. "Communal Penance: Some Preliminary Questions on Sin and Sacrament." *Worship* (June–July, 1973) 45:338-45.

_____. "The Sacrament of Penance in Religious Communities." *Worship* (March 1968) 42:159-68.

Osborne, Kenan, O.F.M. "Why Confess to a Priest?" *Chicago Studies* (Fall 1975) 14:260-78.

O'Shea, Kevin F., C.SS.R. "The Reality of Sin: A Theological and Pastoral Critique." *Theological Studies* (June 1968) 29:241-59.

Palmer, P. "But What Must We Confess?" *Priest* (November 1975) 31:31-3; (December 1975) 31:40-2.

Pelikan, J. "Brother Martin, Pope Martin, and Saint Martin: On the Conditions of Christian Reconciliation." *One in Christ* (November 2 1976) 12:142-56.

Peter, Carl J. "The New Norms for Communal Penance: Will They Help?" *Worship* (January 1973) 45:2-10.

Pierre, K. "Therapeutic Aspects of the Sacrament of Penance." *Priest* (May 1973) 29:18-9.

Poschmann, Bernhard. *Penance and the Anointing of the Sick.* Trans. Francis Courtney. Freiburg: Herder, 1964.

Power, David N. "The Sacramentalization of Penance." *Heythrop Journal* (1977) 18:5-22.

Provdolyubov, Sergij. "The Sacrament of Penance: How to Fast and Prepare for Confession." *Journal of the Moscow Patriarchate* (1985) 12:68-70.

Quinn, J. "Celebrating in the Sacrament of Penance." *Furrow* (June 1976) 27:339-51.

Rahner, Karl, S.J. "Forgotten Truths Concerning the Sacrament of Penance" *Theological Investigations* Trans. Karl-H. Kruger. 21 vols.; Baltimore, MD: Helicon, 1963, 2:135-74.

_____. "Guilt and Remission: The Borderline between Theology and Psychotherapy." *Theological Investigations* Trans. Karl-H. Kruger. 21 vols.; Baltimore, MD: Helicon, 1963, 2:265-82.

_____. "The Meaning of Frequent Confession." *Theological Investigations* Trans. Karl-H. Kruger. 21 vols.; Baltimore, MD: Helicon, 1966, 3:177-89.

_____. "Problems Concerning Confession." *Theological Investigations* Trans. Karl-H. Kruger. 21 vols.; Baltimore, MD: Helicon, 1966, 3:190-208.

Richter, Stephen. *Metanoia: Christian Penance and Confession.* Trans. Raymond Kelly. New York: Sheed and Ward, 1966.

Riga, Peter. "Penance as Sign of the Minister." *Priest* (July–August 1975) 30:25-8.

_____. "Private and Communal Penance." *Priest* (May 1974) 30:25-8.

_____. *Sin and Penance.* Milwaukee, WI: Bruce, 1963.

Rondet, M. "Penance and Brotherly Love." *Review for Religious* (May 1976) 35:330-7.

Sargent, R. "Sacramental Penance: Are We Still Reacting?" *Sisters Today* (January 1975) 46:281-4.

Sievernich, Michael, S.J. "Ist die Suende Abgeschafft?" *Stimmen der Zeit* (June 1988) 206:363-76.

Shall, James V., S.J. "Penance: Redemption of Sins." *Worship* (February 1964) 38:133-41.

Schillebeeckx, Edward, O.P. *Sacramental Reconciliation.* New York: Herder & Herder, 1971.

Sheets, J. "Communal Penance and Private Confession: The New Directives." *Communio* (Spring 1974) 1:99-102.

Simons, G. "Thoughts on the Renewal of Penance." *Sisters* (March 1976) 47:438-41.

Slattery, M. "The New Order of Penance." *Furrow* (May 1974) 25:426-60.

_____. "Restore the *Ordo Paenitentium*—Some Historical Notes." *Living Light* (March 1984) 20:248-53.

Sottocornola, Franco. "Les nouveaux rites de la penitence: Commentaire." *Questions Liturgiques* (1974) 55:89-136.

Staffner, H. "What is Wrong with the Sacrament of Penance?" *Clergy Monthly* (1972) 362–73.

Sullivan, Thomas F. "What Age for First Confession?" *America* (September 1973) 110–3.

Szoka, Apb. Edmund. "The Sacrament of Penance: General Absolution." *Origins* (March 1987) 16:716-21.

Taylor, Michael J., S.J., ed. *The Mystery of Sin and Forgiveness.* New York: Alba, 1973.

Thurian, Max. *Confession.* London: Mowbray, 1985.

Thwaites, Hugh. *Confession.* Chulmleigh: Augustine, 1985.

Toner, J. "The Testimony of Penance: Reflection on the Paschal Mystery." *L'Osservatore Romano* (April 3, 1975), No. 14 [366] 10.

Tormey, J. "Helping Children to Confess." *Catechist* (February 1976) 9:14-7.

Verheule, D. Ambroise, O.S.B. "Le sacrement de la reconciliation à travers les siècles." *Questions Liturgiques* (1977) 58:27-49.

Vorgrimmler, Herbert. *Busse und Krankensalbung.* Freiburg: Herder, 1978.

Walgrove, J. "The Sacrament of Penance." *Furrow* (February 1976) 27:67-76.

Williams, B. "The New Rite of Penance." *Homiletic and Pastoral Review* (October 1975) 76:9-22.

Williams, J. "Notes on the Sacrament of Penance." *L'Osservatore Romano* (February 27, 1975) No. 9 [361] 9–11.

VII. Anointing:

Beckworth, B. "The New Rite of Anointing." *St. Anthony's Messenger* (July 1976) 84:28-33.

Bednarski, G. "Catechesis for the Elderly: The Anointing of the Sick." *Living Light* (Summer 1974) 11:205-16.

Brennan, J. "Ministry of Healing." *Priest* (May 1975) 31:14-6.

Buttrick, George. *God, Pain, and Evil.* New York: Abingdon, 1966.

Cleary, Maureen, B.V.M. "The Anointing of the Sick." *Religion Teacher's Journal* (February 1973) 38–41.

Danilesson, D. "The Healing Family." *Catholic Worker* (June 1976) 42:3.

Empereur, James L. *Prophetic Anointing: God's Call to the Sick, Elderly, and the Dying.* Wilmington, DE: Michael Glazier, 1982.

Grandis, Robert de. "Can Faith Heal?" *U.S. Catholic* (December 1974) 39:35-7.

Gelpi, Donald L., S.J. "The Ministry of Healing" in *Pentecostal Piety.* New York: Paulist, 1972, 3–58.

Gusmer, C. "I Was Sick and You Visited Me: The Revised Rites of the Sick." *Worship* (November 1974) 48:516-25.

Haddock, G. "The Sacrament of Anointing Watered Down." *Homiletic and Pastoral Review* (April 1976) 76:14-5.

Haughey, J., S.J. "Healed and Healing Priests." *America* (August 2, 1975) 133:46-8.

Iula, F. "The Physician's Role as Spiritual Healer." *New Catholic World* (October 1976) 219:218-20.

Jurgens, Arnold, M.H.M. "The Sacrament of the Sick." *African Ecclesiastical Review* (1972) 337–40.

Kaler, Patrick, C.SS.P. "The Sacrament of the Sick in Today's Church" *Ligourian* (March 1983) 71:11-16.

Keating, C. "The Sacrament of Anointing the Sick." *Homiletic and Pastoral Review* (June 1974) 74:8-11.

Kelsey, Morton. *Healing and Christianity.* New York: Harper & Row, 1973.

Lange, J. *Freedom and Healing.* Paramus, NJ: Paulist-Newman, 1976.

Linn, Dennis, S.J., and Matthew Linn, S.J. *Healing of Memories.* Paramus, NJ: Paulist-Newman, 1975.

Maddock, L. "Anointing the Sick." *Today's Parish* (January–February 1973) 24–5.

Martimort, A. "Le nouveau rituel des malades." *La Documentation Catholique* (February 4, 1973) 70:103-4.

Martin, Francis. "The Healing of Memories." *Review for Religious* (May 1973) 22:498-507.

McIntyre M., and E. Curley. "How Do We Think About Anointing the Sick?" *Religion Teacher's Journal* (January 1975) 8:22-3.

McMarrow, K. "Sacrament of the Anointing of the Sick: Historical-Theological Considerations." *American Ecclesiastical Review* (October 1975) 169:507-21.

McNutt, Francis. *Healing.* South Bend, IN: Ave Maria, 1974.

Mongelluzzo, J. "Sacrament of Healing: The Revised Rite of Anointing." *Sign* (May 1976) 55:33-7.

Nauer, B. "Towards a Theology of Healing." *Communio* (Fall 1974) 1:316-20.

Nolan K. "The Sacrament of Anointing and Total Patient Care." *Homiletic and Pastoral Review* (June 1974) 74:53-62.

Nouwen, J. *The Wounded Healer: Ministry in Contemporary Society.* Garden City, NY: Doubleday, 1972.

Ortemann, Claude. *Le sacrement des malades.* Paris: Editions du Cerf, 1971.

O'Sullivan, Eugene. "The Pastoral Care of the Sick: The Challenge of Liturgical Change." *Doctrine and Life* (September 1988) 38:364-71.

Poschmann, Bernhard. *Penance and the Anointing of the Sick.* Trans. Francis Courtney. Freiburg: Herder, 1964.

Ristow, Kate. "Is Anyone Among You Sick? Teaching about the Anointing of the Sick." *Catechist* (January 1989) 22:20-1.

Rogge, L. "The Anointing of the Sick in Historical Perspective." *Linacre Quarterly* (August 1975) 42:205-15.

Rouillard, Phillipe, O.S.B. "Le ministre du sacrement de l'onction des malades." *Nouvelle Révue Théologique* (1979) 101:395-402.

Shlemon, Barbara Leahy, Dennis Linn, S.J., and Matthew Linn, S.J. *To Heal as Jesus Healed.* Notre Dame: Ave Maria Press, 1978.

Slattery, M. "The New Rite for the Sacrament of the Sick." *Furrow* (March 1973) 24:131-7.

Testa, Emmanuel P., O.F.M. *L'Huile de la foi.* Jerusalem: Imprimerie des Pères Franciscains, 1967.

Trutter, Richard. "Communal Anointing." *Today's Parish* (September–October 1972) 9–12.

Twenty-First Liturgical Conference Saint-Serge. *Temple of the Holy Spirit: Sickness and Death in the Liturgy.* Trans. Matthew J. O'Connell. New York: Pueblo, 1983.

van der Poel, C. "The Healing Mission of the Church." *Hospital Progress* (August 1976) 57:84-5.

Vorgrimmler, Herbert. *Busse und Krankensalbung.* Freiburg: Herder, 1978.

Whalen, W. "Towards a Theology of Healing." *Communio* (Fall 1974) 1:316-20.

Wilhelm, R. "Sacrament of Pilgrimage." *Spiritual Life* (Spring 1974) 20:62-8.

Ziegler, John J. "Who Can Anoint the Sick?" *Worship* (January 1987) 61:25-44.

VIII. Eucharist:

Adams, Raymond A., S.J. "The Holy Spirit and the Real Presence." *Theological Studies* (March 1968) 39:37-51.

Aulen, Gustaf. *Eucharist and Sacrifice.* Trans. Eric Wahlstrom. Philadelphia, PA: Michlenberg, 1958.

Balasuriya, Tissa. *The Eucharist and Human Liberation.* Maryknoll, NY: Orbis, 1979.

Bernejo, A. M. "The Propitiatory Nature of the Eucharist: An Inquiry into the Early Sources." *Indian Journal of Theology* (1972) 133–69.

Bishops' Committee on Priestly Life and Ministry. *Fulfilled in Your Hearing: The Homily in the Sunday Assembly.* Washington, DC: National Conference of Catholic Bishops, 1982.

Bouley, Allen. *From Freedom to Formula: The Evolution of the Eucharistic Prayer from Improvization to Written Texts.* Washington, DC: Catholic University Press, 1981.

Bouyer, Louis, S.J. *Eucharist.* Trans. Charles U. Quinn. Notre Dame, IN: Notre Dame University Press, 1966.

Browning, W. "Eucharist and Life: Power in Weakness." *Sisters Today* (June–July 1974) 45:629-33.

Bugnini, A. "La communion dans le main." *Documentation Catholique* (June 17, 1973) 70:565-8.

Bullen, A. "The Eucharist and Young People." *Clergy Review* (November 1975) 60:719-27.

Byron, B. F. "Recent Ecumenical Statements on the Eucharist and Catholic Theology of the Eucharist as Sacrifice." *Australasian Catholic Record* (1972) 265–73.

Byron, W. "Eucharist and Society." *America* (August 7, 1976) 135:43-6.

Carr, A. "Admitting Other Christians to Communion in the Catholic Church." *Homiletic and Pastoral Review* (March 1975) 75:60-73.

Cioppi, L. "*Mysterium Fidei:* Tenth Anniversary of the Encyclical." *L'Osservatore Romano* (September 2, 1975) No. 37 [389] 4.

Clark, Francis, S.J. *Eucharistic Sacrifice and the Reformation.* Oxford: Bladswell, 1967.

Clark, Neville. "Spirit Christology in the Light of Eucharistic Theology." *Heythrop Journal* (July 1982) 23:270-84.

Cooke, Bernard. "Eucharist: Source or Expression of Community." *Worship* (November 1963) 37:630-39.

_____. "Synoptic Presentation of the Eucharist as a Covenant Sacrifice." *Theological Studies* (March 1960) 21:1-44.

Cormack, H. M. "The Act of Christ in the Mass." *Worship* (June 1966) 40:630-9.

Coventry, J. "The Eucharistic and the Sacrifice of Christ." *One in Christ* (November 4, 1975) 11:330-41.

_____. "Intercommunion the Ultimate Goal?" *Music and Liturgy* (Summer 1975) 1:174-8.

Cullman, Oscar. *Early Christian Worship.* Trans. A. Stewart and James B. Torrance. London: S. C. M. Press, 1953.

Cullman Oscar, and F. J. Leenhardt. *Essays on the Lord's Supper.* Trans. by J. G. Davies. Richmond, VA: John Knox Press, 1953.

Dallen, J. "Eucharist and Penance." *Worship* (July 1976) 50:324-8.

Daly, Robert J. *Christian Sacrifice: The Judaeo-Christian Background before Origen.* Washington, DC: Catholic University Press, 1978.

Deiss, L. *It Is the Lord's Supper: The Eucharist of Christians.* Paramus, NJ: Paulist-Newman, 1976.

Diekmann, Godfrey, O.S.B. "The Eucharist Makes the People of God." *Worship* (May 1964) 39:458-68.

Dix, Dom Gregory. *The Shape of the Liturgy.* New York: Seabury, 1983.

Doohan, L. "Eucharist and Group Asceticism." *Sisters Today* (June–July 1975) 46:586-9.

Elert, Werner. *Eucharist and Church Fellowship in the First Four Centuries.* St. Louis, MO: Concordia, 1966.

Emminghuas, Johannes H. *The Eucharist: Essence, Form, Celebration.* Collegeville, MN: The Liturgical Press, 1978.

Falardeau, Ernest R., S.S.S. "The Eucharist: A Challenge and an Opportunity." *Priest* (November 1984) 40:18-20.

Firth, Francis, O.S.B. "The Fathers of the Church: The Earliest Christian Eucharist." *Canadian Catholic Review* (January 1989) 7:36-7.

Fitzer, Joseph. "Teilhard's Eucharist: A Reflection." *Theological Studies* (June 1973) 34:251-64.

Foley, L. "How God Forgives Us." *St. Anthony's Messenger* (February 1976) 83:16-9.

Gallagher, W. "Prayer Crisis and the Eucharist." *Homiletic and Pastoral Review* (January 1974) 74:9-25.

Galot, Jean, S.J. "The Theology of the Eucharistic Presence." *Review for Religious* (July 1963) 20:407-29.

Gamber, Klaus. *Beracha: Eucharistiegebet und Eucharisticfier.* Regensberg: Komissionsverlag F. Pustet, 1986.

Gantoy, Robert, Herve Cnudde, and Dieudonne Dufrasne. *A la récherche de prieres eucharistiques pour notre temps.* Paris: Le Centurion, 1976.

Gelineau, Joseph. *The Eucharistic Prayer: Praise of the Whole Assembly.* Trans. Mary Anselm. Washington, DC: Pastoral Press, 1985.

Gelpi, Donald L., S.J. "Ecumenical Reflections on Christ's Eucharistic Presence" in *Essays on Apostolic Themes.* Peabody, MA: Hendrickson, 1985, 193–207.

Gogan, B. "Worship for Small Groups—The Eucharist." *Furrow* (March 1974) 25:127-35.

Gramlich, M. "In Remembrance of Me." *Cross and Crown* (June 1974) 26:127-34.

Grasse, J. "The Eucharist in the Gospel of Mark." *American Ecclesiastical Review* (November 1974) 168:595-608.

Guzie, Tad W. *Jesus and the Eucharist.* Paramus, NJ: Paulist-Newman, 1974.

Hanshell, D. "Corpus Christi." *Tablet* (June 12, 1976) 230:567-8.

Hanssens, Jean M., S.J. "Le cérémonial de la communion eucharistique dans les rites orientaux." *Gregorianum* (January 1960) 41:30-62.

Häring, Bernard. *The New Covenant.* London: Burnes and Oates, 1965.

Hellwig, Monika. *Eucharist and the Hunger of the World.* Paramus, N.J.: Paulist-Newman, 1976.

Hoffinger, J. "Evangelizing Power of the Eucharist." *Priest* (December 1974) 30:11-6.

Horvath, Tibor. "Who Presided at the Eucharist? A Comment on BEM." *Journal of Ecumenical Studies* (Summer 1985) 22:604-7.

Jeanrond, Werner. "The Church: Eucharistic Community." *Doctrine and Life* (December 1988) 29:171-98.

Jeremias, Joachim. *The Eucharistic Words of Jesus.* Trans. Norman Perrin. New York: Scribners, 1966.

Joussa, Jean-Pierre, O.P. "Quelle théologie de las messe soustend notre catechèse?" *Paroisse et Liturgie* (1965) 47:527-55.

Jungmann, Josef A. *The Mass of the Roman Rite.* Trans. Francis A. Brunner. New York: Benziger, 1951.

Keane, E. "Do Most Catholics Believe in the Real Presence?" *Homiletic and Pastoral Review* (April 1975) 75:11-20.

Keefe, Donald J. "Toward a Eucharistic Morality." *Communio* (Summer 1975) 2:99-125.

Keifer, R. *Blessed and Broken: The Contemporary Experience of God in Eucharistic Celebration.* Wilmington, DE: Michael Glazier, 1982.

_____. "The Eucharistic Prayer." *Worship* (July 1976) 50:316-23.

Kelleher, David, O.F.M.Cap. "The Real Presence." *Homiletic and Pastoral Review* (June 1983) 83:30-32.

Kilmartin, Edward, S.J. "Public Testimony to Hope: Proclaiming the Lord Till He Comes." *New Catholic World* (November–December 1975) 218:283-6.

_____. "Reflections on Modern Eucharistic Theology." *New Catholic World* (July–August 1981) 224:178-81.

Kirby, John C. "Eucharistic Liturgy in the Anglican Communion." *Worship* (October 1968) 42:466-86.

Krump, J. "Eat My Body, Drink My Blood." *U.S. Catholic* (June 1974) 36:6-13.

_____. "Eucharist: Celebration of Presence." *Critic* (May–June 1974) 36:6-13.

Lee, B. "Towards a Process Theology of the Eucharist." *Worship* (April 1974) 48:194-205.

Legere, Thomas E. "Real Presence." *Emmanuel* (November 1988) 94:10-1.

Lubich, Chiara. *The Eucharist.* New York: New City Press, 1977.

Lussier, Ernest. *Getting to Know the Eucharist.* Canfield, OH: Alba, 1974.

_____. *Living the Eucharistic Mystery.* Canfield, OH: Alba, 1976.

Lyonnet, Stanislaus, and Leopold Sabourin. *Sin, Redemption, and Sacrifice.* Rome: Biblical Institute, 1970.

Maloney, Francis J. "John 6 and the Celebration of the Eucharist." *The Downside Review* (October 1975) 93:243-51.

Manton, J. "Is Christ in the Eucharist Too Hard to Swallow?" *Ligourian* (June 1975) 63:50-2.

Marxsen, Willi. *The Lord's Supper as a Christological Problem.* Trans. Lorenz Nieting. Philadelphia, PA: Fortress, 1970.

Mazza, Enrico. *The Eucharistic Prayers of the Roman Rite.* Trans. Matthew J. O'Connell. New York: Pueblo Publishing Co., 1986.

McGregor, Austin. "The Real Presence." *Worship* (February 1967) 41:99-104.

Mierzwa, R. "What Can Bread Teach About Eucharist?" *Religion Teacher's Journal* (January 1976) 9:23-5.

Montclos, Jean de. *Lafranc et Berenger: La controverse eucharistique du XIe siècle.* Louvain: Spicilegium Sacrum Louvaniense, 1971.

Mossi, John, S.J. "The New Eucharistic Prayers of Reconciliation." *Modern Liturgy* (January 1976) 3:28-9.

Murphy-O'Connor, J. "Eucharist and Community in First Corinthians." *Worship* (January 1977) 51:56-69.

Murtagh, J. "Breaking the Bread of God's Word." *Bible Today* (February 1976) 82:634-9.

O'Driscoll, J. A. "Reality of the Real Presence." *Downside Review* (July 1975) 93:201-7.

Oulton, John. *Holy Communion and the Holy Spirit.* London: Society for the Promotion of Christian Knowledge, 1951.

Pancovski, Ivan. "Die heilige Eucharistie in Orthodoxer Sicht," *Ostkirchliches Studien* (September 1985) 34:163-77.

Pearce-Higgins, A. G. "Theology of the Eucharist—A New Approach." *Modern Churchman* (Summer 1955) 18:156-9.

Pearson, Lennart. "Presbyterians and the Eucharist." *Reformed Liturgical Music* (Winter 1985) 19:29-33.

Powers, Joseph M., S.J. *Eucharistic Theology.* New York: Herder & Herder, 1967.

_____. "*Mysterium fidei* and the Theology of the Eucharist." *Worship* (January 1966) 40:17-35.

Quinn, John J. "The Lord's Supper and Forgiveness of Sin." *Worship* (May 1968) 42:281-91.

Rahner, Karl, S.J. "Eucharist and Suffering." *Theological Investigations.* Trans. Karl-H. and Boniface Kruger. Baltimore, MD: Helicon, 1967, 3:161-70.

_____. "On the Duration of the Presence of Christ after Communion." *Theological Investigations.* Trans. Karl-H. and Boniface Kruger. 21 vols.; Baltimore, MD: Helicon, 1966, 4:312-22.

_____. "The Presence of Christ in the Sacrament of the Lord's Supper." *Theological Investigations.* Trans. Karl-H. and Boniface Kruger. 21 vols.; Baltimore, MD: Helicon, 1966, 4:287-311.

_____. "The Word and the Eucharist." *Theological Investigations.* Trans. Karl-H. and Boniface Kruger. Baltimore, MD: Helicon, 1966, 4:253-86.

Rearden, M. "Transubstantiation and Identity." *Irish Theological Quarterly* (July 1975) 42:197-211.

Rosato, P. "Convergent Perspectives on the Eucharist." *Sisters Today* (June–July 1976) 47:628-40.

_____. "World Hunger and Eucharistic Theology." *America* (August 7, 1976) 131:47-9.

Rush, A. "The Eucharist and the Sacrament of the Dying in Christian Antiquity." *Jurist* (Winter–Spring 1974) 34:10-35.

Ryan, John Barry. *The Eucharistic Prayer: A Study in Contemporary Liturgy.* New York: Paulist, 1974.

Torio Esteban, Antonio, O.S.A. "La Eucaristia en San Augustin." *Teologia y Vida* (1988) 29:171-98.

Sanchez Caro, Jose Manuel. *Eucharistia e historia de la salvacion: estudio sobre la plegaria eucharistica oriental.* Madrid: Editorial Catolica, 1983.

Shepard, Robert. "The Eucharistic Presence and Reconciliation of Opposing Realities." *Heythrop Journal* (April 1981) 22:123-34.

Schillebeeckx, Edward, O.P. *The Eucharist.* Trans. N. D. Smith. New York: Sheed and Ward, 1968.

Schneider, T. "Die Neuere Katholische Diskussion über die Eucharitie." *Evangelische Theologie* (November–December 1975) 35:497-524.

Schuler, R. "Corpus Christi 1975." *Sacred Music* (Summer 1975) 102:8-12.

Schweizer, Eduard. *The Lord's Supper According to the New Testament.* Trans. James M. Davis. Philadelphia, PA: Fortress, 1967.

Seasoltz, R. Kevin, ed. *Living Bread, Saving Cup: Readings on the Eucharist.* Collegeville, MN: The Liturgical Press, 1982.

Sheedy, Charles E. *The Eucharistic Controversy of the Eleventh Century Against the Background of Pre-Scholastic Theology.* Washington, DC: Catholic University Press, 1947.

Smolarski, Dennis C., S.J. *Eucharistia: A Study of the Eucharistic Prayer.* New York: Paulist, 1982.

Soubigou, Louis. *Les préfaces de la liturgie étudiées, prechées, meditées.* Paris: P. Lethielleux, 1969.

Southard, R. "Eucharist and Ecumenism: Crisis for Catholics." *Homiletic and Pastoral Review* (April 1960) 34:258-68.

Stuhlmueller, Carroll, C.P. "The Holy Eucharist: Symbol of Christ's Glory." *Worship* (April 1960) 34:258-68.

_____. "The Holy Eucharist: Symbol of the Passion." *Worship* (March 1960) 34:195-205.

Tillard, J. M. R., O.P. *The Eucharist: Pasch of God's People.* Staten Island: Alba House, 1967.

Vollert, Cyril, S.J. "The Eucharist: Controversy over Transubstantiation." *Theological Studies* (September 1961) 22:391-422.

_____. "The Eucharist: Quests for Insights from Scripture." *Theological Studies* (June 1960) 21:404-43.

Wainwright, Goeffrey. *Eucharist and Eschatology.* New York: Oxford University Press, 1981.

Wilson, D. "The Church, the Eucharist, and the Mentally Handicapped." *Clergy Review* (February 1975) 60:69-84.

Wright, J. "The Priesthood and the Eucharist." *L'Osservatore Romano* (August 15, 1974) No. 33 [333] 3–4.

Zimmerman, Marie. "L'Eucharistie: quelques aspects de la pensée de Schillebeeckx." *Révue de Sciences Réligieuses* (July 1975) 49:234-49.